INDIGENOUS DIFFERENCE AND THE CONSTITUTION OF CANADA

There is a unique constitutional relationship b[...]
the Canadian state – a relationship that does not [...]
and the state. It is from this central premise th[...] ..... builds his
argument in this controversial work.

Why does this special relationship exist? What does it entail in terms of Canadian constitutional order? There are, Macklem argues, four complex social facts that lie at the heart of the relationship. First, Aboriginal people belong to distinctive cultures that were and continue to be threatened by non-Aboriginal beliefs, philosophies, and ways of life. Second, prior to European contact, Aboriginal people lived in and occupied North America. Third, prior to European contact, Aboriginal people not only occupied North America; they exercised sovereign authority over persons and territory. Fourth, Aboriginal people participated in and continue to participate in a treaty process with the Crown. Together, these four social conditions are exclusive to the Aboriginal people of North America and constitute what Macklem refers to as indigenous difference.

Exploring the constitutional significance of indigenous difference in light of the challenges it poses to the ideal of equal citizenship, Macklem engages an interdisciplinary methodology that treats constitutional law as an enterprise that actively distributes power, primarily in the form of rights and jurisdiction, among a variety of legal actors, including individuals, groups, institutions, and governments. On this account, constitutional law refers to an ongoing project of aspiring to distributive justice, disciplined but not determined by text, structure, or precedent. Far from threatening equality, constitutional protection of indigenous difference promotes equal and therefore just distribution of constitutional power.

The book examines constitutional rights to Aboriginal people that protect interests associated with culture, territory, sovereignty, and the treaty process, and explores the circumstances in which these rights can be interfered with by the Canadian state. It also examines the relation between these rights and the Canadian Charter of Rights and Freedoms, and proposes extensive reform of existing treaty processes in order to protect and promote their exercise.

Macklem's book offers a challenge to traditional understandings of the constitutional status of indigenous peoples, relevant not only to Canadian debates but also to those in other parts of the world where indigenous peoples are asserting greater autonomy over their collective futures.

PATRICK MACKLEM is Professor of Law, University of Toronto.

Indigenous Difference and the Constitution of Canada

PATRICK MACKLEM

UNIVERSITY OF TORONTO PRESS
Toronto Buffalo London

© University of Toronto Press Incorporated 2001
Toronto Buffalo London
Printed in Canada

ISBN 0-8020-4195-7 (cloth)
ISBN 0-8020-8049-9 (paper)

∞

Printed on acid-free paper

Canadian Cataloguing in Publication Data

Macklem, Patrick
    Indigenous difference and the Constitution of Canada

    Includes bibliographical references and index.
    ISBN 0-8020-4195-7 (bound)   ISBN 0-8020-8049-9 (pbk.)

    1. Indians of North America – Legal status, laws, etc. – Canada.
    2. Indians of North America – Canada – Government relations.
    3. Indians of North America – Civil rights – Canada.
    4. Constitutional law – Canada.   I. Title.

    E92.M335 2001   323.1'197071   C00-932065-2

This book has been published with the help of a grant from the Humanities and Social Sciences Federation of Canada, using funds provided by the Social Sciences and Humanities Research Council of Canada.

The University of Toronto Press acknowledges the financial assistance to its publishing program of the Canada Council for the Arts and the Ontario Arts Council.

University of Toronto Press acknowledges the financial support for its publishing activities of the Government of Canada through the Book Publishing Industry Development Program (BPIDP).

For my parents,
Joy and Peter Macklem

Contents

Acknowledgments

This book has been some years in the making and has benefited from the insights, expertise and wisdom of many colleagues and friends. I am grateful in this respect to Joe Arvay, Michael Asch, Joe Corbiere, René Dussault, Georges Erasmus, the late, great Norman Feltes, Phil Healey, Bill Henderson, Martin Henderson, David Kennedy, Duncan Kennedy, Karl Klare, Will Kymlicka, Tara Letwiniuk, Rod Macdonald, Jim Morrison, Stephen O'Neill, Cathie Parker, Andrew Petter, Tony Reynolds, Peter Russell, Michael Trebilcock, Mary Ellen Turpel-Lafond, Catherine Twinn, Jack Woodward, and Kevin Worthen. I would also like to thank the many students who enrolled in my courses at the Faculty of Law, University of Toronto, over the last several years for testing and clarifying many ideas and arguments. I am particularly grateful to colleagues and friends – Jim Anaya, Joel Bakan, David Beatty, John Borrows, Sujit Choudhry, Gina Cosentino, Dennis Davis, Gus Gibbon, Moira Gracey, Robert Howse, Allan Hutchinson, Ralph Keesickquayash, Karen Knop, Bruce Ryder, David Schneiderman, Joe Singer, Brian Slattery, Kerry Wilkins, David Wiseman, and especially Lisa Austin, Sonia Lawrence, and Mia London – who read an earlier draft of this book and offered extensive and constructive criticisms.

I am indebted to Robert Corbiere, Debbie Maiangowi, Farrell Manitowabi, Henry Peltier, Cecilia Pitawanakwat, Peggy Pitawanakwat, Jim Recollet, Gladys Wakegijig, and Ron Wakegijig of the Wikwemikong Unceded Indian Reserve for introducing me to the mysteries of Manitoulin Island, and Esther Osche of the Whitefish River First Nation for revealing the mountain within. I also owe a special debt of appreciation to Courtney Milne and Sherrill Miller, for their vision and grace.

This book could not have been written without the active encouragement of my colleagues at the Faculty of Law, University of Toronto, especially Dean Ron Daniels, whose personal and institutional support has been invaluable. I am also grateful for the hospitality of the faculty and administration of the UCLA School of Law, where I was a visiting scholar in 1992 and where, without knowing it at the time, this project was first conceived. The librarians at the Bora Laskin Law Library at the University of Toronto and the Newberry Library in Chicago, Illinois, provided valuable research assistance, and the Social Sciences and Humanities Research Council of Canada and the University of Toronto Connaught Committee provided generous financial assistance. I would also like to thank Andrew Wilson for his last-minute research assistance, Allyson May, Heather Ritchie, and Barbara Schon for their editorial assistance, and Virgil Duff and Anne Laughlin of the University of Toronto Press for skilfully shepherding the book through to publication.

Many of the ideas in this book have been presented at workshops and conferences sponsored by the Centre for Applied Legal Studies at the University of the Witwatersrand, the Department of Political Science at the University of Toronto, the Faculty of Law at Tel-Aviv University, the Faculty of Law at the University of Windsor, Harvard Law School, the Institute for the Study of Canada at McGill University, the Program in Latin American Studies at Princeton University, the Robarts Centre for Canadian Studies at York University, and the UCLA American Indian Studies Center. I am grateful to those institutions for affording me the opportunity to test my ideas and to participants for their valuable comments and thoughtful criticisms. Parts of the book build on but significantly revise work previously published in the *Alberta Law Review*, Michael Asch, ed., *Aboriginal and Treaty Rights in Canada* (Vancouver: UBC Press, 1997); the *McGill Law Journal*; the *Osgoode Hall Law Journal*; the *Queen's Law Journal*; the *Stanford Law Journal*; and the *University of British Columbia Law Review*. Copyright to the Nehahupkung and Dreamer's Rock stories that appear in the conclusion belongs to the Whitefish River First Nation. No part of these stories may be reproduced, reprinted, or transmitted in any form without the prior permission of Whitefish River First Nation.

Finally, I would like to thank my brother, David, and sisters, Katherine, Jennifer, and Ann, for their support and encouragement, and Mely Heceta for the gift of time. But the person to whom I owe the greatest thanks is Alyson Feltes, who supported this project from its inception and who, together with our wonderful children, Riel and Sam, taught me love's diference.

INDIGENOUS DIFFERENCE AND THE
CONSTITUTION OF CANADA

Introduction

Between Lake Huron and Georgian Bay lies Manitoulin Island, the largest freshwater island in the world. Recorded in its landscape are the spiritual histories of the Ottawa, Ojibway, and Potawatomi peoples, who constitute the Three Fires Confederacy and who regard Manitoulin Island as their ancestral home. Known as the Island of the Great Spirit, Manitoulin Island contains a number of lakes, many of which are said to be connected by a series of underwater caverns and tunnels. A powerful underwater spirit or manitou known as Mishebeshu, encountered in visions and remembered in myths, is said to dwell in several of Manitoulin's lakes and to travel through underwater tunnels exerting his power on Manitoulin and its residents. Thunderbirds – created by the Great Spirit to cleanse the world by bathing it with rain – often battle with Mishebeshu, pitting sky against water and causing violent thunderstorms to lash the shores of Lake Huron and Georgian Bay.[1]

One of Manitoulin Island's underground caverns is thought to lie in the waters of Manitowaning Bay, on the eastern side of the island near the small village of Manitowaning, or 'den of the manitou.' Manitowaning is the village where Sir Francis Bond Head, the newly appointed lieutenant-governor of the colony of Upper Canada, arrived by canoe

---

1 This account of Manitoulin Island and the Great Spirit is adapted from Basil Johnston, *The Manitous: The Supernatural World of the Ojibway* (Toronto: Key Porter, 1995); Theresa S. Smith, *The Island of the Anishnaabeg: Thunderers and Water Monsters in the Traditional Ojibwe Life-World* (Moscow: University of Idaho Press, 1995); and Courtney Milne, *Spirit of the Land: Sacred Places in Native North America* (Toronto: Penguin Books, 1994). For a colonial history of Manitoulin Island, see W.R. Wightman, *Forever on the Fringe: Six Studies in the Development of Manitoulin Island* (Toronto: University of Toronto Press, 1982).

from Penatanguishene in 1836. Bond Head travelled to Manitowaning to participate in gift-giving, a Crown practice that had begun shortly after the fall of New France, and to negotiate a treaty with Manitoulin Island's residents. He spoke to the several thousand who greeted him, and subsequently negotiated a treaty that set aside Manitoulin Island and its surrounding islands as a place of refuge for Aboriginal peoples threatened by increased settlement in the colony.

Countless colonial encounters on Aboriginal ancestral territories such as the one at Manitowaning in 1836 helped to constitute the country we now call Canada. But, whether they relate to Manitoulin Island, the interior of British Columbia, or the mountains of the Yukon, the spiritual histories and lived experiences of Aboriginal peoples have traditionally existed far beyond the borders of the Canadian constitutional imagination. In this book, I explore a number of constitutional commitments that affirm the central role that Aboriginal peoples, through their prior presence on the continent, their unique cultural identities, and their intersocietal engagements with non-Aboriginal people, have played in the constitution of Canada. My thesis, first and foremost, is that a unique constitutional relationship exists between Aboriginal people and the Canadian state – a relationship that does not exist between other Canadians and Canada. I hope to explain why this relationship exists, why it is unique, and what it entails in terms of the Canadian constitutional order. I also hope to explain why recognition – by citizens, governments, and the judiciary – of this relationship is demanded by elementary principles of justice.

As the history of Manitoulin Island illustrates, four complex social facts lie at the heart of the relationship between Aboriginal people and the Canadian state. First, Aboriginal people belong to distinctive cultures that were and continue to be threatened by non-Aboriginal beliefs, philosophies, and ways of life. Second, prior to European contact, Aboriginal people lived in and occupied vast portions of North America. Third, before European contact, Aboriginal people not only occupied North America, they exercised sovereign authority over persons and territory. Fourth, Aboriginal people participated and continue to participate in a treaty process with the Crown. Together, these social facts – Aboriginal cultural difference, Aboriginal prior occupancy, Aboriginal prior sovereignty, and Aboriginal participation in a treaty process – are exclusive to Aboriginal people in North America and, for the purposes of this book, constitute what I will refer to as indigenous difference.

The complexity of these social facts does not lie in their factual accuracy. Although some might take issue with their precise formulation, few deny their basic truth. Nor is their complexity a function of their exclusivity. Few deny that these facts, individually and collectively, capture differences between Aboriginal people and non-Aboriginal people in Canada. Instead, their complexity lies in their constitutional significance. Canadian constitutional traditions, generally speaking, are cool to constitutional rights that attach to persons or groups on the basis of difference. A familiar version of this perspective is the often-heard refrain that Aboriginal people are equal to other Canadians and therefore should not enjoy 'special rights' under the constitution. But a more sophisticated version argues that constitutional rights ought to reflect fundamental aspects of citizenship shared by all Canadians. Unless they can be shown to possess constitutional significance, these four social facts simply describe factual differences among citizens, and their elevation to the status of constitutional right clashes with the fundamental ideal of equal citizenship.

In this book, I argue that equality – the very ideal thought by many to be threatened by the constitutionalization of differences among citizens – is promoted by the existence of a unique constitutional relationship between Aboriginal people and the Canadian state. Specifically, constitutional protection of interests associated with indigenous difference promotes equal and therefore just distributions of constitutional power. Aboriginal cultural interests warrant constitutional protection because Aboriginal people face unequal challenges in their ability to reproduce their cultures over time. Aboriginal territorial interests warrant constitutional protection because Aboriginal people are entitled to at least the same level of protection that Canadian law provides to non-Aboriginal proprietary entitlements and because they lived on and occupied their territories before the establishment of the Canadian state. Interests associated with Aboriginal sovereignty merit constitutional protection because a just distribution of sovereignty requires a constitutional recognition of the fact that Aboriginal and European nations were formal equals at the time of contact and because the vesting of greater law-making authority in Aboriginal nations will assist in ameliorating contemporary substantive inequalities confronting Aboriginal people. Finally, Aboriginal interests associated with the treaty process warrant constitutional protection because treaties establish basic terms and conditions of Aboriginal and non-Aboriginal co-existence. Although the reasons why interests associated with indigenous difference merit constitutional protection are relatively distinct, they share a common feature: each appeals to a principle of equality.

I also argue that the purpose of constitutional recognition and affirmation of Aboriginal and treaty rights is to protect these interests in the wake of Canada's emergence as a sovereign state. Four relatively distinct sets of constitutional rights work to protect and promote interests associated with indigenous difference. The first set of rights, relating to Aboriginal cultural interests, includes rights to engage in practices, customs, and traditions integral to the distinctive culture of the Aboriginal community claiming the right. The second set of rights, relating to Aboriginal territorial interests, includes rights associated with what is often referred to as Aboriginal title. The third set of rights, which relate to interests associated with Aboriginal sovereignty, includes Aboriginal rights of self-government. Treaty rights, which comprise the fourth set of rights, typically protect interests associated with cultural, territorial, and self-government rights, but they are predicated on successful negotiations with the Crown.

Although they underpin relatively distinct sets of constitutional rights, the social facts that comprise indigenous difference are deeply interconnected. The history of Aboriginal territorial relationships on Manitoulin Island, for example, reveals the often profound and diverse cultural differences between Aboriginal and non-Aboriginal people in Canada. Aboriginal forms of governance also reveal culturally distinct territorial bonds and collective responsibilities. And participation in the treaty process is premised on the fact that Aboriginal people occupied and exercised territorial sovereignty over parts of North America prior to European contact. These interconnections give rise to normative considerations that might be overlooked by an approach that views each aspect of indigenous difference in isolation. By initially disaggregating indigenous difference into its constituent elements, I hope to reveal the diverse ways in which these elements interact and, through their interaction, give rise to interests that merit constitutional protection.

In defending the proposition that indigenous difference possesses constitutional significance, I hope to counter the claim that constitutional recognition of Aboriginal and treaty rights clashes with the fundamental ideal of equal citizenship. But I also hope to address another, very different claim – one that challenges what proponents of equal citizenship tend to assume, that is, the legitimacy of including Aboriginal peoples and Aboriginal territories within the Canadian constitutional order. Two variants of this claim stand out. The first argues that European assertions of territorial sovereignty in North America were premised on the assumption that Aboriginal nations were not sovereign nations at the time of European contact, an assumption in turn founded on the belief that Aboriginal peoples were inferior to European peoples. Given that

Aboriginal peoples were not inferior to European peoples and that Aboriginal nations were sovereign nations at the time of European contact, Canada cannot rightfully exercise sovereign authority and by extension constitutional authority over Aboriginal peoples and Aboriginal territory. The second variant argues that conceptualizing the relationship between Aboriginal peoples and the Canadian state in constitutional terms is foreign to Aboriginal world-views and does cultural violence to Aboriginal ways of understanding. Combining these two positions produces the claim that Aboriginal nations ought to be regarded as independent of the Canadian constitutional order and that the relation between Aboriginal nations and the Canadian state ought to be determined solely by reference to international law.

Canadian sovereign authority does owe its origins to a colonization project that assumed that Aboriginal peoples were inferior to European peoples, and, to the extent it fails to recognize Aboriginal forms of sovereignty, the present distribution of sovereignty in North America is unjust. Although international law has much to say on the matter, however, the constitutional task is not to cede the responsibility to address this injustice to the international arena. Instead, it is to establish constitutional arrangements that protect interests associated with indigenous difference, including interests that relate to indigenous sovereignty. This task requires a non-absolute, pragmatic conception of sovereignty that contemplates a plurality of entities wielding sovereign authority within the Canadian constitutional order. The legitimacy of Canadian sovereignty thus depends on constitutional recognition of territorial and jurisdictional spaces in which Aboriginal societies can take root and flourish, which in turn requires reconceiving Canadian sovereignty in non-absolute terms. It is true that much of Canadian law in general and Canadian constitutional law in particular is forged in discourse and traditions foreign to Aboriginal world-views, and it may be that the gulf between Aboriginal and non-Aboriginal ways of relating to the world is so great as to prevent constitutional arrangements from accomplishing this task. But this cannot be known in advance. Constitutional arrangements that take into account indigenous difference may capture a measure of intercultural allegiance. Proposing and defending such arrangements, in any event, is one of the aims of this book.

Exploring the constitutional status of Aboriginal people in Canada is as much a project of constitutional theory as it is an exercise in legal explanation. In Chapter 1, I address several theoretical issues implicated by this project and advance the claim that constitutional law is an enterprise that aspires to distributive justice; it seeks to ensure that power is distributed in a just manner. In so doing, I hope to reach beyond what might be the book's primary audience and to engage readers with a general interest in constitutional theory. Those more interested in substantive questions concerning the constitutional relationship between Aboriginal people and the Canadian state might wish to by-pass this chapter initially and return to it later if they want to reflect on the method employed in relation to these substantive questions.

Chapters 2 to 5 explore the constitutional significance of indigenous difference. In Chapter 2, I examine a number of threshold issues associated with ascribing constitutional significance to Aboriginal cultural difference. I trace the extent to which contemporary jurisprudence protects Aboriginal cultural interests and argue that tradition, international law, and ultimately distributive justice support attaching greater constitutional significance to Aboriginal cultural difference. In Chapter 3, I argue that Aboriginal territorial interests possess legal significance because of a basic distributive principle of justice with respect to land: prior occupants of land have a stronger claim to its use and enjoyment than newcomers. I also suggest that the legal significance of Aboriginal territorial interests is not merely proprietary but constitutional in nature. In Chapter 4, I argue that, despite the constitution's textual silence, interests associated with Aboriginal sovereignty merit constitutional protection. Chapter 5 explores the constitutional significance of the treaty process. Treaties are constitutional accords that distribute constitutional authority between Aboriginal people and the Canadian state; in light of their distributive dimensions, I suggest ways in which treaties can be interpreted in accordance with principles of distributive justice.

Chapter 6 translates the constitutional significance of indigenous difference into the discourse of rights and freedoms, exploring the relationship between interests associated with indigenous difference and subsection 35(1) of the Constitution Act, 1982, which recognizes and affirms the existing Aboriginal and treaty rights of the Aboriginal peoples of Canada. Properly understood, the purpose of constitutional recognition and affirmation of existing Aboriginal and treaty rights is to provide constitutional protection to interests associated with indigenous difference. I outline the nature and scope of these rights, including the kinds of activities, practices and authority that they authorize. Understanding Aboriginal and treaty rights in light of their underlying interests assists in determining whether and to what extent Parliament and provincial legislatures can justifiably interfere with their exercise.

Chapters 7 to 9 address some of the constitutional and institutional consequences of the claim that interests associated with indigenous difference possess constitutional significance. In Chapter 7, I examine the relation between Aboriginal and treaty rights and constitutional rights that pertain to all Canadians, specifically those enshrined in the Canadian Charter of Rights and Freedoms. The chapter concludes with an exploration of the complex issue of the Charter's impact on the ability of Aboriginal communities to determine membership in the face of federal efforts, in the name of gender equality, to unilaterally extend band membership to individuals who had previously lost their membership and Indian status by operation of federal law. In Chapters 8 and 9, I hope to shed light on some of the social, fiscal, and institutional implications of the main thesis of this book: that distributive justice demands recognition of a unique constitutional relationship between Aboriginal people and the Canadian state. In Chapter 8, I argue that the constitution requires governments in certain circumstances to provide social, fiscal, and institutional entitlements to Aboriginal people; Chapter 9 focuses specifically on positive state obligations in the context of contemporary treaty processes.

Although I aspire in this book to articulate a general theory of the constitutional significance of indigenous difference, I have not addressed the specific constitutional position of Métis peoples. The Métis, who belong to distinctive cultures and communities across Canada, trace their ancestry to marriages, usually between Aboriginal women and European fur traders and fishermen. Perhaps the most well-known Métis collectivity is the Métis Nation, whose national identity was forged primarily through clashes on the prairies with colonial authorities, culminating in the formation of provisional governments led by Louis Riel in what became known as Manitoba and Saskatchewan. The Canadian constitution refers to Métis peoples as Aboriginal peoples and recognizes and affirms their Aboriginal and treaty rights. As Aboriginal peoples, Métis peoples partake of indigenous difference but their unique histories give rise to a constitutional relationship with the Canadian state that may differ in important respects from the relationship that exists between Canada and other Aboriginal peoples.[2]

---

2 For an extended examination of the history and constitutional status of Métis peoples, see Royal Commission on Aboriginal Peoples, *Final Report*, vol. 4, *Perspectives and Realities* (Ottawa: Minister of Supply and Services Canada, 1996), at 199–386.

The last decade has seen a dramatic resurgence of indigenous nationalism in many countries originally forged through colonial expansion. Whether it is the Miskito in Central America, the Meriam in Australia, or the Sami in Sweden, indigenous peoples are advancing claims of cultural autonomy, territory, and self-determination in terms that share important features with what I refer to in this book as indigenous difference. International law, long the exclusive refuge of sovereign states, is beginning to acknowledge that it originated in part through and by a systematic denial of the rightful place of indigenous peoples in the community of nations. Despite the fact that in many ways the constitutional significance of indigenous difference transcends domestic constitutional arrangements, this book does not advance a theory of the constitutional significance of indigenous difference applicable to all states in which indigenous peoples are located. As I argue in the following chapter, determining the conditions of a just constitutional order demands a methodology that is attentive to history and context. At the same time, I hope that my contribution to the debate concerning the constitutional position of Aboriginal peoples in Canada will be relevant in other parts of the world where indigenous peoples are asserting greater autonomy and freedom over their collective futures.

Chapter One

Method

The wild requires that we learn the terrain, nod to all the plants and animals and birds, ford the streams and cross the ridges, and tell a good story when we get back home.

Gary Snyder, *The Practice of the Wild*[1]

The existence of a unique constitutional relationship between Aboriginal people and the Canadian state turns on what the constitution has to say about the matter. Yet determining the meaning of the constitution immediately raises matters of method. By 'method,' I refer to investigatory approaches to a number of interpretive and theoretical questions that are analytically prior to an inquiry into the constitutional status of Aboriginal people. For example, is the written text of the constitution clear, vague, or silent on the relationship between Aboriginal people and the Canadian state? Does the text exhaust the constitution's meaning? What role do judicial decisions play in determining the constitutional status of Aboriginal people? What does it mean to say that certain social facts – in our case, the four facts that comprise indigenous difference – possess constitutional significance? More generally, how do claims of justice relate to constitutional interpretation? And what is the relevance to this inquiry of the debate between those who argue that a universal set of standards exists for assessing the justice of constitutional arrangements and those who claim that normative standards are relative to specific cultural contexts?

---

1 Gary Snyder, *The Practice of the Wild* (New York: North Point Press, 1990), at 24.

In this chapter, I first examine what the text and structure of the constitution have to say about the constitutional position of Aboriginal people and the role that precedent plays in my inquiry. I then explore a common way of understanding constitutional law, known as positivism, that treats constitutional law as a set of textual and structural imperatives and rules promulgated by the judiciary. From a positivist perspective, whether Aboriginal people enjoy a unique constitutional relationship with the Canadian state depends solely on whether the text and structure of the constitution as interpreted by the judiciary support such a claim. I outline a number of positivism's deficiencies, not the least of which is its insistence on a radical separation between law and justice. I also navigate the debate between universalism and relativism and lay the theoretical groundwork for the claim that constitutional recognition of indigenous difference furthers equality. In addition, I explore the utility of the distinction between individual and collective rights and examine the relationship between equality and distributive justice. Each of these topics raises fundamental questions concerning the nature of law and justice and merits a more exhaustive discussion than it receives in this study. But I hope to provide an explanation of the method that informs my analysis in the chapters that follow.

Text, Structure, Precedent

Three provisions of the Constitution of Canada frame my inquiry. First, subsection 35(1) of the Constitution Act, 1982 provides that the 'existing aboriginal and treaty rights of the Aboriginal peoples of Canada are hereby recognized and affirmed.' By recognizing and affirming existing Aboriginal and treaty rights, subsection 35(1) provides explicit textual support for the proposition that Aboriginal people possess a unique constitutional status in Canadian law. Moreover, the fact that Aboriginal and treaty rights are 'recognized and affirmed,' as opposed to created or conferred, implies that such rights owe their existence not to subsection 35(1) but to some other source of law. Second, subsection 91(24) of the Constitution Act, 1867 authorizes Parliament to enact laws in relation to 'Indians, and Lands reserved for the Indians.' By referring to two classes of subject matters that fall within federal legislative authority, Indians and Indian lands – subsection 91(24) authorizes special legislative measures aimed at both a class of persons who can claim Indian legal status and territory set aside for such persons. And, third, section

25 of the Canadian Charter of Rights and Freedoms provides that '[t]he guarantee in this Charter of certain rights and freedoms shall not be construed so as to abrogate or derogate from any aboriginal, treaty or other rights or freedoms that pertain to the aboriginal peoples of Canada.' By insulating Aboriginal and treaty rights from the constraints of the Charter of Rights, section 25 signals that Aboriginal people merit unique constitutional consideration.

The structure of the constitution also suggests that Aboriginal people enjoy a unique constitutional relationship with the Canadian state. Reasoning from structure is a mode of interpretation that derives the existence of particular constitutional entitlements from structural presuppositions of the constitution itself.[2] A structural account of a unique constitutional relationship between Aboriginal people and Canada starts with the presupposition that Canada is a federal state. Parliament and provincial legislatures possess exclusive authority to enact laws in relation to certain classes of subject matters. As noted, the Constitution Act, 1867 assigns two such classes of subject matters, Indians and lands reserved for the Indians, to Parliament. If Aboriginal people did not possess a unique constitutional status in Canada, each province would be entitled to enact laws in relation to Indians and Indian lands located in that province. This result would be at odds not only with the text of subsection 91(24) but, more importantly from a structural perspective, with the federal system of government in Canada. Thus one of the basic

---

2 See Charles L. Black Jr, *Structure and Relationship in Constitutional Law* (Woodbridge: Ox Bow Press, 1968), at 7 (describing constitutional interpretation as including 'a method of inference from the structures and relationships created by the constitution in all its parts or in some principal part'). Some define structural theory more broadly to include what are often referred to as procedural theories. See, for example, Louis Michael Seidman and Mark V. Tushnet, *Remnants of Belief: Contemporary Constitutional Issues* (Oxford: Oxford University Press, 1996), at 166–89. For a classic procedural theory, known as 'legal process,' see Henry Melvin Hart and Albert M. Sacks, *The Legal Process* (Westbury: Foundation Press, 1994) (judicial decision-making ought to attempt to find consensus on a set of jurisdictional and procedural rules concerning which institution should decide particular issues and how such decisions ought to be made, as opposed to substantive principles that purport to dictate what those decisions ought to be); for a modern procedural account, known as 'representation-reinforcing theory,' see John Hart Ely, *Democracy and Distrust* (Cambridge: Harvard University Press, 1980) (the primary role of constitutional review is to ensure the fairness of the political process by making certain that everyone has fair access).

structures of the constitution – the federal distribution of legislative authority – suggests that Aboriginal people enjoy a unique constitutional relationship with the Canadian state.

Given the text and structure of the constitution, why is there a need to demonstrate the constitutional significance of indigenous difference? This need arises in part because reliance on text and structure that intimate that Aboriginal people enjoy a unique constitutional status in Canada raises more questions than it answers.[3] Neither text nor structure provides insight into a wide range of issues critical to understanding the constitutional status of Aboriginal people. For example, what types of activities do Aboriginal and treaty rights authorize? Are Aboriginal and treaty rights individual or collective rights? Do Aboriginal and treaty rights constrain the exercise of legislative power? What is the precise relation between Aboriginal and treaty rights and rights guaranteed by the Charter of Rights? What is the nature and scope of federal legislative authority with respect to Aboriginal people? The written text provides guidance on but ultimately underdetermines both the nature and scope of Aboriginal and treaty rights and the nature and scope of federal legislative authority. The structure of the constitution may provide interpretive assistance, but in no way does it resolve these questions.

The judiciary, through detailed interpretations of the provisions identified above, has begun to explore and resolve some of these issues. For example, the Supreme Court of Canada has held that the legal relationship between Canada and Aboriginal people is 'trust-like, rather than adversarial, and contemporary recognition of Aboriginal rights must be defined in light of this historic relationship.'[4] It has also held that the constitution provides a framework to reconcile the fact that Aboriginal peoples lived on the continent in distinctive societies before European contact with the fact of Canadian sovereignty, and that Aboriginal rights recognized by subsection 35(1) relate to practices, customs, or tradi-

---

3 For analysis of the limits of textual reasoning, see Eric J. Segall, 'The Skeptic's Constitution,' 44 U.C.L.A. L. Rev. 1467, at 1502 (1997) ('[t]he constitutional text is irrelevant to virtually every case the Supreme Court decides'); David A. Strauss, 'Common Law Constitutional Interpretation,' 63 U. Chi. L. Rev. 877, 883 (1996) ('[i]n practice constitutional law generally has little to do with the text'). For analysis of the limitations of structural reasoning, see Seidman and Tushnet, *Remnants of Belief*, at 180 ('it is hard to choose between structural theories or to give the theories determinate content without reference to disputed value judgments'). See, generally, Paul Brest, 'The Fundamental Rights Controversy: The Essential Contradictions of Normative Constitutional Scholarship,' 90 Yale L.J. 1063 (1981).

4 *R. v. Sparrow*, [1990] 1 S.C.R. 1075 at 1108.

tions integral to the distinctive culture of Aboriginal peoples.[5] Treaty rights have been held to constrain the exercise of federal and provincial legislative authority.[6] And provincial legislatures have been held to exceed their legislative authority when they enact laws that single out Indian people,[7] or when provincial laws of general application touch on matters that go to the core of federal jurisdiction over Indians and lands reserved for the Indians.[8]

Precedent thus supports the view that Aboriginal people enjoy a unique constitutional relationship with the Canadian state. Judicial decisions also suggest the role that precedent can play in fixing the meaning of otherwise generally worded and open-ended constitutional provisions.[9] But many questions remain. For example, what does it mean to speak of practices integral to an Aboriginal culture? Do Aboriginal and treaty rights inhere in individuals or collectivities? What is the relation between Aboriginal rights and treaty rights? The judiciary will probably be afforded opportunities to rule on these and related questions, but until this occurs, the constitutional position of Aboriginal people requires elaboration. And even if the judiciary were to establish precedent on these issues, any certainty would be more illusory than real. New cases present different sets of facts, and the judiciary often departs from precedent when it views prior holdings as unsound. More important, precedent does not eliminate normative concerns surrounding the legitimacy of judicial interpretations.[10] Whether the judiciary has provided a legitimate account of the constitutional relationship between Canada and Aboriginal people or convincingly explained the justice of constitutionally recognizing this relationship are questions that cannot be answered by precedent alone. Unless and until these nor-

---

5 *R. v. Van der Peet,* [1996] 2 S.C.R. 507.

6 *R. v. Badger,* [1996] 1 S.C.R. 771.

7 See, for example, *R. v. Sutherland,* [1980] 2 S.C.R. 451.

8 See, for example, *Kruger and Manuel v. The Queen,* [1978] 1 S.C.R. 104; *Four B Manufacturing v. United Garment Workers of America,* [1980] 1 S.C.R. 1031.

9 See specifically Catherine Bell and Michael Asch, 'Challenging Assumptions: The Impact of Precedent in Aboriginal Rights Litigation,' in Michael Asch, ed., *Aboriginal and Treaty Rights in Canada: Essays on Law, Equality, and Respect for Difference* (Vancouver: UBC Press, 1997), 38–74. See generally F. Schauer, 'Precedent,' 39 Stan. L. Rev. 571 (1987); Henry P. Monaghan, 'Our Perfect Constitution,' 56 N.Y.U. L. Rev. 353 (1981).

10 See Schauer, 'Precedent,' at 576 ('a pure argument from precedent depends only on the results of [previous] decisions, and not only [on] the validity of reasons supporting those results').

mative questions are addressed, they will continue to threaten the legitimacy of judicial inquiries into the constitutional status of Aboriginal people in Canada.

Positivism and Distributive Justice

By engaging these normative questions directly, this book strays from the well-travelled path of what legal philosophers call legal positivism – the view that legal rights and relationships exist solely because of positive legislative or judicial action.[11] Positivism insists on a sharp distinction between description and evaluation, or between what the law is and what the law ought to be. In the words of John Austin, a classical positivist scholar, '[t]he existence of the law is one thing; its merit or demerit is another.'[12] A positivist account of constitutional law strives to describe an objectively ascertainable set of rules, generated by legislative or judicial action and understood as constitutional in nature, that govern the exercise of state authority.[13] From a positivist perspective, whether a unique constitutional relationship between Aboriginal people and the Canadian state exists depends on whether the text and structure of the constitution as understood by the judiciary mandates such a relationship. Whether, as a matter of justice or morality, Canadian law ought to recognize such a relationship is an entirely different matter.

The drawbacks of positivism in this context are fivefold. First, by assuming that the constitution is comprised solely of formal rules generated by positive legislative or judicial action, positivism at best dimly comprehends a perspective alluded to earlier, namely, that at least some Aboriginal rights are inherent rights and not contingent on Canadian law. This perspective suggests that although the constitution recognizes and affirms Aboriginal rights, at least some Aboriginal rights owe their ori-

---

11 See generally, John Austin, *The Province of Jurisprudence Determined*, ed. W.E. Rumble (Cambridge: Cambridge University Press, 1995); Hans Kelsen, *General Theory of Law and State*, trans. A. Nedberg (Cambridge: Harvard University Press, 1945); H.L.A. Hart, *The Concept of Law* (Oxford: Clarendon Press, 1961). See also Owen Fiss, 'The Varieties of Positivism,' 90 Yale L.J. 1007 (1981).

12 Austin, *The Province of Jurisprudence Determined*, at 157.

13 Compare Luc B. Tremblay, *The Rule of Law, Justice, and Interpretation* (Montreal and Kingston: McGill-Queen's University Press, 1997), at 25 (positivist constitutional theory regards 'a given legal doctrine as true if its main propositions correspond to a subset of valid material rules of constitutional law laid down in recognized legal sources such as the constitution, a statute, or a case').

gins to the presence of Aboriginal law, not Canadian law,[14] and that, as a result, the Canadian constitutional order houses a plurality of legal systems.[15] Positivism does not dismiss the possibilities of describing Aboriginal rights in this manner, in so far as Aboriginal rights can be defined by reference to legal rights and relationships recognized by Aboriginal legal regimes,[16] but its emphasis on legislative and judicial rule-making is not immediately receptive to legal pluralism in general and an inherent understanding of Aboriginal rights in particular.

Second, positivist accounts of law typically obscure but do not eliminate normative concerns about the legitimacy of particular judicial decisions and reasons offered in support of such decisions. Specifically, in positivist descriptions of Aboriginal rights (for example, 'precedent holds that Aboriginal rights are practices integral to Aboriginal identity that existed pre-contact')[17] normative concerns invariably re-emerge (for example, 'is it just or appropriate to restrict Aboriginal rights to practices that existed pre-contact?'). Such concerns are often addressed by reasons judges offer in support of their rulings, but reasons for decision tend to play a secondary role in positivist accounts. Because they are rendered by the judiciary, reasons for decision no doubt form part

---

14 See, for example, *Coté v. The Queen*, [1996] 3 S.C.R. 139 at 174 (s. 35 protection is not restricted to 'those defining features [of Aboriginal societies] which were fortunate enough to have received the legal recognition and approval of European colonizers').

15 For scholarship on legal pluralism generally, see John Griffiths, 'What Is Legal Pluralism?' 24 Journal of Legal Pluralism 1 (1986); Martha-Marie Kleinhans and Roderick A. Macdonald, 'What Is a *Critical* Legal Pluralism?' 12 Can. J. Law & Soc. 25 (1997); see, specifically, John Borrows, 'With or without You: First Nations (in Canada),' 41 McGill L.J. 630 (1996); Natalie Oman, 'The Role of Recognition in the Delgamuukw Case,' in Jill Oakes et al., eds., *Sacred Lands: Aboriginal World Views, Claims, and Conflicts* (Edmonton: Canadian Circumpolar Institute, 1998), 243–56.

16 See, for example, *Mabo v. Queensland* [No. 2] (1992), 175 C.L.R. 1 at 58, per Brennan J. ('Native title has its origin in and is given content by the traditional laws acknowledged by and the traditional customs observed by the indigenous inhabitants of a territory' and '[t]he nature and incidents of native title must be ascertained as a matter of fact by reference to those laws and customs'). For discussion, see Kent McNeil, 'The Meaning of Aboriginal Title,' in Asch, ed., *Aboriginal and Treaty Rights in Canada*, 135 at 137–41. See also Ian Hamnett, *Chieftainship and Legitimacy* (Boston: Routledge and Kegan Paul, 1975), at 14 ('customary law can be regarded as a set of norms which the actors in a social situation abstract from practice and which they invest with binding authority'); Marc Galanter, 'Justice in Many Rooms: Courts, Private Ordering, and Indigenous Law,' 19 Journal of Legal Pluralism 1 (1981) ('indigenous law' refers to 'concrete patterns of social ordering').

17 See, for example, *R. v. Van der Peet*.

of a positivist account of the nature of law, but they tend not to enjoy the same ascribed status as judicial rules or holdings. Yet reasons for decision provide an opportunity for the judiciary to justify its own rulings. As such, they are central to law's legitimacy, belying positivist attempts to maintain a bright line between legality and normativity. Positivist accounts of the legitimacy of constitutional law – wherein decisions are legitimate if they are authorized by the constitution – do not help matters much.[18] Such accounts too often appear to be question-begging; constitutional law is justified simply because it is law.

Third, positivist accounts of law tend to assume a degree of determinacy in law that on many occasions does not exist.[19] Legal indeterminacy in this context exists in relation to both the choice of constitutional norm and the constitutional norm chosen. With respect to the former, the constitution invariably offers an array of norms from which to begin an inquiry and does not dictate how to choose among them. Is the constitutional status of religious schooling, for example, to be determined by reference to freedom of religion, freedom of association, equal protection of the law, or all three? With respect to the latter, the constitutional norm chosen to guide the inquiry often turns out to be a highly abstract principle which could logically be used both to support and to criticize the specific proposition under scrutiny. The establishment of religious schools both furthers and frustrates values underlying freedom of religion, freedom of association and equal protection of the law. In other words, because abstract constitutional norms often turn out to be contested sites of interpretation, normative stances are necessary to render them useful in particular circumstances. This is not to say that positivist scholarship is unaware of legal indeterminacy. H.L.A. Hart, for example, acknowledges that judges exercise 'discretion' when text or precedent do not provide clear direction.[20] And scholars

---

18 See, for example, Austin, *The Province of Jurisprudence Determined* (a law is valid because it is the command of a sovereign); Kelsen, *General Theory of Law and State* (a legal norm is valid if authorized by another legal norm of a higher rank); Hart, *The Concept of Law* (a law is valid if it complies with 'secondary rules' or laws that authorize the enactment of law).

19 For scholarship addressing legal indeterminacy, see Duncan Kennedy, *A Critique of Adjudication* (Cambridge: Harvard University Press, 1997); Robert W. Gordon, 'Critical Legal Histories,' 36 Stan. L. Rev. 57 (1984); Joseph Singer, 'The Player and the Cards: Nihilism and Legal Theory,' 94 Yale L.J. 1 (1984); Karl Klare, 'Law-Making as Praxis,' 40 Telos 123 (1979); and Duncan Kennedy, 'Legal Formality,' 2 J. Legal Studies 351 (1973).

20 See Hart, *The Concept of Law*.

have argued that the law requires that discretion be exercised in particular ways and for specific ends,[21] and that the law itself authorizes the judiciary to rely on normative considerations when exercising discretion.[22] But legal indeterminacy nonetheless destabilizes the distinction that lies at the heart of positivism, namely, the distinction between description and evaluation, or between what the law is and what the law ought to be.

Fourth, positivist modes of reasoning can lead to the trap of thinking that constitutional rights do not exist if precedent is silent on the matter. But judicial silence should not be automatically equated with constitutional silence.[23] As stated, the judiciary has yet to confront many issues involving the constitutional status of Aboriginal people, and the possibility that a unique constitutional relationship exists between Aboriginal people and the Canadian state in itself does not necessarily entail that the judiciary should immediately recognize this relationship in its entirety. There may be independent reasons for taking a minimalist approach to its recognition. In Chapters 8 and 9, for example, I argue that Aboriginal and treaty rights do more than restrict governmental action; properly understood, they impose certain positive social, fiscal, and institutional obligations on federal, provincial, and territorial governments. Yet the positive dimensions of Aboriginal and treaty rights pose complex questions of legislative and social policy that are not amenable to judicial assessment. In such circumstances, a minimalist interpretive strategy may well be warranted.[24] However, where few formal legal sources can be found in support of recognizing positive dimensions of a constitutional right, an undue emphasis on positivist modes of

---

21 See, for example, Neil MacCormick, *Legal Reasoning and Legal Theory* (Oxford: Clarendon Press, 1978) (arguing judges decide hard cases under a detailed judicial duty to do justice according to law).

22 For an extensive discussion of positivist theory in this regard, see Anthony J. Sebok, *Legal Positivism in American Jurisprudence* (Cambridge: Cambridge University Press, 1998) (arguing that positivism can explain how law can both incorporate and cabin normative considerations).

23 For a discussion of judicial minimalism, see Cass R. Sunstein, *One Case at a Time: Judicial Minimalism on the Supreme Court* (Cambridge: Harvard University Press, 1999).

24 See Lawrence G. Sager, 'Justice in Plain Clothes: Reflections on the Thinness of Constitutional Law,' 88 Northwestern U.L. Rev. 410 (arguing that social and economic rights call for a minimalist approach to constitutional enforcement). See also Lawrence G. Sager, 'Fair Measure: The Legal Status of Underenforced Constitutional Norms,' 91 Harv. L. Rev. 1212 (1978) (arguing that the legal scope of constitutional norms often is not coterminous with the scope of judicial enforcement).

reasoning may prematurely terminate the inquiry. In such cases, positivism tends to generate unduly conservative, and often inaccurate, descriptions of the law. This risk of inaccuracy arises as a result of erroneously treating constitutional law as a static body of manifest legal rules instead of an active, evolving, and interpretive inquiry into not only what constitutional law is but what it ought to become.

Finally, even where the judiciary has not remained silent on the matter, the constitution is more than what judges say it is.[25] Precedent has a unique way of infiltrating and shaping inquiries into the justice of certain constitutional arrangements not only by virtue of the normative force of its content but also because of its ability to provide a ready-made set of legal categories with which to begin an inquiry. As stated by Abram Chayes, 'the ability of a judicial pronouncement to sustain itself ... and the power of judicial action to generate assent over the long haul become the ultimate touchstones of legitimacy.'[26] As such, judicial decision making is deeply implicated in the conceptualization of the constitutional status of Aboriginal people in Canada. But in as much as Canadians seek a just constitutional order, the possibility that the judiciary has spoken on the subject will not end the inquiry. In Chayes's words, 'judicial action only achieves such legitimacy by responding to and indeed stirring the deep and durable demands for a just society.'[27] Judicial rulings at best are contributions to an ongoing debate concerning constitutional justice. Blind acceptance of the validity of judicially generated legal categories and constructions is especially fatal in the context of the constitutional relationship between Aboriginal people and the Canadian state – a relationship that raises profound normative questions concerning the legitimacy of assertions of Canadian sovereignty over Aboriginal societies that predate the emergence of the Canadian state.

---

25 Compare Paul Brest, 'Constitutional Citizenship,' 34 Cleveland State L. Rev. 175 at 181 (1986) ('[I]f the judges exercise a monopoly over constitutional decisionmaking, then other citizens and their representatives are excluded from participating in what are among the polity's most fundamental decisions'); Sager, 'Fair Measure,' at 1264 ('the Court should welcome the efforts of Congress and the state courts to shape elusive constitutional norms at their margins').

26 Abram Chayes, 'The Role of the Judge in Public Law Litigation,' 89 Harv. L. Rev. 1281 at 1316 (1976).

27 Ibid. For a detailed examination of the merits and demerits of the judicial arena in relation to Aboriginal claims, see Lisa Marie Strelein, 'Indigenous Self-Determination Claims and the Common Law in Australia' (PhD thesis, Australian National University, 1998) (on file with author).

This book treats constitutional law as more than a limited number of textual and structural imperatives and a finite set of legal rules that passively constrain the exercise of political power. Constitutional law is an enterprise that actively distributes power, primarily in the form of rights and jurisdiction, among a variety of legal actors, including individuals, groups, institutions, and governments. By 'power,' I mean the constitutional authority not only to engage or not to engage in certain activities but also to mobilize what Joel Handler describes as 'the rules of the game – values, beliefs, rituals, as well as institutional procedures – which systematically benefit certain groups at the expense of others.'[28] The fact that a legal actor possesses a measure of constitutional authority does not mean it possesses the material ability to accomplish what the constitution authorizes. A myriad of factors – economic, social, political, and legal – affects the ability of a legal actor to translate formal constitutional authority into material reality. But constitutional law distributes fundamental baseline entitlements among legal actors and, in so doing, it can have profound effects on the material circumstances of individuals and groups in society. This is especially true in the context of Aboriginal and treaty rights, which confer explicit territorial and law-making authority on Aboriginal people. Aboriginal title, for example, in so far as it vests an exclusive right to land in an Aboriginal nation, enables that nation to engage in or authorize and share in the proceeds arising from the development of renewable and non-renewable resources, including mineral resources, timber, and wildlife.

Judges may not experience their actions as possessing distributive dimensions; judges typically describe their constitutional role in supervisory terms. As guardians of the constitution, they see themselves as responsible for ensuring that exercises of political power comply with constitutional requirements. That judges experience their actions in this manner and in fact perform this task is no doubt true, but such descriptions obscure the distributive consequences of the supervisory role. When the judiciary rules on the division of legislative authority between Parliament and provincial legislatures, for example, it is not simply constraining the exercise of legislative power. It is distributing power between two levels of government. Nor are the distributive dimensions of constitutional law restricted to jurisdictional disputes.

---

28 Joel Handler, 'Poverty, Dependency, and Social Welfare: Procedural Justice for the Poor,' in Bryant G. Garth and Austin Sarat, eds., *Justice and Power in Sociolegal Studies* (Evanston: Northwestern University Press, 1998), 136–65 at 140.

The judiciary also distributes power, in the form of rights and freedoms, among individuals and groups, through its interpretations of rights and freedoms guaranteed by the Charter of Rights and Aboriginal and treaty rights guaranteed by section 35 of the constitution.

A focus on the distributive dimensions of constitutional law reveals its relation to distributive justice. As a distributive enterprise, constitutional law implicates an aspiration that power be distributed in a just manner. This aspiration is often expressed positively in the form of constitutional rules, either by explicit textual reference or by judicial interpretation. For example, section 15 of the Charter guarantees equality before and under the law and the equal protection and benefit of the law, thereby instructing the judiciary to ensure that legislatures distribute statutory power in a manner consistent with principles of equality. But the constitutional aspiration that power be distributed in a just manner is not exhausted by section 15. Nor does it depend merely on text or precedent. Instead, it operates as a 'background norm' in that it illuminates the legitimacy or illegitimacy of a wide array of particular distributions of power.[29] The legitimacy of the constitutional distribution of voting rights, for example, turns not simply on whether it is mandated by text, structure, or precedent, but also on whether the principle of 'one citizen, one vote'[30] is a distributively just means of allocating votes. Similarly, whether provincial legislatures deserve equal treatment in the distribution of legislative authority or whether Quebec ought to possess special status within the Canadian federation is a question that implicates the justice of the existing distribution of legislative authority. Debates over the distributive justice of 'one citizen, one vote' or of special status for Quebec illustrate the fact that Canadians aspire to belong to a just constitutional order. 'In such discussions,' in the words of Jürgen Habermas, 'participants clarify the way they want to understand themselves as citizens of a specific republic, as inhabitants of a specific region, as heirs to a specific culture, which traditions they want to perpetuate and which they want to discontinue.'[31] Constitutional law, on

---

29 Cass R. Sunstein, *After the Rights Revolution: Reconceiving the Regulatory State* (Cambridge: Harvard University Press, 1990), at 157 (discussing the role of contestable background norms in legal interpretation).

30 See Constitution Act, 1982, s. 3 ('[e]very citizen of Canada has the right to vote in an election of members of the House of Commons or of a legislative assembly').

31 Jürgen Habermas, 'Struggles for Recognition in the Democratic Constitutional State,' in Amy Gutman, ed., *Multiculturalism: Examining the Politics of Recognition* (Princeton: Princeton University Press, 1994), at 125.

this account, refers to an ongoing project of aspiring to distributive justice, disciplined but not determined by text, structure, or precedent.

This is not to say that comprehending constitutional law in terms of a commitment to distributive justice either resolves constitutional indeterminacy or insulates constitutional law from political controversy.[32] Those in favour of special status for Quebec typically identify certain aspects of Québécois identity, such as its culture and civil law tradition, as worthy of constitutional recognition. Those who advocate equality of the provinces typically deny that Québécois culture and tradition merit differential treatment in the distribution of legislative authority. Whether the former or the latter position constitutes a just distribution of legislative authority is deeply contestable and shot through with political considerations. Equally controversial is the claim that constitutional recognition of indigenous difference promotes a just distribution of constitutional power. As stated in the Introduction, many Canadians regard constitutional recognition of indigenous difference to be incompatible with individual equality. But the contestability of the justice of particular distributive outcomes should not impede an inquiry into the constitutional significance of indigenous difference. In fact, it underscores the need to determine what distributive outcomes might follow from constitutional recognition of indigenous difference and whether such outcomes are consistent or inconsistent with a commitment to distributive justice.

The Role of External Theory

In recent years, there has been an explosion of interest among philosophers and legal theorists in the conditions of a just constitutional order. Two scholars dominate the field. John Rawls has argued that a just constitutional order is one in which each person possess an equal right to the most extensive set of equal basic liberties compatible with a similar system of liberty for all, and that social and economic inequalities are to be arranged so that they are to the greatest benefit of the least advantaged.[33] Rawls derives these two principles of justice by arguing that

---

32 See Tom Campbell, *Justice* (Atlantic Highlands: Humanities Press International, 1988), at 3 (principles of distributive justice 'are ideological battlegrounds which exhibit some of the most basic differences in moral and political outlook').

33 See John Rawls, *A Theory of Justice* (Cambridge: Harvard University Press, 1971).

equally situated free and rational individuals, stripped of any specific knowledge of their society and of their individual circumstances, would agree that they constitute just principles of determining how basic institutions should be arranged to distribute benefits and burdens through social cooperation.[34] Ronald Dworkin has argued that a just constitutional order is one that accords individuals 'equal concern and respect.'[35] He argues that much of democratic life rightly involves the enactment of laws that strive to satisfy the preferences of citizens. But he distinguishes between personal preferences, which call for the assignment of a set of goods or opportunities to the preference holder, and external preferences, which call for an assignment of a set of goods or opportunities not to the preference holder but to other members of the community. Dworkin calls for constitutional rights to be entrenched and interpreted in a manner that prevents the state from constraining the liberty of some in order to satisfy the external preferences of others.[36]

Scholarship on the subject often appears to bracket social reality when working out the normative content of constitutional law.[37] Bracketing social reality tends to spawn a methodology that generates abstract, acontextual, and ahistorical principles that are then used to assess whether existing institutions meet the requirements of a just constitutional order. Rawls places hypothetical individuals behind a 'veil of

---

34 Ibid., at 153–6. In his recent writings Rawls has introduced the idea of an 'overlapping consensus,' consisting of 'all the reasonable opposing religious, philosophical, and moral doctrines likely to persist over generations and to gain a sizable body of adherents,' which can support a political conception of justice: see John Rawls, *Political Liberalism* (New York: Columbia University Press, 1993), at 15.

35 See Ronald Dworkin, *Taking Rights Seriously* (Cambridge: Harvard University Press, 1977), at 277.

36 Ibid., at 275–8. In more recent writings, Dworkin has introduced the idea of 'law as integrity,' which posits that 'rights and responsibilities flow from past decisions and so count as legal, not just when they are explicit in these decisions but also when they follow from the principles of personal and political morality the explicit decisions presupposed by way of justification': see *Law's Empire* (Cambridge: Harvard University Press, 1986), at 96. He has also sought to advance the view that his work does not endorse any particular set of moral values: see ibid., at 358–9; but see Ronald Dworkin, *Freedom's Law: The Moral Reading of the American Constitution* (Cambridge: Harvard University Press, 1996), at 75 ('the Constitution guarantees the rights required by the best conceptions of the political ideals of equal concern and basic liberty').

37 For the view that much of contemporary constitutional theory brackets social reality, see Jürgen Habermas, *Between Facts and Norms: Contributions to a Discourse Theory of Law and Democracy* (Cambridge: MIT Press, 1996), at 43 (criticizing philosophical theories of justice for 'los[ing] touch with contemporary societies').

ignorance' concerning their 'place in society' to determine the components of a just constitutional order;[38] Dworkin speaks of the need to
ground the justice of constitutional law in a 'vast over-arching theoretical system of complex principles.'[39] Such a methodology often supports
the conclusion that just institutions already exist in Western constitutional orders,[40] thereby providing little assistance in determining how
they can be promoted or established in the event that existing institutions are found wanting.[41] And it does not lend itself easily to assessing
whether existing institutional arrangements were established in a manner consistent with principles of justice.

This book claims that the conditions of a just constitutional order
cannot be determined without paying close attention to aspects of social
reality – in particular, the four complex facts that comprise indigenous
difference. Close attention to social reality entails a method that is con-
sciously empirical, historical, contextual, and critical. It is empirical in
its assumption that part of the task of constitutional theory is to determine whether and which social facts possess constitutional significance.
It is historical through its inquiry into the birth and development of
Canada as a sovereign state. It is contextual in its presumption that the
conditions of a just constitutional order may vary from country to country, and in its claim that the specific distributive principle brought to
bear on the justice of particular distributions depends on the nature of
the good in question.[42] And it is critical in its assessment of the justice of
existing distributions of constitutional power and in its determination of

---

38 Rawls, *A Theory of Justice*, at 12.
39 Ronald Dworkin, 'In Praise of Theory,' 29 Ariz. L.J. 353 at 354 (1997).
40 Compare Stanley Fish, *Doing What Comes Naturally: Change, Rhetoric, and the Practice of
    Theory in Literary and Legal Studies* (Durham: Duke University Press, 1989), at 370 (*Law's
    Empire* 'urges us to adopt "law as integrity," but since that is the form our judicial prac-
    tice already and necessarily takes, the urging is superfluous'); Pierre Schlag, 'Normativ-
    ity and the Politics of Form,' in Paul F. Campos, Pierre Schlag, and Steven D. Smith,
    Against the Law (Durham: Duke University Press, 1996), 29–99 at 56, n. 74 ('as jurispru-
    dence goes, [*Law's Empire*] is in the genre of cheerleading').
41 Habermas, *Between Facts and Norms*, at 58 ('all this holds only on the assumption that
    just institutions already exist .... [I]t is another question how these can be *established* or
    at least promoted in present circumstances') (emphasis in original).
42 For analyses of contextual methodologies, see Martha Minow and Elizabeth Spelman,
    'In Context,' 63 S. Cal. L. Rev. 1597 (1990); C. Wells, 'Situated Decisionmaking,' 63 S.
    Cal. L. Rev. 1727 (1990); Thomas Grey, 'Holmes and Legal Pragmatism,' 41 Stan. L.
    Rev. 787 (1989).

how just distributions can be established or promoted in light of contemporary social reality.[43]

This book thus shares much with what several scholars have referred to as external theories of law.[44] In contrast to an internal perspective, which seeks to understand law on its own terms, an external perspective treats law as a component of social reality and attempts to explicate its sociological functions. Some argue that law works to institutionalize and legitimate a market economy at the expense of alternative economic arrangements;[45] others argue that law works to institutionalize and legitimate patriarchal values at the expense of feminist aspirations;[46] still others argue that law works to institutionalize and legitimate dominant cultural values at the expense of marginalized systems of belief.[47] However diverse such stances may appear at first glance, they share a methodology that describes law in terms of its sociological functions, thereby

---

43 Compare Roberto Mangabeira Unger, *What Should Legal Analysis Become?* (London: Verso, 1996), at 132 ('[c]riticism explores the disharmonies between the professed social ideals and programmatic commitments of society, as well as the recognized group interests, and the detailed institutional arrangements that not only constrain the realization of those ideals, programs, and interests but also give them their developed meaning').

44 See Dworkin, *Law's Empire*, at 13–14 (drawing a distinction between internal and external points of view on law); Hart, *The Concept of Law*, at 86–8 (drawing a distinction between the external observer who does not accept the rules and the internal participant who uses the rules as guides to conduct).

45 Some advance this claim with praise: see, for example, Richard Epstein, *Takings: Private Property and the Power of Eminent Domain* (Cambridge: Harvard University Press, 1985), at 332 ('[a] system of private rights provides an exhaustive and internally consistent normative baseline of entitlements against which all the complex schemes of justice can be tested'). Others decry it: see Joel Bakan, *Just Words: Constitutional Rights and Social Wrongs* (Toronto: University of Toronto Press, 1997), at 61 ('[l]iberal rights discourse is sustained by, and helps sustain, the various elements of liberal and capitalist hegemony').

46 Catherine MacKinnon, *Toward a Feminist Theory of the State* (Cambridge: Harvard University Press, 1989), at 224 (law conceals 'the substantive way in which man has become the measure of all things').

47 See, for example, Kenneth B. Nunn, 'Law as a Eurocentric Enterprise,' 15 Law & Inequality 323 at 328 (1997) ('law is part of a broader cultural endeavor that attempts to promote European values and interests at the expense of all others'); see also Mary Ellen Turpel, 'Aboriginal Peoples and the Canadian Charter: Interpretive Monopolies, Cultural Differences,' 6 Can. Human Rights Yearbook 3 (1989–90) ('[t]he rights paradigm and interpretive context of Canadian constitutional law is so unreceptive to cultural differences that, as a result, it is oppressively hegemonic in its perception of its own cultural authority').

treating law as part of a broader set of economic, social, and political set of practices that comprise social reality.

I adopt an external perspective on constitutional law in three respects. First, by arguing that the Canadian constitutional order can and ought to be understood in light of certain social facts, I place constitutional law alongside social life and argue that the meaning of the constitution is in part a function of certain aspects of social reality. Second, by focusing on the distributive dimensions of constitutional law, I hope to illuminate the relationship between constitutional law and the material circumstances facing Aboriginal people in Canadian society. Third, I argue that the justice of particular distributions of power, whether in the form of rights or jurisdiction, turns in part on the extent to which legal authority materially empowers those entitled to its exercise. In each respect, I view constitutional law in light of its functions and as comprehensible in terms of a broader set of practices that constitute social life.

In other respects, however, this book stands at a distance from external theory. Despite my focus on the distributive dimensions of constitutional law, I do not attempt to reduce constitutional law's functions to a singular performance, nor do I view them as immutable. My account does not treat constitutional law solely as a function of social reality, nor does it reduce the normative implications of constitutional law to its distributive consequences. Instead, I seek to split the difference between internal and external perspectives on law.[48] Pure externalism ultimately disables one from judging the justice of existing distributions by reference to ideals internal to the constitutional enterprise and from proposing ways in which constitutional law can better achieve just distributions of power. Pure internalism, by turning constitutional law inside out, fails to explain what aspects of social reality receive constitutional attention and ignores

---

48 Compare Schlag, 'Normativity and the Politics of Form,' at 89 ('law has an *inside* and an *outside*; it is bounded') (emphasis in original); Unger, *What Should Legal Analysis Become?* at 179 (calling for legal scholarship to 'split the difference between rationalism and historicism'); Habermas, *Between Facts and Norms*, at 79 ('[l]aw is two things at the same time: a system of knowledge and a system of action' and '[i]t is equally possible to understand law as a text, composed of legal propositions and their interpretations, and to view it as an institution, that is, as a complex of normatively regulated action'); and Sally Falk Moore, *Law as Process* (Cambridge: Harvard University Press, 1978), at 57 (law 'can generate rules and customs and symbols internally, but ... it is also vulnerable to rules and decisions and other forces emanating from the larger world by which it is surrounded').

the distributive consequences of constitutional law. I acknowledge constitutional law's external dimensions in so far as I argue that the meaning of the constitution turns on the existence of certain social facts and that constitutional law operates to distribute power among legal actors in society, and I identify external factors that might explain why Aboriginal interests receive insufficient constitutional attention. But I also acknowledge that constitutional law possesses an internal dimension in so far as it is an enterprise that implicates an aspiration to distributive justice.[49] Given that 'power is maintained partly on the acceptance of its justifications,'[50] I critically examine justifications supporting existing distributions of power that affect Aboriginal interests. I also argue that alternative distributions that conform to principles of distributive justice can be established or promoted which will have a material effect on contemporary Aboriginal reality.

Equality as an Organizing Principle

If constitutional law implicates an aspiration that power be distributed in a just manner, what constitutes a just distribution of power? A short answer to this question is that an equal distribution is a just distribution.[51] But a longer answer acknowledges that the concept of equality

---

49 Compare Klare, 'Law-Making as Praxis,' at 134 ('Must we not recognize that legal culture can and has provided a context and a moral basis for resistance to injustice?').

50 Robert Gordon, 'Unfreezing Critical Reality: Critical Approaches to Law,' 15 Florida State U. L. Rev. 196 at 217 (1987). See also Habermas, *Between Facts and Norms*, at 36 ('the acceptance of validity claims, which generates and perpetuates social facts, rests on the context-dependent acceptability of reasons that are constantly exposed to the risk of being invalidated by better reasons').

51 See, e.g., Aristotle, *Politics*, ed. G.P. Gould, trans. H. Rackham (Cambridge: Harvard University Press, 1990), at 370–3; Aristotle, *Nichomachean Ethics*, ed. and trans. Martin Ostwald (Indianapolis: Bobbs-Merrill, 1962), at 119–20 (distributive justice produces equality). Following Plato, Aristotle divided equality into numerical and proportional equality, the former referring to distributions that treat all individuals within the set as indistinguishable, and the latter referring to distributions that treat all individuals within the set in proportion to a relevant characteristic, such as merit. See Plato, *Laws*, ed. G.P. Goold, trans. R.G. Bury (London: Heinemann, 1984), at 412–15. Aristotle confined proportional equality to distributive justice and numerical equality to corrective justice. See Aristotle, *Nichomachean Ethics*, at 118–19; see also Michael Walzer, *Spheres of Justice: A Defense of Pluralism and Equality* (New York: Basic Books, 1983), at xv ('distributive justice is ... an art of differentiation ... [a]nd equality is simply the outcome of that art'). For a detailed discussion of Aristotelian theories of equality, see Wolfgang von Leyden, *Aristotle on Equality and Justice: His Political Argument* (Houndsmills: Macmillan, 1985).

itself does not appear to supply the criteria by which to determine the justice of particular distributions. Equality is said to exist simply when equals are treated equally and unequals are treated unequally.[52] In general, when used descriptively, equality refers to the relationship that exists between two things measured by a common standard and found to be indistinguishable by reference to that standard.[53] Used prescriptively, equality refers to a relation that ought to exist between two classes of people who are similar or different in relevant respects.[54] Equality therefore requires that distributive outcomes reflect relevant similarities and differences that exist among people, but it does not specify which similarities or differences might be relevant to the justice of any given distribution.

It is often said that all Canadian citizens are equal before and under the law and that constitutional recognition of indigenous difference runs counter to fundamental principles of individual equality. According to this perspective, indigenous difference is not a relevant difference among citizens for the purpose of distributing constitutional rights. In contrast, I argue that indigenous difference is constitutionally relevant to the distribution of rights that protect interests associated with Aboriginal cultural difference, territory, sovereignty, and the treaty process. Arguments to the contrary tend wrongly to reduce indigenous difference to racial or cultural difference,[55] overlook the fact that similar treatment of people who possess relevant differences can constitute

---

52 Aristotle, *Nichomachean Ethics*, at 118–20. Compare Hart, *The Concept of Law*, at 155 ('justice is traditionally thought of as maintaining or restoring a *balance* or *proportion*, and its leading precept is often formulated as "Treat like cases alike"; although we need to add to the latter "and treat different cases differently"') (emphasis in original).

53 Peter Westen, *Speaking of Equality: An Analysis of the Rhetorical Force of 'Equality' in Moral and Legal Discourse* (Princeton: Princeton University Press, 1990), at 40–1.

54 Ibid., at 61.

55 Compare Adeno Addis, 'Individualism, Communitarianism, and the Rights of Ethnic Minorities,' 66 Notre Dame L. Rev. 1219 (1991) (cultural difference should not be reduced to racial difference); Turpel, 'Aboriginal Peoples and the Canadian Charter': (indigenous difference should not be reduced to racial difference); David Schneiderman, 'Theorists of Difference and the Interpretation of Aboriginal and Treaty Rights,' 14 Int'l J. Can Stud. 35 (1996) (indigenous difference should not be reduced to cultural difference); and Isabelle Schulte-Tenckhoff, 'Reassessing the Paradigm of Domestication: The Problematic of Indigenous Treaties,' 4 Rev. Const. Stud. 239 (1998) (indigenous difference should not be reduced to cultural difference). See also Chapter 2, below.

inequality, and ignore scholarship that defends Aboriginal rights on the basis that they further principles of equality.[56]

Two concerns appear to underpin the claim that indigenous difference is not a relevant difference for the purpose of distributing constitutional rights among Canadian citizens. First, constitutional recognition of indigenous difference might be thought illegitimate because it privileges the collective over the individual by attaching rights to individuals by virtue of their membership in a group. Second, collective differences between Aboriginal and non-Aboriginal people arguably are not relevant for the purpose of distributing constitutional rights. The first concern should be dispensed with at the outset. In so far as they attach to collectivities and protect interests that individuals share with others,[57] Aboriginal and treaty rights are often described as collective, as opposed to individual, rights.[58] But to suggest that collective rights are incompatible with notions of individual equality ignores the fact that equality itself possesses collective dimensions. If equality requires determining relevant similarities and differences among individuals, it requires determining whether two classes of people are sufficiently similar in relevant respects to warrant similar treatment or sufficiently different in relevant respects to warrant differential treatment. Equality, in other words, requires regarding people in light of the fact that they belong to particular collectivities or classes of persons and determining which similarities and differences warrant legal protection.[59]

---

56 See, for example, Will Kymlicka, *Multicultural Citizenship: A Liberal Theory of Minority Rights* (Oxford: Clarendon Press, 1995). See also Duncan Ivison, 'Decolonizing the Rule of Law: Mabo's Case and Postcolonial Constitutionalism,' 17 Oxford J. Leg. Stud. 252 at 254 (1997) (arguing that 'accommodation of differences is essential to treating [Aboriginal] people equally in diverse political communities').

57 For the view that some individual interests possess collective aspects, see Leslie Green, 'Two Views of Collective Rights,' 4 Can. J. Law & Jur. 315 (1991); see also Leighton McDonald, 'Can Collective and Individual Rights Coexist?' 22 Melbourne U. L. Rev. 310 (1998). For a collective interest analysis of 'cultural autonomy' see Denise Réaume, 'Justice between Cultures: Autonomy and the Protection of Cultural Affiliation,' 29 U.B.C. L. Rev. 117 (1995).

58 See, for example, *Delgamuukw v. British Columbia*, [1997] 3 S.C.R. 1010; see also *Amodu Tijani v. Secretary, Southern Nigeria*, [1921] 2 A.C. 399 (P.C.).

59 Joseph Tussman and Jacobus TenBroek, 'The Equal Protection of Laws,' 37 Cal. L. Rev. 341, at 343 (1949) ('the demand for equal protection cannot be a demand that laws apply universally to all persons. The legislature, if it is to act at all, must impose special burdens upon or grant special benefits to special groups or classes of individuals').

The second concern is more challenging. Why is indigenous difference a relevant difference for the purpose of distributing constitutional
entitlements? The relevance of certain similarities or differences among
individuals seems to turn on what standard or criterion is employed to
structure distributions. 'To each according to his or her need,' for
example, identifies need as a standard or criterion to be employed in
distributions, which in turn deems certain similarities and differences to
be relevant to distributive outcomes. Similarly, merit as a distributive criterion renders relevant certain similarities and differences among people, namely, their ability or skill at performing or accomplishing certain
activities or tasks. Criteria such as need and merit call for distributions
on the basis of particular attributes of classes of people; they stipulate
that people are equal and deserving of equal treatment when they share
such attributes and that people are unequal and deserving of differential treatment when they do not share such attributes. Assessing the justice of a distributive outcome thus involves determining whether it has
taken into account similarities and differences deemed relevant by the
criterion structuring the distribution in question. Whether indigenous
difference possesses constitutional relevance, according to this line of
reasoning, depends on the criteria chosen to structure the distribution
of constitutional rights.

But, as stated by Douglas Rae, 'the question is not "Whether equality",
but "Which equality?"'[60] Beyond a certain level of generality, equality
admits of many specific conceptions that attempt to supply criteria capable of assessing the justice of particular distributive outcomes.[61] Accordingly, distributive justice does not turn solely on fidelity to the criteria
employed in particular distributions. It also turns on the appropriate-
ness of the criteria themselves. In other words, what counts as a relevant
similarity or difference among people also depends on the object of the

---

60 Douglas Rae, et al., *Equalities* (Cambridge: Harvard University Press, 1981), at 19
   (emphasis deleted). See also Westen, *Speaking of Equality*, at 126 ('[e]very normative
   dispute can be framed as a contest between ... one proposed equality and another');
   David E. Cooper, *The Illusions of Equality* (London: Routledge and Kegan Paul, 1980),
   at 14 ('many of the interesting debates are not about the bare question, "should we
   have equality?", but about which of the various competing equalities we should have').
61 Westen, *Speaking of Equality*, at 61. Compare Rawls, *A Theory of Justice*, at 4–5 (distinction
   between concept of justice and conceptions of justice); Dworkin, *Law's Empire*, at 70–2,
   134–6 (distinction between concept of equality and conceptions of equality).

distribution under assessment. In the words of Charles Taylor, '[c]rite-
ria of distributive justice are meant to give us the basis for knowing what
our share is, and therefore when we are being grasping.'[62] But the fairness of a share, and who ought to receive one, cannot be determined
without reference to what is being shared. A focus on certain similarities
or differences among people may do justice in relation to some goods,
but can be at best irrelevant or at worst unjust in relation to the distribution of other goods.[63]

For example, need may well be an appropriate distributive principle
in relation to the distribution of health care, but less relevant in relation to the distribution of other types of goods, such as the right to
vote. Similarly, certain differences among people may well be irrelevant
when distributing political rights within a particular collectivity, but relevant when distributing political power among collectivities.[64] Assessing
the justice of the latter type of distribution requires asking which collectivities ought to be entitled to exercise political power. Asserting that
certain differences are irrelevant to this inquiry because they are irrelevant to the distribution of political rights within particular collectivities
often tends to assume the legitimacy of including a group that seeks
political autonomy in the very collectivity from which it seeks distance.
Whether indigenous difference is a relevant difference for the purpose
of distributing constitutional entitlements thus depends on the nature
of the entitlement in question. If indigenous difference is relevant to
the distribution of constitutional entitlements, then taking indigenous
difference into account will further, not frustrate, equality. And to the
extent that equal distributions are consistent with distributive justice,

---

62 Charles Taylor, *Philosophy and the Human Sciences: Philosophical Papers* (Cambridge: Cam-
    bridge University Press, 1985), at 2:300. Compare James Boyd White, *Justice as Transla-
    tion: An Essay in Cultural and Legal Criticism* (Chicago: University of Chicago Press,
    1990), at 233 ('the radical question of justice ... [is] not, "How much do I get?" but
    "Who are we to each other?"').

63 See Walzer, *Spheres of Justice*, at 6 ('principles of justice are themselves pluralistic in
    form; ... different social goods ought to be distributed for different reasons, in accor-
    dance with different procedures, by different agents; and ... all these differences derive
    from different understandings of the social goods themselves').

64 For an apparent endorsement of this claim, see Walzer, *Spheres of Justice*, at 62. While
    Walzer argues that American political culture is premised on equal treatment of citi-
    zens without regard to racial or cultural difference, he appears to accept that this par-
    ticular conception of equality is of little use in determining whether a group or
    collectivity has the right to govern itself.

acknowledging the constitutional significance of indigenous difference is consistent with the aspiration that power be distributed in a just manner.

What of the fact that Aboriginal people in Canada and elsewhere constitute peoples, in the sense that 'they comprise distinct communities with a continuity of existence and identity that links them to the communities, tribes, or nations of their ancestral past?'[65] That Aboriginal people constitute peoples is relevant to many areas of the law, especially international law, which regards a people as possessing a right of self-determination.[66] In the following section, I explore the significance of self-determination discourse to the task of determining the extent to which indigenous difference merits constitutional protection. But whether Aboriginal people constitute peoples in international law is of secondary importance to this task. The concept of indigenous difference includes many of the factors that lead scholars to conclude that Aboriginal people comprise peoples, including aspects of Aboriginal ancestry and continuity of identity, but the term 'people,' like the terms 'minority' and 'nation,' serves little purpose in my inquiry, other than providing a shorthand for the proposition that Aboriginal people constitute a class or classes of people who occupy a unique position in the Canadian constitutional order.

The Significance of Self-Determination

Although equality is the primary focus of this book, the constitutional relevance of indigenous difference can be articulated by reference to

---

65 S. James Anaya, *Indigenous Peoples in International Law* (Oxford: Oxford University Press, 1996), at 3. See also U.N. Subcommission on Prevention of Discrimination and Protection of Minorities, *Study of the Problem of Discrimination Against Indigenous Populations*, U.N. Doc. E/CN.4/Sub.2/1986/7/Add. 4, para. 379 (1986) ('Indigenous ... peoples ... are those which, having a historical continuity with pre-invasion and pre-colonial societies that developed on their territories, consider themselves distinct from the other sectors of the societies now prevailing in those territories').

66 Articles 1(2) and 55 of the United Nations Charter refer to 'the principle of equal rights and self-determination of peoples.' However, articles 2(1) and 2(4) of the Charter also affirm the 'sovereign equality' and 'territorial integrity' of member states: Charter of the United Nations, adopted 26 June 1945, entered into force 24 Oct. 1945, as amended.

other fundamental values,[67] such as respect for life,[68] liberty,[69] freedom of association,[70] or self-determination.[71] Of these other values, self-determination is perhaps the most significant, given its place as a core legal principle of international law. International law is often invoked in support of the normative proposition that all peoples, or nations, should be entitled to determine their own political future or destiny free of external interference.[72] The principle of self-determination, in the words of James Anaya, has arisen 'within international law's expanding lexicon of human rights concerns and accordingly is posited as a

---

67 Compare Schlag, 'Normativity and the Politics of Form,' at 39 (criticizing normative legal thought as monistic, for seeking 'to prescribe a single authoritative norm to rule within the described jurisdiction of the enterprise'); Cass R. Sunstein, 'General Propositions and Concrete Cases (With Special Reference to Affirmative Action and Free Speech),' 31 Wake Forest L. Rev. 369 at 381 (1996) ('Human morality recognizes irreducibly diverse goods, which cannot be subsumed under a single "master" value. The same is true for the moral values reflected in law. ... It would be absurd to try to organize legal judgments through a single conception of value').

68 See Brian Slattery, 'Aboriginal Sovereignty and Imperial Claims,' 29 Osgoode Hall L.J. 681 (1991) (rights to life and basic necessities ground Aboriginal rights of self-government).

69 See Leon Trakman, 'Native Cultures in a Rights Empire Ending the Dominion,' 45 Buff. L. Rev. 189 (1997) (liberty should be understood as encompassing a responsibility to respect Aboriginal interests).

70 See Aviam Soifer, *Law and the Company We Keep* (Cambridge: Harvard University Press, 1995), at 542 ('if ever freedom of association should have constitutional clout, it ought to be in cases brought by remaining Native Americans that assert tribal rights').

71 See Anaya, *Indigenous Peoples in International Law*, see also Royal Commission on Aboriginal Peoples, *Final Report*, vol. 2, *Restructuring the Relationship* (Ottawa: Minister of Supply and Services Canada, 1996).

72 See, generally, Antonio Cassese, *Self-Determination of Peoples: A Legal Reappraisal* (Cambridge: Cambridge University Press, 1995); Martti Koskenniemi, 'National Self-Determination Today: Problems of Legal Theory and Practice,' 43 Int'l & Comp. L.Q. 241 (1994); Guyora Binder, 'The Case for Self-Determination,' 29 Stan. J. Int'l Law 223 (1993); Edward M. Morgan, 'The Imagery and Meaning of Self-Determination,' 20 N.Y.U. J. Int'l Law 355 (1988); Nathaniel Berman, 'Sovereignty in Abeyance: Self-Determination and International Law,' 7 Wisc. Int'l L.J. 51 (1988). See, specifically, Russel Lawrence Barsh, 'Indigenous Peoples in the 1990s: From Object to Subject of International Law?,' 7 Harv. Human Rights J. 33 (1994); Mary Ellen Turpel, 'Indigenous Peoples' Rights of Political Participation and Self-Determination: Recent International Legal Developments and the Continuing Struggle for Recognition,' 25 Cornell Int'l L.J. 579 (1992); Maivân Clech Lâm, 'Making Room for Peoples at the United Nations: Thoughts Provoked by Indigenous Claims to Self-Determination,' 25 Cornell Int'l L.J. 603 (1992); Catherine J. Iorns, 'Indigenous Peoples and Self-Determination: Challenging State Sovereignty,' 24 Case Western. Res. J. Int'l L. 199 (1992).

fundamental right that attaches collectively to groups of living human beings.'[73]

International legal sources supporting a right of self-determination include article 1(2) of the United Nations Charter, which lists the principle of self-determination as one of the purposes of the United Nations.[74] Article 55 of the Charter calls for the promotion of a number of social and economic goals '[w]ith a view to the creation of conditions of stability and well-being which are necessary for peaceful and friendly relations among nations based on respect for the principle of equal rights and self-determination of peoples.'[75] Similarly, the International Covenant on Civil and Political Rights provides that '[a]ll peoples have the right of self-determination ... [and to] freely determine their political status and freely pursue their economic, social and cultural development.'[76] Self-determination has also been described as a right by the International Court of Justice.[77]

At its inception in the early twentieth century, the principle of self-determination was primarily invoked in the international sphere as a political justification for the liberation of Eastern European nations under the yoke of foreign domination.[78] It later served increasingly as a clarion call for colonies seeking to shed imperial shackles and assume independent statehood. In the 1950s, Belgium attempted to extend the principle of self-determination not only to colonies that wished to rid themselves of their imperial masters, but also to populations within independent states, so that indigenous populations and cultural minorities could assert a right of self-determination under international law.[79]

---

73 S. James Anaya, 'The Capacity of International Law to Advance Ethnic or Nationality Rights Claims,' 75 Iowa L. Rev. 837 at 841 (1990).

74 U.N. Charter, ('[t]he purposes of the United Nations are ... [t]o develop friendly relations among nations based on respect for the principle of equal rights and self-determination of peoples').

75 Ibid., art. 55.

76 International Covenant on Civil and Political Rights, art. 1, opened for signature 19 Dec. 1966, 999 U.N.T.S. 171 (entered into force 23 Mar. 1976). Article 1 of the International Covenant on Economic, Social and Cultural Rights contains identical language. Opened for signature 19 Dec. 1966, 993 U.N.T.S. 3 (entered into force 3 Jan. 1976).

77 *Namibia*, [1971] I.C.J. 16 at 31; *Western Sahara*, [1975] I.C.J. 12 at 31.

78 See, generally, Umozurike Oji Umozurike, *Self-Determination in International Law* (Hamden: Archon, 1972), at 11–26.

79 See, generally, Fernand van Langenhove, *The Question of Aborigines before the United Nations: The Belgian Thesis* (Brussels: Royal Colonial Institute, 1954).

The Belgian initiative was unsuccessful; in passing the Declaration on the Granting of Independence to Colonial Territories,[80] the General Assembly of the United Nations implemented what is known as the 'salt water thesis,' which restricts the right of self-determination to overseas colonies. The Declaration stated that '[a]ny attempt aimed at the partial or total disruption of the national unity and the territorial integrity of a country is incompatible with the Purposes and Principles of the Charter of the United Nations.'[81] In the words of Patrick Thornberry, 'The effect is that colonial boundaries function as the boundaries of the emerging States. Minorities, therefore, may not secede from States, at least, international law gives them no right to do so. The logic of the resolution is relatively simple: peoples hold the right of self-determination; a people is the whole people of a territory; a people exercises its right through the achievement of independence.'[82]

As with constitutional law, international law is not a static body of manifest legal rules but an active, evolving, and interpretive inquiry into both what the law is and what it ought to become. And international law increasingly is acknowledging the arbitrariness of restricting the right of self-determination to overseas colonies. Positivistic limitations on the principle of self-determination under international law, such as the salt water thesis, should not obscure its normative dimensions[83] or the emergence of a more flexible formulation of the principle of self-determination based in part on the relevance of indigenous difference. Indigenous organizations themselves certainly describe their objectives in terms of self-determination. The World Council of Indigenous Peoples, at its second general assembly, described self-determination as one of the 'irrevo-

---

80 G.A. Res. 1514, 15 U.N. GAOR Supp. (No. 16), at 66, U.N. Doc. A/7218 (1969).

81 GAOR 15th Session, Supplement 16, 66.

82 Patrick Thornberry, *International Law and the Rights of Minorities* (Oxford: Clarendon Press, 1991), at 18 (emphasis deleted). For critiques of the 'salt water' thesis, see, generally, Lung-Chu Chen, 'Self-Determination and World Public Order,' 66 Notre Dame L. Rev. 1287 (1991); see, specifically, Russel Lawrence Barsh, 'Indigenous Peoples and the Right to Self-Determination in International Law,' in Barbara Hocking, ed., *International Law and Aboriginal Human Rights* (Sidney: Law Book, 1988), at 68.

83 See, generally, Dov Ronen, *The Quest for Self-Determination* (New Haven: Yale University Press, 1979), at 7 (self-determination 'is an expression, in succinct form, of the aspiration to rule one's self and not to be ruled by others'); see, specifically, Iorns, *Indigenous Peoples*, at 225 (indigenous self-determination refers to 'the idea of freedom from oppressors and the right to determine their future, their own form of government, as well as the extent of self-government').

cable and inborn rights which are due to us in our capacity as Aboriginals.'[84] The International Indian Treaty Council described indigenous populations as 'composed of nations and peoples, which are collective entities entitled to and requiring self-determination,' which in turn is described as including external and internal features.[85] External self-determination encompasses all the features of independent statehood, whereas internal self-determination includes rights to maintain and promote interests associated with indigenous difference through parallel political institutions.[86]

The emergence of a more flexible formulation of the principle of self-determination is also reflected in the Draft Declaration on the Rights of Indigenous Peoples, prepared by a subcommission of the United Nations Commission on Human Rights. The Draft Declaration proposes to recognize that 'Indigenous peoples have the right to self-determination' and '[b]y virtue of that right they freely determine their political status and freely determine their economic, social and cultural development.'[87] Accordingly, the Draft Declaration proposes to recognize indigenous rights of autonomy and self-government, the right to manifest, practice and teach spiritual and religious traditions, rights to territory, education, language, and cultural property, and the right to maintain and develop indigenous economic and social systems.[88]

An explanatory note accompanying an earlier version of the Draft Declaration draws the aforementioned distinction between 'external' and 'internal' self-determination. It defines internal self-determination

---

84 Quoted in Thornberry, *International Law and the Rights of Minorities*, at 18.

85 U.N. Doc. E/CN.4/Sub.2/476/Add.5, Annex III, 2. See also Grand Council of the Crees (of Quebec), *Submission: Status and Rights of the James Bay Crees in the Context of Quebec's Secession from Canada* (Commission on Human Rights, 48th Sess., 1992).

86 For an illuminating analysis of external self-determination, see Karen C. Knop, 'The Making of Difference in International Law: Interpretation, Identity and Participation in the Discourse of Self-Determination' (S.J.D. thesis, Faculty of Law, University of Toronto, 1998) (on file with author). For discussions of internal self-determination, see Patrick Thornberry, 'The Democratic or Internal Aspect of Self-Determination with Some Remarks on Federalism,' in C. Tomuschat, ed., *Modern Law of Self-Determination* (Dordrecht: Martinus Nijhoff, 1993); Thomas Franck, 'The Emerging Right to Democratic Governance,' 86 Amer.J. Int'l L. 46 (1992). See also *Reference re Secession of Quebec*, [1998] 2 S.C.R. 217.

87 Draft Declaration on the Rights of Indigenous Peoples (as agreed to by the members of the working group at its 11th session) E/CN.4/Sub.2/1994/2/Add.1 (20 Apr. 1994), art. 3.

88 Ibid.

as 'entitling a people to choose its political allegiance, to influence the political order in which it lives and to preserve its cultural, ethnic, historical or territorial identity.' [89] An indigenous right of external self-determination is contingent upon the failure of the state in which indigenous peoples live to accommodate indigenous aspirations for internal self-determination: 'Once an independent State has been established and recognized, its constituent peoples must try to express their aspirations through the national political system, and not through the creation of new States. This requirement continues unless the national political system becomes so exclusive and non-democratic that it no longer can be said to be representing the whole people." At that point, and if all international and diplomatic measures fail to protect the peoples concerned from the State, they may perhaps be justified in creating a new State.'[90] Acceptance by the world community of the Draft Declaration would usher in a new international legal order, one in which indigenous peoples would no longer be denied the right of self-determination simply because they live within existing state structures.

What is the relevance of these developments to the claim that Aboriginal nations ought to be treated as independent of the Canadian constitutional order? They suggest the emergence of a more flexible formulation of the principle of self-determination in international law, one that extends to Aboriginal people in Canada and that calibrates its content to the capacity and willingness of the Canadian state to protect interests associated with indigenous difference. Under this formulation, a failure by Canada to constitutionally protect interests associated with indigenous difference increases the likelihood that Aboriginal nations possess a right of external self-determination under international law. However, if Canada protects interests associated with indigenous difference in accordance with the right of internal self-determination, it is unlikely that international law, under this formulation, would treat Aboriginal nations as independent of the Canadian constitutional order. Canada's international legal obligations, in other words, require domestic constitutional arrangements that implement the right of internal self-determination that Aboriginal peoples possess under interna-

---

89 Erica-Irene Daes, Chairperson of the Working Group on Indigenous Populations, *Explanatory Note concerning the Draft Declaration on the Rights of Indigenous Peoples*, E/CN.4/Sub.2/1993/26/Add.1 (released 19 July 1993).
90 Ibid.

tional law. In Chapter 4, I argue that these domestic arrangements must be predicated on a non-absolute, pragmatic conception of sovereignty that contemplates a plurality of entities wielding sovereign authority within the Canadian constitutional order.[91]

Notwithstanding the emerging distinction between external and internal self-determination in international law, the discourse of self-determination is difficult to adapt to the objective of allowing Aboriginal peoples to participate in Canadian, as well as their own, forms of government. The principle of self-determination supports constitutional recognition of Aboriginal governmental authority but it is not clear why, having exercised rights of self-determination, Aboriginal peoples ought also to possess the right to continue to enjoy benefits associated with Canadian citizenship.[92] In other words, the principle of self-determination yields a group right to decide to be self-governing,[93] but it does not appear to confer a right on the group in question to unilaterally decide the extent to which it is entitled to participate in the polity from which it seeks a measure of distance. If a group exercises its right to exclude others from its political institutions, on what basis can it demand representation in the political institutions of those whom it has excluded? Although there may be normative reasons in support of continued representation, the principle of self-determination, standing alone, does not appear to provide them.

The distinction between internal and external self-determination avoids this concern by defining internal self-determination as including rights of political participation within the state structure in which indigenous peoples find themselves in addition to rights of self-government and political autonomy. But simply redefining the principle as includ-

---

91 Compare James Tully, 'The Struggles of Indigenous Peoples for and of Freedom,' in D. Ivison et al., eds., *Political Theory and the Rights of Indigenous Peoples* (Oakleigh: Cambridge University Press, forthcoming), at 33 (internal self-determination coupled with an absolute conception of state sovereignty constitutes 'indirect colonial rule').

92 Compare Jeremy Waldron, 'Minority Cultures and the Cosmopolitan Alternative,' 25 U. Mich. L. Rev. 751, at 779 (1992) ('Indigenous communities ... are not entitled to accept the benefits of ... protection and subsidization and at the same time disparage and neglect the structures, institutions, and activities that make it possible for indigenous communities to secure the aid, toleration, and forebearance of the large numbers of other citizens and other small communities by which they are surrounded').

93 See Avishai Margalit and Joseph Raz, 'National Self-Determination,' 87 J. Philo. 439 (1990).

ing that which it appears to exclude does not eliminate the necessity of normatively justifying such a definition. The question remains: why should indigenous peoples be entitled both to rights of self-government and autonomy and the right to continue to participate in political structures from which they seek a measure of distance? In light of concerns that constitutional protection of interests associated with indigenous difference clashes with the fundamental ideal of equal citizenship, an answer to this question cannot rest solely on an assertion of a flexible international right of self-determination. As will be seen, it also rests on the constitutional significance of the four social facts that comprise indigenous difference.

Universalism and Relativism

This book stakes out what I believe is a distinct position among current debates concerning the justice of constitutional arrangements by side-stepping an important debate concerning the nature of human rights. Some scholars believe in the existence of certain values so fundamental to humanity that they provide universal standards for determining the justice of particular constitutional arrangements.[94] Others believe that normative standards are relative to specific cultural contexts,[95] and that there exists no universal means of judging the merits of culturally specific ways of life. Universalists charge that relativists sanction violations of human rights in the name of cultural difference, whereas relativists argue that universalism is a cloak for the projection of culturally specific beliefs onto cultures that possess different inner logics.[96]

Rights to be free of racial or cultural discrimination are often posited as universal human rights, inhering in all persons as a prerequisite to human dignity and freedom. The Universal Declaration of Human Rights, to take one international legal instrument, recognizes that all individuals 'are equal before the law and are entitled without any discrimination to equal protection of the law,' and that every individual

---

94 See, for example, Jack Donnelly, *Universal Human Rights in Theory and Practice* (Ithaca: Cornell University Press, 1989).

95 See, generally, Alison Dundes Renteln, *International Human Rights: Universalism versus Relativism* (Newbury Park: Sage Publications, 1990).

96 See Iris Marion Young, *Justice and the Politics of Difference* (Princeton: Princeton University Press, 1990), at 59 (defining cultural imperialism as the establishment of a dominant group's experience and culture as a universal norm).

possesses the right to vote and to take part in government.[97] The Universal Declaration suggests the existence of a 'limited international normative order'[98] that treats equality and antidiscrimination rights as universally shared by all individuals and to be respected by all governments. Constitutional recognition of Aboriginal-specific cultural, territorial, and self-government rights appears to threaten not only domestic constitutional commitments to the ideal of equality of citizenship but also universal commitments to equality and human rights.

Universality, however, is often purchased at the expense of determinacy, resulting in principles pitched at such an abstract level that they are of limited use in assessing the justice of particular constitutional arrangements. For example, it is not difficult to construct arguments that 'the will to live and to be free,' one basis for the assertion of universal rights,[99] both undercuts and underpins the legitimacy of a unique constitutional relationship between Aboriginal people and the Canadian state. One variant would stress the relationship between Aboriginal forms of government and individual and collective identities; the other would stress values of antidiscrimination and individual autonomy. Deriving one conclusion instead of the other requires the injection of normative concerns that cannot claim the same degree of universality that might attach to the more abstract premise of the will to live and be free.

Moreover, there is no universally accepted way to choose which universal norm ought to govern the assessment of the legitimacy of particular constitutional arrangements. For example, how does the right to equal protection of the law and the right to vote and take part in government, to the extent that they are interpreted as hostile to constitutional recognition of Aboriginal forms of government, square with article 27 of the International Covenant on Civil and Political Rights, which provides that 'persons belonging to [ethnic] minorities shall not be denied the right, in community with the other members of their group, to enjoy

---

97 G.A. Res. 217A, U.N. GAOR, 3d Sess., pt. 1, at 71, U.N. Doc. A/810 (1948), arts. 7 and 21, respectively.

98 Douglas Lee Donoho, 'Relativism versus Universalism in Human Rights: The Search for Meaningful Standards,' 27 Stan. J. Int'l L. 345, at 357 (1991).

99 Abdullahi Ahmed An-Na'im, *Toward an Islamic Reformation: Civil Liberties, Human Rights, and International Law* (Syracuse: Syracuse University Press, 1990), at 164 ('universal human rights are based on the two primary forces that motivate all human behavior, the will to live and the will to be free').

their own culture'?[100] Those in favour of constitutional recognition of Aboriginal forms of government would enlist article 27 in its defence; those opposed would refer to equal protection. It is true that contestability in relation to the choice of the governing universal norm does not itself refute universalism. However, as we have seen, a flexible formulation of the right of self-determination is emerging in international law, making it difficult to determine on which side of the dispute universalism lies.

One strength of cultural relativism lies in its ability to circumvent problems of indeterminacy that bedevil any attempt to establish universality. The relativist can concede that some principles may be shared by all but argue that they exist at a level of abstraction so high that their articulation is of no use in assessing the legitimacy of particular constitutional arrangements. Any principle that deserves the mantle of universality does so by virtue of its indeterminacy. Because its meaning will be rendered concrete in radically diverse ways by different communities, any attempt to insist on one particular interpretation constitutes interpretive imperialism. Specifically, cultural relativism often underpins challenges to the legitimacy of constitutional principles and practices that do not take into account Aboriginal world-views and ways of life.[101] It is often said that because Aboriginal people have different ways of relating to others and to the world, as well as different ways of resolving disputes, it is unjust to govern Aboriginal people by normative standards that emanate from, and are only meaningful to, non-Aboriginal society. Rupert Ross, for example, writes eloquently of the injustices invariably are produced when the Canadian legal system fails to acknowledge cultural differences between Aboriginal and non-Aboriginal people. He argues for reforms that respect such cultural differences and facilitate cross-cultural communication.[102]

I do not challenge the fact that Aboriginal people have culturally different ways of relating to others and to the world; in fact, in the next chapter, I argue that interests associated with Aboriginal cultural differ-

---

100 19 Dec. 1966, art. 27, 999 U.N.T.S. 171.

101 See, for example, Turpel, 'Aboriginal Peoples and the Canadian Charter' (challenging the cultural authority of Canadian constitutional law as it relates to Aboriginal people). See more generally, Nunn, 'Law as a Eurocentric Enterprise,' at 324 ('law is the creation of a particular *type* of culture') (emphasis in original).

102 Rupert Ross, *Dancing with a Ghost: Exploring Indian Reality* (Markham: Octopus, 1992), at 186.

ence merit constitutional protection. But cultural relativism, as opposed to cultural difference, is an unstable perspective on which to rest constitutional recognition of indigenous difference. First, there is nothing logically necessary about equating cultural relativism with the protection of cultural difference. One could derive a denial of the relevance of cultural difference from some versions of cultural relativism,[103] namely, those that claim that different moral beliefs are the products of differing cultural contexts but do not ascribe normative significance to this fact.[104] Second, at least some versions of relativism are self-refuting. For example, should relative or universal status be ascribed to the relativist's claim that 'evaluations are relative to the cultural background out of which they arise'?[105] It cannot be a universal truth, for relativism dismisses such a concept; on the other hand, if it is relative to a particular culture, then relativism itself is relative.[106]

Many critics have argued that adhering to cultural relativism forces the toleration of intolerance. With its premise that moral values are con-

---

103 Cultural relativism is often broken down into a number of different versions. A common list includes descriptive relativism, normative relativism, and meta-ethical relativism. Descriptive relativism is factual in nature: it points out that as a matter of fact different moral beliefs exist by virtue of differing cultural contexts. For refinements of this version, see M. Spiro, 'Cultural Relativism and the Future of Anthropology,' 1 Cultural Anthropology 259 at 260–1 (1986). Normative relativism is based on the more contentious claim that differing moral values have no validity outside of their particular cultural contexts and, as such, are incommensurable. The work of Ruth Benedict is often associated with this view. See Ruth Benedict, *Patterns of Culture* (Boston: Houghton Mifflin, 1934), at 278 (there are 'coexisting and equally valid patterns of life'). Meta-ethical relativism holds that one cannot objectively justify the moral beliefs of one culture over the moral beliefs of another, although there may exist certain shared or universal values. See, generally, Donoho, 'Relativism versus Universalism in Human Rights,' at 351–2; William K. Frankena, *Ethics* (Englewood Cliffs, N.J.: Prentice-Hall, 1973), at 109–10; Paul F. Schmidt, 'Some Criticisms of Cultural Relativism,' 70 J. Philo. 780 (1955).

104 Similarly, one could derive recognition of the relevance of indigenous difference from some versions of universalism: see, e.g., Anaya, *Indigenous Peoples in International Law*, at 75–96.

105 Melville J. Herskovits, *Man and His Works: The Science of Cultural Anthropology* (New York: Knopf, 1948), at 63.

106 Many have made this point. See for example, Schmidt, 'Some Criticisms of Cultural Relativism,' 70 J. Phil. 780 at 781 (1955) ('the cultural relativist cannot have it both ways: he cannot claim that the truth of factual judgments is relative to their cultural background and at the same time believe in the objectivity of sociological and anthropological investigations'). See also Grace A. de Laguna, 'Cultural Relativism and Science,' 51 Phil. Rev. 141 (1942).

tingent on cultural practices, relativism disarms social criticism; as one critic writes, '[i]ts tolerance might be less charitably interpreted as the cowardice of moral abstention.'[107] The critic is disarmed because once the wall of cultural autonomy is raised as a defence, little more can be said on a matter.[108] One version of this charge notes that relativism does not have egalitarian consequences; since all it does is assert that values are culturally specific, it provides no means of challenging culturally specific inegalitarianism.[109] Another scholar has even argued that, pushed to its extreme, relativism permits intolerance on the part of the external observer: if all moral beliefs are relative, '[w]e might just as well hate them all.'[110] Still others have claimed that, by elevating principles of tolerance to the international context, cultural relativists commit the very sin they accuse universalists of committing, namely, the imposition of ethnocentric views about how groups ought to relate to one another.[111]

Relativist claims tend to totalize the concept of culture – as if one single uniform, dominant culture exists within a particular society instead of intersecting and competing structures of belief.[112] When people have

---

107 R.J. Vincent, *Human Rights and International Relations* (Cambridge: Cambridge University Press, 1986), at 55; I.C. Jarvis, 'Rationalism and Relativism,' 34 Brit. J. Sociology 44 at 46 (1983) ('behind relativism nihilism looms'); Clyde Kluckhohn, 'Ethical Relativity: Sic et Non,' 52 J. Phil. 663 (1995) ('one is compelled to accept any cultural pattern as vindicated precisely by its cultural status'). But see Herskovits, *Man and His Works*, at 245 ('To recognize that right, and justice, and beauty may have as many manifestations as there are cultures is to express tolerance, not nihilism').

108 Compare Donnelly, *Universal Human Rights*, at 116 ('no matter how firmly someone else, or even a whole culture, believes differently, at some point we simply must say that those contrary beliefs are wrong'); and Vincent, *Human Rights and International Relations*, at 55 ('[h]owever true it is that we all tend to devolve upon our own worlds the responsibility of being in the right against others, this is not a reason to withdraw from moral argument in world politics all together').

109 See Clifford Geertz, *The Interpretation of Cultures* (New York: Basic Books, 1973), at 192–200; see also Fish, *Doing What Comes Naturally*, at 351–4 (non-foundationalism does not entail any particular political consequences).

110 Robert Redfield, *The Primitive World and Its Transformations* (Ithaca: Cornell University Press, 1962), at 147.

111 See, e.g., Frank E. Hartung, 'Cultural Relativity and Moral Judgments,' 21 Phil. Sci. 118 at 121 (1954) (relativism 'is an ethnocentric circumlocution, a round-about way of saying that our liberal tradition is the best tradition, and that all ought to follow').

112 See Rhoda Howard, *Human Rights in Commonwealth Africa* (Totowa N.J.: Rowman & Littlefield, 1986), at 23–5; see also Annie Bunting, 'Theorizing Women's Cultural Diversity in Feminist International Human Rights Strategies,' 20 J. Law & Society 6 at 9 (1993) ('multiply-constituted nature and competing understandings of any given culture are rarely discussed' in relativistic accounts).

conflicting or overlapping collective affiliations, an assertion of cultural relativism adds little insight and may justify protecting only those aspects of a culture that differ from those of the observer, resulting in only traditional forms of culture being respected by external observers. Cultural relativism may ignore how powerful cultures exercise power over weak ones. Interactions with external forces, including legal norms, often tend to reverberate through cultures in unpredictable ways and leave lasting imprints on cultural identities. Aboriginal practices that arose in response and in reaction to European contact, such as participating in the fur trade or incorporating elements of European religious beliefs into Aboriginal consciousness,[113] and that ensured the continuation and survival of Aboriginal communities, may not be shielded by blanket assertions of cultural relativism. As discussed in the following chapter, the boundaries of culture are more porous than cultural relativism presupposes. A particular culture that is both similar to and different from a more dominant culture may only be able to assert its identity in terms of its difference and not in its more subtle variations of difference and similarity.

The debate between universalism and relativism shows no sign of abating in the near future. Pending its outcome, grounding the constitutional significance of indigenous difference in either relativist or universalist premises is inherently unstable.[114] The risk of constitutional instability is sufficient justification, if not to 'move beyond' it,[115] then at least to put the debate aside and engage in the more immediate task of assessing the constitutional relevance of indigenous difference in light of principles that potentially possess normative significance to Aboriginal and non-Aboriginal people alike.[116] Such principles can serve as

---

113 See, e.g., John Borrows, 'A Genealogy of Law: Inherent Sovereignty and First Nations Self-Government,' 30 Osgoode Hall L.J. 291 (1992).

114 But see Donnelly, *Universal Human Rights in Theory and Practice*, at 118 ('where there is a thriving indigenous cultural tradition and community, arguments of cultural relativism offer a strong defense against outside interference – including disruptions that might be caused by introducing "universal" human rights').

115 See Richard J. Bernstein, *Beyond Objectivism and Relativism: Science, Hermeneutics, and Praxis* (Philadelphia: University of Pennsylvania Press, 1983) at 1–44 (arguing that a new understanding of rationality permits one to move beyond philosophical debates concerning objectivism and relativism).

116 Compare Abdullahi Ahmed An-Na'im, 'Toward a Cross-Cultural Approach to Defining International Standards of Human Rights: The Meaning of Cruel, Inhuman or Degrading Treatment or Punishment,' in An-Na'im, ed., *Human Rights in Cross-*

standards for determining the justice of existing constitutional arrangements and suggest ways in which just distributions of power can be
established or promoted in light of contemporary social reality without
having to wait for a conclusive determination of whether universalism or
cultural relativism is actually 'true.' In the next chapter, I argue that
interests associated with Aboriginal cultural difference warrant constitutional protection not because of any incommensurability between
Aboriginal and non-Aboriginal values, but because such protection promotes a just distribution of constitutional power. By proceeding in this
way, I hope to capture a measure of intercultural agreement among
Aboriginal people and non-Aboriginal people on the constitutional significance of indigenous difference.

Cultural Perspective: A Quest for Consensus (Philadelphia: University of Pennsylvania
Press, 1992), at 19, 27 ('[C]ultural consensus on the goals and methods of cooperation in the protection and promotion of human rights ... can be achieved through
internal cultural discourse and cross-cultural dialogue ... Cross-cultural dialogue
should be aimed at broadening and deepening international ... consensus'); Amelie
Oskenberg Rorty, 'Relativism, Persons, and Practices,' in Michael Kraus, ed., *Relativism: Interpretation and Confrontation* (Notre Dame: University of Notre Dame Press,
1989), 418–440, at 418 ('nothing follows from [relativism] about the impossibility of
cross-cultural interpretation, communication, or evaluation, particularly among cultures engaged in practical interactions with one another').

Chapter Two

Culture

[A] person needed to establish lines of communication with the non-human realm. He would do so through a vision encounter with a more or less individualized, personalized manifestation of the power that pervaded the wild realm of nature. The passage from the human sphere to the nonhuman sphere was ritually dangerous and hedged with taboos. Contact could be achieved only if the human supplicant were purged of the taint of human existence. Bathing cleaned off the smell of sweat and the odor of smoke from the plank houses; fasting and emetics cleaned out all trace of food from the belly; isolation in wild and desolate places protected the seeker from the contamination of human companionship.

Pamela Amoss, *Coast Salish Spirit Dancing*[1]

Aboriginal people belong to distinctive cultures that have been and continue to be threatened by assimilative forces within Canadian society.[2] They are not alone in this respect; other Canadian citizens also belong to distinctive cultures threatened by assimilation. Moreover, there is no one single Aboriginal culture; Aboriginal cultures are as varied and distinct as the cultures that comprise non-Aboriginal societies. Given that Aboriginal and certain non-Aboriginal cultures alike are threatened by

---

1 Pamela Amoss, *Coast Salish Spirit Dancing: The Survival of an Ancient Religion* (Seattle: University of Washington Press, 1978), at 12–13.
2 Compare Iris Young's definition of 'social group' as 'a collective of persons differentiated from at least one other group by cultural forms, practices, or ways of life.' See Iris Marion Young, *Justice and the Politics of Difference* (Princeton: Princeton University Press, 1990), at 43.

assimilation, as well as the existence of deep diversity among Aboriginal cultures, what does it mean to speak of Aboriginal cultural difference as an aspect of indigenous difference? Aboriginal cultural difference exists by virtue of the distinctive content of the cultures in which Aboriginal people participate. Some aspects of Aboriginal cultures, including practices that Aboriginal people engaged in before contact with Europeans as well as ways in which Aboriginal people have resisted, responded to, adapted, and incorporated non-Aboriginal ways of life into their collective identities, are unique to Aboriginal people. It is in this sense that Aboriginal cultural difference is exclusive to Aboriginal people and, I argue in this chapter, merits constitutional protection.

The claim that Aboriginal cultural difference possesses constitutional significance is not controversial – it conforms to a judicial willingness to constitutionally protect practices, customs, and traditions integral to distinctive Aboriginal cultures. It also conforms to Canadian constitutional traditions and Canada's international legal obligations, and it is consistent with a judicial proclivity to view the diverse cultural identities of all Canadians as worthy of some measure of constitutional respect. But, as will be seen, this judicial tendency is a relatively recent phenomenon. Canadian constitutional law historically declined to attach constitutional significance to Aboriginal cultural difference and to the extent it received judicial notice, Aboriginal cultural difference was typically cast in terms of inferiority. Judicial devaluation of Aboriginal cultural difference was consistent with broader political efforts to assimilate Aboriginal people into Canadian society through legislative and policy initiatives designed to ensure that, in the words of a deputy superintendent-general of Indian Affairs, 'there is not a single Indian in Canada that has not been absorbed into the body politic.'[3]

Although the judiciary now accords a measure of constitutional protection to Aboriginal cultural difference, current jurisprudence is flawed in three respects. First, it unreasonably restricts constitutional protection to pre-contact cultural practices integral to Aboriginal cultural identities. Second, it fails adequately to explain why interests associated with Aboriginal cultural difference merit constitutional protection. Third, and perhaps most important, it treats Aboriginal cultural difference as though it were the only aspect of indigenous difference worthy of consti-

---

3 As quoted in J. Rick Ponting and Roger Gibbins, *Out of Irrelevance: A Socio-Political Introduction to Indian Affairs in Canada* (Toronto: Butterworths, 1980), at 3–30.

tutional protection, ignoring the fact that indigenous difference also includes Aboriginal prior occupancy, Aboriginal prior sovereignty, and Aboriginal participation in a treaty process. Tradition, international law, and ultimately principles of distributive justice support attaching constitutional significance to Aboriginal cultural difference, but Aboriginal cultural difference is best understood as one of several sets of constitutional interests underlying Aboriginal and treaty rights. Constitutional protection of indigenous difference ought to extend beyond protection of certain customs, practices, and traditions integral to Aboriginal cultures to include protection of interests associated with territory, sovereignty, and the treaty process.

Comprehending Culture

In February 1988, several members of the Coast Salish nation in British Columbia took another member, David Thomas, against his will to a ceremonial long house. Apparently in accordance with Coast Salish traditions, they kept him there for four days to undergo initiation ceremonies required to become a spirit dancer.[4] According to facts found at trial, he was denied food, forced to walk naked in a creek, and carried by a group of men who bit him and dug their fingers into his stomach. Upon his release, Thomas filed suit claiming nonpecuniary, aggravated, punitive, and special damages for assault, battery, and false imprisonment. Counsel for the Coast Salish defendants argued that the spirit dance initiation ceremony was a cultural practice to which members could be subjected without their consent and that it constituted an existing Aboriginal right recognized and affirmed by subsection 35(1) of the Constitution Act, 1982. The trial judge disagreed, holding that the defendants had failed to introduce evidence sufficient to establish the existence of an Aboriginal right and that, even if the spirit dance constituted such a right, 'those aspects of it which were contrary to English common law, such as the use of force, assault, battery and wrongful imprisonment, did not survive' the introduction of English law in British Columbia.[5]

For present purposes, the case of *Norris v. Thomas* is relevant for neither its reasons nor its result; as will be seen, subsequent jurisprudential

---

4 For a detailed description of spirit dancing, see Amoss, *Coast Salish Spirit Dancing*.

5 *Norris v. Thomas*, [1992] 2 C.N.L.R. 139 (B.C.S.C.). For an illuminating discussion of the case, see Claude Denis, *We Are Not You: First Nations and Canadian Modernity* (Peterborough: Broadview Press, 1997).

developments have superseded the framework relied upon by the trial judge to dispose of the claim. Instead, its relevance lies in its striking facts, which reveal a number of threshold problems associated with ascribing constitutional significance to Aboriginal cultural difference. The first is the elasticity of the concept of culture itself. When attempting to define the term, most scholars typically isolate certain background conditions that provide a common intelligibility to human experience, such as language, religion, and shared beliefs about social organization and human behaviour,[6] but determining which of these conditions should be included and which excluded from an operating definition is no easy task. Moreover, depending on one's definition, cultures can be found anywhere and everywhere, from the culture of the family farm to the culture of the urban neighbourhood.[7] A truly open-ended definition of culture threatens to encompass all aspects of social life,[8] but a more selective definition runs the risks of excluding important background conditions from analysis and glossing over the fact that the formation of cultural identity involves a host of interconnected aspects of social existence.

The elasticity of the concept of culture is perhaps even more pronounced in the context of Aboriginal cultural difference, and it dramatically affects the degree of constitutional protection that might be accorded to Aboriginal people. No doubt the Coast Salish spirit dance is a practice central to Coast Salish cultural difference. But should constitutional protection of Coast Salish cultural difference extend to practices that involve the application of cultural norms to unwilling individuals? An answer to this question depends in part on which background conditions merit inclusion in one's definition of culture. For

---

6 But see Christopher Herbert, *Culture and Anomie: Ethnographic Imagination in the Nineteenth Century* (Chicago: University of Chicago Press, 1991), at 1 (questioning the 'belief that human life consists of the multifarious phenomena of a condition or a set of conditioning factors or processes called "culture"').

7 See Brian Walker, 'Plural Cultures, Contested Territories: A Critique of Kymlicka,' 30 Can. J. Pol. Sci. 211 (1997) (invoking the family farm and the urban neighbourhood to illustrate the complexity of cultural institutions on which we rely for sharing meaning).

8 See, for example, Howard M. Kallen, *Cultural Pluralism and the American Idea: An Essay in Social Philosophy* (Philadelphia: University of Pennsylvania Press, 1956), at 44 ('a group's culture embraces the total economy of their life together'). Compare Northrop Frye, *The Eternal Act of Creation: Essays, 1979–1990* (Indianapolis: Indiana University Press, 1993), at 168 (customs, institution, and products constitute the 'structure' of a culture).

example, Aboriginal cultures are informed by ancient forms of sovereignty. On the one hand, an expansive definition of Aboriginal culture could encompass Aboriginal forms of government, including rights to enforce Aboriginal law against unwilling individuals. If constitutional protection ought to be accorded to Aboriginal cultural difference, and if Aboriginal cultural difference is defined to include Aboriginal governmental authority, then Aboriginal governmental authority will receive constitutional protection.[9] Under this formulation, Coast Salish laws that seek to enforce cultural norms against unwilling individuals arguably ought to receive constitutional protection as aspects of Coast Salish cultural difference. On the other hand, a restrictive definition of culture, one that does not include forms of governmental authority, might not protect the operation of Aboriginal laws that involve the application of cultural norms to unwilling individuals.

The elasticity of the concept of culture also presents itself in relation to Aboriginal territorial interests. While there are many distinctive Aboriginal perspectives on the significance of ancestral territory, Aboriginal relationships with land are profoundly spiritual in ways that elude non-Aboriginal ways of understanding the environment. Aboriginal people tend to regard their relationships to land in terms of an overarching collective responsibility to cherish and protect the earth as the giver of life. In the words of Venus Walker of the Haudenasaunee Confederacy, 'we look to the earth as a sacred mother who holds everything in the palm of her hand to give us things so that every day and every night our families are in good health.'[10] An expansive definition of Aboriginal culture could result in the constitutional protection of Aboriginal territorial interests. If Aboriginal cultural difference merits constitutional protection and includes unique Aboriginal relationships with land, constitu-

---

9 See, for example, Will Kymlicka, *Multicultural Citizenship: A Liberal Theory of Minority Rights* (Oxford: Clarendon Press, 1995) (arguing that a national minority ought to enjoy self-governing authority in order to protect its societal culture); see also Yael Tamir, *Liberal Nationalism* (Princeton: Princeton University Press, 1993) (deriving the right of self-government from an individual right to practise one's culture); and S. James Anaya, 'On Justifying Special Ethnic Rights: Comments on Pogge,' in Ian Shapiro and Will Kymlicka, eds., *Ethnicity and Group Rights* (New York: New York University Press, 1997), 222–31 at 226 ('[i]ncreasingly, autonomous governance for indigenous communities is acknowledged to be instrumental to their capacities of control over the development of the multifaceted aspects of their distinctive cultures').

10 Venus Walker, Royaner, Wolf Clan, Oneida, presentation before the House of Commons Special Committee on Indian Self-Government, 1 June 1983, *Minutes of Proceedings and Evidence of the Special Committee*, Issue no. 21 (translated from Oneida).

tional protection of Aboriginal cultural difference will extend to certain Aboriginal territorial interests.

Even though they figure profoundly in the formation and reproduction of Aboriginal cultural identities, I have resisted the temptation to treat Aboriginal governmental authority and territory solely under the rubric of cultural interests, in part because interests associated with Aboriginal territory and sovereignty merit constitutional protection in themselves and for reasons relatively independent of the constitutional significance of Aboriginal cultural difference. In Chapter 6, I argue that these interests give rise to an Aboriginal right of self-government that in turn authorizes the enforcement of cultural norms against unwilling individuals in certain circumstances. Whether the Coast Salish can force an individual to participate in a spirit dance, for example, depends not simply on whether the spirit dance is integral to Coast Salish culture but also on the nature and scope of Coast Salish governmental authority.[11] But I also treat interests associated with Aboriginal territory and sovereignty separately to counter a trend in current jurisprudence to reduce indigenous difference to cultural difference, as if cultural difference is all that constitutionally differentiates Aboriginal people from non-Aboriginal people.[12] The problem of culture's elasticity ought to be addressed in a manner sensitive to the possibility that there is more to the constitutional significance of indigenous difference than the fact that Aboriginal people belong to distinctive cultures threatened by assimilation.

A second problem associated with ascribing constitutional significance to cultural difference arises from a common tendency to speak erroneously of cultures as self-contained sets of practices that exclusively inform individual and collective identities. The plaintiff in *Norris v. Thomas*, for example, was a member of the Coast Salish Nation but, by seeking redress in Canadian courts according to Canadian law, he also asserted a Canadian legal allegiance. As Edward Said has said, '[n]o one today is purely *one* thing.'[13] Some scholars argue that it is misleading to speak of

---

11 In Chapter 7, I argue that the enforcement of a law of this kind involves an 'internal restriction' and is subject to the Charter of Rights and Freedoms: see text accompanying notes 75–7, Chapter 7, below.

12 For a similar critique, see David Schneiderman, 'Theorists of Difference and the Interpretation of Aboriginal and Treaty Rights,' 14 Int'l J. Can. Stud. 35 (1996).

13 Edward Said, *Culture and Imperialism* (New York: Vintage Books, 1993), at 336 (emphasis in original). See also James Clifford, *The Predicament of Culture: Twentieth-Century Ethnography, Literature, and Art* (Cambridge: Harvard University Press, 1988), at 95 ('it becomes increasingly difficult to attach human identity and meaning to a coherent "culture" or "language"').

cultures apart from a wide array of cultural fragments emanating from a wide variety of cultural sources. While such fragments provide meaningful options to individuals and collectivities in the forging of identities, given the nature and extent of intercultural interaction where one culture ends and another begins cannot be determined. Because of its fragmentary and overlapping quality, it seems inappropriate to speak of cultural membership in terms of exclusive conformity to a single set of practices and ways of life as opposed to a plurality of cultural allegiances. According to this view, cultures do not possess self-contained or ascertainable boundaries; what is relevant is not that individuals belong to particular cultures but that they have access to and choice among a range of meaningful options from which to forge their identities.[14]

While I assume a strong relation between culture and identity I am sceptical about the possibility of belonging to a single culture that offers a relatively fixed set of practices and ways of life.[15] There is an elective aspect to cultural membership. Individuals are not locked into belonging to particular cultures but instead can and do assimilate, break cultural bonds, and change cultural allegiances over time. This is not to say that change is easy or frequent, but cultural membership does not preclude choice.[16] Accordingly, I refer to cultural identity as an active web of interlocking and intersecting allegiances among individuals and communities. Such allegiances are constructed in part by law but they continually cut across and frustrate efforts at legal definition.[17] The dynamic dimension of cultural identity poses a dramatic challenge to the ability of constitutional discourse to address the constitutional sig-

---

14 See, for example, Jeremy Waldron, 'Minority Cultures and the Cosmopolitan Alternative,' 25 U. Mich. L. Rev. 751 at 783–5 (1992) ('[m]eaningful options may come to us as items or fragments from a variety of cultural sources').

15 Compare James Tully, *Strange Multiplicity: Constitutionalism in an Age of Diversity* (Cambridge: Cambridge University Press, 1995), at 54 ('citizens are in cultural relations that overlap, interact, and are negotiated and reimagined'); Natalie Benva Oman, 'Sharing Horizons: A Paradigm for Political Accommodation in Intercultural Settings' (Ph.D. thesis, McGill University, 1997), at 44 ('a hasty espousal of the idea that identities should be conceived of in solely individual terms as self-fashioned and wholly unconstrained, without reference to assailable notions of collective identity, flies in the face of actual practice').

16 Compare Tamir, *Liberal Nationalism*, at 33 ('[r]eflection always begins from a defined social position, but contextuality need not preclude choice').

17 See Sally Engle Merry, 'Resistance and the Cultural Power of Law,' 29 Law & Society Rev. 11 (1995) (discussing scholarship that emphasizes the culturally productive role of law and the power of cultural resistance). See also Clifford, *The Predicament of Culture* and Martha Minow, 'Identities,' 3 Yale J. Law & Humanities 97 (1991).

nificance of cultural difference. In the words of Joseph Carens, 'the normative problem is to think about what justice prohibits, permits, and requires in the face of this sort of multiplicity.'[18] If cultural difference is an interest underlying certain rights that attach to Canadian citizens, such rights must not be defined by the imposition of a rigid constitutional grid of right and duty that cannot account for the shifting nature of cultural identities.

A final threshold problem associated with ascribing constitutional significance to cultural difference is that cultures themselves can undergo deep transformations over time. According to Eric Wolf, '[i]n the rough-and-tumble of social interaction, groups are known to exploit the ambiguities of inherited forms, to impart new evaluations or valences to them, to borrow forms more expressive of their interests, or to create wholly new forms to answer to changed circumstances.'[19] Aboriginal cultures include cultural forms, practices, and ways of life that have been affected, transformed, and even generated in response to contact with non-Aboriginal society. To the extent that colonization can be understood in part as a process that involved the construction of Aboriginal people as culturally different from, and inferior to, non-Aboriginal settlers, many scholars view contact and colonization as actually producing certain aspects of Aboriginal cultural identities.[20] Attempts to define

---

18 Joseph Carens, *Culture, Citizenship and Community: A Contextual Exploration of Justice at Evenhandedness* (Oxford: Oxford University Press, 2000), at 66.

19 Eric R. Wolf, *Europe and the People without History* (Berkeley: University of California Press, 1982), at 387. See also Chandran Kukathas, 'Explaining Moral Variety,' 11 Soc. Phil & Pol'y 1 at 6 (1994) ('[b]ecause they are the product of interaction, and are subject to numerous influences, cultures are ... mutable'); Bernard Williams, *Ethics and the Limits of Philosophy* (London: Fontana Collins, 1985), at 158 ('cultures, subcultures, fragments of cultures, constantly meet one another and exchange and modify practices and attitudes'). For an attempt to categorize cultures in terms of the extent to which they are open to transformation, see Robert Justin Lipkin, 'Liberalism and the Possibility of Multi-Cultural Constitutionalism: The Distinction between Deliberative and Dedicated Cultures,' 29 U. Rich. L. Rev. 1263 (1995).

20 On the production of Aboriginal identities, see María Teresa Sierra, 'Indian Rights and Customary Law in Mexico: A Study of the Nahuas in the Sierra de Puebla,' 29 Law & Society 227 at 229 (1995) ('what today is identified as Indian tradition is better understood as the product of processes of domination and colonization'); and Alan Knight, 'Racism, Revolution, and Indigenismo: Mexico, 1910–1940,' in R. Graham, ed., *The Idea of Race in Latin America, 1870–1940* (Austin: University of Texas Press, 1990), 71–114 at 75 ('it was the European who created the Indian'). It has also been argued that colonization was a process that forged non-Aboriginal identity: see, for example,

Aboriginal cultural identities solely by reference to pre-contact ways of life not only risk stereotyping Aboriginal people in terms of historical differences with non-Aboriginal people that may or may not have existed in the distant past, they also profoundly underdescribe important aspects of contemporary Aboriginal cultural identities.

In chapter 6, I argue that the transformative nature of cultural difference renders problematic the claim that Aboriginal cultures possess a core set of practices that must by their very nature possess a pre-contact referent. Such a claim either ignores the myriad ways in which Aboriginal cultural identities have been produced through contact and colonization and countless historical interactions between Aboriginal and non-Aboriginal people, or it assumes that post-contact Aboriginal identities can adequately be explained by non-Aboriginal cultural categories.[21] As such, a pre-contact referent excludes from the outset constitutional consideration of important dimensions of contemporary Aboriginal cultural identities. Of course, one could argue that while some aspects of Aboriginal cultural identities may have developed in response to contact, pre-contact Aboriginal cultural practices exhaust the constitutional significance of Aboriginal cultural difference – a claim that pos-

---

Annelise Riles, 'Aspiration and Control: International Legal Rhetoric and the Essentialization of Culture,' 106 Harv. L. Rev. 723 at 737 (1993) ('[t]his essentialized European identity depended ... upon an opposition of Europe to non-Europe that articulated in symbolic terms inequalities of power between Europeans and their colonial subjects').

On the production of cultural identities generally, see Joan Scott, 'Multiculturalism and the Politics of Identity,' in John Rajchman, ed., *The Identity in Question* (New York: Routledge, 1995), 3,11 ('subjects are produced through multiple identifications, ... [and] the project of history is not to reify identity but to understand its production as an ongoing process of differentiation, ... subject to redefinition, resistance and change'); Wendy Brown, *States of Injury: Power and Freedom in Late Modernity* (Princeton: Princeton University Press, 1995), at 66 (persons cannot be 'reduced to observable social attributes and practices defined empirically, positivistically, as if their existence were intrinsic and factual, rather than effects of discursive and institutional power'); and Akhil Gupta and and James Ferguson, 'Beyond Culture: Space, Identity and the Politics of Difference,' 7 Cultural Anthropology 6 at 14 (1992) (calling for scholarship that explores 'the processes of *production* of difference in a world of culturally, socially, and economically interconnected and interdependent spaces') (emphasis in original).

21 Compare Rosemary J. Coombe, *The Cultural Life of Intellectual Properties: Authorship, Appropriation, and the Law* (Durham: Duke University Press, 1998), at 20 ('[i]t is ethnocentric to believe that when others become involved in cash economies, open to multinational advertising strategies, and engaged in consumer choices, our own commonsense categories then suffice to make sense of their lives').

sesses some currency with the judiciary and one with which I also take issue in Chapter 6.

In summary, constitutional protection of cultural difference must take into account its conceptual elasticity. Aboriginal cultural difference, in particular, can serve as a constitutional category that protects everything from ancient customs, practices, and traditions to Aboriginal territory and sovereignty. Constitutional protection of cultural difference must also be sensitive to the fact that individuals are not locked into particular cultures but may instead express a plurality of cultural allegiances, assimilate, break cultural bonds, and change cultural allegiances over time. Finally, cultures themselves undergo dramatic transformations in response to internal and external circumstances and developments. In the next section, I assess current efforts on the part of the judiciary to protect Aboriginal cultural difference from non-Aboriginal incursion. As will be seen, the three threshold problems described above plague judicial efforts to provide a secure doctrinal base for the constitutional protection of Aboriginal cultural difference.

Aboriginal Rights as Cultural Rights

To the extent that Aboriginal cultural difference historically possessed legal significance in Canada, it served as a reason for denying Aboriginal people rights to own and exercise authority over ancestral territories,[22] rights otherwise guaranteed by treaty,[23] rights to vote,[24] rights to engage in cultural practices,[25] and rights to educate their children according to traditional ways,[26] as well as a host of other injustices. Aboriginal people

---

22 See Chapters 3 and 4 respectively.

23 See, for example, *R. v. Syliboy*, [1929] 1 D.L.R. 307 (N.S. Co. Ct.). See also Chapter 5, below.

24 Indians did not possess the right to vote in federal elections until 1960. See, generally, Jack Woodward, *Native Law* (Scarborough, Ont.: Carswell, 1990), at 145–50.

25 See An Act to Amend the Indian Act, S.C. 1884, s. 3 ('[e]very Indian or other person who engages in or assists in celebrating the Indian festival known as the "Potlach" is guilty of a misdemeanour, and shall be liable to imprisonment for a term of not more than six nor less than two months in any gaol or other place of confinement'). The prohibition was lifted in 1951. For a detailed account, see Douglas Cole and Ira Chaikin, *An Iron Hand upon the People: The Law against the Potlatch on the Northwest Coast* (Vancouver: Douglas and McIntyre, 1990).

26 For an exhaustive study of education policy, see J. Barman, Y. Hébert, and D. McCaskill, eds., *Indian Education in Canada* (Vancouver: UBC Press, 1986); see also Royal Commission on Aboriginal Peoples, *Final Report*, vol. 1, *Looking Forward, Looking Back* (Ottawa: Supply and Services Canada, 1996), at 333–409.

were actively urged – indeed, legally coerced – to abandon their cultures and to assimilate with non-Aboriginal society. The nineteenth-century precursor to the federal Indian Act, for example, provided for the 'civilization' and voluntary 'enfranchisement' of status Indian men of good character as determined by a board of examiners.[27] Upon enfranchisement, individuals would no longer possess Indian status under the Act. They would instead acquire the rights of non-Aboriginal citizens and receive individual possession of up to fifty acres of land within the reserve and a per capita share in the principal of treaty annuities and other band moneys. When Aboriginal men refused to seek enfranchisement voluntarily, the Act was amended to make enfranchisement mandatory for all status Indian men who obtained higher education.[28]

Canadian devaluation of Aboriginal cultural difference was especially evident in education policy. Residential schools were founded on the belief that it was necessary to reclaim Aboriginal children from the 'uncivilized state' in which they were raised by bringing them 'into contact from day to day with all that tends to effect a change in ... views and habits of life.'[29] The federal Department of Indian Affairs argued that it was 'highly desirable, if it were practicable, to obtain entire possession of all Indian children after they attain to the age of seven or eight years, and keep them at schools ... until they have had a thorough course of instruction.'[30] First established in 1880, residential schools were funded by the federal government and operated by governments and churches. In 1920, the Indian Act was amended to require that all Indian children attend residential school for ten months a year. While the majority of residential schools ceased operating in the 1970s, the last one closed only in 1984. To the extent that Aboriginal cultural difference received legal attention in the past, it typically served as a proxy for Aboriginal inferiority and thus as a justification for assimilation.

Since the enactment of the Constitution Act, 1982, Canadian courts have begun to attach constitutional significance to the fact of Aboriginal cultural difference. In *R. v. Sparrow*, the Supreme Court of Canada addressed the meaning of subsection 35(1) of the Constitution Act, 1982, which constitutionally recognizes and affirms 'existing aboriginal ... rights.'[31] At issue was the constitutionality of federal fishing regula-

---

27 An Act to encourage the gradual Civilization of the Indian Tribes in this Province, and to amend the Laws respecting Indians, S.C. 1867, c. 26.
28 An Act to amend and consolidate the laws respecting Indians, S.C. 1876, c. 18.
29 Department of Indian Affairs, *Annual Report* (1889), at xi.
30 Department of Indian Affairs, *Annual Report* (1890), at xii.
31 [1990] 1 S.C.R. 1075.

tions imposing a permit requirement and prohibiting certain methods of fishing. The Musqueam First Nation, located in British Columbia, had fished since ancient times in an area of the Fraser River estuary known as Canoe Passage. According to anthropological evidence at trial, salmon is not only an important source of food for the Musqueam but also plays a central role in Musqueam cultural identity. The Musqueam regard salmon as a race of beings that had, in 'myth times,' established a bond with humans, which required salmon to come each year to give themselves to humans, who in turn treated them with respect by performing certain rituals. The Musqueam argued at trial that the federal fishing requirements interfered with their Aboriginal fishing rights and, as a result of subsection 35(1), were invalid. In its landmark decision, the Court found for the Musqueam nation and held that Aboriginal rights recognized and affirmed by subsection 35(1) include practices that form an 'integral part' of an Aboriginal community's 'distinctive culture.' If such rights 'existed' as of 1982, that is, if such rights had not been 'extinguished' by state action before 1982, then any law that unduly interferes with their exercise must meet relatively strict standards of justification. Specifically, such a law must possess a 'valid legislative objective,' and any allocation of priorities after implementing measures that secure the law's objective must give 'top priority' to Aboriginal interests. The court also indicated that in future cases it might require that such laws infringe the right in question as little as possible, and that infringements be accompanied by fair compensation.

Strictly speaking, the court in *Sparrow* did not explicitly state that the practice of fishing among the Musqueam constituted an Aboriginal right because it forms an integral part of Musqueam culture. But subsequent jurisprudence makes it clear that Aboriginal rights are designed to protect integral aspects of Aboriginal cultures. In *R. v. Van der Peet*, a member of the Sto:lo First Nation of British Columbia was charged with selling salmon contrary to federal law.[32] The trial judge held that fishing for food and ceremonial purposes was a significant and defining feature of Sto:lo culture and as such merited constitutional protection. He further held, however, that the Sto:lo, at the time of contact with European settlers, did not participate in a regularized market system in the exchange of fish. As a result, he found that the Sto:lo could not assert an Aboriginal right to fish for commercial purposes. On appeal to the

---

32 [1996] 2 S.C.R. 507.

Supreme Court of Canada, a majority of the court, per Lamer C.J., held that 'to be an aboriginal right an activity must be an element of a practice, custom or tradition integral to the distinctive culture of the aboriginal group claiming the right at the time of contact.'[33] In so holding, the court signalled a willingness to regard Aboriginal cultural difference as an interest worthy of constitutional protection.

Although *Van der Peet* purports to protect Aboriginal cultural difference, it is flawed in three respects. First, and discussed in more detail in Chapter 6, the test it proposes for ascertaining what constitutes an Aboriginal right is ill-suited to the task. It relies on a core-periphery distinction that excludes from the ambit of constitutional recognition practices that are not 'integral' to the cultural identity of an Aboriginal community. Moreover, the test requires a pre-contact referent. Only contemporary practices, customs, and traditions that can be traced back to pre-contact practices, customs, and traditions will receive constitutional protection. Because the evidence did not support the conclusion that the Sto:lo engaged in commercial fishing at the time of contact with European settlers, the court held that they could not assert an Aboriginal right to fish for commercial purpose.

More fundamental is a second problem with the court's approach: it fails to explain why Aboriginal cultural difference is worthy of any constitutional protection at all. The court referred to Aboriginal prior occupancy and reasoned that Aboriginal people are unique among 'all other minority groups in Canadian society' because of 'one simple fact: when Europeans arrived in North America, aboriginal peoples were already here, living in communities on the land, and participating in distinctive cultures, as they had done for centuries.'[34] In the court's view, this fact works both positively, supporting constitutional protection of cultural difference, and negatively, restricting such protection to Aboriginal cultures as opposed to extending it to all cultures threatened by assimilative forces in Canadian society.

Neither use is entirely convincing, in part because the court really relies on two facts, not one, to defend constitutional protection of Aboriginal cultural practices. The first fact, Aboriginal cultural difference (Aboriginal peoples participate in 'distinctive cultures'), may well work positively to justify constitutional protection of Aboriginal cultural

---

33 Ibid., at 549.
34 Ibid., at 538.

practices. Whether it operates in this manner depends on the strength of reasons for concluding that Aboriginal cultural interests merit constitutional protection. But because Aboriginal people are not the only people who participate in distinctive cultures in Canada, the fact of Aboriginal cultural participation cannot work negatively to restrict constitutional protection of cultural practices to Aboriginal people. The second fact, Aboriginal prior occupancy ('Aboriginal people were already here'), factually and, as the next chapter argues, normatively does distinguish Aboriginal people from non-Aboriginal people but it is not clear what it adds to the positive claim that Aboriginal cultural practices deserve constitutional protection. Why should the fact that Aboriginal people occupied the continent before European contact have any bearing on the claim that Aboriginal cultural practices deserve protection? Prior occupancy may well have something to do with the justice of recognizing Aboriginal territorial claims but, unless it is relied on merely as evidence of the significance of a particular cultural practice, its relation to the protection of Aboriginal cultural practices is difficult to fathom.

Nor is it clear why the fact of prior occupancy works negatively to exclude non-Aboriginal cultural practices from constitutional protection. Perhaps prior occupancy is thought of as proxy for the idea that, unlike other groups who participate in distinctive cultures in Canada, Aboriginal people did not choose to immigrate to Canada and accept pre-existing laws that conflict with their cultural practices.[35] But while consent may accurately describe the experience of many individuals who immigrated to Canada, it glosses over the fact that ancestors of many African-Canadians, for example, did not voluntarily immigrate to North America; they were forcibly removed from their traditional homes and sold into slavery.[36] Other immigrants fled their countries of birth because of economic, religious, or political persecution; to speak of informed consent in such a context is problematic at best.[37] Even if it were not problematic to equate immigration with notional consent,

---

35 See, for example, Thomas R. Berger, *Fragile Freedoms: Human Rights and Dissent in Canada* (Toronto: Clarke, Irwin, 1981), at 244.

36 For an outline of the history of slavery prior to Canadian statehood, see H.C. Pentland, *Labour and Capital in Canada, 1650–1860* (Toronto: Lorimer, 1981), at 1–23.

37 But see Kymlicka, *Multicultural Citizenship*, at 10–33. Kymlicka draws a distinction between national minorities and ethnic groups along similar lines; he advocates the distribution of cultural rights to ethnic groups, and the distribution of cultural rights and self-government rights to national minorities.

such consent should not bar immigrants from being entitled to enlist the constitution in aid of efforts to reconstitute their cultural identities in their adopted country.[38]

But the third shortcoming is perhaps the most serious of all. By protecting only practices, customs, and traditions integral to Aboriginal cultures, the court treats Aboriginal cultural difference as the only aspect of indigenous difference that possesses constitutional significance. In so doing, it implicates problems associated with the elasticity of the concept of culture discussed earlier. The extent of this shortcoming turns in part on which interests are characterized as cultural interests or, put differently, which background conditions are said to comprise Aboriginal cultural identity. A narrow definition of culture excludes from the outset additional aspects of indigenous difference that distinguish Aboriginal people from other cultural groups and which might merit constitutional protection. A broader definition, by including much of what constitutes indigenous difference, blunts the critique that indigenous difference should not be equated with cultural difference. If territorial interests, for example, are construed as cultural interests, then what constitutionally distinguishes Aboriginal people from non-Aboriginal people is more fundamental than a set of interests relating, say, to spirituality.

But equating indigenous difference with cultural difference takes the establishment of the Canadian state as a normative given. Aboriginal people are constructed as cultural minorities within Canada, with the key issue being which cultural practices deserve constitutional protection. This approach ignores the possibility that an inquiry into the constitutional significance of indigenous difference requires an exploration not only of whether the Canadian state ought to respect Aboriginal cultural difference but also whether and to what extent the state is entitled to treat Aboriginal people as subject to Canadian sovereign authority.[39]

---

38 See Kenneth L. Karst, *Belonging to America: Equal Citizenship and the Constitution* (New Haven: Yale University Press, 1989), at 212–13 (describing immigrant challenges to traditional political beliefs as efforts 'to expand the meanings that define ... civic culture').

39 See Kymlicka, *Multicultural Citizenship*, at 116 ('the equality argument assumes that the state must treat its citizens with equal respect ... [b]ut there is the prior question of determining which citizens should be governed by which states'); Richard Spaulding, 'Peoples as National Minorities,' 47 U.T.L.J. 35, 54 (1997) ('there are really two planes of justice involved ... the justice of the authority of sovereign government, and the justice of actions of sovereign governments toward their citizens').

This latter inquiry raises fundamental questions about the establishment of the Canadian state, including the legitimacy of assertions of
Canadian sovereignty and the justice of the distribution of legislative
authority and property rights in Canada. The discourse of minority cultural rights does not fully capture the jurisdictional and territorial
dimensions of such an inquiry.[40]

Of course, if Aboriginal cultural difference is the only aspect of indigenous difference that has constitutional significance, these questions
may well deserve to go unaddressed. But if other aspects of indigenous
difference also possess constitutional significance, then constitutional
protection of Aboriginal cultural practices captures only a small part of
the constitutional relationship between Aboriginal people and the
Canadian state.

Cultural Difference and Constitutional Tradition

The question remains: why does Aboriginal cultural difference merit
constitutional protection? One possible reason is that such protection is
consonant with Canadian constitutional traditions. In addition to the
protection that Canadian law currently provides to Aboriginal peoples,
there are several constitutional provisions that acknowledge the cultural
heterogeneity of Canada. The federal structure of Canadian government
was designed in part 'to minimize ethnic competition between French
and English by separating the united province of Canada into two provinces, Quebec and Ontario, to be dominated by French and English
majorities respectively.'[41] Section 133 of the Constitution Act, 1867 provides for minority language protection in federal and Quebec political
institutions.[42] Section 93 of the Constitution Act, 1867 provides certain
safeguards in the area of religious education.[43] The Charter of Rights
and Freedoms expresses a commitment to the preservation of minority
culture, including provisions for minority-language education rights and
an interpretive clause that emphasizes 'the preservation and enhance-

---

40 Compare the forceful words of the International Indian Treaty Council, '[t]he ultimate goal of their colonizers would be achieved by referring to indigenous people as
   minorities.' Quoted in Jules Deschenes, 'Proposal concerning a Definition of the Term
   "Minority,"' U.N. Doc. E/CN.4/Sub.2/1985/31, at para. 33.
41 Alan C. Cairns, *Charter versus Federalism: The Dilemmas of Constitutional Reform* (Montreal
   and Kingston: McGill-Queen's University Press, 1992), at 35.
42 (U.K.) 30 & 31 Vict., c. 3. See also the Manitoba Act, R.S.C. 1970, App. II, No. 8.
43 Ibid.

ment of the multicultural heritage of Canadians.'[44] Precedent also supports the proposition that a long-standing Canadian constitutional tradition exists of respecting the rights of cultural minorities. In the recent *Secession Reference*, for example, the Supreme Court of Canada held the accommodation of cultural minorities to be a fundamental animating principle of the Canadian constitutional order.[45] According to this line of reasoning, Aboriginal cultural difference would merit constitutional protection by virtue of Canadian constitutional traditions of acknowledging and accommodating cultural difference.

This is not to suggest that Canadian courts have been enthusiastically enforcing collective cultural rights. While the Supreme Court has emphasized the significance of cultural difference in a number of cases when interpreting rights and freedoms guaranteed by the Charter, such rights and freedoms have been defined primarily in individualistic terms.[46] In delineating the nature and scope of freedom of expression, for example, the court stated that Canada is 'a multicultural society in which the diversity and richness of various cultural groups is a value to be protected and enhanced.'[47] At the same time, it also defined freedom of expression primarily in terms of individual autonomy: according

---

44 See, generally, Katherine Swinton, 'Multiculturalism and the Canadian Constitution,' in H.P. Glenn and M. Ouelette, eds., *Culture, Justice and Law* (Montreal: Canadian Institute for the Administration of Justice, 1994).

45 *Reference re Secession of Quebec*, [1998] 2 S.C.R. 217 at 261–2 ('the protection of minority rights is ... an independent principle underlying our constitutional order').

46 See generally Joel Bakan, *Just Words: Constitutional Rights and Social Wrongs* (Toronto: University of Toronto Press, 1997); Allan Hutchinson, *Waiting for CORAF: A Critique of Law and Rights* (Toronto: University of Toronto Press, 1995). For the view that constitutional recognition of cultural difference challenges individualistic definitions of Charter rights, see Vern DaRe, 'Beyond General Pronouncements: A Judicial Approach to Section 27 of the Charter,' 33 Alberta L. Rev. 551 at 562-63 (1995) (judicial protection of groups is warranted in some contexts involving indirect attacks on multicultural practices).

   For analyses of group rights in the context of Aboriginal peoples, see Leon Trakman, 'Native Cultures in a Rights Empire Ending the Dominion,' 45 Buff. L.Rev. 189 (1997); Darlene M. Johnston, 'Native Rights as Collective Rights: A Question of Group Self-Preservation,' 2 Can. J. Law & Juris. 19 (1988); Robert N. Clinton, 'The Rights of Indigenous Peoples as Collective Group Rights,' 32 Ariz. L. Rev. 739 (1990); Randy Kapashesit and Murray Klippenstein, 'Aboriginal Group Rights and Environmental Protection, 36 McGill L.J. 925 (1991); and Kevin J. Worthen, 'One Small Step for Courts, One Giant Leap for Group Rights: Accommodating the Associational Role of "Intimate" Government Entities,' 71 N.C.L. Rev. 595 (1993).

47 See, for example, *R. v. Keegstra*, [1990] 3 S.C.R. 697 at 757.

to the court, it is 'a widely accepted premise of Western thought that the proper end of man is the realization of his character and potentialities as a human being.'[48] Similarly, freedom of religion purports to guarantee that 'every individual [is] free to hold and to manifest whatever beliefs and opinions his or her conscience dictates.'[49] Indeed, the court's description of Aboriginal rights as rights to engage in particular practices central to cultural identity is consistent with the judiciary's individualistic approach to cultural difference. Nonetheless, the judiciary has acknowledged the constitutional significance of cultural membership, even if such acknowledgement has taken the form of individual as opposed to collective rights protection.

Although constitutional protection of Aboriginal cultural difference may be consistent with Canadian constitutional tradition, it is important to ask why tradition ought to govern the matter. That Canadians have engaged in certain social and legal practices for a long time is no doubt worthy of constitutional attention;[50] tradition, for example, partly explains the unique role that constitutional conventions play in the Canadian constitutional order.[51] And respect for tradition demonstrates constitutional prudence, which many cherish as a constitutional virtue.[52] But tradition alone cannot ground the constitutional significance of Aboriginal cultural difference. There are multiple, conflicting traditions concerning cultural minorities in Canada. Moreover, given the historical fate of Aboriginal cultural difference in the Canadian legal imagination, it cannot be said that Canada has a tradition of respecting Aboriginal cultural difference. Between 1884 and 1951, for example, the federal Indian Act prohibited 'any Indian festival, dance, or other ceremony [involving] the giving away or paying or giving back of money, goods or articles of any sort ... or ... [involving] the wounding or mutilation of the dead or

---

48 Ibid., at 804, per McLachlin J. dissenting on other grounds, quoting T. Emerson, 'Toward a General Theory of Freedom of the First Amendment,' 72 Yale L.J. 877 at 879 (1963).

49 *R. v. Big M Drug Mart*, [1985] 1 S.C.R. 295 at 346.

50 See Anthony T. Kronman, 'Precedent and Tradition,' 99 Yale L.J. 1029 at 1066 (1990) (law should honour the past 'because the world of culture that we inherit from it makes us who we are').

51 See Andrew David Heard, *Canadian Constitutional Conventions: The Marriage of Law and Politics* (Toronto: Oxford University Press, 1991).

52 See Alexander Bickel, *The Least Dangerous Branch* (New Haven: Yale University Press, 1965); Philip Bobbitt, *Constitutional Fate: Theory of the Constitution* (New York: Oxford University Press, 1982).

living body of any human being or animal,'[53] a prohibition that arguably included the Coast Salish spirit dance at issue in *Norris v. Thomas*. An argument from tradition must proceed on the premise that Canada has a tradition of respecting cultures other than Aboriginal cultures. But stated this way, and assuming this premise to be correct,[54] it is not clear whether tradition underpins or undermines attaching constitutional significance to Aboriginal cultural difference.[55]

Some have responded to the concern that there are often multiple traditions with conflicting levels of generality by claiming that only unitary, consistent, and specific traditions deserve constitutional attention.[56] Again, given Canada's historical treatment of Aboriginal people, proving the existence of a tradition of respect, let alone consistency, seems highly unlikely. But even if it were possible to demonstrate such a tradition, its existence would not provide a satisfactory explanation of why Aboriginal cultural difference is worthy of constitutional protection. Constitutional law is partly concerned with determining which traditions possess constitutional significance;[57] grounding constitutional protection of Aboriginal cultural difference in tradition presupposes a point of reference that requires evaluation. At best, tradition supports but does not require attaching constitutional significance to Aboriginal cultural difference.

---

53 Indian Act, S.C. 1886, s. 114.
54 See generally Ninette Kelley and Michael J. Trebilcock, *Making of the Mosaic: History of Canadian Immigration Policy* (Toronto: University of Toronto Press, 1999).
55 Compare Cass R. Sunstein, 'Against Tradition,' 13 Soc. Phil & Policy 207, 214 (1996) ('constitutional traditionalism ... is too vague and broad-gauged'); Robert L. Hayman, Jr, 'The Color of Tradition: Critical Race Theory and Postmodern Constitutional Traditionalism,' 30 Harv. C.R.-C.L. L. Rev. 57, 78 (1995) ('[t]raditions constrain us ... but their meanings are too unstable for [their external] signs to be definitive').
56 See, for example, *Michael H. v. Gerald D.*, 109 S.Ct. 2333 at 2344, n. 6 (1989) (requiring 'the most specific level at which a relevant tradition protecting, or denying protection to, the asserted right can be identified'). For a critique of this requirement, see Laurence H. Tribe and Michael C. Dorf, 'Levels of Generality in the Definition of Rights,' 57 U. Chi. L. Rev. 1057 (1990).
57 See Sunstein, *Against Tradition*, at 228 ('[a] principal point of constitutionalism is to subject past practices to critical assessment'). See also Tribe and Dorf, 'Levels of Generality in the Definition of Rights,' at 1087 ('the law has never given its blessing to behavior simply because it is "traditional"'); Jack Balkin, 'Tradition, Betrayal, and the Politics of Deconstruction,' 11 Card. L. Rev. 1613 at 1617 (1993) ('the existence of a tradition may be a reason for rejecting it as controlling').

Downloading International Law

Canada's international legal obligations also support constitutional protection of Aboriginal cultural interests. Several international legal norms support claims of minority cultural integrity within sovereign states. Various articles of the United Nations Charter, for example, affirm cultural cooperation and cultural development.[58] Article 27 of the International Covenant on Civil and Political Rights recognizes rights of members of 'ethnic, religious or linguistic minorities ... to enjoy their own culture, to profess and practise their own religion [and] to use their own language.'[59] The U.N. Convention Against Genocide provides added support for the concept of cultural autonomy,[60] as does the UNESCO Declaration of Cultural Co-operation, which affirms a right and duty of all peoples to protect and develop minority cultures throughout the world.[61] The U.N. Convention on Racial Discrimination calls for positive governmental action to 'ensure the adequate development and protection of certain racial groups or individuals belonging to them.'[62]

Several international documents specifically refer to indigenous populations when calling for the protection of minority cultures within sovereign states. For example, Convention 107 of the International Labour Organization,[63] adopted in 1957, while advocating the 'integration' of

---

58 U.N. Charter, arts. 13, 55, 57, and 73.

59 Adopted 16 Dec. 1966, 999 U.N.T.S. 171 (entered into force, 23 Mar. 1976).

60 Convention on the Prevention and Punishment of the Crime of Genocide, 9 Dec. 1948, 78 U.N.T.S. 277 (entered into force 12 Jan. 1961). Art. II defines 'genocide' as 'acts committed with intent to destroy, in whole or in part, a national, ethnical, racial, or religious group, as such ...'. For links between the concept of genocide and the treatment of American Indians, see Lyman H. Legters, 'The American Genocide,' in Fremont J. Lyden and Lyman H. Legters, eds., *Native Americans and Public Policy*, 101–12 (Pittsburgh: University of Pittsburgh, 1992).

61 Declaration of the Principles of International Cultural Cooperation, proclaimed by the General Conference of the United Nations Educational, Scientific and Cultural Organization at its fourteenth session on 4 Nov 1966, reprinted in *United Nations, Human Rights: A Compilation of International Instruments*, U.N. Doc. ST/HR/1/Rev.3 (1988), at 409.

62 International Convention on the Elimination of All Forms of Racial Discrimination, art. 2, para. 2, opened for signature 7 Mar. 1966, 660 U.N.T.S. 195 (entered into force 4 Jan. 1969).

63 *The Protection and Integration of Indigenous and Other Tribal and Semi-Tribal Populations in Independent Countries, Conventions and Recommendations Adopted by the International Labour Conference, 1919–66* (Geneva: ILO, 1966), at 901 and 909. Canada is not party to the convention.

indigenous populations into national communities, also calls upon governments to develop coordinated and systematic action to protect indigenous populations and to promote their social, economic, and cultural development.[64] While many scholars regard ILO Convention 107 as somewhat dated in its emphasis on integration, its existence 'became the basis for a much enhanced international concern for indigenous peoples,' and suggests some support in international customary law for constitutional recognition of Aboriginal cultural difference.[65]

The International Labour Organization recently adopted a revision of Convention 107, known as Convention 169.[66] Convention 169 proposes to recognize 'the aspirations of [indigenous] peoples to exercise control over their own institutions, ways of life and economic development and to maintain and develop their identities, languages and religions, within the frameworks of the States in which they live.'[67] It then lists an impressive range of rights that attach to indigenous peoples and responsibilities that attach to governments in relation to indigenous peoples which would facilitate the protection of indigenous ways of life. Article 7, for example, provides: 'The peoples concerned shall have the right to decide their own priorities for the process of development as it affects their lives, beliefs, institutions, spiritual well-being and the lands they occupy or otherwise use, and to exercise control, to the extent possible, over their own economic, social and cultural development. In addition, they shall participate in the formulation, implementation and evaluation of plans and programmes for national and international development which may affect them directly.'[68] By including indigenous

---

64 Ibid., arts. 2(1), 2(2).

65 Anaya, *Indigenous Peoples in International Law*, at 45. For an assessment of the ILO Convention, see Patrick Thornberry, *International Law and the Rights of Minorities* (Oxford: Clarendon Press, 1991), at 334–68. See also José Martinez-Cobo, *Analytical Compilation of Existing Legal Instruments and Proposed Draft Standards Relating to Indigenous Rights*, U.N. Doc. M/HR/86/36, Annex V, for a summary of submissions by indigenous groups sharply criticizing the Convention on a number of grounds.

66 Convention (No. 169) concerning Indigenous and Tribal Peoples in Independent Countries, 27 June 1989, International Labour Conference (entered into force 5 Sept. 1991).

67 Ibid., preamble.

68 Ibid. For commentary, see Anaya, *Indigenous Peoples in International Law*, at 47–9; Lee Swepson, 'A New Step in the International Law on Indigenous and Tribal Peoples: ILO Convention No. 169 of 1989,' 15 Okla. City U. L. Rev. 677 (1990); Russel L. Barsh, 'An Advocate's Guide to the Convention on Indigenous and Tribal Peoples,' 15 Okla. City U. L. Rev. 209 (1990).

authority to make decisions on development priorities and imposing extensive consultation and participation requirements on states, Convention 169 provides for an understanding of Aboriginal rights that currently is only implicit in domestic jurisprudence on the constitutional relationship between Aboriginal peoples and the Canadian state.

Moreover, as discussed in the previous chapter, the Draft Declaration on the Rights of Indigenous Peoples, prepared by a subcommission of the United Nations Commission on Human Rights, proposes to recognize that 'Indigenous peoples have the right to self-determination' and '[b]y virtue of that right they freely determine their political status and freely determine their economic, social and cultural development.'[69] The Draft Declaration proposes the recognition of a number of rights relating to the cultural integrity of Aboriginal societies, including the right to manifest, practise, and teach spiritual and religious traditions; rights to territory, education, language, and cultural property; the right to maintain and develop indigenous economic and social systems; and rights of self-government.[70]

The international legal instruments referred to above support the view that Aboriginal cultural difference possesses constitutional significance in Canada. Constitutional protection of Aboriginal cultural interests is consistent with broader domestic and international efforts to preserve the cultural integrity not only of Aboriginal peoples but also of other peoples threatened by dominant assimilative forces in modern nation states. By Convention 169 and the emerging consensus surrounding the Draft Declaration on the Rights of Indigenous Peoples, international law recognizes that indigenous difference merits legal protection. Acknowledging that Aboriginal people enjoy a unique constitutional relationship with the Canadian state is consistent with Canada's membership in the international legal order.

International law is also relevant in that it offers a range of specific doctrinal techniques to protect Aboriginal cultural difference that could be directly downloaded into domestic constitutional law.[71] Most relevant is the jurisprudence of the United Nations Human Rights Com-

---

69 Draft Declaration on the Rights of Indigenous Peoples (as agreed to by the members of the working group at its 11th session) E/CN.4/Sub.2/1994/2/Add.1 (20 Apr. 1994), art. 3.

70 Ibid. For commentary, see Anaya, *Indigenous Peoples in International Law*, at 49–58.

71 See generally Kelley C. Yukich, 'Aboriginal Rights in the Constitution and International Law,' 30 U.B.C. L. Rev. 235 (1996).

mittee addressing article 27 of the International Covenant on Civil and Political Rights. Article 27 provides that ethnic minorities shall not be denied the right to enjoy their own cultures, to profess and practise their own religions, or to use their own languages. In *Lovelace v. Canada*, the Human Rights Committee held provisions in Canada's Indian Act that stripped an Indian woman of Indian status for marrying a non-Indian to be at odds with article 27.[72] Translated to the context of the Canadian constitutional order, the Human Rights Committee's views in *Lovelace* suggest that membership is a cultural interest that warrants constitutional protection.[73]

Other decisions rendered by the Human Rights Committee contemplate the idea that the right to enjoy one's culture includes rights to engage in economic activities essential to cultural reproduction. In *Ivan Kitok v. Sweden*,[74] for example, under Swedish law an ethnic Sami was denied rights to herd reindeer. The committee held that 'reindeer husbandry is so closely connected to the Sami culture that it must be considered part of the Sami culture itself,' and where economic activity is 'an essential element in the culture of an ethnic community' it falls under the protection of the Covenant.[75] Similarly, in *Ominayak and the Lubicon Lake Band v. Canada*, the committee expressed the view that article 27 contemplates the protection of economic and social activities necessary to the continued existence of an ethnic minority.[76] By linking protection of rights to the future as opposed to the past, *Ominayak* represents an alternative to the approach taken in *Van der Peet*, where, as

---

72 U.N. Doc. CCPR/C/DR/[XII]/R6/24 (31 July 1983).

73 For more discussion, see Chapter 7.

74 (Communication 197/1985), *Official Records of the Human Rights Committee* 1987/88, at 2:442 (U.N. Doc. A/43/40 (1988)).

75 Ibid., at paras. 4.3, 9.2. See generally, Benedict Kingsbury, 'Claims by Non-State Groups in International Law,' 25 Cornell Int'l L.J. 481 at 491 (1992); Martin Scheinin, 'The Right to Enjoy a Distinct Culture: Indigenous and Competing Uses of Land,' in Theodore S. Orlin, Allan Rosas and Martin Scheinen, eds., *The Jurisprudence of Human Rights: A Comparative Interpretive Approach* (Turku: Åbo Akademi University Institute for Human Rights, 2000).

76 U.N. Doc. A/45/40, Vol. II, App. A (1990). See also Kingsbury, 'Claims by Non-State Groups in International Law,' at 490 (arguing that *Ominayak* implies that the right to culture is violated where members are not allocated the land and control of resource development necessary to pursue economic activities of central importance to their culture'). And see Dominic McGoldrick, 'Canadian Indians, Cultural Rights and the Human Rights Committee,' 40 Int. & Comp. L.Q. 658 (1991).

stated, the Supreme Court of Canada extended constitutional protection only to pre-contact practices integral to Aboriginal culture.[77]

But the fact that international law supports attaching constitutional significance to Aboriginal cultural difference does not end the inquiry. Canada is party to the International Covenant on Civil and Political Rights and, as such, is obligated under international law to obey its dictates. But Canada is not party to Convention 169 and, when finalized, the Draft Declaration will only provide an indication of what a majority of states views as appropriate domestic treatment of indigenous peoples. The utility of international legal principles in this context should not be discounted.[78] Domestic courts have demonstrated a willingness to interpret constitutional guarantees in light of non-binding international law. In *R. v. Jones*, for example, Wilson J. relied on article 8 of the European Convention for the Protection of Human Rights and Fundamental Freedoms,[79] a convention to which Canada is not party, to conclude that the Charter protects the right of parents to educate their children according to their religious convictions.[80] However, unless one accepts the positivist view that a law obtains legitimacy by its very enactment,[81] the fact that international law calls for constitutional protection of Aboriginal cultural difference simply deflects normative questions surrounding the constitutional significance of Aboriginal cultural difference to the inter-

---

77 Yukich, 'Aboriginal Rights in the Constitution and International Law.'

78 For more discussion, see Robert A. Williams Jr, 'Encounters on the Frontiers of International Human Rights Law: Redefining the Terms of Indigenous Peoples' Survival in the World,' [1990] Duke L.J. 660 at 668 ('international human rights law and norms have come to assume a more authoritative and even constraining role on state actors in the world'). But see Robert Laurence, 'Learning to Live with the Plenary Power of Congress over the Indian Nations,' 30 Ariz. L. Rev. 413, 428 (1998) ('I have no faith in the ability of public international law to put bread on American Indian tables').

79 213 U.N.T.S. 222 (1950).

80 [1986] 2 S.C.R. 284 at 319–20. See also *Reference Re Public Service Employees Act (Alta.)*, [1987] 1 S.C.R. 313 at 348, per Dickson C.J. ('[t]he various sources of international human rights law ... must ... be relevant and persuasive sources for interpretation of the Charter's provisions'); *Slaight Communications Inc v. Davidson*, [1989] 1 S.C.R. 1038 at 1056–7 ('Canada's international human rights obligations should inform not only the interpretation of the content of the rights guaranteed by the Charter but also the interpretation of what can constitute a pressing and substantial s. 1 objective'); *Baker v. Canada*, [1999] S.C.J. No. 39, at para. 70, per L'Heureux-Dubé J. ('the values reflected in international human rights law may help inform the contextual approach to statutory interpretation and judicial review').

81 See text accompanying notes 11–27, Chapter 1.

national sphere: for example, why should cultural minorities possess special collective rights of cultural preservation at international law? Moreover, although this question has not gone unanswered in the literature,[82] the fact that international law mandates protection of Aboriginal cultural difference does not resolve normative concerns associated with the view that constitutional protection of Aboriginal cultural interests clashes with the ideal of equal citizenship. Nor do doctrinal choices offered by international law resolve these concerns; such choices represent techniques that presuppose the constitutional significance of Aboriginal cultural interests and therefore require normative justification of their domestic deployment.

Cultural Difference and Equality of Resources

Although precedent, tradition, and international law point to its protection, Aboriginal cultural difference merits constitutional protection as a matter of distributive justice. Cultural forms, practices, and ways of life provide a shared intelligibility to human existence and, as such, shape the formation of individual identity. The relation between culture and identity is both social and temporal. It is social because cultures provide socially meaningful options to an individual making decisions about how to lead his or her life. In the words of Will Kymlicka, 'freedom involves making choices amongst various options, and ... culture not only provides these options, but also makes them meaningful to us.'[83] And it is temporal in two senses. First, participation in cultural practices generates a shared sense of continuity with the past.[84] Second, the reproduc-

---

82 See, for example, Anaya, *Indigenous Peoples in International* at 75–125 (the principle of self-determination underpins the protection of indigenous cultural difference).

83 See Kymlicka, *Multicultural Citizenship*, at 6. For commentary on *Multicultural Citizenship*, see Leighton McDonald, 'Regrouping in Defence of Minority Rights: Kymlicka's Multicultural Citizenship,' 34 Osgoode Hall L.J. 291 (1996); Richard Spaulding, 'Peoples as National Minorities,' 47 U.T.L.J. 35 (1997); Robert Howse, 'Liberal Accommodation,' 46 U.T.L.J. 311 (1996). For discussion of the relation between culture and identity, see Avishai Margalit and Joseph Raz, 'National Self-Determination,' 87 J. Phil. 439, 447 (1990) ('our sense of our own identity depends on criteria of belonging').

84 See Stanley J. Tambiah, 'The Nation-State in Crisis and the Rise of Ethnonationalism,' in Edwin N. Wilmsen and Patrick McAllister, eds., *The Politics of Difference: Ethnic Premises in a World of Power* (Chicago: University of Chicago Press, 1996), 124–43 at 142 ('[i]t is through these participatory processes, which inscribe relations of identity, that one's sense of continuity with others through time and space is generated and shared').

tion of the options produced by cultural participation bequeaths their availability to future generations.[85] The social and temporal significance of culture is not diminished by threshold problems, discussed earlier in this chapter, associated with attempting to comprehend the significance of cultural difference, namely, that individuals rarely belong solely to one culture and that to a certain extent they can elect to change their cultural affiliations. Cultural pluralism and cultural transformation simply multiply the range of options available to individuals. And cultures matter not only to those who belong to them but also because, as stated by Charles Taylor, 'they have important things to say to all human beings.'[86]

Few would deny the presumptive value of culture in general or of Aboriginal cultures in particular. But culture does not possess constitutional significance simply because it is presumptively valuable. What is it about Aboriginal cultural difference that renders it worthy of constitutional protection? Will Kymlicka again provides insight. He argues that 'a comprehensive theory of justice in a multicultural state' demands equal concern and respect for all citizens, but equal concern and respect does not demand equal treatment of all citizens in all cases.[87] What they do demand is that the state allow 'people to choose a conception of the good life, and ... to reconsider that decision, and adopt a new and hopefully better plan of life.'[88] Such choice occurs in the context of an individual's culture – a set of social practices that provide individuals with meaningful ways of life across a range of human activities.[89]

Kymlicka distinguishes between national minorities, that is, previously self-governing, territorially concentrated cultures that have been incorporated into a larger state, and ethnic groups, which constitute loose

---

85 Compare Charles Taylor, 'The Politics of Recognition,' in Amy Gutman, ed., *Multiculturalism: Examining the Politics of Recognition* (Princeton: Princeton University Press, 1994), 25–73 at 41, n. 16 ('[f]or the populations concerned, ... what is at stake .... [is] survival through indefinite future generations').

86 Taylor, 'The Politics of Recognition,' at 66.

87 Kymlicka, *Multicultural Citizenship*, at 6.

88 Ibid., at 80.

89 Kymlicka employs the term 'societal culture.' Compare Ronald Dworkin, *A Matter of Principle* (Cambridge: Harvard University Press, 1985), at 230 (cultures must be protected from 'structural debasement or decay'). For a critique of the utility of the concept of societal culture, see Joseph Carens, *Culture, Citizenship, and Community*. See also Robert Justin Lipken, 'Can Liberalism Justify Multiculturalism?' 45 Buff. L. Rev. 1 at 17 (1997) (criticizing the ambiguity of Kymlicka's definition of culture).

associations of immigrants who left their culture behind in favour of a new cultural affiliation with their adopted country. In his view, states should be required to tend to the viability of national minority cultures because cultural protection redresses 'unequal circumstances which put the members of minority cultures at a systemic disadvantage in the cultural market-place, regardless of their personal choices.'[90] Members of ethnic groups, having left their original culture in favour of another, do not need access to a distinctive culture to exercise meaningful freedom of choice, although Kymlicka does argue that 'special efforts should be made to accommodate the cultural differences of immigrants' by 'adapting the institutions and practices of mainstream society so as to accommodate ethnic differences.'[91]

Distinguishing between national minorities and ethnic groups on the basis of choice arguably does not adequately address the fact, discussed earlier in this chapter, that ancestors of many Canadians did not voluntarily immigrate to North America; they were forcibly removed from their traditional homes and sold into slavery. Others fled their countries of birth because of economic, religious or political persecution. Nor should the choice of their ancestors necessarily bar immigrants from enlisting the Canadian constitution in aid of efforts to reconstitute their cultural identities in their adopted country. And if culture possesses constitutional significance because of its intimate relationship to identity, it is not clear why members of national minorities are entitled to benefit from a richer array of constitutionally protected cultural possibilities than what the constitution provides to members of ethnic groups.

Moreover, characterizing Aboriginal nations as 'previously self-governing' groups that have been 'incorporated' into a larger state presupposes the legitimacy of the assertion of state sovereignty that purported to accomplish such an incorporation. It also suggests that such groups are no longer self-governing absent delegation of self-governing authority by the larger state.[92] But to the extent that the constitution does not

---

90 Kymlicka, *Multicultural Citizenship*, at 113. Kymlicka argues that cultural protection is also supported by certain historical agreements and the value of cultural diversity.

91 Kymlicka, *Multicultural Citizenship*, at 97.

92 See Dale Turner, 'From Vallalolid to Ottawa: The Illusion of Listening to Aboriginal People,' in Jill Oakes et al., eds., *Sacred Lands: Aboriginal World Views, Claims, and Conflicts* (Edmonton: Canadian Circumpolar Institute, 1998), 53–68 at 62–3 (critiquing Kymlicka's description of Aboriginal people as 'previously self-governing' and 'incorporated' into the Canadian state).

protect interests associated with indigenous difference, the legitimacy of Canadian sovereignty over Aboriginal peoples and Aboriginal territory is far from self-evident. And while the constitution may not have explicitly recognized an Aboriginal right of self-government before 1982, this silence does not mean that Aboriginal forms of sovereignty did not survive the establishment of the Canadian state.

For present purposes, what is useful about Kymlicka's work is that it opens the door to a contextual explanation of why Aboriginal cultural interests are worthy of constitutional protection. For a variety of historical, social, and legal reasons associated with colonization, Aboriginal people face steep challenges in their efforts to maintain and reproduce their distinctive cultures. Attaching constitutional significance to Aboriginal cultural difference facilitates the reproduction of Aboriginal cultures and helps to redress the social inequality between Aboriginal people and non-Aboriginal people. In this light, Aboriginal cultural difference is a constitutionally relevant difference between Aboriginal and non-Aboriginal people. Constitutional recognition of the value of Aboriginal cultural difference furthers equality by distributing protection of cultural interests to those who otherwise lack the resources necessary for cultural reproduction.[93]

It is true that members of non-Aboriginal cultures in Canada also face steep costs associated with cultural reproduction. As I stated at the outset of this chapter, it is the content of Aboriginal cultures, not the fact of cultural difference, that is unique to Aboriginal people. Locating the constitutional significance of Aboriginal cultural difference in the need to redress inequalities associated with the costs of cultural reproduction opens the door for members of other cultures in Canada to claim that their cultural differences also warrant constitutional recognition. The constitution recognizes the significance of cultural difference in its instruction to the judiciary to interpret the Charter in a manner that emphasizes the preservation and enhancement of the multicultural her-

---

93 Compare Tully, *Strange Multiplicity*, at 191 ('[i]f a contemporary constitution is to be culturally neutral, it should not promote one culture at the expense of others, but mutually recognize and accommodate the cultures of all the citizens in an agreeable manner'); Anne Phillips, *The Politics of Presence: The Political Representation of Gender, Ethnicity, and Race* (Oxford: Clarendon Press, 1995), at 93 ('[w]hereas histories of inequality, deprivation, or exclusion have placed individuals in different relationships to economic and political power, we do not treat them equally when we treat them as if they are the same'). See generally, Ronald Dworkin, *What Is Equality? Part II: Equality of Resources*, 10 Philo. & Pub. Aff. 283 (1981).

itage of Canadians. This requirement may well entail judicial acknowledgement of relative inequalities in the costs of cultural reproduction
when interpreting the Charter's guarantees.[94]

But the fact that many cultural minorities also face steep costs associated with cultural reproduction should not obscure either the unique-
ness or constitutional significance of other aspects of indigenous difference. As I argue in the following three chapters, Aboriginal cultural
interests are but one set of several interests that ought to inform the
nature and scope of Aboriginal and treaty rights. There is more to the
constitutional relation between Aboriginal people and the Canadian
state than the constitutional protection of Aboriginal cultural difference. Indigenous difference should not be reduced to cultural difference; constitutional protection should also extend to interests associated
with Aboriginal territory, Aboriginal sovereignty, and the treaty-making
process.

---

94 Compare Tully, *Strange Multiplicity*, at 8 ('[a] just form of constitution must begin with
the full mutual recognition of the different cultures of its citizens').

Chapter Three

Territory

All landscapes have a history, much the same as people exist within cultures, even tribes. There are distinct voices, languages that belong to particular areas. There are voices inside rocks, shallow washes, shifting skies; they are not silent. And there is movement, not always the violent motion of earthquakes associated with the earth's motion or the steady unseen swirl through the heavens, but other motion, subtle, unseen, like breathing.

Joy Harjo, *Secrets from the Center of the World*[1]

Perhaps the most commonly noted aspect of indigenous difference is that Aboriginal people lived in and occupied portions of North America prior to European contact. Canadian law acknowledges the legal significance of the fact that Aboriginal people occupied the continent from 'time immemorial.'[2] The law of Aboriginal title recognizes that, if they can demonstrate that their ancestors exclusively occupied territory at the time Britain asserted sovereignty and that they continue to occupy the territory in question, Aboriginal people enjoy the right of exclusive use and occupation of such territory for a variety of purposes, which need not be related to distinctive aspects of Aboriginal cultural identity.[3] In this chapter, I argue that Aboriginal prior occupancy possesses

---

1 Joy Harjo, *Secrets from the Center of the World* (Tucson: University of Arizona Press, 1989).
2 *Calder v. A.G.B.C.*, [1973] S.C.R. 313 at 368, per Hall J., dissenting on other grounds.
3 *Delgamuukw v. British Columbia*, [1997] 3 S.C.R. 1010. See also *Guerin v. The Queen*, [1984] 2 S.C.R. 335, per Dickson J. at 376–9 ('Aboriginal title [is] a legal right derived from the Indians' historic occupation and possession of their tribal lands').

legal significance because of a basic distributive principle of justice with respect to land: prior occupants of land have a stronger claim to its use and enjoyment than newcomers.

Despite Canadian law's acceptance of Aboriginal title, the law of Aboriginal title historically failed to protect ancestral territories from non-Aboriginal incursion and exploitation. This failure was in part a function of broader economic and social developments associated with colonial expansion and Canada's emergence as a nation state. But it was also the result of a judicial devaluation of the legal significance of Aboriginal prior occupancy, which occurred through an unwillingness to regard Aboriginal territorial interests as worthy of at least the same level of legal protection that the law accords to non-Aboriginal proprietary interests. It also occurred through the acceptance of a legal fiction that the Crown was the original occupant of all the lands of the realm.

In this chapter, I argue that Aboriginal territorial interests merit at least the same level of legal protection as the law extends to non-Aboriginal proprietary interests. Such a proposal finds resistance in many quarters, but two lines of critique are common. The first takes issue with the legal significance of Aboriginal prior occupancy, either questioning whether Aboriginal occupancy constitutes occupancy within the eyes of the law or arguing that prior occupancy – whether by Aboriginal or non-Aboriginal people – is an inappropriate principle on which to distribute rights with respect to land. I argue in response that a commitment to distributive justice demands a definition of occupancy that does not privilege non-Aboriginal use and enjoyment of land to the exclusion of Aboriginal modes of use and enjoyment. Unless the judiciary is willing to jettison prior occupancy as a general principle of distribution informing Canadian property law, Aboriginal people are entitled to its specific application. Proponents of the second line of critique accept the legal significance of Aboriginal prior occupancy but argue that delineation of Aboriginal territorial interests is more appropriately pursued in land claims negotiations than in the courtroom. This critique assumes a separation of law and politics that belies law's distributive function. The law of Aboriginal title is intimately connected to the relative bargaining power of parties involved in negotiations. Because law distributes bargaining power among the parties, it cannot and should not cede responsibility in this manner.

Notwithstanding the claim that Aboriginal territorial interests merit at least the same level of legal protection as is provided to non-Aboriginal proprietary interests, in one important respect Aboriginal territorial interests merit greater protection than what the law accords to non-Aboriginal proprietary interests. In the final section of this chapter, I argue that Aboriginal territorial interests deserve independent constitutional protection. First, Aboriginal territorial interests are profoundly constitutive of Aboriginal identity. Second, Aboriginal interests in land are best understood as territorial, and not merely proprietary, in nature. Finally, constitutional protection is due because Aboriginal people occupied the continent prior to the establishment of the Canadian state.

The Legal Significance of Prior Occupancy

Claims of prior occupancy possess legal significance because they correspond to a commonly invoked principle of distributing rights with respect to land that suggests that a prior occupant of land has a stronger claim to that land than subsequent arrivals. Typically a person comes to own property under Canadian law by purchasing it from its prior owner. But the primary legal mode of acquiring property that belongs to no one is to take possession by occupancy. The law of personal and real property in Canada views occupancy as proof of title in the absence of a better claim by another.[4]

The notion that occupancy is the origin of title has a notable and diverse philosophical and jurisprudential heritage. Jean-Jacques Rousseau traced the origin of property to the 'first claimant.'[5] Immanuel Kant recognized that the first person to appropriate land creates rights with respect to that land in certain circumstances.[6] Sir William Blackstone, in his *Commentaries on the Laws of England*, wrote that 'occupancy is the thing by which the title was in fact originally gained; every man seising to his own continued use such spots of ground as he found most agreeable to his own convenience, provided he found them unoccu-

---

4 On claiming title to previously unowned chattels, see *Pierson v. Post*, 3 Cai. R. 175 (N.Y. Sup. Ct. 1805); *Sutton v. Moody* (1697), 1 Ld. Raym. 250; and *Blades v. Higgs* (1865), 11 H.L.C. 621. On claiming title to previously unowned land, see *Calder v. A.G.B.C.*, at 375, per Hall J., dissenting on other grounds ('possession is itself proof of ownership'). See, generally, Kent McNeil, *Common Law Aboriginal Title* (Oxford: Clarendon Press, 1989), at 6–78.

5 J.J. Rousseau, *Discourse on Inequality* (Harmondsworth: Penguin, 1984), at 109.

6 Immanuel Kant, *The Metaphysics of Morals*, trans. J. Ladd (Indianapolis: Bobbs-Merrill, 1965), at 44–56; see also G.W.F. Hegel, *Philosophy of Right*, trans. T.M. Knox (Oxford: Clarendon Press, 1942), at 37–41 (discussing right of appropriation over all things).

pied by any one else.'[7] Blackstone argued that prior occupancy gives rise to 'a sort of ownership, from which it would have been unjust, and contrary to the law of nature, to have driven him by force.'[8] More recently, Robert Nozick has argued that state action that does not respect just acquisitions or transfers of property is itself unjust.[9] Similarly, Richard Epstein views first possession to be foundational to 'any sound legal system.'[10]

Not all scholars who accept the legal significance of prior occupancy are willing to acknowledge the legal significance of Aboriginal prior occupancy. John Locke, for example, argued that uncultivated land in North America was not occupied and therefore was free to be taken up by settlers.[11] Similarly, the eighteenth-century Swiss natural law theorist, Emmerich de Vattel, wrote that 'uncertain occupancy of vast regions can not be held as a real and lawful taking of possession; and when the Nations of Europe, which are too confined at home, come upon lands which the savages have no special need of and are making no present

7 William Blackstone, *Commentaries on the Laws of England*, ed. E. Christian (London: A. Strathan, 1809), at 2:8–9.

8 Ibid., at 3. See, also J.W. Harris, *Property and Justice* (Oxford: Clarendon Press, 1996), at 216 (arguing that communal claims of prior occupancy are stronger than individual claims).

9 Robert Nozick, *Anarchy, State, and Utopia* (New York: Basic Books, 1974), at 151. For commentary, see David Lyons, 'The New Indian Claims and Original Rights to Land,' in J. Paul, ed., *Reading Nozick: Essays on Anarchy, State, and Utopia*, 355–79 (Oxford: Blackwell, 1982).

10 Richard Epstein, *Simple Rules for a Complex World* (Cambridge: Harvard University Press, 1995), at 59–70. See also Richard Epstein, 'Possession as the Root of Title,' 13 Georgia L. Rev. 1221 (1979). In *Simple Rules*, Epstein defends 'the rule of first possession' by contrasting it with a rule of second possession, 'whereby the second person who comes onto land ... is the person who owns it' (at 60). Epstein is right to dismiss the latter rule as an 'invitation to social disaster' (at 61), but no doubt he did not have underlying Crown title in mind when he stated that '[a] rule of this [second] sort has never been tried' (at 61).

11 John Locke, *Two Treatises of Government*, ed. P. Laslett (Cambridge: Cambridge University Press, 1988), at 299 ('Yet there are still *great Tracts of Ground* to be found, which (the Inhabitants thereof not having joined with the rest of Mankind) in consent of the Use of their common money) *lie waste*, and are more than the People, who dwell on it, do, or can make use of, and so still be in common'). See, generally, Jeremy Waldron, *The Right to Private Property* (Oxford: Clarendon Press, 1988), at 137–252; James Tully, *A Discourse on Property: John Locke and His Adversaries* (Cambridge: Cambridge University Press, 1980).

and continuous use of, they may lawfully take possession of them and establish colonies in them.'[12]

Part of the resistance among classical scholars to the idea that Aboriginal prior occupancy gives rise to legally enforceable interests in ancestral territories can be explained by their views on why occupancy counts, and what counts as occupancy, for the purpose of recognizing title. Embedded in their concerns are two related approaches to defining occupancy for the purpose of enforcing rights against competing claimants. The first, exemplified by Locke's writings and known as the labour theory of property, asserts that occupancy must be coupled with productive use. Locke argued that occupancy alone does not count for much; in his view, an occupant of land, in the absence of a better claim, can claim ownership only by mixing his or her labour with it.[13] As a result, uncultivated lands, despite an Aboriginal presence, ought to be regarded as free to be taken up by others who want to put them to productive use. The second approach is hinted at by de Vattel's reference to the 'uncertain occupancy' of land by Aboriginal people and is known as the notice theory of property. This approach requires that an occupant provide clear notice to others of an intent to claim territory as his or her own. Notice can be accomplished by productive use, as in the case of a farmer who cultivates land, signalling to others an intent to use the land to the exclusion of others. But notice need not involve productive use: an occupant who fences off land signals a possessory intent to the outside world without using the land for any productive purpose.[14]

On either theory, as stated by Carol Rose, 'the audience presupposed ... is an agrarian or commercial people – a people whose activities with respect to the objects around them require an unequivocal delineation of lasting control so that those objects can be either managed or

---

12 Emmerich de Vattel, *The Law of Nations* (New York: AMS Press, 1975), Bk 1, chap. 18, at para. 209.

13 Locke, *Two Treaties of Government*, at 287–8.

14 See Carol M. Rose, *Property and Persuasion: Essays on the History, Theory, and Rhetoric of Ownership* (Boulder, Colo.: Westview, 1994), at 11–23. Some scholars treat notice as a necessary but not sufficient condition of occupancy: see Karl Olivecrona, 'Locke's Theory of Appropriation,' 24 Philosophical Quarterly 220 at 228 (1974). Others view notice as a necessary and sufficient condition of occupancy: see Clark Wolf, 'Contemporary Property Rights, Lockean Provisos, and the Interests of Future Generations,' 105 Ethics 791 at 795 (1995).

15 Rose, *Property and Persuasion*, at 19.

traded.'[15] Locke and de Vattel did not view Aboriginal people in North America who belonged to migratory societies or who did not engage in agrarian or commercial activities akin to their European counterparts as occupants for the purpose of assessing competing claims to land. For many classical scholars, either Aboriginal use did not count as occupancy or Aboriginal people failed to signal their intent to claim territory as their own in a manner acceptable to European communicative standards.

Defining occupancy by European standards of cultivation and notice excludes from the outset legal consideration of the fact that many Aboriginal people related and continue to relate to land in ways that defy traditional European understandings of productive use and notice. Some Aboriginal societies did put territory to productive use along the lines demanded by the classical scholars. In territory now constituting areas of New England, Nova Scotia, New Brunswick, and Quebec, for example, Aboriginal people cleared land for corn fields and farming purposes.[16] However, many Aboriginal societies were migratory in nature, organized around seasonal hunting, fishing, and trapping. Migration tended to be regular and patterned in ways that displayed continued occupation and use of ancestral territory for hunting, fishing, and trapping purposes. The Dene and Cree peoples, for example, occupied large territories, enabling them to organize seasonal activities such as hunting, fishing, and harvesting to suit their collective needs. Other Aboriginal societies, especially those that relied on the sea and its resources, were organized into relatively permanent settlements, with clearly regulated territorial boundaries that extended beyond village communities. Pacific coast peoples, such as the Haida, lived in villages close to waters that provided their members with food and sustenance.[17]

---

16 See William Cronon, *Changes in the Land: Indians, Colonists, and the Ecology of New England* (1st ed.) (New York: Hill and Wang, 1983) for a discussion of Aboriginal farming practices. See also Olive Patricia Dickason, 'For Every Plant There Is a Use: The Botanical World of Mexica and Iroquoians,' in Kerry Abel and Jean Friesen, eds., *Aboriginal Resource Use in Canada: Historical and Legal Aspects* (Manitoba: University of Manitoba Press, 1991); R. Douglas Hurt, *Indian Agriculture in America: Prehistory to the Present* (Lawrence: University of Kansas Press, 1987).

17 See, generally, Royal Commission on Aboriginal Peoples, *Final Report*, vol. 2, *Restructuring the Relationship* (Ottawa: Minister of Supply and Services Canada, 1996), at 448–64 and authorities cited therein. For an excellent discussion of diverse land tenure practices of First Nations in the western sub-Arctic, plateau, and northwest coast regions of

Aboriginal use and enjoyment of ancestral territories did not go unnoticed by classical scholars. De Vattel, for example, argued that 'wandering families, like those of pastoral tribes, which move from place to place according to their needs, ... can not be justly deprived of lands of which they are making use.'[18] And Locke argued that lands that are 'more than the People, who dwell on it, do, or can make use of,' are free to be taken up for settlement.[19] But Locke, like de Vattel, regarded European forms of use as necessary to constitute occupancy for the purpose of determining ownership. According to James Tully, '[i]n his depiction of Amerindian property, Locke highlights one specific form of activity – industrious labour and the products of industrious labour – and does not recognize the native system of national territories, the bundle of property rights and responsibilities in activities and their locales, and the customs governing distribution.'[20] As Tully points out, there is no necessary link between, on the one hand, privileging prior occupancy and, on the other hand, defining occupancy by reference to traditional European standards of use or notice. Indeed, attending to indigenous difference requires a pluralistic understanding of occupancy for the purposes of determining title. The fact that Aboriginal people occupied ancestral territory in ways and for purposes unfamiliar to European standards should not disentitle them from claiming rights of ownership in relation to that territory.

Herein lies the deep legal significance of Aboriginal prior occupancy. If prior occupants have a stronger claim to use and enjoy land than newcomers, then Aboriginal prior occupancy entitles Aboriginal people to receive at least the same legal protection in relation to ancestral territories as Canadian law accords to non-Aboriginal property holders. As will be seen, Canadian law does acknowledge that Aboriginal prior occupancy possesses a measure of legal significance, despite the fact that many Aboriginal nations did not occupy ancestral territories in a manner cognizable to traditional European understandings. But, until

---

British Columbia, see Greg Poelzer, 'Land and Resource Tenure: First Nations Traditional Territories and Self-Governance,' in Roslyn Kunin, ed., *Prospering Together: The Economic Impact of Aboriginal Title Settlements in B.C.* (Vancouver: Laurier Institution, 1998), 85–109.

18 de Vattel, *The Law of Nations*, bk II, chap. VII, at para. 97.

19 Locke, *Two Treaties of Government*, at 299.

20 James Tully, *An Approach to Political Philosophy: Locke in Contexts* (Cambridge: Cambridge University Press, 1993), at 154.

recently, the law refused to accept the deeper normative implication of Aboriginal prior occupancy: that Aboriginal territories ought to receive at least the same level of protection as non-Aboriginal property interests.

A stronger objection to attaching legal significance to the fact of Aboriginal prior occupancy is found in scholarship that does not distinguish between Aboriginal and non-Aboriginal forms of occupancy but questions the legitimacy of prior occupancy itself as a distributive principle. Some scholars take issue with the notion that prior occupancy ought to serve as a criterion for the distribution of proprietary entitlements in modern societies. They argue that prior occupancy should not thwart state efforts to distribute wealth and resources among citizens. Valuing prior occupancy typically relies on libertarian theories of historical entitlement that account for 'the justice or injustice of distributions of resources, not in terms of the distributive outcomes in question (such as whether the holdings are equal, or proportionate to the distribution of something else, like need or moral desert), but rather in terms of the procedures by which the distribution was arrived at.'[21] In contrast, liberal end-state theories typically 'maintain that the justice of holdings (and our rights to them) depends not on how they came about, but rather on the moral character of the structure (or pattern) of the set of holdings of which they are a part.'[22] According to this line of critique, assessing the justice of a distribution of rights with respect to land by inquiring into the extent to which the law respects Aboriginal prior occupancy wrongly attaches moral or legal significance to individual or collective actions that constituted occupancy sometime in the distant past.[23]

This is not to say that end-state theories rule out legal protection of Aboriginal territorial interests. Aboriginal people may well be entitled to demand state protection of rights with respect to land and resources, not because they were the first occupants, but because such protection would result in a just distributive outcome among all citizens, perhaps by making Aboriginal people better off without making others worse

---

21 Waldron, *The Right to Private Property*, at 257.

22 A. John Simmons, 'Historical Rights and Fair Shares,' 14 Law and Philosophy 149 at 150–151 (1994).

23 For an assessment of the strengths and weaknesses of prior or first occupancy as a normative or philosophical basis for the assertion of property rights, see Lawrence C. Becker, *Property Rights: Philosophic Foundations* (London: Routledge and Kegan Paul, 1977), at 24–31.

off,[24] or because it would accord Aboriginal people equal concern and respect.[25] Will Kymlicka, for example, while expressing scepticism about the moral significance of Aboriginal prior occupancy has nonetheless defended Aboriginal land rights on the basis that Aboriginal people in Canada are significantly disadvantaged compared to non-Aboriginal people and that Aboriginal title is a means of offsetting such disadvantage.[26] On this account, Aboriginal land rights help to secure a measure of substantive equality for Aboriginal people by ameliorating social and economic conditions that they face precisely because they lack an adequate land base.

While theories of historical entitlement bear the burden of investing the past with moral significance, end-state theories bear the burden of explaining why history does not matter. And history, of course, does matter to end-state theorists to the extent that they take past distributions as given when they attempt to determine whether proposed distributions would make certain people better off without making others worse off or would accord equal concern or respect to all citizens. It may well be that an end-state theory is an appropriate way to assess the justice of distributions of certain goods whereas a theory of historical entitlement is appropriate to assess the justice of distributions of other types of goods.[27] Indeed, I argued in the previous chapter along lines similar to Kymlicka's thesis that the constitutional significance of Aboriginal cultural difference lies not in the justice or injustice of past actions but in the need to redress systemic disadvantage in the ability of Aboriginal people to reproduce their distinctive cultural identities.

---

24 For a defence of this distributive principle, see John Rawls, *A Theory of Justice* (Cambridge: Harvard University Press, 1971).

25 For a defence of this distributive principle, see Ronald Dworkin, *Taking Rights Seriously* (Cambridge: Harvard University Press, 1977).

26 See Will Kymlicka, *Liberalism, Community, and Culture* (Oxford: Oxford University Press, 1989), at 158–61. Kymlicka's argument on this point ought to be read in light of his subsequent scholarship; see Kymlicka, *Multicultural Citizenship: A Liberal Theory of Minority Rights* (Oxford: Clarendon Press, 1995), at 117 (Aboriginal people constitute 'national minorities' and 'the way a national minority was incorporated often gives rise to certain group-differentiated rights').

27 See Michael Walzer, *Spheres of Justice: A Defense of Pluralism and Equality* (New York: Basic Books, 1983), at 6 ('principles of justice are themselves pluralistic in form ... different social goods ought to be distributed for different reasons, in accordance with different procedures, by different agents; ... and these differences derive from different understandings of the social goods themselves').

In the context of assessing the justice of the distribution of title in Canada, however, it is unnecessary to decide between these two approaches to determine the extent to which Aboriginal prior occupancy possesses legal significance. A focus on equality splits the difference between libertarian historical entitlement and liberal end-state theories. Property rights historically have been distributed and enforced in part by Canadian law in accordance with a certain respect for prior occupancy. Until Canadian property law jettisons its commitment to prior occupancy as a means of assessing competing claims to land, formal equality demands that Aboriginal people benefit from its application. To hold otherwise would be to treat Aboriginal people differently than non-Aboriginal people in the application of a basic premise of Canadian property law.

An insight worth preserving from end-state theories is that a just distribution of property rights involves more than respect for prior occupancy. But this does not mean that prior occupancy possesses no legal significance at all. It may well be that the legal significance of prior occupancy ought to be tempered by competing normative commitments.[28] Canadian law recognizes this possibility by constructing property rights in common law as opposed to constitutional terms, thereby allowing the state to regulate and even expropriate private property in the name of the broader public interest.[29] But any tempering of the significance of prior occupancy should not be at the expense of Aboriginal territorial interests alone. Given that Canadian law recognizes that prior occupancy gives rise to enforceable property rights in land in the absence of a better claim on title, it ought to extend this presumption to Aboriginal prior occupancy. Aboriginal prior occupancy possesses legal significance because Aboriginal people deserve to be treated equally by Canadian property law.

The Law of Aboriginal Title

Given that Aboriginal territorial interests are worthy of legal protection, does Canadian property law provide such interests with the legal protection they deserve? As stated, the law of Aboriginal title acknowledges that Aboriginal people lived on and occupied the continent prior to European contact and, as a result, possess certain interests worthy of

---

28 See Morris Cohen, 'Property and Sovereignty,' 13 Cornell L.Q. 8 (1927).
29 *British Columbia v. Tener*, [1985] 1 S.C.R. 533.

legal protection. This body of law prescribes ways of handling disputes between Aboriginal and non-Aboriginal people, especially disputes over land. It recognizes Aboriginal title, that is, Aboriginal occupation and use of ancestral lands, including territory where Aboriginal people hunted, fished, trapped, and gathered food, not just Aboriginal village sites or cultivated fields.[30] It describes rights associated with Aboriginal title in collective terms, as vesting in Aboriginal communities.[31] It purports to restrict non-Aboriginal settlement on Aboriginal territory until the Aboriginal interest in such territory has been surrendered to the Crown.[32] It prohibits sales of Aboriginal land to non-Aboriginal people without the approval of and participation by Crown authorities.[33] And it prescribes safeguards for the manner in which such surrenders can occur and imposes fiduciary obligations on government in its dealings with Aboriginal lands and resources.[34]

Although Canadian law has recognized that Aboriginal relationships with ancestral territory possess legal significance, however, the law of Aboriginal title historically failed to protect Aboriginal territorial interests from non-Aboriginal settlement and exploitation. This failure was in part a function of broader social and historical realities associated with colonial expansion. Governments and settlers either misunderstood or ignored the law of Aboriginal title. Crown respect for the law of Aboriginal title was eroded by the decline of the fur trade and the waning of Aboriginal and non-Aboriginal economic interdependence. And the increased demands on Aboriginal territory occasioned by population growth and westward expansion, followed by a period of paternalistic administration marked by involuntary relocations, only exacerbated the erosion of respect.

---

30 See, for example, *Hamlet of Baker Lake v. Minister of Indian Affairs and Northern Development*, [1980] 1 F.C. 518 (F.C.T.D.).

31 See, for example, *Amodu Tijani v. Secretary, Southern Nigeria*, [1921] 2 A.C. 399 (P.C.).

32 See, for example, *Guerin v. The Queen*, at 383 ('[t]he purpose of this surrender requirement is clearly to interpose the Crown between the Indians and prospective purchasers or lessees of their land, so as to prevent the Indians from being exploited').

33 See, for example, *Canadian Pacific Ltd. v. Paul*, [1988] 2 S.C.R. 654 at 677 (Aboriginal title cannot be transferred, sold or surrendered to anyone other than the Crown).

34 See, for example, *Guerin v. The Queen*, at 382 (Aboriginal title 'gives rise upon surrender to a distinctive fiduciary obligation on the part of the Crown to deal with the land for the benefit of the surrendering Indians'); see also *R. v. Sparrow*, [1990] 1 S.C.R. 1075 at 1108 ('the Government has the responsibility to act in a fiduciary capacity with respect to Aboriginal peoples').

Notwithstanding these external factors, the failure of the law to protect Aboriginal territorial interests can also be traced internally to legal choices of the judiciary. On more than one occasion, the judiciary suggested that Aboriginal prior occupancy might not possess any independent legal significance at all.[35] The possibility that Aboriginal prior occupancy might not generate independently enforceable interests with respect to land served as a legal backdrop for almost a century of relations between the Crown and Aboriginal peoples, shaping legal expectations of governments, corporations, citizens, and other legal actors. It contributed to a perception that governments and third parties were relatively free to engage in a range of activity on ancestral lands – a perception which, in turn, legitimated unparalleled levels of government and third-party development and exploitation of Aboriginal territories.

Moreover, until recently, the legal significance that the judiciary attached to Aboriginal prior occupancy was minimal. Courts resisted characterizing Aboriginal title in proprietary terms, preferring instead to characterize it as a right of occupancy,[36] a personal or usufructuary right,[37] or, more recently, as a sui generis interest.[38] Constructing Aboriginal title as a non-proprietary interest enabled its regulation and indeed its extinguishment by appropriate executive action,[39] disabled

---

35 See, for example, *St. Catherines Milling and Lumber Co. v. The Queen* (1888), 14 A.C. 46
    (P.C.) (Aboriginal rights with respect to land and resources did not predate but were
    created by the Royal Proclamation and, as such, are 'dependent on the good will of the
    Sovereign') and *In re Southern Rhodesia*, [1919] A.C. 211 at 233 (P.C.) (some 'Aboriginal
    tribes .... are so low in the scale of social organization that their usages and conceptions
    of rights and duties are not to be reconciled with the institutions or the legal ideas of
    civilized society,' and, as a result, their Aboriginal title should not be recognized by
    colonial law).
36 *Johnson v. M'Intosh*, 8 Wheat. 543 at 588 (1823).
37 *St. Catherines's Milling and Lumber Co v. The Queen*, at 54; see also *Smith v. The Queen*,
    [1983] 1 S.C.R. 554.
38 *Canadian Pacific Ltd. v. Paul*, at 658 (Aboriginal title refers to an 'Indian interest in
    land [that] is truly *sui generis*'); see also *R. v. Sparrow*, at 1112 ('[c]ourts must be care-
    ful ... to avoid the application of traditional common law concepts of property as they
    develop their understanding of ... the *sui generis* nature of Aboriginal rights').
39 See, for example, *Ontario (A.G.) v. Bear Island Foundation*, [1991] 2 S.C.R. 570 at 575
    ('whatever may have been the situation upon signing of the Robinson-Huron Treaty,
    that right was in any event surrendered by arrangements subsequent to that treaty by
    which the Indians adhered to the treaty in exchange for treaty annuities and a
    reserve').

Aboriginal title-holders from obtaining interim relief,[40] and frustrated access to the common law presumption of compensation in the event of expropriation.[41] Courts also indicated a willingness to view Aboriginal title as a set of rights to engage only in traditional practices on Aboriginal territory, that is, those practices that Aboriginal people engaged in at the time the Crown acquired territorial sovereignty.[42] Each of these legal choices had a profound effect on the ability of Aboriginal people to rely on Canadian law to protect ancestral territories from non-Aboriginal incursion.

It is true that, in at least three relevant respects, Aboriginal title differs from other proprietary interests under Canadian law. First, Aboriginal title is collective in nature, held by communities not individuals.[43] Second, Aboriginal title is inalienable except to the Crown, and the Crown is under a fiduciary obligation to deal with surrendered land in the interests of those who surrendered it.[44] Third, Aboriginal title is an inherent legal interest – it receives protection under Canadian law

---

40 A number of cases have held that Aboriginal title does not constitute an interest in land sufficient to support the registration of a caveat or certificate of *lis pendens*, which would temporarily prevent activity on ancestral territory pending final resolution of a dispute. See, for example, *Uukw v. A.G.B.C.* (1987), 16 B.C.L.R. (2d) 145 (B.C.C.A.); *Lac La Ronge Indian Band v. Beckman*, [1990] 4 W.W.R. 211 (Sask. C.A.); and *James Smith Indian Band v. Saskatchewan (Master of Titles)*, [1994] 2 C.N.L.R. 72 (Sask. Q.B.); but see *Ontario (A.G.) v. Bear Island Foundation*. See, generally, Kent Roach, 'Remedies for Violations of Aboriginal Rights,' 21 Man. L.J. 498 (1992), Roger Townshend, 'Interlocutory Injunctions in Aboriginal Rights Cases,' [1991] 3 C.N.L.R. 1.

41 See, for example, *British Columbia v. Tener*, [1985] 1 S.C.R. 533 at 559, quoting *Attorney-General v. De Keyser's Royal Hotel Ltd.*, [1920] A.C. 508 at 542, per Lord Atkinson ('a statute is not to be construed so as to take away the property of a subject without compensation').

42 See, for example, *Hamlet of Baker Lake v. Minister of Indian Affairs*, at 559 ('the common law ... can give effect only to those incidents of that enjoyment that were ... given effect by the [Aboriginal] regime that prevailed before'); *A.G. Ont. v. Bear Island Foundation*, [1985] 1 C.N.L.R. 1 at 3 (Ont. S.C.) ('the essence of Aboriginal rights is the right of Indians to live on the lands as their forefathers lived'). For a detailed critique of this view, see Kent McNeil, 'The Meaning of Aboriginal Title,' in Michael Asch, ed., *Aboriginal and Treaty Rights in Canada: Essays on Law, Equality and Respect for Difference* (Vancouver: UBC Press, 1997), at 135–54.

43 See *Delgamuukw v. British Columbia*, at 1082, per Lamer C.J. ('aboriginal title cannot be held by individual Aboriginal persons; it is a collective right to land held by all members of an Aboriginal nation').

44 See *Guerin v. The Queen*, at 376 per Dickson J. ('the Indian interest in land is inalienable except upon surrender to the Crown').

because of occupancy that occurred prior to the establishment of the Canadian state.[45] Aboriginal title is sui generis because it is a collective, inalienable, and inherent legal interest; as such, it is difficult to integrate into a property regime that views ownership in terms of individual or joint estates in land conferred by a fictional or actual Crown grant.

The unique attributes of Aboriginal title do not, however, justify a level of legal protection less than what non-Aboriginal proprietary interests receive under Canadian law. Specifically, they do not justify allowing executive regulation and extinguishment without legislative authorization, restrictions on access to interim relief measures, or a refusal to apply a presumption that compensation is owed in the event of expropriation. Nor do they justify restricting Aboriginal title to the legal protection of practices Aboriginal people engaged in at the time the Crown acquired sovereignty. The sui generis nature of Aboriginal title should not have been used as an excuse to define the legal interest in ways that foreclosed Aboriginal people from relying on Canadian property law to protect ancestral territories from non-Aboriginal incursion.[46]

The Supreme Court of Canada addressed many of the jurisprudential shortcomings described above in *Delgamuukw v. British Columbia*, a case in which hereditary chiefs of the Gitksan and Wet'suwet'en nations claimed Aboriginal title to 58,000 square kilometres of the interior of British Columbia. The Gitksan sought to prove historical use and occupation of part of the territory in question by entering as evidence their 'adaawk,' a collection of sacred oral traditions about their ancestors, histories, and territories. The Wet'suwet'en entered as evidence their 'kungax,' a spiritual song or dance or performance that ties them to their territory. Both the Gitksan and Wet'suwet'en also introduced evidence of their feast hall, in which they tell and retell their stories and identify their territories to maintain their connection with their lands over time. The trial judge admitted the evidence but accorded it little independent

---

45 Ibid. (source of Aboriginal title lies in 'the Indians' historic occupation and possession of their tribal lands'). See also *Calder v. A.G.B.C.*

46 Compare Catherine Bell and Michael Asch, 'Challenging Assumptions: The Impact of Precedent in Aboriginal Rights Litigation,' in Michael Asch, ed., *Aboriginal and Treaty Rights in Canada: Essays on Law, Equality, and Respect for Difference* (Vancouver: UBC Press, 1997), 38–74 at 49 ('the concept of *sui generis*' has been used 'to deny classification of Aboriginal title as fee simple ownership with all the rights flowing therefrom'). See also Joseph William Singer, 'Sovereignty and Property,' 86 Northwestern L. Rev. 1 (1991) (critiquing American law for its differential treatment of Aboriginal and non-Aboriginal property rights-holders).

weight, stating that, because of its oral nature, it could not serve as evidence of a detailed history of extensive land ownership.[47] He concluded that ancestors of the Gitksan and Wet'suwet'en peoples lived within the territory in question prior to the assertion of British sovereignty, but predominantly at village sites already identified as reserve lands. As a result, he declared, the Gitksan and Wet'suwet'en did not own or possess Aboriginal title to the broader territory.[48]

On appeal, the Supreme Court of Canada ordered a new trial. Although its reasons for doing so were predominantly procedural in nature, it took the opportunity to provide a definition of Aboriginal title that swept away many of the procedural and substantive hurdles Aboriginal people faced in their attempts to obtain legal recognition of their rights to ancestral territories. Specifically, the court held that Aboriginal title is a communally held right in land and, as such, comprehends more than the right to engage in specific activities which may themselves constitute Aboriginal rights. Based on the fact of prior occupancy, Aboriginal title confers the right to exclusive use and occupation of land for a variety of activities, not all of which need be aspects of practices, customs, or traditions integral to the distinctive cultures of Aboriginal societies. The court held further that the trial judge erred by placing insufficient weight on the oral evidence of the Gitksan and Wet'suwet'en appellants: 'the laws of evidence must be adapted in order that this type of evidence can be accommodated and placed on an equal footing with the types of historical evidence that courts are familiar with, which largely consists of historical documents.'[49]

For present purposes, the relevance of *Delgamuukw* lies in its refusal to conclude that Aboriginal title, because of its sui generis nature, warrants a level of protection less than that accorded to non-Aboriginal proprietary interests under Canadian law. But *Delgamuukw* is also important because it accords constitutional protection to Aboriginal territorial interests. In a subsequent section, I defend the constitutional status of Aboriginal title despite the fact that non-Aboriginal proprietary interests receive only common law protection. My point here is

---

47 *Uukw v. B.C.*, [1987] 6 W.W.R. 155 at 181 (B.C.S.C.).
48 [1991] 3 W.W.R. 97 at 383 (B.C.S.C.).
49 *Delgamuukw v. British Columbia*, at 1069. For an extensive, anthropological analysis of Aboriginal title in general and *Delgamuukw* in particular, see Dara Culhane, *The Pleasure of the Crown: Anthropology, Law and First Nations* (Burnaby: Talonbooks, 1998).

simply that the law before *Delgamuukw*, by not providing Aboriginal territorial interests with at least the same level of legal protection provided to non-Aboriginal proprietary interests, failed to accord Aboriginal prior occupancy the legal significance it deserves. The law further weakened the protection of Aboriginal territorial interests by upholding the legal fiction that the Crown was the original occupant of all the lands of the realm, including the ancestral territories of Aboriginal peoples in North America.

The Fiction of Original Crown Occupancy

During the period of initial European contact and colonial expansion in North America, it was accepted practice among European nations that the first to discover vacant land acquired sovereignty over that land to the exclusion of other potential discoverers.[50] With populated land, sovereignty was acquired by the discovering nation not by simple settlement, but by conquest or cession, but such land could be deemed vacant if its inhabitants were insufficiently Christian or civilized. International law subsequently deemed North America to be vacant, and regarded the acquisition of territorial sovereignty by European powers as occurring through the mere act of discovery and settlement.[51] One expression and consequence of the sovereign power of the Canadian state is that Aboriginal territorial interests are governed by Canadian law. Based on the legal fiction that the Crown was the original occupant of all the lands of the realm, Canadian property law holds that the

50 See, generally, I. Brownlie, *Principles of Public International Law*, 5th ed. (Oxford: Clarendon Press, 1998, at 127–71.
51 For the classic statement in this regard, see *Johnson v. M'Intosh*, at 573 ('[t]he character and religion of [North America's] inhabitants afforded an apology for considering them as a people over whom the superior genius of Europe might claim an ascendancy'). See also John Westlake, *Chapters on Principles of International Law* (Cambridge: Cambridge University Press, 1894), at 136–8, 141–3 (drawing a distinction between 'civilization and want of it'); William E. Hall, *A Treatise on International Law*, 8th ed. (Oxford: Clarendon Press, 1924), at 47 (international law only governs states that are 'inheritors of that civilization'); Lassa F.L. Oppenheim, *International Law*, 3rd ed. (London: Longmans, 1920) (law of nations does not apply to 'organized wandering tribes'); and Charles C. Hyde, *International Law Chiefly as Interpreted and Applied by the United States* (Boston: Little Brown, 1922), at 164 ('native inhabitants possessed no rights of territorial control which the European explorer or his monarch was bound to respect').

Crown enjoys underlying title to all of Canada.[52] Property owners possess and own their land as a result of grants from the Crown. Ownership confers a right to use and enjoy the land in question and a right to exclude others from entering onto one's land.

The fiction of original Crown occupancy was developed to legitimate feudal landholdings in England, along with another fiction that the actual occupants of the land enjoyed rights of ownership as a result of Crown grants. The law imagined the Crown as granting lands to landholders, with the result that ownership, or fee simple, passed as a result of these grants to landholders. As Kent McNeil has explained, this process never truly occurred; the Crown was not the original occupant and therefore owner of the land and by and large it did not confer actual grants to landholders. These fictions were developed to rationalize the existing pattern of landholdings in England, and they served this purpose well.[53]

McNeil makes the further critical point that the fiction of underlying Crown title has had dramatically different consequences in the colonial context. Underlying Crown title in England was accompanied by legal recognition of initially fictional grants to actual occupants, thereby legitimating the existing pattern of landholdings. Only half of this equation was imported to Canada, thereby severely disrupting the existing pattern of landholdings. Although the Crown was imagined as the original occupant of all of Canada, actual Aboriginal occupants were not recognized as owning their land as a result of a series of fictional Crown grants. The Crown was thus relatively free to grant third-party interests to whomever it pleased, which it did: to settlers, mining companies, forestry compa-

---

52 See *R. v. Sparrow*, at 1103 ('while British policy towards the Aboriginal population was based on respect for their right to occupy their traditional lands, ... there was from the outset never any doubt that ... the underlying tile ... to such lands vested in the Crown').

53 See, generally, Kent McNeil, *Common Law Aboriginal Title* (Oxford: Clarendon Press, 1989). On the utility of legal fictions, see Lon Fuller, *Legal Fictions* (Stanford: Stanford University Press, 1967), at 111 (legal fictions are in part a function of the 'inveterate hang of the human mind toward an organized simplicity'). See also Henry Maine, *Ancient Law* (1861; London: Dent, 1917), at 76–7 ('[t]his conflict between belief or theory and notorious fact is at first sight extremely perplexing; but what it really illustrates is the efficiency with which Legal Fictions do their work in the infancy of society'); Duncan Kennedy, *A Critique of Adjudication* (Cambridge: Harvard University Press, 1997), 200–2 (examining legal fictions as modes of collective denial produced by specific conflicts).

nies, and others. To the extent that it refused to acknowledge the full legal significance of Aboriginal occupancy, Canadian property law vested extraordinary proprietary power in the Crown. When coupled with its legislative power, the Crown's proprietary authority authorized a vast array of competing claims to ancestral territories.[54]

As stated, the law of Aboriginal title partially acknowledges the legal significance of Aboriginal prior occupancy. It provides that, under certain circumstances, Aboriginal nations can claim rights of possession and use of remnants of ancestral territory subject to surrender to or extinguishment by the Canadian state. But, until recently, it also assumed that 'there has been all along vested in the Crown a substantial and paramount estate, underlying the Indian title, which became a plenum dominium whenever that title was surrendered or otherwise extinguished.'[55] And, again until recently, the burden that Aboriginal title placed on the Crown's underlying interest never meaningfully checked the exercise of Crown proprietary power, let alone the exercise of the Crown's legislative authority. As a result, Aboriginal title existed at the margins, meaningful only in geographic spaces left vacant by Crown or third-party non-use.

More specifically, the federal and provincial governments possess both proprietary and legislative authority. I address federal and provincial legislative authority in detail in chapter 4. But proprietary authority flows from the fact that the federal and provincial governments possess title to certain public lands, often called Crown lands. Each level of government, as owner of Crown lands, possesses proprietary authority over such lands akin to the authority that a private property owner enjoys over his or her property. As owner, the federal or provincial government can exploit, sell, mortgage, lease, or license activities on Crown lands, subject to any legislative or constitutional restrictions that constrain the exercise of such proprietary authority.[56]

---

54 McNeil, *Common Law Aboriginal Title*. See also Kent McNeil, 'The Temagami Indian Claim: Loosening the Judicial Straight-Jacket,' in Matt Bray and Ashley Thomson, eds., *Temagami: A Debate on Wilderness* (Toronto: Dundurn Press, 1990), at 200–5. For an insightful discussion of the functional effects of the fiction of original Crown occupancy in Australia, see Nehal Bhuta, 'Mabo, Wik and the Art of Paradigm Management,' 22 Melbourne U. L. Rev. 24 (1998).

55 *St. Catherine's Milling v. The Queen.*

56 In 1867, the various assets and liabilities of the confederating colonies were apportioned between the federal and provincial governments by the Constitution Act, 1867.

The judiciary has long maintained that Aboriginal title places a burden on Crown title. But, until recently, the extent of this burden was by no means clear. The Crown tended to regard itself as entitled to act like a private property owner in relation to Crown lands subject to Aboriginal title. In truth, the content of the Crown's proprietary authority over lands subject to Aboriginal title bears a direct relation to the content of Aboriginal title. The greater the content of Aboriginal title, the lesser the content of the Crown's proprietary authority. By resisting the proposition that Aboriginal title is a proprietary interest, the judiciary increasingly legitimated the assumption that Crown title vests full proprietary authority in the Crown to lands subject to Aboriginal title.

By referring to Aboriginal title as 'a right to the land itself,'[57] the Supreme Court of Canada in *Delgamuukw* finally made it clear that proprietary authority over land subject to Aboriginal title vests in the Aboriginal nation, and not in the Crown.[58] Moreover, to the extent that the Crown possesses any proprietary authority over lands subject to Aboriginal title, constitutional protection of Aboriginal title checks the ability of the Crown to exercise such authority to the detriment of Aboriginal title-holders. Such actions must further a compelling and substantial governmental objective and be consistent with the special fiduciary relationship between the Crown and Aboriginal people. Consultation and compensation for such interference will ordinarily be required. And provincial proprietary authority cannot be exercised in a way that invades Parliament's exclusive legislative authority over Indians and Indian lands, which includes lands subject to Aboriginal title.[59] Given the contemporary definition and constitutional status of Aboriginal

---

By s. 117 of the Act, the four original provinces retained all their public property not otherwise disposed of by the Act, and s. 109 confirmed this by stipulating that all lands, mines, minerals, and royalties belonging to the colonies at the time of union shall continue to belong to the provinces, subject to any trusts existing in respect thereof, and to any interest other than that of the province. Accordingly, when colonies joined Confederation as provinces, they possessed Crown title to all lands to which they previously possessed title as colonies. However, by s. 109, such title continued to be subject to any trusts or interests, including Aboriginal title, other than that of the province: see *St. Catherine's Milling and Lumber Co. v. The Queen*, *Delgamuukw v. British Columbia*, at 1117.

57 *Delgamuukw v. British Columbia*, at 1095.

58 See, generally, Kent McNeil, *Defining Aboriginal Title in the Nineties: Has the Supreme Court Finally Got it Right?* (Toronto: Robarts Centre for Canadian Studies, 1998), at 8–13.

59 See, generally, *Delgamuukw v. British Columbia*, at 1080–91.

title, the idea of Crown title underlying lands subject to Aboriginal title carries only symbolic consequences for the future.

But the concept of underlying Crown title was anything but symbolic in the past. Sustained by the fiction of original Crown occupancy, the concept of underlying Crown title effectively legitimated a distribution of proprietary authority in Canada that either ignored or downplayed the fact of Aboriginal prior occupancy. And given that *Delgamuukw* only provides constitutional protection to Aboriginal title that had not been lawfully extinguished before 1982, it assumes that Aboriginal title can only be asserted in geographic spaces left vacant by Crown or third-party non-use. In the next section, I explore the extent to which the law can begin to address the injustices associated with its historic failure to protect Aboriginal territorial interests in particular and the existing distribution of proprietary authority in general.

The Distribution of Title

Legal acceptance of the fiction of original Crown occupancy combined with the non-proprietary status of Aboriginal title produced a distribution of proprietary authority that has severely disadvantaged, in fact and in law, Aboriginal people in their efforts to maintain the integrity of their ancestral territories against non-Aboriginal incursion. Can the law address the consequences of its failure to protect Aboriginal territorial interests? Some argue that the law is too blunt an instrument to reflect the complex political, economic, jurisdictional, and remedial judgments necessary to resolve competing claims to territory.[60] And even if the law could tailor its rules and remedies to address these issues systematically, negotiations are said to be clearly preferable to court-imposed solutions. Litigation is expensive and time-consuming whereas negotiation permits parties to address each other's real needs and reach complex and mutually agreeable trade-offs.[61] A negotiated agreement is more likely to garner legitimacy than a court-ordered solution, if only because the parties participated more directly and constructively in its

---

60 See Royal Commission on Aboriginal Peoples, *Final Report*, vol. 2, at 561–2. See also *Pacific Fishermen's Defence Alliance v. Canada*, [1987] 3 F.C. 272 at 284 (T.D.) ('[b]ecause of their socio-economic and political nature, it is indeed much preferable to settle Aboriginal rights by way of negotiation than through the Courts').

61 See Melvin Aron Eisenberg, 'Private Ordering through Negotiation: Dispute Settlement and Rulemaking,' 89 Harv. L. Rev. 637 (1976).

creation. And negotiations have the potential to mirror the nation-to-nation relationship that underpins the law of Aboriginal title and structures relations between Aboriginal nations and the Crown.[62]

Arguments that favour negotiation over litigation, however, overlook the distributive function of judicial choices regarding the scope and content of Aboriginal title. For example, when the Crown and an Aboriginal nation negotiate the terms of a land claims agreement, each begins negotiations armed with a certain amount of bargaining power, which it exercises with an eye to wresting concessions from the other. Much criticism has been levelled against the processes the federal government has put in place that structure and regulate negotiations; as discussed in Chapter 9, existing comprehensive and specific land claims processes suffer from a number of structural and institutional flaws that render them ineffectual instruments for achieving mutual co-existence.[63] Yet even if the parties were to agree on procedurally fair processes for the resolution of comprehensive and specific claims, such procedural reform could not address the real problem: the dramatic inequality of bargaining power that exists between the parties.

The key point here is that the relative bargaining power of the parties is a function of the distribution of property rights accomplished by legal choice.[64] As Joseph Singer has said, '[t]he definition and distribution of property rights create both power and vulnerability.'[65] Imagine an Aboriginal nation involved in negotiations with the Crown over access to and control of certain territory. Imagine further that Canadian law holds

---

62 See Kent Roach, *Constitutional Remedies in Canada* (Aurora: Canada Law Book, 1995), 15–3 ('negotiation ... has historical origins in the treaty-making process'). For an account of obstacles that Aboriginal negotiators face in negotiating land claims and self-government agreements with the Crown, see Bradford W. Morse, 'Common Roots but Modern Divergences: Aboriginal Policies in Canada and the United States,' 10 St. Thomas L. Rev. 115 at 139–48 (1997).

63 Royal Commission on Aboriginal Peoples, *Final Report*, vol. 2, at 527–56. See also Royal Commission on Aboriginal Peoples, *Treaty Making in the Spirit of Co-existence: An Alternative to Extinguishment* (Ottawa: Supply and Services Canada, 1995); William B. Henderson and Derek T. Ground, 'Survey of Aboriginal Land Claims,' 26 Ottawa L. Rev. 187 (1994); Indian Claims Commission, *Indian Claims Commission Proceedings*, vol. 2, Special Issue on Land Claims Reform (Ottawa: Supply and Services, 1995).

64 See, generally, Robert L. Hale, 'Coercion and Distribution in a Supposedly Non-Coercive State,' 38 Pol. Sci. Q. 470 (1923) (bargaining power is constituted in part by the background distribution of property rights).

65 Joseph William Singer, 'Sovereignty and Property,' 86 Northwestern L. Rev. 1 at 56 (1991).

that (a) the nation in question enjoys Aboriginal title to such territory; (b) Aboriginal title confers exclusive rights to a wide range of activities in the territory, including exclusive rights to develop surface and subsurface renewable and non-renewable resources; (c) the Crown possesses no proprietary authority over the territory in question; and (d) any existing third-party interests are subject to the exercise of rights associated with Aboriginal title. Contrast this with the following scenario: (a) the law has not recognized that the Aboriginal nation possesses title to anything more than a few scattered villages within the territory in question; (b) legal recognition of Aboriginal title does not prevent the Crown from regulating Aboriginal activity or authorizing third-party activity on the land; (c) the law views the remainder of the territory as 'Crown lands'; and (d) the law recognizes and enforces rights associated with third-party interests, such as timber rights, on both land conceived of as subject to Aboriginal title and lands within the territory not conceived as subject to Aboriginal title. The two scenarios represent two distributions of baseline entitlements, producing two distributions of bargaining power and structuring two negotiated outcomes. Whether the first, the second, or some other scenario exists is a function of legal choice – choice that has dramatic consequences in terms of Aboriginal power and vulnerability in negotiations with the Crown.

Nor was the distribution of bargaining power between the Crown and Aboriginal people a one-shot affair, occurring sometime in the distant past when the law initially accepted assertions of underlying Crown title. The distribution of baseline entitlements is an ongoing process, occurring and recurring every time a court rules on the nature and extent of Aboriginal title, Crown title, and third party interests. Indeed, the legal framing of disputes between Aboriginal people and the Crown – what makes a political dispute a legal dispute – signals the distributive function of law. Public highways are characterized as running through 'Crown land' with the question being whether an Aboriginal person possesses certain 'rights of access.' Fee simple interests are characterized as stable, durable, and exclusionary, and as paramount in the event of conflict with a right associated with Aboriginal title. And, as described previously, Aboriginal title is characterized as sui generis, a label that has served as an excuse to allow extinguishment by executive action, to disable Aboriginal litigants from accessing effective interim relief, to frustrate access to the common law presumption of compensation in the event of expropriation, and to restrict Aboriginal use and enjoyment to traditional practices.

As these scenarios illustrate, it is not a question of whether the law ought to become involved in a process to resolve competing claims to territory; Canadian law is already involved in categorizing territory by actively establishing and maintaining rights associated with property and non-proprietary entitlements of the Crown, Aboriginal people and third parties. These rights form baselines that constitute the relative bargaining power of the parties.[66] To speak of law as too blunt an instrument to resolve the complex and competing interests implicated in the protection of Aboriginal lands and resources ignores the fact that the law is already there, establishing baselines, defining rights, and forming and maintaining a range of interests at stake.[67] Instead of asking whether the law should intervene, the distributive dimension of law requires determining on whose behalf the law should intervene – an inquiry that reveals law's relation to distributive justice.

The Constitutional Dimensions of Aboriginal Title

Even though it has historically failed in its actual protection of Aboriginal territorial interests, the law of Aboriginal title rightly views Aboriginal prior occupancy as possessing legal significance. But, apart from a few exceptions,[68] rights associated with Aboriginal title prior to 1982

---

66 See generally Kennedy, *A Critique of Adjudication*, at 240–6 (arguing that non-regulatory understandings of the common law conceal its distributive dimension and naturalize existing distributions); Joseph W. Singer, 'Property and Social Relations: From Title to Entitlement,' in G.E. van Maanen and A.J. van der Walt, eds., *Property Law on the Threshold of the 21st Century* (Apeldorn: Maklu, 1996), at 69–90 (arguing that property law is inescapably distributive); and Duncan Kennedy and Frank Michaelman, 'Are Property and Contract Efficient?' 8 Hofstra L. Rev. 711 (1980) (arguing that the common law is no less regulatory than regulation).

67 Compare John Brigham, *The Constitution of Interests: Beyond the Politics of Rights* (New York: New York University Press, 1996), at 154 ('[t]he law of property is what makes some people poor and some not').

68 These exceptions lay in cases where there was explicit reference to Aboriginal interests in constitutional documents, such as the Royal Proclamation of 1763 (U.K.), R.S.C. 1985, App. II, No. 1 (prescribing conditions for the disposal of ancestral territory); Constitution Act, 1867 (U.K.), 30 & 31 Vict., c. 3, s. 91(24) (assigning exclusive legislative authority over 'Indians, and Lands reserved for the Indians' to Parliament); Rupert's Land and North-Western Territory Order, 1870 (U.K.), R.S.C. 1985, App. II, No. 9, and Adjacent Territories Order, 1880 (U.K.), R.S.C. 1985, App. II, No. 14 (admission of northern territory to Canada conditional on 'adequate provision for the protection of Indian tribes whose interests and well-being are involved in the transfer'); Manitoba Act, 1870 (U.K.), 33 Vict. c. 3, s. 31, reprinted in R.S.C. 1985, App. II,

were conceptualized in common law terms. As such, they were subject to the exercise of legislative authority. The right to fish as an incident of Aboriginal title, for example, could be regulated and even extinguished by appropriate legislative action.[69] Does Aboriginal prior occupancy possess constitutional significance beyond the protection accorded to it by Canadian property law? Could it serve as a basis for a set of rights that subject the exercise of state power to constitutional standards of justification?

We saw in the previous chapter that the Supreme Court of Canada has invested Aboriginal prior occupancy with constitutional significance. In *Van der Peet*, Chief Justice Lamer stated that Aboriginal people are unique among 'all other minority groups in Canadian society' because of 'one simple fact: when Europeans arrived in North America, aboriginal peoples were already here, living in communities on the land, and participating in distinctive cultures, as they had done for centuries.'[70] According to the chief justice, Aboriginal prior occupancy justifies constitutional protection of certain Aboriginal cultural practices. But why should the fact that Aboriginal people lived in North America prior to the arrival of Europeans have any bearing on whether their cultural practices deserve constitutional protection? Constitutional protection of Aboriginal cultural practices is justified instead by the need to offset the disproportionate costs of cultural reproduction that Aboriginal people bear compared to other cultural groups in Canada. If prior occupancy possesses constitutional significance, its significance lies not as a justification for constitutional protection of Aboriginal cultural

---

No. 9, and Adjacent Territories Order, 1880 (U.K.), R.S.C. 1985, App. II, No. 14 (admission of northern territory to Canada conditional on 'adequate provision for the protection of Indian tribes whose interests and well-being are involved in the transfer'); Manitoba Act, 1870 (U.K.), 33 Vict. c. 3, s. 31, reprinted in R.S.C. 1985, App. II, No. 8 (providing for land allotment for Métis people); and British Columbia Terms of Union, 1871 (U.K.), reprinted in R.S.C. 1985, App. II, No. 10 ('the charge of the Indians, and the trusteeship and management of the lands reserved for their use and benefit, shall be assumed by the Dominion Government'). See also the natural resource agreements entered into between Canada and the three prairie provinces, given constitutional effect by the Constitution Act, 1930 (U.K.), 20-21 Geo., c. 26, reprinted in R.S.C. 1985, App. II, No. 26 (guaranteeing Indians the right to take game and fish 'for food' on specified territory).

69 See, for example, *R. v. Derricksan* (1976), 71 D.L.R. (3d) 159 (S.C.C.) (Parliament by virtue of its authority to enact laws in relation to 'Sea Coast and Inland Fisheries' can regulate the exercise of an Aboriginal right to fish).

70 *R. v. Van der Peet*, at 538 (emphasis removed).

interests but as part of a justification for constitutional protection of Aboriginal territorial interests.

In *R. v. Adams*,[71] the court signalled a willingness to separate cultural from territorial interests. At issue in *Adams* was whether a claim to an Aboriginal right to fish must be tied to a claim to Aboriginal title to the area in which the fishing took place. Holding that 'aboriginal rights cannot be inexorably linked to Aboriginal title,' Chief Justice Lamer further held that 'claims to title to the land are simply one manifestation of a broader based conception of aboriginal rights.'[72] This separation allows for constitutional protection of customs, practices, and traditions integral to the distinctive culture of an Aboriginal community even where the community cannot demonstrate that its occupancy of the land on which the activity takes place supports a claim of title. The question left unanswered in *Adams* is whether the separation of culture from territory leads to parallel constitutional protection of Aboriginal territorial interests or merely the constitutional protection of certain cultural practices. Do all rights associated with Aboriginal title receive constitutional protection or only those rights that relate to traditional cultural practices?

Admittedly, a huge gulf does not exist between Aboriginal cultural interests and Aboriginal territorial interests. Aboriginal people typically engage in cultural practices on ancestral territory and cultural practices are often intimately connected to Aboriginal relations with ancestral territory. But it is not necessarily the case that all Aboriginal practices occurring on Aboriginal territory are integral to Aboriginal cultural identity. A set of practices only loosely connected to Aboriginal cultural identity could receive constitutional protection – for example, mineral exploration – on the basis that Aboriginal territorial interests deserve independent constitutional protection. Territorial interests could also receive constitutional protection against a provincial or federal initiative – again, for example, mineral exploration – in the absence of any direct threat posed to Aboriginal cultural practices by the initiative.

In *Delgamuukw v. British Columbia*, the Supreme Court of Canada indicated that Aboriginal territorial interests warrant independent constitutional protection. Aboriginal title, according to the court, is a right recognized and affirmed by subsection 35(1) of the Constitution Act, 1982. The Supreme Court held that a court faced with a claim of Aborig-

---

71 [1996] 3 S.C.R. 101.
72 Ibid., at 118, 119.

inal title need not distinguish between distinctive, pre-contact Aboriginal cultural practices and practices that developed as a result of European influences. The act of occupation alone is sufficient to ground Aboriginal title; it is not necessary to prove that the land was a distinctive or integral part of the Aboriginal nation prior to European contact. And, as stated, Aboriginal title confers the right to exclusive use and occupation of land for a variety of activities, not all of which need be aspects of practices, customs, or traditions integral to the distinctive cultures of Aboriginal societies.

Despite the boldness of its holding, the Supreme Court provided little argument as to why Aboriginal title is worthy of a level of protection greater than what the law provides to non-Aboriginal proprietary interests. It simply held that a 'plain reading' of the constitution, as well as precedent, was conclusive of the issue. The court argued that the plain meaning of subsection 35(1) suggests that it provides constitutional status to those rights that were 'existing' prior to 1982. Given that Aboriginal title was a common law right in existence prior to 1982, Aboriginal title receives constitutional protection. With respect to precedent, the court relied on its earlier ruling in *Van der Peet* to the effect that subsection 35(1) constitutionalized Aboriginal rights in existence prior to 1982 in support of the proposition that the constitution recognizes and affirms Aboriginal title.

Any assessment of the constitutional status of Aboriginal title must take into account the fact that private, non-Aboriginal proprietary interests do not receive direct constitutional protection. The constitution does not explicitly protect non-Aboriginal private property holders whose property interests are adversely affected by state action, whether in the form of governmental regulation or the more extreme measure of expropriation.[73] And the reasons Canadian property law offers to defend the social institution of private property, generally speaking, are not of the kind that might support constitutional protection of private property.[74] While some scholars have attempted to fashion indirect con-

---

73 See, generally, Alexander Alvaro, 'Why Property Rights Were Excluded from the Charter of Rights and Freedoms, 24 C.J.P.S. 309 (1991).

74 See Frank I. Michaelman, 'Socio-Political Functions of Constitutional Protection for Private Property Holdings (In Liberal Political Thought),' in van Maanen and van der Walt, eds., *Property Law on the Threshold of the 21st Century*, 433–50 at 442 ('[l]iberal thought cannot defend, on the basis of socio-political functions, a constitutionally mandated practice of judicial intervention on behalf of private property against the vicissitudes of ordinary politics and ordinary government').

stitutional protection of private property, such as through the reference in the Charter's preamble to the rule of law,[75] such indirect protection would not be of the same order as recognizing that Aboriginal territorial interests underlie constitutional recognition of Aboriginal and treaty rights. If Aboriginal territorial interests are worthy of constitutional recognition, there must be something unique about such interests, compared to non-Aboriginal property interests, to warrant constitutional protection.

Three features of Aboriginal territorial interests explain why they warrant independent constitutional protection. First, Aboriginal people have unique spiritual relationships with ancestral territories that transcend particular cultural customs, practices, and traditions that may be engaged in by communities on ancestral land. Examples abound of this deep connection between spiritual identity and land. Members of the Blackfoot Confederacy, for example, view the land as a gift from the Creator as a mother, a giver of life, and the provider of all things necessary to sustain existence.[76] For the Gitksan in British Columbia, ownership of territory is a marriage of the chief and the land. Each chief has an ancestor who encountered and acknowledged the life of the land and received authority from such encounters.[77] Although Aboriginal systems of belief are diverse, Aboriginal relationships with land are often structured by beliefs that manifest an overarching spiritual responsibility to protect, nurture, and cherish the earth as the giver of life.[78] For the reasons outlined in Chapter 2, Aboriginal cultural difference, including Aboriginal beliefs about ancestral territories, merits constitutional protection in the face of interference by the Canadian state.[79]

In as much as Aboriginal spiritual beliefs form part of the cultural dif-

---

75 See, for example Philip W. Augustine, 'Protection of the Right to Property Under the Canadian Charter of Rights and Freedoms,' 18 Ottawa L. Rev. 55 (1986).

76 Leroy Little Bear, *The Relationship of Aboriginal People to the Land and the Aboriginal Perspective on Aboriginal Title* (research study prepared for the Royal Commission on Aboriginal Peoples, 1993) (on file with author).

77 Gisday Wa and Delgam Uukw, *The Spirit in the Land* (opening statement of the Gitksan and Wet'suwet'en Hereditary Chiefs in the Supreme Court of British Columbia, 11 May 1987), at 7–8.

78 See, generally, Royal Commission on Aboriginal Peoples, *Final Report*, vol. 2, at 448–64.

79 Compare *Delgamuukw v. British Columbia*, at 1089 ('[i]f lands are so occupied, there will exist a special bond between the group and the land in question such that the land will be part of the definition of the group's distinctive culture').

ference between Aboriginal and non-Aboriginal people in Canada, they illustrate one way in which aspects of indigenous difference intersect and interact with one another in ways that possess normative significance. But the spiritual dimensions of Aboriginal relationships with land only partly explain why Aboriginal territorial interests possess constitutional significance. Non-Aboriginal people may also relate to land in profoundly spiritual ways, yet such relations are not immediately seen as giving rise to constitutional entitlements. It may be that non-Aboriginal relationships with land also warrant constitutional protection in circumstances where there exists a close link between land and spiritual identities. For present purposes, my claim is simply that a deep connection between spiritual identity and land is a necessary but insufficient reason in itself for independent constitutional protection of Aboriginal territorial interests.

The second reason why Aboriginal territorial interests warrant constitutional protection is rooted in the difference between property and territory. Aboriginal territorial interests relate to land that is not only the property but also the territory of the right-holder. To speak of property is to speak primarily of ownership. Territory signifies a space to which individuals experience an attachment that partly constitutes their identification with a broader social and political collectivity.[80] Indeed, a person can experience territorial attachment without possessing any property rights in the land in question. Many Canadians own no land in Canada but nonetheless claim national attachment as Canadian citizens to territory that comprises Canada as a sovereign state. The law of Aboriginal title acknowledges the territorial status of ancestral lands in its acceptance of the collective nature of Aboriginal title.[81] But, when framed in common law terms, the law of Aboriginal title comprehends

---

80 Steven Grosby, 'Territoriality: The Transcendental, Primordial Feature of Modern Societies,' 1 Nations and Nationalism 143 at 148–49 (1995) ('the use of the word "territory" refers not merely to a geometrically delineated space; it rather refers to the transcendental significance of that space; it refers to the life-ordering and life-sustaining significance of a space which makes that space into a meaningful structure'). See also Matthew Chapman, 'Indigenous Peoples and International Human Rights: Towards a Guarantee for the Territorial Connection,' 26 Anglo-Am. L. Rev. 357 at 360 (1997) ('the "territorial connection" is a dynamic *and adaptable* social phenomenon in which territory clearly provides not merely a means of economic subsistence but also sustains religious and cultural values') (emphasis in original).

81 See *Delgamuukw v. British Columbia*, at 1082–3; *Amodu Tijani v. Secretary, Southern Nigeria*.

Aboriginal territorial interests as merely akin to ownership and not as constitutive of national identity. Common law recognition of Aboriginal territorial interests fails to capture the territorial dimensions of such interests.

Finally, perhaps the most significant reason why Aboriginal territorial interests deserve constitutional protection is the one with which I began this chapter – Aboriginal prior occupancy. While the fact that Aboriginal people lived in and occupied ancestral lands before the arrival of European settlers possesses general legal significance for the reasons advanced earlier, one aspect of their prior occupancy specifically warrants constitutional protection of ancestral lands. Aboriginal people occupied ancestral lands not only before the arrival of Europeans but before the establishment of the Canadian state. That is, Aboriginal people possessed title to their territories according to their own laws prior to the establishment of a sovereign entity that assumed the legislative power to redistribute title to its citizens. In the words of Swepson and Plant, 'rights of ownership already accrue to indigenous populations, and are not ceded to them through the actions of nation-states.'[82] Canada became a sovereign state against the backdrop of a pre-existing distribution of territory among Aboriginal nations. Constitutional protection of Aboriginal title acknowledges the fact that Canada was and continues to be constituted on Aboriginal territories. It ensures that legislative power will be exercised in a manner that respects Aboriginal prior occupancy.

This aspect of the constitutional significance of Aboriginal territorial interests is reflected in the Royal Proclamation of 1763, which observed that 'great Frauds and Abuses' had been committed by individuals purchasing lands from the Indians, and that it would be both strategic and equitable to take preventive action in the future.[83] According to imperial dispatches and correspondence sent in advance of the Proclama-

---

82 L. Swepson and R. Plant, 'International Standards and the Protection of the Land Rights of Indigenous and Tribal Populations,' 124 International Lab. Rev. 91 at 97 (1985).

83 The most accurate printed text of the Proclamation is provided in Clarence S. Brigham, ed., British Royal Proclamations Relating to America, Transactions and Collections of the American Antiquarian Society, vol. 12 (Worcester, Mass.: American Antiquarian Society, 1911), at 212–18. A less accurate version is reproduced in R.S.C. 1985, App. II, No. 1. The original text, entered on the Patent Roll for the regal year 4 Geo. III, is found in the United Kingdom Public Record Office: c. 66/3693 (back of roll).

tion, the course chosen was to guarantee to Aboriginal nations 'a Readiness upon all occasions to do them Justice,'[84] and in particular, to afford them 'Royal Protection from any Incroachment on the Lands they have reserved to themselves, for their hunting Grounds, & for their own Support & Habitation.'[85] The Proclamation constitutionally forbids the purchase of Aboriginal lands from persons other than the Crown and establishes constitutional ground rules to govern the voluntary cession of Indian lands to the Crown 'if, at any Time, any of the said Indians should be inclined to dispose of the said Lands.'[86] There is much debate concerning the legal effect and contemporary scope of the Royal Proclamation,[87] but to concentrate on its terms and reach is to miss the fact that the Proclamation illustrates the more basic point that Canada was literally constituted on ancestral territories. To ignore this aspect of Aboriginal prior occupancy would be to ignore a foundational feature of Canadian constitutional identity. In contrast, constitutional recognition of Aboriginal prior occupancy provides a degree of legitimacy to the distribution of private property in Canada.[88]

---

84 Circular letter from Lord Egremont to the Superintendent for the Southern Indians and several colonial governors, text in William L. Saunders, ed., *The Colonial Records of North Carolina*, 10 vols. (Raleigh, N.C: P.M. Hale, 1886–90), at 974–6 (ordering a promise be made to the Indians to dispel the idea that the English 'entertain a settled Design of extirpating the whole Indian Race, with a View to possess & enjoy their lands').

85 Egremont (Secretary of State for the Southern Department) to Amherst (Commander in Chief of the British forces in America), 27 Jan. 1763, 'Fitch Papers,' *Collections of the Connecticut Historical Society*, 31 vols. (Hartford: Connecticut Historical Society, 1860–1967), 18:224.

86 See also *Mitchel v. U.S.*, 9 Pet. 717 (U.S. Fla., 1835), at 747; *R. v. Koonungnak* (1963), 45 W.W.R. 282, at 302 (N.W.T. Terr. Ct.); *Doherty v. Giroux* (1915), 24 Que. K.B. 433 at 435; and *R. v. Baby* (1855), 12 U.C.Q.B. 346 at 360.

87 See, generally, Brian Slattery, *The Legal Status and Land Rights of Indigenous Canadian Peoples, as Affected by the Crown's Acquisition of the Territories* (Saskatoon: Native Law Centre, 1989); see also John Borrows, 'Wampum at Niagara: The Royal Proclamation, Canadian Legal History, and Self-Government,' in Michael Asch, ed., *Aboriginal and Treaty Rights in Canada*, 155–72.

88 Compare Jennifer Nedelsky, 'Should Property be Constitutionalized? A Relational and Comparative Approach,' in van Maanen and van der Walt, eds., *Property Law on the Threshold of the 21st Century*, at 418 (arguing that in light of conquest and colonization, 'the *distribution* of property is manifestly unjust') (emphasis in original). While Nedelsky argues that this is reason to question constitutional protection of private property, my claim is that constitutionalization of Aboriginal title mitigates some of the injustice associated with the distribution of private property produced by the common law.

Taken together, these three features distinguish Aboriginal territorial interests from non-Aboriginal proprietary interests and explain why Aboriginal title warrants constitutional protection independent of and in addition to constitutional protection of particular customs, practices, and beliefs of Aboriginal people. Aboriginal people have unique spiritual relationships with their ancestral lands, ancestral lands are integral to Aboriginal social and political identity, and Aboriginal people lived in and occupied ancestral lands prior to the establishment of the Canadian state. While the first feature illustrates the close proximity of the territorial and cultural dimensions of indigenous difference, the second and third involve the intersection of these two dimensions. In so doing, they implicate issues relating to Aboriginal governance and the nature and scope of the distribution of legislative authority in Canada. These issues form the subject of the next chapter.

Chapter Four

Sovereignty

Upon mature consideration we have thought fit to own the Five Nations or Cantons of the Indians, viz: the Maquaes, Sinecas, Cayougues, Oneydes, and Onondagues, as our subjects, and resolve to protect them as such.

Royal Instructions to British Colonial Governors, 1670–1776[1]

When representatives of the British colonies in North America decided to form a new confederation and call it Canada, they met in Charlottetown, Prince Edward Island, to complete the drafting of a set of constitutional principles that would serve to guide the new country in the future. But for a single reference to federal jurisdiction over 'Indians, and Lands reserved for the Indians,' the Constitution Act, 1867[2] makes no mention of the fact that, prior to European contact, Aboriginal people belonged to nations structured by ancient forms of government exercising sovereign authority over persons and territory.[3] In the oft-

---

1 Leonard Woods Labaree, ed., *Royal Instructions to British Colonial Governors, 1670–1776* (1935; reprinted New York: Octagon, 1967), at 2:463.

2 (U.K.), 30 & 31 Vict., c. 3.

3 For a useful definition of 'nation,' see Konstantin Symmons-Symonolewicz, 'The Concept of Nationhood: Toward a Theoretical Clarification,' 12 Canadian Review of Studies in Nationalism 215 at 221 (1985) (defining 'nation' as a 'territorially based community of human beings sharing a distinct variant of modern culture, bound together by a strong sentiment of unity and solidarity, marked by a clear historically-rooted consciousness of national identity, and possessing, or striving to possess, a genuine political self-government').

quoted words of Chief Justice Marshall of the U.S. Supreme Court, 'America, separated from Europe by a wide ocean, was inhabited by a distinct people, divided into separate nations, independent of each other and of the rest of the world, having institutions of their own, and governing themselves by their own laws.'[4]

Why did the birth of Canada include no explicit constitutional acknowledgement of the fact of Aboriginal prior sovereignty? In attempting to answer this question, I first explore a range of meanings attributed to sovereignty, as well as a number of factors that account for its contestability in the context of Aboriginal claims, and assess the warnings offered by some that sovereignty is an inappropriate vehicle for realizing Aboriginal aspirations.

Sovereignty's Meaning

What does it mean to speak of Aboriginal sovereignty as an interest that merits constitutional protection? The meaning of sovereignty is not entirely shared across particular groups, societies or cultures, nor does it somehow inhere in the nature of the word. Instead, its meaning or value is a function of interpretive acts by those who possess it and those who seek it. Because sovereignty is a contested site of interpretation, it remains open to transformation and application to diverse forms of human association.[5] However, the contestability of sovereignty does not in itself preclude the possibility of a shared understanding among those who possess it and those who seek it of its meaning and value.

International law provides perhaps the most common understanding of sovereignty: sovereignty denotes the formal independence of a state

---

4 *Worcester v. Georgia*, 31 U.S. (6 Pet.) 515 at 542–3 (1832).
5 See Lassa F.E. Oppenheim, *International Law: A Treatise*, 3rd ed. (London: Longman, 1920), at 1:129 ('there exists perhaps no conception the meaning of which is more controversial than that of sovereignty'). R.B.J. Walker, *Inside/Outside: International Relations as Political Theory* (Cambridge: Cambridge University Press, 1993), at 166 ('the very attempt to treat sovereignty as a matter of definition and legal principle encourages a certain amnesia about its historical and culturally specific character'); Thomas J. Biersteker and Cynthia Weber, 'The Social Construction of Sovereignty,' in Biersteker and Weber, eds., *Sovereignty as a Social Construct* (Cambridge: Cambridge University Press, 1996), at 1 ('[s]overeignty is ... an inherently *social* construct') (emphasis in original); and Jens Bartleson, *A Genealogy of Sovereignty* (Cambridge: Cambridge University Press, 1995), at 2 ('the relationship between the very term sovereignty, the concept of sovereignty and the reality of sovereignty is historically open, contingent and unstable').

and represents the 'totality of international powers' that international law recognizes as attaching to states.[6] 'States' claims to sovereignty,' in the words of Thomas Biersteker and Cynthia Weber, 'construct a social environment in which they can interact as an international society of states, while at the same time the mutual recognition of claims of sovereignty is an important element in the construction of states themselves.'[7] Sovereignty, under this formulation, refers to powers typically exercised by an independent state. It establishes the state as an international legal subject and divides international from national competence.[8] Understood in this manner, sovereignty is an inappropriate term to refer to an Aboriginal interest or set of interests that warrants constitutional protection if the task at hand is to explore the possibility that constitutional arrangements can and should be established that create territorial and jurisdictional spaces short of independent statehood for Aboriginal peoples. In any event, independent statehood lies within the province of international, not constitutional, law.

However, more flexible understandings of sovereignty are capable of housing Aboriginal aspirations. International law increasingly recognizes that subunits of states exercise a measure of sovereignty in the international arena. In contrast to a formal demarcation between international and national competence, sovereignty can be understood as a set of 'disaggregated rights to be pragmatically bundled, rearranged and balanced.'[9] Moreover, international law – whether formally or pragmatically understood – does not exhaust sovereignty's meaning. In addition to its external aspect constitutional law comprehends sovereignty as referring to political and legal authority within states.[10] In this internal

---

6 James Crawford, *The Creation of States in International Law* (Oxford: Clarendon Press, 1979), at 27.

7 Biersteker and Weber, 'The Social Construction of State Sovereignty,' at 1–2. See also J.L. Brierly, *The Law of Nations: An Introduction to the International Law of Peace*, 4th ed. (Oxford: Clarendon Press, 1949), at 48–9 ('for the practical purposes of the international lawyer sovereignty is not a metaphysical concept, nor is it of the essence of statehood; it is merely a term which designates an aggregate of particular and very extensive claims that states habitually make for themselves in their relations with other states').

8 For description and critique of this view, see David Kennedy, 'Receiving the International,' 10 Conn. J. Int'l L. 1 (1995).

9 Ibid., at 9. See also David Elkins, *Beyond Sovereignty: Territory and Political Economy in the Twenty-First Century* (Toronto: University of Toronto Press, 1995).

10 Ingrid Detter de Lupis, *International Law and the Independent State*, 2nd ed. (Aldershott: Gower, 1987), at 3. See also Harold J. Laski, 'The Foundations of Sovereignty,' in *The Foundations of Sovereignty and Other Essays* (New York: Harcourt, Brace, 1921), 1–29.

sense, sovereignty need not be vested in single authority. Degrees of sovereign authority, as any federalist knows, can be simultaneously wielded by a number of different entities – states, provinces, and, as the American experience demonstrates, Indian nations – which possess inherent sovereign authority over persons and territory.[11] None of these entities wields absolute sovereign power over and against other competing sources of power; within a federal system, levels of government are often viewed as sovereign within their respective spheres of authority.[12] Aboriginal conceptions of sovereignty likewise often imply the sharing of authority among jurisdictions. Gerald Alfred, for example, writes of a Mohawk conception of sovereignty based 'upon a mutual respect among communities for the political and cultural imperatives of nationhood – a flexible sharing of resources and responsibilities in the act of maintaining the distinctiveness of each community.'[13] This conception, according to Alfred, does not preclude a recognition 'that certain jurisdictions require a sharing of authority with other governments.'[14]

The internal dimension of sovereignty aptly describes what is at issue when assessing whether forms of Aboriginal sovereignty merit constitutional protection. A grant or recognition of some measure of sovereignty to a particular collectivity permits that collectivity to express its collective difference. Those who possess sovereignty are thus typically

---

11 The inherent sovereignty of Indians in the United States obtains constitutional expression through and by the concept and reality of 'domestic dependent nation' status. See *Cherokee Nation v. Georgia*, 30 U.S. (5 Pet.) 1 at 17 (1831), per Marshall C.J. ('tribes which reside within the acknowledged boundaries of the United States can. ... be denominated domestic dependent nations'). As such, Indian nations are viewed in law as free to exercise inherent jurisdiction over internal tribal affairs, subject to overriding Congressional plenary authority. See, for example, *U.S. v. Kagama*, 118 U.S. 375 (1886), and *Lone Wolf v. Hitchcock*, 187 U.S. 553 (1903) (recognizing Congressional plenary power over Indian nations). For commentary, see Nell Jessup Newton, 'Federal Power over Indians: Its Sources, Scope, and Limitations,' 132 U. Pa. L. Rev. 195 (1984). American states traditionally have been held to have no or very limited legislative power to regulate the affairs of Indians on reservations. See, for example, *Williams v. Lee*, 358 U.S. 217 (1959) (state law inapplicable where it infringes right to self-government). See, generally, Frank Pommersheim, 'Tribal-State Relations: Hope for the Future?' 36 S. Dak. L. Rev. 239 (1991).

12 For a history of the concept of federalism, see S. Rufus Davis, *The Federal Principle: A Journey through Time in Quest of Meaning* (Berkeley: University of California Press, 1978).

13 Gerald R. Alfred, *Heeding the Voices of Our Ancestors: Kahnawake Mohawk Politics and the Rise of Native Nationalism* (Toronto: Oxford University Press, 1995), at 102.

14 Ibid., at 147.

reluctant to relinquish any measure of it. A conquered people that yearns to rid itself of its colonial past seeks sovereignty as a vehicle for and an expression of this desire; it seeks to be free to express its collective identity. Similarly, a conquering nation values its sovereignty because sovereignty permits the domestic and international expression of its collective identity, as well as the continued projection on and enforcement of that identity against those it has conquered.

Both those who possess and those who seek sovereignty thus share an appreciation of its value. Disagreement occurs when descending into specifics about the uses of sovereignty – what sovereignty ought to permit as opposed to why it is valuable. It is a function of differing views on whether a collectivity ought to be entitled to exercise its sovereign authority in particular ways and for particular purposes. Disagreement over the uses to which sovereignty ought to be put actually illustrates agreement among otherwise divergent collectivities over the value and meaning of sovereignty. Each side cherishes its own collective difference and values sovereignty as a way of expressing that difference and protecting it from the encroaching views of the other. Collective difference, far from being a reason for refusing to recognize a community's sovereignty, is in fact a precondition of such recognition. The value of sovereignty lies in the legal space it establishes for a community to construct, protect, and transform its collective identity. Sovereignty, simply speaking, permits the legal expression of collective difference.[15]

Constitutional protection of Aboriginal sovereignty is a means by which Aboriginal people can assert some degree of control over the form, content, and direction of their individual and collective identities. Given that sovereignty can be understood both pragmatically, as not necessarily referring to the totality of powers that attach to a nation state, and internally, as referring to political and legal authority within Canada, Aboriginal sovereignty can be viewed as an interest that warrants constitutional protection. Aboriginal sovereignty in this sense does not differ from other manifestations of internal sovereign authority in Canada. It represents one strand in a larger web of entities that exercise some degree of sovereign authority over land and people. One can speak of a distribution of sovereignty, heterogeneous in its forms and sources, entitling a wide class of entities, including Aboriginal people, to exercise sovereign authority.

---

15 See Bartleson, *A Genealogy of Sovereignty*, at 189 ('modern sovereignty is, above all, a principle of difference').

Some writers have advised Aboriginal people to disregard the concept of sovereignty in their quest for greater self-determination. Menno Boldt and Anthony Long, for example, argue that by making claims of sovereignty, 'Indian leaders are legitimizing European-western-type philosophies and structures of authority and decision-making within contemporary Indian communities.'[16] They equate sovereignty with statehood and statehood with a hierarchy of power relationships that do violence to cultural traits and values shared by Aboriginal people, such as 'the reaching of decisions by consensus, institutionalized sharing, respect for personal autonomy, and a preference for impersonal controls and behaviour.'[17] Instead, they advocate the extension of certain collective rights to Aboriginal people to preserve their national status and collective identities.

Such concerns miss the point. Aboriginal people may not be able to express their individual and collective identities if they exercise sovereignty in a way that mimics European structures of authority. Sovereignty exercised in this way may threaten the continued existence of traditional Aboriginal forms of government.[18] However, this possibility should not stand as a reason for denying Aboriginal peoples enhanced law-making authority over their individual and collective identities. Those concerned about the potential erosion of Aboriginal identities ought instead to direct their energies towards influencing how sovereignty is exercised once Aboriginal people are viewed as sovereign within their spheres of authority. Nothing inherent in the concept of sovereignty dictates a particular institutional form. If sovereignty means allowing the legal expression of collective difference, it refers to a relation between two or more entities and not to particular structures of authority internal to one. A relation between sovereigns is a relation of equality in which each views itself and the other as independent and distinct. A group's distinctiveness can take many forms but it need not take a particular form for that group to be sovereign.

---

16 Menno Boldt and J. Anthony Long, 'Tribal Traditions and European-Western Political Ideologies: The Dilemma of Canada's Native Indians,' in Boldt and Long, eds., *The Quest for Justice: Aboriginal Peoples and Aboriginal Rights* (Toronto: University of Toronto Press, 1985), 333 at 342.

17 Ibid., at 334.

18 Compare Homi Bhabha, *The Location of Culture* (London: Routledge, 1994), at 85, 112 ('mimicry' is simultaneously 'one of the most elusive and effective strategies of colonial power and knowledge' and a 'strategic reversal of the process of domination').

Discovery and the Distribution of Sovereignty

When the fathers of Confederation agreed to the principles enshrined in the Constitution Act, 1867, none questioned the exercise of legislative authority by the Dominion of Canada over Aboriginal people in Canada. In the words of the Supreme Court of Canada, 'while British policy towards the aboriginal population was based on respect for their right to occupy their traditional lands, ... there was from the outset never any doubt that sovereignty and legislative power ... vested in the Crown.'[19] The assertion of territorial sovereignty over Aboriginal people implicit in the establishment of colonies on the continent and in the enactment of the Constitution Act, 1867 conformed to dominant understandings of international legal principles governing the distribution of sovereignty.

To speak of distributing sovereignty may conjure up an image of a single authority meting out fair shares but this need not be the case. The initial distribution of sovereignty over North America among European powers was generated not by a single decision-making authority, but by and through a series of acts of mutual recognition by European powers. Each colonizing power viewed itself and others as entitled to claim sovereignty to territory if it could establish a valid claim according to the rules and principles that governed European imperial practice. According to 'the doctrine of discovery,' sovereignty could be acquired over unoccupied territory by discovery.[20] Sovereignty over occupied territory could be acquired only by conquest or cession. However, international law deemed North America to be unoccupied, or terra nullius, for the purposes of distributing sovereignty. European settlement thus vested

---

19 *R. v. Sparrow*, [1990] 1 S.C.R. 1075 at 1103.

20 See, generally, James Crawford, *The Creation of States in International Law* (Oxford: Clarendon Press, 1979), at 173–85. With respect to unoccupied land, discovery was a necessary but not necessarily sufficient condition for a valid claim of sovereignty under international law. Some have argued that effective occupation was also required: see R.Y. Jennings, *The Acquisition of Territory in International Law* (Manchester: Manchester University Press, 1963). See also *Island of Palmas*, 11 R.I.A.A. 829 (1928) (discovery vests inchoate title that requires effective occupation for its completion). Others have claimed that symbolic acts accompanying an assertion of sovereignty, such as the planting of a flag, was sufficient: see Oppenheim, *International Law: A Treatise*, at 557–8; William E. Hall, *A Treatise on International Law* (8th ed.) (Oxford: Clarendon Press, 1924), at 126–7; and A.S. Keller, O.J. Lissitzyn, and F.J. Mann, *Creation of Rights of Sovereignty through Symbolic Acts, 1400–1800* (New York: Columbia University Press, 1963); see also 'Clipperton Island Arbitration' (English text found in 26 Am. J. Int'l L. 390 (1932)) (symbolic occupation sufficient to vest sovereignty).

sovereignty in settling nations despite an indigenous presence. Because North America was treated as vacant, neither conquest nor cession was necessary to transfer sovereignty from Aboriginal nations to European powers.[21]

International law deemed North America to be terra nullius under the doctrine of discovery because European powers viewed Aboriginal nations as insufficiently Christian or civilized to justify recognizing them as sovereign over their lands and people.[22] An Aboriginal nation did not constitute 'a legal unit in international law.'[23] In the words of Chief Justice Marshall: 'the character and religion of [North America's] inhabitants afforded an apology for considering them as a people over whom the superior genius of Europe might claim an ascendancy. The potentates of the old world found no difficulty in convincing themselves that they made ample compensation to the inhabitants of the new, by bestow-

---

21 See, generally, I. Brownlie, *Principles of Public International Law*, 5th ed. (Oxford: Clarendon Press, 1998), at 125–67. When international law came to comprehend the acquisition of territorial sovereignty despite an indigenous presence in these terms is a matter of some dispute. See, specifically, Brian Slattery, 'Did France Claim Canada upon "Discovery"?' in J.M. Bumsted, ed., *Interpreting Canada's Past* (Toronto: Oxford University Press, 1986), at 1:2–26. See, generally, Sharon Korman, *The Right of Conquest: The Acquisition of Territory by Force in International Law and Practice* (Oxford: Clarendon Press, 1996), at 41–66. For the view that international law on the subject did not '*precede* and thereby effortlessly resolve the problem' but instead 'was created out of the unique issues generated by the encounter between cultures,' see Anthony Anghie, 'Francisco de Vitoria and the Colonial Origins of International Law,' in Eve Darian-Smith and Peter Fitzpatrick, eds., *Laws of the Postcolonial* (Ann Arbor: University of Michigan Press, 1999), 89–107 at 90 (emphasis in original).

22 See, e.g., John Westlake, *Chapters on Principles of International Law* (Cambridge: Cambridge University Press, 1894), at 136–8, 141–3 (drawing a distinction between 'civilization and want of it'); Hall, *A Treatise on International Law*, at 47 (international law only governs states that are 'inheritors of that civilization'); Oppenheim, *International Law*, 126 (the law of nations does not apply to 'organized wandering tribes'); and Charles C. Hyde, *International Law Chiefly as Interpreted and Applied by the United States* (Boston: Little Brown, 1922), at 164 ('native inhabitants possessed no rights of territorial control which the European explorer or his monarch was bound to respect'). See, generally, S. James Anaya, 'The Rights of Indigenous Peoples and International Law in Historical and Contemporary Perspective,' Harvard Indian Law Symposium (1990), 191; Gerrit W. Gong, *The Standard of 'Civilization' in International Society* (Oxford: Clarendon Press, 1984). Compare David Strang, 'Contested Sovereignty: The Social Construction of Colonial Imperialism,' in Biersteker and Cynthia Weber, *State Sovereignty as a Social Construct*, 22–49 at 43 ('the imperial moment took place within and was carried forward by a collective delegitimation of the sovereignty of non-Western polities').

23 *Cayuga Indians (Great Britain) v. United States* (1926), 6 R.I.A.A. 173 at 176.

ing on them civilization and Christianity, in exchange for unlimited independence.'[24] Thus, when the British Parliament passed the Constitution Act, 1867 and further distributed internal sovereignty between the federal and provincial governments in the new Dominion of Canada, the Crown did not seriously question the legitimacy of its assertion of sovereignty over Aboriginal people and Aboriginal lands in Canada.[25]

Nowhere in the jurisprudence devoted to the distribution of internal sovereignty or, more precisely, the distribution of legislative authority between Parliament and provincial legislatures, is there any sustained examination of the legitimacy of the assertion of Canadian sovereignty over Aboriginal people in Canada.[26] As discussed in Chapter 3, underlying Crown title vests in the Crown an underlying proprietary interest in ancestral lands that until recently,[27] and notwithstanding a number of exceptions,[28] gave rise to the legal expectation that the Crown possessed the unilateral authority to regulate and extinguish Aboriginal territorial interests. Underlying Crown sovereignty bears a similar relationship to the legislative authority of the Crown as that which exists between underlying Crown title and the Crown's proprietary authority. Its acceptance enables Parliament and provincial legislatures, subject to the recent enactment of subsection 35(1) of the Constitution Act, 1982, to pass laws regulating Aboriginal people without their consent.

---

24 *Johnson v. M'Intosh*, at 573.
25 This is not to say that Crown sovereignty was not questioned in particular regulatory contexts: see, for example, Hamar Foster, 'Forgotten Arguments: Aboriginal Title and Sovereignty in Canada Jurisdiction Act Cases,' 21 Man. L.J. 343 (1992); Mark D. Walters, 'The Extension of Colonial Criminal Jurisdiction over the Aboriginal Peoples of Upper Canada: Reconsidering the Shawanakiskie Case (1822–26),' 46 U.T.L.J. 273 (1996). Nor is it to say that the assertion of Crown sovereignty had the effect of extinguishing Aboriginal sovereignty: see Royal Commission on Aboriginal Peoples, *Report*, vol. 2, *Restructuring the Relationship*, pt 1 (Ottawa: Minister of Supply and Services Canada, 1996), at 202–13, and authorities cited therein.
26 But see *Logan v. Styres* (1959), 20 D.L.R. (2d) 416 (Ont. C.A.), where a member of the Six Nations Confederacy, composed of the Mohawk, Oneida, Onondaga, Cayuga, Seneca, and Tuscarora nations, argued unsuccessfully that members of the Six Nations were not subjects of the Crown and therefore outside the reach of the federal Indian Act, R.S.C. 1952, c. 149. In dismissing the argument, King J. argued that the Six Nations were once 'faithful allies of the Crown' but became 'loyal subjects of the Crown' by accepting reserve land from it.
27 See *Delgamuukw v. British Columbia*, [1997] 3 S.C.R. 1010; see also text accompanying Notes 36–42, Chapter 3.
28 See note 68, Chapter 3.

Subsection 91(24) of the Constitution Act, 1867 confers on Parliament legislative jurisdiction over 'Indians, and Lands reserved for the Indians,'[29] which has been held to authorize Parliament to pass laws directly in relation to Aboriginal people. In addition, Parliament is also entitled to pass laws pursuant to other heads of power listed in section 91 that have the effect of regulating Aboriginal interests.[31] By contrast, a provincial legislature is not entitled to pass legislation directly in relation to Indians or lands reserved for the Indians; legislation to this effect would be in essence legislation in relation to a federal head of power and therefore ultra vires a provincial legislature.[31] Generally speaking, however, a province is entitled to pass legislation with a valid provincial purpose governing Aboriginal people as long as such legislation does not invade federal jurisdiction. Such a provincial law will intrude on federal jurisdiction over 'Indians, and Lands reserved for the Indians' if it does not have a uniform territorial operation, that is, if it is not a law of 'general application' or if it 'touches the core of Indianness.'[32]

A provincial law might 'touch the core of Indianness' in at least two ways. First, a provincial law that 'impairs the status or capacity of Indians' will be held to 'touch the core of Indianness,' and therefore will not apply of its own force to Indians or Indian lands. 'Status' and 'capacity' have been interpreted as referring to legal status under federal law, namely, 'Indian status ... [or] rights so closely connected with Indian status that they should be regarded as necessary incidents of status such ... as registrability, membership in a band, the right to participate in the election of chiefs and band councils, [or] reserve privileges.'[33] Second, a provincial law that affects the exercise of Aboriginal rights recognized by subsection 35(1) of the Constitution Act, 1982 will necessarily 'touch the core of Indianness' and therefore will not apply of its own force to Indians or Indian lands.[34]

Provincial laws that intrude on federal authority over Indians and that

---

29 Supra, note 2.
30 See, for example, *R. v. Derriksan* (1976), 71 D.L.R. (3d) 159 (S.C.C.) (federal law regulating Aboriginal rights held intra vires), and *R. v. George*, [1966] S.C.R. 267 (federal law regulating treaty rights held intra vires).
31 See, for example, *R. v. Sutherland*, [1980] 2 S.C.R. 451.
32 *Dick v. The Queen*, [1985] 2 S.C.R. 309 at 315, 326; *Delgamuukw v. British Columbia*, at 1121.
33 *Four B Manufacturing v. United Garment Workers of America*, [1980] 1 S.C.R. 1031.
34 *Delgamuukw v. British Columbia*, at 1121.

would not apply of their own force nonetheless can, with federal approval, apply to Indians. Section 88 of the federal Indian Act, for example, functions to adopt, or incorporate by reference, some provincial laws that would otherwise be inapplicable to Indians.[35] The fact that Parliament has authorized the application of certain provincial laws that intrude on federal authority over Indians, however, does not insulate such laws from the dictates of subsection 35(1) of the Constitution Act, which recognizes and affirms existing Aboriginal and treaty rights. As is the case with provincial proprietary authority, a province (or Parliament) cannot exercise its legislative authority so as to interfere with the exercise of Aboriginal rights absent a compelling and substantial legislative objective, nor can such authority be exercised in a manner inconsistent with the special fiduciary relationship between the Crown and Aboriginal peoples. Valid legislative objectives include the development of agriculture, forestry, mining and hydroelectric power, general economic development, protection of the environment or endangered species, the building of infrastructure, and the settlement of foreign populations to support those aims.[36] In such circumstances, the Crown is under at least a duty of consultation and, in most cases, the duty will be significantly deeper than consultation.[37] Fair compensation will ordinarily be required when a provincial (or federal) law infringes Aboriginal title.[38]

Thus the issue underlying every jurisdictional dispute over matters pertaining to Aboriginal people is not whether the Canadian state has authority to regulate Aboriginal people but rather which level of government is entitled to regulate the matter in question. The unspoken assumption is that Aboriginal sovereignty is not an interest that warrants constitutional protection. Principles governing the distribution of legislative authority between Parliament and provincial legislatures accept without question a hierarchical relationship of sovereign and subject between the Canadian state and Aboriginal people.[39] It may well have been the case that, prior to 1982, it would have been inappropriate for

---

35 *Dick v. The Queen.*
36 *Delgamuukw v. British Columbia*, at 1111.
37 Ibid., at 1112–13.
38 Ibid., at 1113.
39 See generally Bruce Ryder, 'The Demise and Rise of the Classical Paradigm in Canadian Federalism: Promoting Autonomy for the Provinces and First Nations,' 36 McGill L.J. 308 (1991).

the judiciary to treat Aboriginal sovereignty as an interest meriting constitutional protection. Although nothing in the text of the Constitution Act, 1867 dictates the conclusion that Canada possesses jurisdiction to pass laws affecting its Aboriginal population without that population's consent, courts have been loath to assess the legitimacy of claims of sovereignty made by their parent states. Known in law as the act of state doctrine, the judiciary has traditionally excluded executive and legislative action in relation to the acquisition of new territory from the purview of domestic courts.[40]

Whatever may have been the case prior to 1982, the passage of subsection 35(1) of the Constitution Act, 1982 dramatically changed the role of the judiciary as it relates to the constitutional status of Aboriginal people in Canada. Much has been written on the possibility that subsection 35(1) recognizes and affirms an inherent Aboriginal right of self-government.[41] Whether it does turns in no small measure on whether Aboriginal sovereignty merits constitutional protection – an issue that requires the judiciary to address whether European assertions of territorial sovereignty or subsequent actions by colonial governments extinguished Aboriginal sovereignty. Such an inquiry will necessarily involve assessing the legitimacy of the claim that a settler nation can assert territorial sovereignty over Aboriginal people and Aboriginal lands without resort to conquest or cession. Subsection 35(1) thus subjects 'acts of state' against Aboriginal people to constitutional scrutiny. The judiciary can no longer shirk the task of assessing the constitutional significance of Aboriginal prior sovereignty. In Brian Slattery's words, 'courts cannot take refuge in the act of state doctrine without

---

40 See, e.g., *Cook v. Sprigg*, [1899] A.C. 572; *Vajesingji Joravarsingji v. Sec. of State for India* (1924), L.R. 51; and *Coe v. Commonwealth of Australia* (1979), 53 A.L.J.R. 403. For discussion, see Kent McNeil, *Common Law Aboriginal Title* (Oxford: Clarendon Press, 1989), at 131, n. 104 and Brian Slattery, *The Legal Status and Land Rights of Indigenous Canadian Peoples, as affected by the Crown's Acquisition of the Territories* (Saskatoon: Native Law Centre 1989), at 45–59.

41 See, for example, Michael Asch, 'Aboriginal Self-Government and the Construction of Canadian Constitutional Identity,' 30 Alta. L. Rev. 465 (1992); John J. Borrows, 'A Genealogy of Law: Inherent Sovereignty and First Nations Self-Government,' 30 Osgoode Hall L.J. 291 (1992); Frank Cassidy and Robert L. Bish, *Indian Government: Its Meaning in Practice* (Halifax: Institute for Research on Public Policy, 1991); David C. Hawkes, *Aboriginal Self-Government: What Does It Mean?* (Kingston: Institute of Intergovernmental Relations, 1985); Kent McNeil, 'Envisaging Constitutional Space for Aboriginal Governments,' 19 Queen's L.J. 95 (1993); and Brian Slattery, 'First Nations and the Constitution,' 71 Can. Bar Rev. 261 (1992).

forfeiting their moral authority and acting as passive instruments of colonial rule.'[42]

Sovereignty and Formal Equality

Questioning the justice of European claims of territorial sovereignty in North America has a long history. Francisco de Vitoria, writing in 1539, for example, stated that Aboriginal peoples in North America 'undoubtedly possessed true dominion, both in public and private affairs.'[43] In 1832, Chief Justice Marshall of the U.S. Supreme Court noted that '[i]t is difficult to comprehend the proposition that the inhabitants of either quarter of the globe could have rightful original claims of dominion over the inhabitants of the other, or over lands they occupied; or that the discovery of either by the other should give the discoverer rights in the country discovered which annulled the pre-existing rights of its ancient possessors.'[44] But what is lacking in many arguments in favour of constitutional recognition of Aboriginal governmental authority is an account of why the fact of prior sovereignty of a particular group of citizens possesses constitutional significance. While it is no doubt true that Aboriginal communities formed sovereign nations prior to European settlement and colonization, why should a state that accords Aboriginal people full rights of citizenship[45] continue to respect this fact? Why is Aboriginal prior sovereignty a relevant reason for differential distributions of political rights and responsibilities among citizens?

Whether Aboriginal prior sovereignty merits constitutional protection turns on the justice of the distribution of sovereignty in North America, which itself depends on whether this distribution respects basic norms of equality. Equality demands that like cases be treated alike and different cases be treated differently. Formal equality requires

---

42 Slattery, 'Aboriginal Sovereignty and Imperial Claims,' 29 Osgoode Hall L.J. 681 at 692 (1991). See also John Borrows, 'Sovereignty's Alchemy: An Analysis of Delgamuukw v. The Queen,' 37 Osgoode Hall L. J. 537 (1999).

43 Francisco de Vitoria, 'De Indis' (1539), in Anthony Pagden and Jeremy Lawrence, eds., *Fransisco de Vitoria: Political Writings* (Cambridge: Cambridge University Press, 1991), at 251.

44 *Worcester v. Georgia*, 31 U.S. (6 Pet.) 515 at 542–3 (1832).

45 Aboriginal people in Canada are citizens of Canada by virtue of the Citizenship Act, R.S.C. 1985, c. C-29. Indian people received the right to vote in federal elections in 1960. See Jack Woodward, *Native Law* (Scarborough, Ont.: Carswell, 1990), at 145–50.

that all potential participants of a distribution be treated as formal equals unless a valid reason, relating to the nature of the good in question, favours differential treatment. Substantive equality suggests that sovereignty should be distributed with a view to ameliorating social and economic disparities among groups in society.[46] In my view, these two principles of distribution do not fall prey to the problems of indeterminacy and ethnocentrism associated with universalist positions on human rights.[47] They are sufficiently determinate to permit critical judgments about particular distributions. And if I am correct in asserting some inter-cultural agreement on the validity of assessing the justice of distributions of sovereignty according to these principles, then their deployment does not raise the problem of ethnocentrism.

As I have said, formal equality requires that all potential recipients of a distribution be treated as formal equals unless a valid reason exists, related to the good in question, for differential treatment.[48] In the present context, formal equality demands scrutiny of the validity of reasons underlying differential treatment of Aboriginal people. Aboriginal people should not be arbitrarily excluded from distributions of goods or benefits that accrue to others nor should they arbitrarily be provided with goods and benefits that do not accrue to others. This is not to suggest that indigenous difference ought always to be ignored. But if indigenous difference is offered as a justification for differential treatment in a distribution of a particular good, then such difference must bear some defensible relation to the good in question.

Many criticisms have been levied against the traditional principles of international law that authorized or legitimated assertions of European

---

46 Compare Kenneth L. Karst, *Belonging to America: Equal Citizenship and the Constitution* (New Haven: Yale University Press, 1989), at 9 (citizenship 'begins in the formal recognition of membership in the community, but ... goes unfulfilled when substantive inequalities effectively bar people from full membership'). See also C. Edwin Baker, 'Outcome Equality or Equality of Respect: The Substantive Content of Equal Protection,' 131 *U. Penn. L. Rev.* 933 (1983) (equality of respect comprehends both the right to participate equally in political processes and requires the state to guarantee certain basic resources and opportunities), Bernard Williams, 'The Idea of Equality,' in Williams, ed., *Problems of the Self* (Cambridge: Cambridge University Press, 1973), 230–49 (drawing a distinction between equality of opportunity and equality of result, and arguing that the former requires the latter).

47 See text accompanying notes 99–102, Chapter 1.

48 See C. Perelman, *The Idea of Justice and the Problem of Argument* (London: Routledge & Kegan Paul, 1963), at 16 (formal equality is 'a principle of action in accordance with which beings of one and the same essential category must be treated in the same way').

sovereignty in North America.[49] These criticisms share, either explicitly or implicitly, a commitment to the principle of formal equality. International legal principles that legitimated assertions of sovereignty by European nations over lands occupied by Aboriginal nations did not treat Aboriginal nations as formal equals. International law regarded North America as vacant because it viewed Aboriginal nations to be inferior to European nations.[50] As a result, European powers were able to convince themselves of the justice of their assertions of sovereignty over Aboriginal people and Aboriginal territories. European acts that simultaneously excluded Aboriginal people from the distribution of sovereignty effected by principles of international law and practice and included them under sovereign imperial authority violated their formal equality. Had the law treated Aboriginal nations as formal equals, prior sovereignty would have entitled them to assert continued sovereignty in the face of settlement. Given its inherent ethnocentricism, the proposition of Aboriginal inferiority cannot stand as a valid reason for excluding Aboriginal nations from the distribution of sovereignty on the continent. Both the original exclusion of Aboriginal nations from the community of nations entitled to assert sovereignty over North America and the continuing refusal to recognize the inherent sovereignty of Aboriginal people offend formal equality. Fully respecting the formal equality of Aboriginal nations means placing them in the legal position they would have been in had they been recognized as formally equal to European nations – as possessing sovereignty over their land and peoples.

Despite the fact that assertions of European sovereignty in North America were steeped in ethnocentric assumptions about indigenous difference, is the assertion of contemporary Canadian sovereignty over Aboriginal peoples and Aboriginal territory necessarily illegitimate? The

---

49 See, e.g., Michael Asch, *Home and Native Land: Aboriginal Rights and the Canadian Constitution* (Toronto: Methuen, 1984), at 41–54; Robert Williams Jr, 'The Algebra of Federal Indian Law: The Hard Trail of Decolonizing and Americanizing the White Man's Jurisprudence,' [1986] Wisc. L. Rev. 219; Joseph W. Singer, 'Sovereignty and Property,' 86 Northwestern L. Rev. 1 (1991); Slattery, 'Aboriginal Sovereignty and Imperial Claims'; Anaya, 'The Rights of Indigenous Peoples'; Michael Asch and Norman Zlotkin, 'Affirming Aboriginal Title: A New Basis for Comprehensive Claims Negotiations,' in Michael Asch, ed., *Aboriginal and Treaty Rights in Canada: Essays on Law, Equality, and Respect for Difference* (Vancouver: UBC Press, 1997); Sharon Venne, 'Understanding Treaty 6: An Indigenous Perspective,' in Asch, ed., *Aboriginal and Treaty Rights in Canada*, at 173; and Borrows, 'Sovereignty's Alchemy.'

50 See text accompanying notes 19–25 supra.

legitimacy of Canadian sovereignty depends on the reasons that can be offered in its defence. Although one justification will no doubt be the initial assertion of sovereignty, other reasons may emerge over time that independently support the assertion of sovereignty. Demonstrating the moral bankruptcy of the historical justification may not end the inquiry. For example, there may be pragmatic reasons to respect Canadian sovereign authority. Chief Justice Marshall of the U.S. Supreme Court alluded to this possibility in the context of his discussion of the doctrine of discovery when he said that 'if the principle has been asserted in the first instance, and afterward sustained; if a country has been acquired and held under it; if the property of the great mass of the community originates in it, it becomes the law of the land, and cannot be questioned.'[51]

A similar pragmatic stance marks the reluctance evident in international law to second-guess the legitimacy of state borders. According to James Anaya, there exists

> a normative trend within international legal process toward *stability through pragmatism* over instability, even at the expense of traditional principle. Sociologists estimate that today there are around 5,000 discrete ethnic or national groupings in the world, and each of these groups is defined – and defines itself – in significant part by reference to history. This figure dwarfs the number of the independent states in the world today, approximately 176. Further, of the numerous stateless cultural groupings that have been deprived of something like sovereignty at some point in their history, many have likewise deprived other groups of autonomy at some point in time. If international law were to fully embrace ethnic autonomy claims on the basis of the historical sovereignty approach, the number of potential challenges to existing state boundaries, along with the likely uncertainties of having to assess competing sovereignty claims over time, could bring the international system into a condition of legal flux and make international law an agent of instability rather than stability.[52]

---

51 *Johnson v. M'Intosh*, at 591.
52 S. James Anaya, 'The Capacity of International Law to Advance Ethnic or Nationality Rights Claims,' 75 Iowa L. Rev. 837 at 840 (1990) (emphasis in original). See also Robert A. Williams Jr, 'Sovereignty, Racism, Human Rights: Indian Self-Determination and the Postmodern World Legal System,' 2 Rev. Constitutional Studies 146, at 157 (1995) (when asserting sovereignty, 'indigenous peoples are driving head-on into the very historical foundations of the consolidation of the western settler-states').

But pragmatism need not preclude constitutional protection of interests associated with indigenous difference, including those associated with Aboriginal sovereign authority. Most assertions of Aboriginal sovereignty do not advocate 'the partial or total disruption of ... national unity and territorial integrity.'[53] Instead, they appear to promote 'a legally plural notion of law in which state law is only one of many levels, without privileged centrality.'[54] Interests that have arisen in light of the establishment of Canadian laws and institutions that receive protection through and by the exercise of Canadian sovereign authority are not automatically threatened by the constitutional protection of Aboriginal sovereign authority. Whether such interests ought to be threatened will depend on the scope of rights that protect Aboriginal sovereignty, which in turn ought to be defined by an open, and indeed pragmatic, assessment of all relevant interests at stake.

To the extent that the Canadian constitutional order protects interests associated with indigenous difference, however, Canadian sovereignty is rooted in more than pragmatism. Although Crown sovereignty was, in the words of Chief Justice Marshall, asserted 'in the first instance, and afterward sustained,' in a manner that violated the formal equality of Aboriginal nations, it has given birth to a complex set of interests grounded in the lived experiences of Canadian communities – Aboriginal and non-Aboriginal – that receive expression and protection through and by the exercise of Canadian sovereign authority. Neither the presence nor significance of this set of interests means that Canadian sovereignty in the Canadian constitutional order is absolute; indeed, the legitimacy of Canadian sovereignty rests on its capacity to co-exist with Aboriginal sovereignty. The constitutional task is to establish arrangements that enable Aboriginal along with federal and provincial governments to exercise sovereign authority in a manner that expresses and protects the lived experiences of the overlapping communities they serve. This task includes determining which level of government – federal, provincial, or Aboriginal – should prevail in the event that one level exercises sovereign authority in a manner that conflicts with or threatens the sovereign authority of another.

Concluding that the denial of sovereignty at the time of settlement

---

53 Williams, 'Sovereignty, Racism, Human Rights,' at 158.
54 Sally Engle Merry, 'Resistance and the Cultural Power of Law,' 29 Law & Soc. Rev. 11 at 23 (1995). See also Boaventura de Sousa, 'Law: A Map of Misreading: Toward a Postmodern Conception of Law,' 14 J. Law and Society 279 (1987).

violated formal equality thus does not necessarily lead to the inevitable creation of independent states. One can be both 'Aboriginal' and 'Canadian'; to constitutionally acknowledge these collective affiliations need not transform membership in one collectivity into an exclusive experience. Intersecting and overlapping collective affiliations can and obviously do exist among individuals and communities; the fact of one collective affiliation should not deny the possibility of another.[55] To hold otherwise would be to do violence to the experience of many Aboriginal people who hold multiple allegiances to many different categories of experience. Moreover, some forms of federalism already accept the notion that citizens have overlapping identities. Reflecting the multidimensionality of citizen allegiance by distributing internal sovereignty into multiple and discrete units of political governance is a common occurrence in contemporary political life.[56] Sovereignty, in the words of Hurst Hannum, has a 'malleable nature.'[57] Recognizing Aboriginal sovereign authority as part of the Canadian constitutional order would enable Aboriginal governments to reflect allegiances within a federal arrangement that also includes institutional structures that give voice to allegiances which cut across indigenous difference.

Circumstances might prevent such a federal union. If one takes the position that constitutional recognition of Aboriginal governmental authority is incompatible with continued citizenship in Canada, then the choice facing Aboriginal people is the stark one between integration and separation. Parties could 'find themselves in positions where absolute

55 Compare John Borrows, '"Landed" Citizenship: Narratives of Aboriginal Political Participation,' in Will Kymlicka and Wayne Norman, eds., *Citizenship in Diverse Societies* (Oxford: Oxford University Press, 2000), 326–42 at 333 ('[o]ur values *and* identities are constructed and reconstructed through local, national, and sometimes international experiences') (emphasis in original); Kimberlé Crenshaw, 'Demarginalizing the Intersection of Race and Sex: A Black Feminist Critique of Antidiscrimination Doctrine, Feminist Theory and Antiracist Politics,' [1989] U. Chi. L. Forum 139 (critiquing the tendency of anti-discrimination law 'to treat race and gender as mutually exclusive categories of experience and analysis,' thereby 'distort[ing] Black women's experiences' and creating obstacles to social and political change).

56 See Richard Simeon, 'Aboriginal Self-Government and Canadian Political Values,' in David Hawkes and Evelyn J. Peters, eds., *Issues in Entrenching Aboriginal Self-Government* (Kingston: Institute of Intergovernmental Relations, 1987), at 49, 53 ('the essential message of federalism is that it is a regime of multiple loyalties').

57 Hurst Hannum, *Autonomy, Sovereignty, and Self-Determination: The Accommodation of Conflicting Rights* (Philadelphia: University of Pennsylvania Press, 1996), at 13.

stances – either separatism or forced unity on the majority's terms – are the only remaining options.'[58] However, the proposition that Aboriginal people ought to have been accorded formal equality at the time of contact suggests that this position is misguided. If Aboriginal nations had been treated as formal equals in the distribution of sovereignty effected by European expansion, their sovereignty would have been respected. It was not and, as a result, allegiances of Aboriginal people became multidimensional. The multidimensionality of Aboriginal allegiances is in fact partly a function of the denial of formal equality and, as such, should not be used as a weapon to force Aboriginal people to choose between two unpalatable scenarios.

It is also possible that some Aboriginal nations might reject the option of participating in the Canadian constitutional order as a third order of government and instead assert a right of self-determination to obtain independence from the Canadian state. As discussed in Chapter 1, a flexible formulation of the principle of self-determination is emerging in international law, one that extends the right of self-determination to Aboriginal people in Canada and calibrates the content of this right to the capacity and willingness of Canada to protect interests associated with indigenous difference. Under this formulation, a failure by Canada to constitutionally protect those interests increases the likelihood that Aboriginal nations possess a right of external self-determination under international law. If, however, Canada protects interests associated with indigenous difference in a manner consistent with the right of internal self-determination, international law is unlikely to treat Aboriginal nations as independent of the Canadian constitutional order. In other words, international law is consistent with the proposition that, despite its suspect origins, Canadian sovereignty over Aboriginal peoples and territory is not per se illegitimate; its legitimacy rests on the extent to which the constitutional order protects interests associated with indigenous difference. If the distribution of constitutional power protects interests associated with indigenous difference and Canadian sovereignty is understood in non-absolute terms, an Aboriginal nation seeking independence cannot simply claim that European powers illegitimately asserted sovereign authority over its people and territory. It must instead explain why it is appropriate today to disrupt a just distribution of sovereignty to secure Aboriginal autonomy.

---

58 Ibid., at 11.

Sovereignty and Substantive Equality

Substantive equality is the second principle relevant to the justice of the distribution of sovereignty. A commitment to substantive equality mandates an examination of the concrete material conditions of individuals and groups in society and the ways in which state structuring can ameliorate adverse social and economic circumstances.[59] Unlike formal equality, a commitment to substantive equality requires more than an examination of legal form; it calls for scrutiny of actual effects of laws and practices on the social and economic condition of individuals and groups. Whether a particular distribution violates formal equality depends on whether it is based on a valid reason, related to the good in question, for distinguishing between two or more classes of people. Whether a particular distribution violates substantive equality depends on the extent to which it increases or decreases social or economic disparity.

The desire to narrow the gap between advantage and disadvantage is not all that drives an aspiration to substantive equality. While substantive equality most often involves proportional comparisons, it can also include 'numerical' considerations.[60] For example, despite the lack of explicit proportional dimensions, a substantive equality claim can include the demand that the state provide all individuals with a minimum set of social entitlements. As stated by Thomas Nagel, 'the degree of preference to the worst off depends not just on their position relative to the better off, but also on how badly off they are, absolutely.'[61] Substantive equality calls for preferential weight to be given to improving the material circumstances of socially and economically disadvantaged groups as opposed to measures that further empower advantaged groups in society.

A commitment to substantive equality need not entail an embrace of equality of result.[62] Equality of result is one of several normative standpoints that accompany concerns about substantive inequality. Other standpoints include commitments to equality of respect and equality of

---

59 See Owen Fiss, 'Groups and the Equal Protection Clause,' 5 Phil. & Pub. Affairs 107 (1975) (arguing that equal protection ought to be interpreted to accord with a 'group disadvantaging principle' to guard against measures that worsen the social and economic conditions of disadvantaged groups).

60 See text accompanying note 51, Chapter 1.

61 Thomas Nagel, *Equality and Partiality* (New York: Oxford University Press, 1991), at 12.

62 Compare C. Jencks et al., *Inequality: A Reassessment of the Effect of Family and Schooling in America* (New York: Harper & Row, 1973), at 3–14 (systems should be structured to foster equality of result).

resources. Proponents of equality of respect argue that everyone is entitled to the resources and opportunities necessary for full and equal participation in the community.[63] Advocates of equality of resources call for individuals to be compensated for costs they bear as a result of natural or social endowment, compensation that ensures the market operates fairly and that individuals bear the cost of choices freely made.[64] These standpoints do not address formal legal categories as much as they attempt to discern whether and to what extent substantive inequalities are justified or deserve relief.

How do substantive equality concerns relate to constitutional recognition of Aboriginal governmental authority? Aboriginal communities have been and continue to be oppressed by various social and economic forces which have had a profound effect on their social and economic status. A commitment to substantive equality suggests that the state should attempt to remedy the oppression that Aboriginal people experience in their daily lives; acknowledging that Aboriginal sovereignty is an interest worthy of constitutional protection would allow Aboriginal people to obtain greater control over their individual and collective identities. It would mandate removal of alien forms of economic, social, political, and legal organization that have been imposed on Aboriginal people. Such an initiative need not be informed by a desire to achieve equality of result such that Aboriginal people enjoy the same social and economic position as non-Aboriginal people. Instead, the objective can be cast in terms of equality of resources; as Kymlicka proposes, the goal would be to relieve Aboriginal people of many of the costs associated with reproducing their cultures in the face of alien institutional structures.[65]

---

63 See, e.g., Baker, 'Outcome Equality or Equality of Respect.'

64 See, e.g., Ronald Dworkin, 'What Is Equality? Part II Equality of Resources,' 10 Phil. & Pub. Aff. 283 at 293–304 (1981).

65 See text accompanying notes 87–90, chapter 2. Measures that represent a commitment to substantive equality of groups can include reforms that make it easier for a group to maintain its cultural difference by relieving it of some of the costs associated with its reproduction. Accordingly, Kymlicka's insight that Aboriginal people must expend a disproportionate amount of resources simply trying to maintain their cultural difference, although formulated in the context of trying to reconcile Aboriginal rights with equality of individuals, can be recast in substantive equality terms. Although not framed in terms of the demands of equality, Karst makes a similar point in *Belonging to America*, at 82 ('the larger society has an obligation – the obligation of citizens to each other – to see that the Indian peoples have the resources they need if [their] choices are to be real').

The justice of the distribution of sovereignty in North America should be assessed by reference to both substantive and formal demands of equality. Determining the substantive justice of the distribution of sovereignty requires asking whether and to what extent its distribution ameliorates adverse social and economic conditions of disadvantaged groups. This approach does not mean that all economically and socially disadvantaged groups are entitled to a measure of sovereignty. From a substantive perspective, whether a particular disadvantaged group is entitled to exercise sovereign authority depends on whether sovereignty provides the most appropriate means of ameliorating the continuing disadvantage in question. And deciding whether sovereignty would remedy disadvantage requires a context-specific judgment, based in part on an assessment of the nature and extent of the disadvantage.[66]

The motivation for reform distinguishes substantive equality from formal equality. Formal equality calls for the constitutional protection of Aboriginal sovereignty to rectify unjust distributions of sovereignty caused by European imperial expansion and maintained by the existing distribution of legislative authority in Canada. A distribution of sovereignty guided by substantive equality concerns looks simply to the present-day material circumstances of a particular group. In some cases, self-governing institutions may be an inappropriate way to improve the condition of the group in question. However, a commitment to substantive equality generates support for constitutional recognition of Aboriginal governmental authority in the hope that vesting Aboriginal people with greater control over their individual and collective identities will ameliorate their social and economic disadvantage.[67]

Equality and Other Cultural Groups

Focusing on the formal and substantive dimensions of equality helps to

---

66 For useful discussions of contextual judgments, see Martha Minow and Elizabeth Spelman, 'In Context,' 63 S. Cal. L. Rev. 1597 (1990), and Ruth Anna Putnam, 'Justice in Context,' 63 S. Cal. L. Rev. 1797 (1990).

67 Although couched in different terminology, for the view that what I refer to as arguments based on substantive equality are more desirable justifications for differential treatment of Indian people than arguments based on formal equality, see Bryan Schwartz, *First Principles, Second Thoughts: Aboriginal Peoples, Constitutional Reform and Canadian Statecraft* (Montreal: Institute for Research on Public Policy, 1986), at 48 ('Most Canadians would respond better to a claim for fiscal transfers to Aboriginal governments if they were characterized as a step towards the improvement of the lives and opportunities of Aboriginal peoples, rather than as the correction of a wrong done ... in the past').

explain why parallel systems of government are particularly suited to Aboriginal peoples as opposed to other groups located in Canada. Immigrant populations and other cultural groups will probably have greater difficulty relying on principles of formal equality to justify differential treatment in distributions of political rights and responsibilities. Formal equality requires constitutional recognition of Aboriginal sovereignty because Aboriginal nations were not treated as equal to European nations when sovereignty was distributed at the time of contact. Immigrant populations cannot make a similar claim. Although immigrant populations have been denied formal equality through countless acts of exclusion, public and private, from social, economic, and political life, such denials have not taken the form of European assertions of sovereignty over land and peoples.

More specifically, while historical wrongs inflicted on other racial and cultural groups in Canada can be viewed as violations of formal equality, the distribution of sovereignty generated by the doctrine of discovery in North America did not violate the formal equality of non-Aboriginal people. Such people were either colonists, immigrants, or slaves. Colonists retained allegiance to the sovereign authority of their parent state until revolution, war, or treaty transferred sovereignty to a new political entity.[68] Immigrants tended to immigrate from nations recognized as sovereign; if such nations were not recognized as sovereign, recognizing the sovereignty of immigrants would not rectify any injustice associated with this original non-recognition. The taking of slaves may have constituted an infringement of the formal equality of the nation from which they were taken and, more obviously, denied the formal equality and contributed to the substantive inequality of those coerced into slavery. Nevertheless, it is not clear that distributing sovereignty to descendants of enslaved people would rectify the denial of formal equality that slavery represented, since this denial occurred through the practice of slavery and not through the distribution of sovereignty in North America. In contrast, constitutional recognition of Aboriginal sovereignty rectifies the denial of formal equality of Aboriginal nations caused by the refusal to recognize Aboriginal nations as sovereign entities at the time

---

68 Whether the law of conquest produces just distributions of sovereignty is a question beyond the scope of this inquiry. It should be noted, however, that after the conquest of the French, Quebec's laws and institutions, indeed self-governing authority, continued in force until they were expressly overruled by the British Parliament. In other words, recognition of French prior sovereignty informed British, and continues to inform Canadian, constitutional treatment of Quebec.

of contact and the continuing refusal to acknowledge the constitutional significance of prior Aboriginal sovereignty.

Depending on their social and economic circumstances, other racial and cultural groups may be able to make substantive equality claims, but constitutional recognition of parallel systems of government may not most appropriately remedy the oppression these groups experience. It is not immediately apparent why or how the social and economic conditions facing African–North Americans, for example, would be improved by implementing unique governmental institutions. Nor is it clear that those conditions exist because African–North Americans do not enjoy parallel governmental institutions. Many would argue instead that African–North American adversity stems from historic, racist exclusion from the mainstream of North American economic, social, educational, and political life.[69]

This is not to suggest that non-Aboriginal people could not make persuasive cases for some measure of sovereignty by reference to principles of formal and substantive equality. African-Americans, for example, have often advanced nationalist claims. As early as 1852, African-Americans were referred to as a 'nation within a nation' in the United States.[70] The 1920s saw the articulation of a Back to Africa Movement, which called for political self-determination of Africans and African-Ameri-

---

69 But for the view that the substantive inequality of African-Americans will only be ameliorated by 'organized and deliberate self-segregation' and the development of a cooperative black economy, see W.E.B. Du Bois, 'A Negro Nation within the Nation,' in *W.E.B. Du Bois Speaks: Speeches and Addresses: 1923–1963*, ed. P.S. Foner (New York: Pathfinder, 1970), 77 at 85. See also Harold Cruse, *Rebellion or Revolution?* (New York: William Morrow, 1968), at 72 ('the tendency to seek assimilation among whites has militated against the cultivation of a strong sense of racial identification within the Negro community'). For an earlier race-conscious, but market-oriented, perspective, see Booker T. Washington, *The Negro in Business* (Boston: Jenkins & Company, 1907). For the view that the African-American will not 'be totally liberated from the crushing weight of poor education, squalid housing and economic strangulation until he is integrated, with power, into every level of American life,' see Martin Luther King, *Where Do We Go from Here: Chaos or Community?* (Boston: Beacon Press, 1968), at 61–2. See also James Baldwin, *The Fire Next Time* (New York: Dell, 1963). For an exhaustive exploration of these and related themes, see Harold Cruse, *Plural but Equal: A Critical Study of Blacks and Minorities and America's Plural Society* (New York: William Morrow, 1987).

70 Martin R. Delany, *The Condition, Elevation, Emigration and Destiny of the Colored People of the United States* (Salem: Ayer Company, 1988), at 203. See, generally, Gary Peller, 'Race Consciousness (Frontiers of Legal Thought),' [1990] Duke L.J. 758.

cans.[71] More recently, Malcolm X, first with the Nation of Islam and later in his overtures to grassroots organizations, powerfully personified African-American nationalism with all of its ambiguities and rhetorical force.[72] There have been calls for the establishment of an independent sovereign state, the 'Republic of New Africa,' in Mississippi, Louisiana, Alabama, Georgia, and South Carolina.[73] It is beyond the scope of this book to assess the justice of these types of claims except to say that full independence and complete separation presumably always remain an option for any group within a state. However, claims for some degree of sovereignty short of independence, in which a particular group desires to continue to share some benefits from continued association with a larger surrounding or adjacent entity, ought to be tested against the principles of distribution that sovereignty, as a good, contemplates. Under principles of formal and substantive equality, Aboriginal people have clearer and more immediate claims for constitutional protection of interests associated with sovereignty than do other groups in Canada. In the following chapter, I address the final aspect of indigenous difference that merits constitutional attention: namely, the fact that Aboriginal people participated and continue to participate in a treaty process with the Crown.

71 See Marcus Garvey, *Philosophy and Opinions of Marcus Garvey* (New York: Atheneum, 1992). See, generally, E. David Cronon, *Black Moses: The Story of Marcus Garvey and the Universal Negro Improvement Association* (Madison: University of Wisconsin Press, 1955).
72 See Malcolm X, *Malcolm X Speaks: Selected Speeches and Statements* (New York: Merit, 1965).
73 See Robert H. Brisbane, *Black Activism: Racial Revolution in the United States, 1954–1970* (Valley Forge: Judson Press, 1974), at 183–5.

Chapter Five

The Treaty Process

*As an abstraction, sovereignty flew lightly from one shore to another. In prac-
tice, however, it had to be confined within the limits of the kings' effective, deliv-
erable power, which were real and strong ... Though distant kings never forgot
for a minute their claims to sovereignty, colonists on the spot filed such claims
away for use at appropriate times and places. Meanwhile the colonists made
treaties with Indian tribes in the same manner that their kings treated with
each other.*

Francis Jennings, *The Ambiguous Iroquois Empire*[1]

When Sir Francis Bond Head, the lieutenant-governor of Upper Canada, arrived at the village of Manitowaning on Manitoulin Island in
1836, he was met by several thousand people who had assembled for an
annual ceremony of gift-giving with the British. This practice had begun
at a meeting between representatives of the British Crown and more
than twenty Aboriginal nations at Niagara Falls in 1764, shortly after the
British army had taken control of French garrisons on the Great Lakes.
At that meeting, the parties affirmed an alliance of peace initially
formed in 1677 and known as the Covenant Chain.[2] But the American

---

1 Francis Jennings, *The Ambiguous Iroquois Empire: The Covenant Chain Confederation of
   Indian Tribes with English Colonies from Its Beginnings to the Lancaster Treaty of 1744* (New
   York: W.W. Norton), at 401–2.
2 For an extended study of the Covenant Chain, see Jennings, *The Ambiguous Iroquois
   Empire*; for a description and analysis of the Treaty of Niagara, see John Borrows,
   'Wampum at Niagara: The Royal Proclamation, Canadian Legal History and Self-
   Government,' in Michael Asch, ed., *Aboriginal and Treaty Rights in Canada: Essays on
   Law, Equality and Respect for Difference* (Vancouver: UBC Press, 1997), 155.

Revolution subsequently caused a massive influx of Loyalists into Upper Canada and cast doubt on the future of the Covenant Chain – at least as it applied to Aboriginal nations in the United States. Bond Head spoke to those assembled at Manitowaning, noting that '[s]eventy snow seasons' had passed since meeting 'at the crooked place.' Referring to 'various circumstances' that had occurred since that time, including 'an unavoidable increase in the white population,' Bond Head called on those present to make 'new arrangements' with the Crown.[3]

What Bond Head had in mind, and what he subsequently negotiated with the Ojibway and Ottawa on Manitoulin Island, was a treaty that established Manitoulin Island and its surrounding islands as a place of refuge for Aboriginal people threatened by increased non-Aboriginal settlement. By the treaty's terms, the Crown agreed to 'withdraw' its disputed claims to Manitoulin Island and its surrounding islands and to recognize the Aboriginal title of the Ottawa and Ojibway nations to these islands as well as their Aboriginal right to fish in the surrounding waters.[4] In return, the Ottawa and Ojibway agreed to 'relinquish' or modify their rights of exclusive use and enjoyment in favour of non-exclusive rights in order to enable other Aboriginal people to relocate to the region in the future.[5]

The Manitoulin Island 1836 Treaty is but one of approximately five hundred treaties that exist between Aboriginal nations and the Canadian state.[6] The year 1850 is often used to distinguish between two types of treaties.[7] The text of most treaties signed before 1850 involved a one-

---

3 Canada, *Indian Treaties and Surrenders* (Saskatoon: Fifth House Publishers, 1992), at 1:112.

4 The written text of Treaty 45 is silent with respect to fisheries, but the historical significance of the fisheries to the Ottawa and Objibway is well documented: see, for example, Victor P. Lytwyn, 'Ojibwa and Ottawa Fisheries Around Manitoulin Island: Historical and Geographical Perspectives on Aboriginal and Treaty Fishing Rights,' 6 Native Studies Review 1 (1990).

5 Canada, *Indian Treaties and Surrenders*, at 1:112, 113. In order to facilitate non-Aboriginal settlement, Bond Head also negotiated another treaty in the same year, known as Treaty No. 45½, which resulted in the cession of land in the Lower Saugeen Peninsula, and a relocation of Saugeen Ojibway people to the Bruce Peninsula: Canada, *Indian Treaties and Surrenders*, at 1:113.

6 Donald J. Purich, *Our Land: Native Rights in Canada* (Toronto: James Lorimer, 1986), at 95.

7 Compare James [sákéj] Youngblood Henderson, 'Empowering Treaty Federalism,' 58 Sask. L. Rev. 241 (1994) (drawing distinction between 'Georgian' and 'Victorian' treaties).

time payment by the Crown for the surrender of relatively small tracts of land. The text of the 1781 Treaty between the Crown and the Chippewa and Mississauga nations, for example, provides for the surrender of Aboriginal territory to the Crown in return for three hundred suits of clothing. Occasionally the text of a pre-1850 treaty provides for annual payments, such as in another treaty negotiated between the Chippewa nation and the Crown in 1827, according to which the Chippewas purportedly agreed to surrender over two million acres of land in return for a paltry eighteen thousand acres of reserve land and an annual payment of eleven hundred pounds.[8] Some pre-1850 treaties did not refer to land surrenders but were peace and friendship treaties. Some Aboriginal people agreed to lay down their arms and support the British Crown in its war against the French typically in exchange for reciprocal obligations attaching to the Crown. For example, the text of the Treaty of 1752 guarantees the Mi'kmaq nation in Nova Scotia the right to hunt and fish in return for its agreement to 'submit to the King' and 'forbear all acts of hostility towards English subjects.'[9] Similarly, in a treaty signed in 1760 by General Murray and the Huron nation, the Huron nation agreed to make peace with British forces in return for a guarantee of 'the free exercise of their Religion, their Customs, and their Liberty of trading with the English.'[10]

Treaties negotiated during and after 1850 covered much more land and provided for annual payments. The written text of the Robinson-Huron Treaty, for instance, one of two treaties negotiated in 1850 by William Benjamin Robinson, provincial commissioner of Upper Canada,[11] purports to accomplish the surrender of all land held by Aboriginal parties to the agreement north of Lake Huron to the border between Canada and what was then known as Rupert's Land. In exchange, the Aboriginal parties were guaranteed a lump sum payment

---

8 Canada, *Indian Treaties and Surrenders from 1680 to 1902*, at 1:71.

9 The text of this treaty is reproduced in *Simon v. The Queen*, [1985] 2 S.C.R. 387; see also text accompanying notes 45–53, infra.

10 The text of this treaty is reproduced in *R. v. Sioui*, [1990] 1 S.C.R. 1025; see also text accompanying notes 55–9, infra.

11 The other was known as the Robinson-Superior Treaty, which purports to extinguish the rights of Aboriginal signatories to all land north and east of Lake Superior to the boundary between Canada and Rupert's Land, and contained terms similar to those of the Robinson-Huron Treaty. Both are found in Canada, *Indian Treaties and Surrenders*, at 1:147, 149.

of two thousand pounds, an annuity of five hundred pounds, three areas of reserve lands, and the right to hunt and fish on unoccupied lands.[12] Eleven numbered treaties negotiated between 1871 and 1921 cover land from the Quebec and Ontario border to the northwest edge of Canada. The text of Treaty 6, for example, purports to accomplish the surrender of approximately 120,000 square miles of territory in what is now central Saskatchewan and Alberta in return for one square mile of reserve land per family of five; continued hunting and fishing rights; a one-time payment of twelve dollars for each Indian beneficiary; farm stock and equipment, seed, a flag, and a medal, and a horse, harness, and wagon for each Indian chief; annual payments of $1,500 as well as an additional thousand dollars a year for three years for provisions; a promise to maintain a school on reserve land; and an undertaking to provide for a medicine chest for the benefit of Indians and assistance in the case of pestilence or famine.[13]

What legal consequences flow from the fact that Aboriginal people entered into treaties with the Crown? This question turns in part on the legal form that a treaty assumes in Canadian law. Is a treaty legally enforceable? If so, is it a form of contract? Or is it a form of constitutional accord? Determining the legal effect of a treaty also depends on its substantive terms, which raises issues relating to the interpretation of treaty guarantees as well as the relationship between the written text and the circumstances surrounding the treaty's negotiation, including oral promises and the expectations of the parties. Courts initially regarded treaties as unenforceable in a court of law. This approach gradually gave way to a conception of a treaty as akin to a contract between the Crown and a group of citizens. As a result of the enactment of the Constitution Act, 1982, which recognizes and affirms 'existing ... treaty rights,' the judiciary has come to regard treaty rights as a form of constitutional rights. And while courts initially interpreted substantive treaty rights by reference to non-Aboriginal legal norms and values, they have recently begun to develop a new interpretive framework that seeks to include

---

12 Ibid., 149.
13 The complete texts of the numbered treaties are available in Alexander Morris, *The Treaties of Canada with the Indians of Manitoba and the North-West Territories* (1880; reprint ed., Toronto: Coles Publishing, 1971). For an analysis of events leading up to the negotiation of Treaties Six and Seven, see John Leonard Taylor, 'Two Views on the Meaning of Treaties Six and Seven,' in Richard Price, ed., *The Spirit of the Alberta Indian Treaties* (Edmonton: Pica Press, 1987), 9–45.

Aboriginal perspectives on the meaning of the substance of treaty rights.

Beneath the surface of jurisprudence addressing the form and substance of treaty rights are deeper questions about the normative significance of the treaty process. Aboriginal people are alone among Canadian citizens in having entered into treaties with the Crown; participation in the treaty process thus constitutes one aspect of indigenous difference, an aspect that has constitutional significance. Treaties are constitutional accords that distribute constitutional authority among the parties. The status of treaties as constitutional accords and the new interpretive framework provided by the judiciary have dramatic implications for the legal effect of clauses that purport to extinguish Aboriginal title and self-government in exchange for benefits to be provided by the Crown.

Form and Substance in Treaty Jurisprudence

Treaties between Aboriginal and European nations negotiated early in the history of European expansion formalized efforts to achieve peaceful co-existence between Aboriginal nations and newcomers to the continent. A 1665 peace treaty between the French Crown and four Aboriginal nations belonging to the Iroquois Confederacy, for example, confirmed a cessation of conflict and a state of peace between the parties. The text of the treaty indirectly acknowledged the Aboriginal parties' continuing title to their territories and certain territorial rights of the French Crown in the settlements of Montreal, Trois-Rivières, and Quebec City.[14] Although the 1665 treaty and others like it signalled a nation-to-nation relationship of mutual respect, the parties did not initially regard them as creating legal rights enforceable in a court of law. Instead, the treaty served as evidence of an ongoing relationship; rights and obligations flowed not from the document itself but from the rela-

---

14 *Treaty of Peace between the Iroquois and Governor de Tracy*, New York Papers 111 A28. The text of the treaty can be found in Clive Parry, ed., *The Consolidated Treaty Series* (Dobbs Ferry: Oceana, 1969–1986), at 9:363; and E.B. O'Callaghan, ed., *Documents Relative to the Colonial History of the State of New York* (Albany: Weed, Parsons, 1856–61), at 3:21. For more discussion of the treaty, see Royal Commission on Aboriginal Peoples, *Treaty Making in the Spirit of Co-Existence: An Alternative to Extinguishment* (Ottawa: Minister of Supply and Services Canada, 1995), at 18–20.

tionship formalized by the treaty.[15] The early treaty process was but a part of a larger set of intersocietal encounters, some friendly, others hostile, through which Aboriginal and non-Aboriginal participants generated norms of conduct and recognition that structured their ongoing relationships. According to Jeremy Webber, 'the distinctive norms of each society furnished the point of departure, determining the spirit of interaction, colouring the first interpretations of the other's customs, and shaping the beginnings of a common normative language.'[16] This early process of generating norms of conduct and recognition operated against the backdrop of a colonial legal imagination that had yet to experience a radical separation of law and politics, in which certain issues are regarded as legal and others as political.

With the gradual emergence of law as a relatively autonomous sphere of social life, the judiciary began to address the legal consequences of the treaty process. It initially regarded treaties as political agreements unenforceable in a court of law. International law provides that an agreement between two 'independent powers' constitutes a treaty binding on the parties to the agreement.[17] But because courts regarded Aboriginal nations as uncivilized and thus not independent, they refused to view Crown promises in treaties with Aboriginal people as legally enforceable obligations under international or domestic law.

---

15 Compare William Blackstone, *Commentaries on the Laws of England*, ed. E. Christian (London: A. Strathan, 1809), at 1:428 (vision of a contract as dependent on the existence of a social relation and pre-existing rights and obligations). See also Patrick Atiyah, *The Rise and Fall of Freedom of Contract* (Oxford: Clarendon Press, 1979), at 143 (eighteenth-century legal consciousness invoked the notion of promise 'to support an independently existing duty'), and Owen Kahn-Freund, 'Blackstone's Neglected Child: The Contract of Employment,' 93 L.Q.R. 508 at 512 (1977) ('the contract is only an *accidentale*, not an *essentiale* of the relation').

16 Jeremy Webber, 'Relations of Force and Relations of Justice: The Emergence of Normative Community between Colonists and Aboriginal Peoples,' 33 Osgoode Hall L.J. 623 at 627 (1995). See also Robert A. Williams Jr, *Linking Arms Together: American Indian Treaty Visions of Law & Peace, 1600–1800* (New York: Oxford University Press, 1997), at 28 (early Aboriginal and non-Aboriginal encounters produced a normative world 'held together by the jurisgenerative force of the common interpretive commitments to a law created and shared by the different peoples of Encounter era North America').

17 See, e.g., Ian Brownlie, *Principles of Public International Law*, 5th ed. (Oxford: Clarendon Press, at 58–70). It should be noted that, even if treaties between the Crown and First Nations were accorded 'international treaty' status, this fact alone would not render them enforceable in domestic courts; implementing legislation would be required: see *A.G. Canada v. A.G. Ontario (Labour Conventions)*, [1937] A.C. 326 (P.C.).

This view was gradually replaced by an approach that regarded a treaty as a form of contract. Aboriginal people were imagined as possessing legal personality similar to that possessed by non-Aboriginal people in Canada and were therefore capable of entering into domestically binding agreements with the Crown. Because treaties assumed the legal form of contract, however, their terms were subject to the exercise of unilateral legislative authority. Prior to 1982, this had the effect of permitting Parliament to unilaterally regulate or extinguish existing treaty rights.

More recently, in its interpretation of the substance of treaty guarantees, the judiciary has shifted in the opposite direction, namely, towards legal recognition of indigenous difference. When courts viewed treaties as contractual agreements, they initially interpreted their substance in a manner that was blind to Aboriginal expectations of the treaty process. Treaty rights were interpreted solely by reference to non-Aboriginal legal norms and values; in the words of Dale Turner, treaties were 'textualized in the language of the dominant European culture.'[18] This mode of interpretation resulted in expansive definitions of the meaning of land surrenders and narrow definitions of treaty benefits flowing to Aboriginal people. Recent jurisprudence is more accommodating of Aboriginal understandings of the treaty process in general and of the substance of treaties in particular. This shift has resulted in more expansive definitions of treaty rights, although, as will be seen, the meaning of land surrenders effected by treaties continues to be steeped in non-Aboriginal understandings of title and transfer.

The 1929 case of *R. v. Syliboy*[19] illustrates the tendency of early jurisprudence to formally view treaties as little more than political arrangements between Aboriginal people and the Crown. Justice Patterson's judgment in *Syliboy* also illustrates the early tendency to interpret the substance of treaty rights by reference to non-Aboriginal legal norms and values. In *Syliboy*, the grand chief of the Mi'kmaq nation was convicted of illegal hunting on Cape Breton Island, contrary to Nova Scotia's Lands and Forests Act, 1926. Chief Syliboy admitted to the act but asserted a right to hunt and trap under a treaty entered into in 1752 by the governor of the Province of Nova Scotia and various representatives of the Mi'kmaq nation. Article 4 of the treaty provided that 'the

---

18 Dale Turner, 'From Valladolid to Ottawa: The Illusion of Listening to Aboriginal People,' in Jill Oakes et al., eds., *Sacred Lands: Aboriginal World Views, Claims, and Conflicts* (Edmonton: Canadian Circumpolar Institute, 1998), 53–68 at 64.

19 [1929] 1 D.L.R. 307 (N.S. Co. Ct.).

said Tribe of Indians shall not be hindered from but have free liberty to hunt and fish as usual.'[20]

In dismissing the appeal, Patterson J. held that the Mi'kmaq nation was an 'uncivilized people' and thus not an 'independent power' possessing the status to enter into a treaty with another nation.[21] He stated that '[a] civilized nation first discovering a country of uncivilized people or savages held such country as its own until such time as by treaty it was transferred to some other civilized nation.'[22] Accordingly, '[t]he savages' rights of sovereignty were never recognized.'[23] Patterson J. found support for his conclusion that the Mi'kmaq did not claim to be an independent power in 'the very fact' that they sought from the governor the right to hunt in Nova Scotia.[24] In his words, 'if they were [an independent power], why go to another nation asking this privilege or right and giving promise of good behaviour that they might obtain it?'[25] He added that 'the Treaty of 1752 is not a treaty at all; ... it is at best a mere agreement made by the Governor and a handful of Indians.'[26] Justice Patterson held in the alternative that even if the Treaty of 1752 were in fact a treaty, it did not extend to Cape Breton Island. First, Cape Breton Island was not part of the Province of Nova Scotia when the treaty was negotiated and, second, the signatories did not represent the precise community of Mi'kmaq people to which Chief Syliboy belonged. He also held the view that, if the Treaty of 1752 were a treaty, it had expired due to the outbreak of hostilities. In any case, the treaty contemplated provincial regulation of hunting. He concluded by characterizing the treaties as a form of political agreement unenforceable in a court of law and the benefits that flowed to the Mi'kmaq not in terms of legal right but as an expression of the good will of the state.

Syliboy is an example of some of the formal and substantive difficulties Aboriginal people have historically faced in trying to enforce treaty rights in Canadian courts. Patterson J. regarded differences between the

---

20 1 Nova Scotia Archives, p. 683, as quoted in Patterson J. in *R. v. Syliboy*, [1929] 1 D.L.R. 307 (N.S. Co. Ct.).

21 *R. v. Syliboy*, at 313.

22 Ibid.

23 Ibid.

24 Ibid.

25 Ibid.

26 Ibid. Patterson J. was also of the view that the governor did not have treaty-making authority as there was no evidence he was specially deputed by the constituted authorities of Great Britain for this purpose.

Mi'kmaq nation and European nations in terms of Aboriginal inferiority, with that inferiority serving as the reason why the 1752 treaty was formally unenforceable in a court of law. *Syliboy* also illustrates the early judicial tendency to rely on non-Aboriginal norms and values when interpreting the substance of treaties. Rejecting the possibility that the Treaty of 1752 extended to Cape Breton Island, Patterson J. determined the scope of the treaty by reference to legal-geographic boundaries that had little or no meaning to the Mi'kmaq people. His resistance to the formal proposition that the treaty agreement created binding legal obligations was rooted in a view of Aboriginal people as different from and inferior to non-Aboriginal people – and his holding that the substance of the agreement did not extend in any event to Cape Breton Island was premised on the legitimacy of non-Aboriginal geographical understandings.

The Contractualist Vision

As law gradually emerged as a relatively autonomous sphere of social life, the idea that a treaty was legally unenforceable in a court of law gave way to the view that a treaty is a form of contract with the Crown. As contracts, treaties distribute binding rights and obligations among the parties. But the type of contract that a treaty was thought to embody was akin to an ordinary legal contract that a private citizen might enter into with the Crown. Thus treaty rights, like ordinary contractual rights, are enforceable only in the event of Crown inaction, in circumstances in which the Crown has failed to live up to its promises set out in the treaty. Such rights do not check the exercise of legislative authority because the principle of legislative supremacy prevents the Crown from contractually binding itself from enacting certain types of legislation.[27]

In *Pawis v. The Queen*,[28] for example, four members of the Ojibway nation were charged with violating federal fishery regulations. All four had been fishing in a traditional manner for food for themselves and other band members in places in which they had fished regularly in the past. In their defence, they appealed to a treaty right to hunt and fish pursuant to the Robinson-Huron Treaty of 1850. The treaty provided that in consideration of the surrender of lands covered by the treaty, the Ojibway possessed 'the full and free privilege to hunt over the territory

---

27 See, for example, *Re Canada Assistance Plan*, [1991] 2 S.C.R. 525 (Parliament can enact legislation despite contractual arrangements to the contrary).
28 (1979), 102 D.L.R. (3d) 602 (F.C.T.D.).

now ceded by them, and to fish in the waters thereof, as they have theretofore been in the habit of doing.'[29] The accuseds argued that the Crown had breached its treaty obligations and was in breach of trust by the enactment of fishery regulations.

Dismissing these arguments, Marceau J. first held that the Robinson-Huron Treaty was 'tantamount to a contract.'[30] Viewing a treaty as a form of legal contract enables its enforcement in a court of law but also triggers certain issues specific to actions in contract. For example, parties are subject to limitation periods; as a result, systematic past breaches of treaty rights by the Crown cannot be invoked in aid of an action in breach of contract. Marceau J. held that any breach of contract occurred not at the date of the apprehension of the four accuseds but rather when federal authorities first enacted the fisheries regulations in question. As a result, '[t]he breach of contract they allege, and the damage they say was thereby caused to the Ojibways, occurred long before they were born.'[31] The limitation period for maintaining an action in breach of contract long expired prior to their apprehension.

Viewing a treaty as a form of contract also enables courts to resort to the technique of implication. In *Pawis*, Marceau J. held that the treaty contained an implied term, 'in like manner that clauses that are customary or necessary are supplied in ordinary contracts between individuals,' that the right to hunt and fish is subject to state regulation.[32] He assumed that the Crown could not contractually bind itself not to enact legislation regulating methods of fishing. Analogizing to property ownership, he concluded that '[t]he right acquired by the Indians in those treaties was ... necessarily subject in its exercise to restriction through acts of the legislature, just as the person who acquires from the Crown a grant of land is subject in its enjoyment to such legislative restrictions as may later be passed as to the use which may be made of it.'[33] The enactment of fishery regulations in accordance with a valid exercise of legislative authority could not constitute breach of contract: '[h]ow can a legal act be at the same time an act to be sanctioned as an illegal breach of contract?'[34]

While *Pawis* signalled a shift in judicial approach to the form of trea-

---

29 Ibid., at 605.
30 Ibid., at 607.
31 Ibid., at 613.
32 Ibid., at 610.
33 Ibid.
34 Ibid.

ties, it continued the judicial tendency to interpret the substance of treaty rights by reference to non-Aboriginal norms and values. Marceau J. held that the substance of the treaty did not contain a promise that the Crown would not regulate the right to fish. Specifically, he held that the reference to 'full and free privilege to fish' did not exclude state regulation. He reached this conclusion by interpreting the treaty right to hunt and fish by reference to a non-Aboriginal, contractualist understanding of the meaning of a 'full and free privilege to fish.' Justice Marceau stated that a 'free privilege to fish ... simply means that no consideration is to be exacted from those entitled to hunt and fish in exercise of the right.'[35] The reference to 'full ... privilege to fish' was interpreted through the prism of property ownership, and seen as 'connot[ing] a plenary quality, a completeness of the right ... strictly as regards the right of the owner or possessor of the land.'[36] Thus, in Marceau J.'s view, the 'full and free privilege to hunt and fish' does not refer to the methods used but to the purpose for which the activity was carried on; '[t]he words have nothing to do with the manner of fishing.'[37] He concluded that 'the wording does not import any intention that there be unrestricted rights in perpetuity to fish regardless of the general laws regulating the means of hunting and fishing.'[38]

The judicial tendency to interpret the substance of treaty guarantees narrowly is also exemplified by *Johnston v. The Queen*.[39] In *Johnston*, the appellant appealed a conviction of a failure to pay hospital tax as was required by Saskatchewan legislation. The Saskatchewan Hospitalization Act created a general obligation to pay hospital tax but exempted both Indians living on reserves and Indians living off reserves for less than twelve months. Those entitled to obtain general hospital services from the federal government were also exempted from paying the tax. Johnston, who had been living off his reserve for more than twelve months, argued that Treaty 6 entitled him to general hospital services from the federal government. The text of Treaty 6 includes the following term:

That a medicine chest shall be kept at the house of each Indian Agent for the use and benefit of the Indians at the direction of such agent.

---

35 Ibid., at 609.
36 Ibid.
37 Ibid.
38 Ibid., at 610.
39 (1966), 56 D.L.R. (2d) 749 (Sask. C.A.).

That in the event hereafter of the Indians comprised within the treaty being overtaken by any pestilence, or by a general famine, the Queen, on being satisfied and certified thereof by her Indian Agent or Agents, will grant to the Indians assistance of such character and to such extent as her Chief Superintendent of Indian Affairs shall deem necessary and sufficient to relieve the Indians from the calamity that shall have befallen them.[40]

The magistrate held that the provision for a medicine chest required that the federal government provide 'all medical services, including medicines, drugs, medical supplies and hospital care free of charge.'[41] On appeal, Chief Justice Culliton was faced with a choice between a broad interpretation and a narrow interpretation of the clause, with few interpretive aids to assist him. Upholding Johnston's conviction, he opted for the latter. Referring to the meaning 'conveyed by the words themselves in the context in which they are used,' he interpreted the clause as an undertaking by the Crown to keep at the house of the Indian agent a medicine chest for the use and benefit of the Indians at the direction of the agent. He added that he could 'find nothing historically, or in any dictionary definition, or in any legal pronouncement, that would justify the conclusion that the Indians, in seeking and accepting the Crown's obligation to provide a "medicine chest" had in contemplation provision of all medical services, including hospital care.'[42]

In refusing to read the medicine chest provision as requiring the Crown to provide free medical care, Chief Justice Culliton adopted an interpretive stance towards the substance of a treaty rights that relied on the meaning of the written text at the time it was negotiated. This approach implicates historical understandings, that is, the intent of those involved in treaty negotiations, but the chief justice went no further than the official record of Alexander Morris, who negotiated Treaty 6 on behalf of the Crown.[43] This is not to suggest that determining the understanding of the Aboriginal negotiators would have been an easy task,[44] but rather to note the adoption of a process that deter-

---

40 Morris, *The Treaties of Canada.*

41 *Johnson v. The Queen*, at 751.

42 Ibid., at 753. For an opposite conclusion, see *Dreaver v. The King*, an unreported judgment of the Exchequer Court of Canada, referred to in *Johnston v. the Queen*, at 753.

43 Morris, *Treaties of Canada.*

44 For the view that '[t]he intent was that Indians should receive from the Federal Government whatever medical care could be made available,' see Indian Chiefs of Canada, 'Citizens Plus,' in *The Only Good Indian* (Don Mills: New Press, 1983), at 35.

mines the meaning of treaty rights solely by reference to non-Aboriginal understandings of treaty terms.

In summary, treaty jurisprudence first regarded Aboriginal people as different from and inferior to non-Aboriginal people. Aboriginal people thus lacked the authority to enter into binding reciprocal arrangements with the Crown. Treaties were imagined as not having the force of law, and amounted to little more than non-binding political arrangements entered into by the Crown with Aboriginal people. The judiciary subsequently came to accept that Aboriginal people possessed the legal status to enter into enforceable agreements. Aboriginal people became imagined as similar to other subjects of the realm, entitled to enter into contractual arrangements with the Crown and to sue for non-compliance. But, as legal contracts, the rights treaties conferred were subject to legislative regulation and extinguishment. Judicial interpretation of the substance of treaty guarantees was initially characterized by a refusal to treat Aboriginal expectations differently from non-Aboriginal expectations. Abstract treaty guarantees were infused with concrete meaning by a reliance on non-Aboriginal norms and values. As the following section illustrates, however, treaty jurisprudence has recently come to embrace indigenous difference, acknowledging that markedly different Aboriginal expectations of the substantive meaning of treaty entitlements ought to inform the interpretive enterprise.

A New Interpretive Framework

The judiciary has recently begun to incorporate Aboriginal understandings of the nature and effect of the treaty process when it interprets the substance of vague treaty guarantees. In *Simon v. The Queen*,[45] for example, the appellant was convicted of an offence under Nova Scotia's Lands and Forests Act. The issue before the Supreme Court of Canada was whether the Treaty of 1752, the same treaty at issue in *Syliboy*, provided for a right to hunt that precluded the application of the provincial law. Chief Justice Dickson for the court stated that Patterson J.'s judgment in *Syliboy* 'reflects the biases and prejudices of another era in our history.'[46] He went on to hold that the Treaty of 1752 was validly created by competent parties, that it contained a right to hunt which applied to

---

45 (1985), 24 D.L.R. (4th) 390 (S.C.C.).
46 Ibid., at 400.

the appellant's activities in question, and that it had not been terminated by hostilities between the Mi'kmaq and the British in 1753 or by extinguishment through occupancy by non-Aboriginal people under Crown grant or lease. He held further that the appellant was covered by the treaty and that, as a result of section 88 of the Indian Act, the hunting rights contained in the treaty exempted the appellant from prosecution under the Nova Scotia legislation.

In his judgment, Chief Justice Dickson articulated four principles that together constitute a new interpretive framework for understanding the legal effect of treaties between Aboriginal people and the Crown. First, 'Indian treaties should be given a fair, large and liberal construction in favour of the Indians.'[47] Second, treaties ought to 'be construed not according to the technical meaning of their words, but in the sense that they would naturally be understood by the Indians.'[48] Third, the treaty right to hunt ought to 'be interpreted in a flexible way that is sensitive to the evolution of changes in normal hunting practices.'[49] Fourth, the right to hunt contemplates 'those activities reasonably incidental to the act of hunting itself.'[50]

This new interpretive framework represents a significant shift in judicial approach to the substance of treaty guarantees; it challenges the blind acceptance of the legitimacy of non-Aboriginal norms and values in the process of determining the meaning of vague treaty rights and calls for heightened sensitivity to Aboriginal expectations surrounding the negotiation of a treaty. *Simon*, however, is ambivalent on the critical question of the extinguishment or regulation of treaty rights. The reason offered by Dickson C.J. as to why Nova Scotia's Lands and Forests Act did not apply to the appellant's activities was not that the treaty right shielded the appellant from provincial regulation, but that section 88 of the federal Indian Act shielded the treaty right from provincial regulation.[51] And although he stated that he did 'not wish to be taken as expressing any view on whether, as a matter of law, treaty rights may be extinguished,'[52] Dickson C.J. also stated that it 'seems appropriate to

---

47 Ibid., at 402.

48 Ibid., quoting *Jones v. Meehan*, 175 U.S. 1 (1899).

49 Ibid., at 403.

50 Ibid. For commentary on these interpretive principles, see Leonard I. Rotman, 'Taking Aim at the Canons of Treaty Interpretation in Canadian Aboriginal Rights Jurisprudence,' 46 U.N.B.L.J. 11 (1997).

51 *Simon v. The Queen*, at 410.

52 Ibid., at 406.

demand strict proof of the fact of extinguishment in each case where
the issue arises.'[53]

Retaining the possibility of the extinguishment or regulation of treaty
rights implies that treaties retain the legal form of contract and that legislatures are entitled, within their respective sphere of jurisdiction and
subject to paramountcy principles, to pass laws that regulate or extinguish treaty rights. Absent the protective shield of section 88 of the federal Indian Act, treaty rights would not trump provincial regulation or
extinguishment. According to this view, treaty rights can be asserted
against valid provincial laws not because treaties restrict the exercise of
legislative authority but because federal law provides that provincial laws
of general application shall not infringe treaty guarantees. Moreover,
nothing in section 88 provides that treaty rights are paramount over federal legislation.[54] Understood as subject to the exercise of federal legislative authority, treaty rights provide protection against executive, but
not legislative, action by the federal government.

A similar judicial orientation to the form and substance of treaties is
evident in *R. v. Sioui*.[55] The respondents in *Sioui* were members of the
Huron band on the Lorette Indian reserve in Quebec. They were convicted of cutting down trees, camping, and making fires in a provincial
park, contrary to provincial legislation. They alleged that they were
engaged in ancestral customs and religious rites protected by a treaty
entered into by the Huron and the Crown in 1760. Justice Lamer held for
the respondents, ruling that the agreement between the Huron and the
Crown constituted a treaty into which the parties were competent to
enter, that it had not been extinguished, and that the respondents were
exempt from the relevant provincial regulations by virtue of section 88 of
the Indian Act.

In his analysis of the scope of the treaty right, Lamer J. provided a
broad interpretation of the treaty's provision for 'the free Exercise of
[the Huron] religion, [and] their Customs.'[56] Because the text of the
treaty makes no mention of the territory over which treaty rights may be
exercised, Quebec argued that they did not extend to activities per-
formed in park territory. Lamer J. held that this issue had to be resolved
'by determining the intention of the parties ... at the time it was con-

---

53 Ibid., at 405.
54 See *R. v. George*, [1966] S.C.R. 267.
55 [1990] 1 S.C.R. 1025.
56 Ibid., at 1074.

cluded.'[57] He acknowledged the possibility of different interpretations
of the parties' common intention and, adding another principle to the
interpretive framework articulated in *Simon*, stated that the court must
choose 'from among the various possible interpretations of the common intention the one which best reconciles the Hurons' interests and
those of the conquerer.'[58] Lamer J. was of the opinion that 'the rights
guaranteed by the treaty could be exercised over the entire territory fre-
quented by the Hurons at the time, so long as the carrying on of the customs and rites is not incompatible with the particular use made by the
Crown of this territory.'[59] Yet, like Chief Justice Dickson's reasons in
Simon, Justice Lamer's judgment left intact the contractualist assumption that a legislature possessed the legislative authority to regulate or
extinguish treaty rights. The provincial legislation making it an offence
to cut down trees in the park was inapplicable to the respondents not by
virtue of the existence of the treaty right itself but by virtue of its combined effect with section 88 of the Indian Act.

Simon and *Sioui* together provide an interpretive framework more
attuned to Aboriginal interests, one that calls for broad readings of the
substance of treaty guarantees and a relaxation of procedural requirements usually associated with actions in breach of contract. Both judgments consider the expectations of Aboriginal negotiators at the time
the treaty was entered into, and neither relies unduly on non-Aboriginal
values when giving meaning to abstract treaty rights. Yet despite a statement by Lamer J. in *Sioui* that '[t]he very definition of a treaty ... makes
it impossible to avoid the conclusion that a treaty cannot be extin-

---

57 Ibid., at 1068.
58 Ibid., at 1069.
59 Ibid., at 1070. It should be noted, however, that Lamer J. excluded the free exercise of
   religion on private property from the scope of the treaty right. He did this by claiming
   that the intent of the parties conformed to non-Aboriginal legal categories, in particular, the distinction between public and private ownership, while at the same time
   acknowledging that the Huron were probably unaware of the consequences of private
   ownership: 'I readily accept that the Hurons were probably not aware of the legal consequences, and in particular of the right to occupy to the exclusion of others, which the
   main European legal systems attached to the concept of private ownership. Nevertheless I cannot believe that the Hurons ever believed that the treaty gave them the right to
   cut down trees in the garden of a house as part of their right to carry on their customs.'
   Relying on the intent of the parties to support the invocation of the public/private distinction in the context of an agreement where one party is unaware of the legal consequences of the concept of private ownership is, to say the least, highly problematic.

guished without the consent of the Indians concerned,'[60] both judgments ultimately rest on the existence of section 88 of the Indian Act, which legislatively provides that treaty rights will be paramount over conflicting provincial legislation. Parliament has jurisdiction over 'Indians, and Lands Reserved For Indians,' enabling it to shield treaty rights from provincial regulation. Federal legislation renders treaty rights paramount over conflicting provincial law but a treaty standing alone remained subordinate to legislative authority. Still conceived of as a form of legal contract, treaties were not imagined in these cases as binding the legislative authority of the Canadian state.

Sioui and *Simon* indicated a shift in traditional interpretive approaches to the substance, but not to the form, of treaty rights. But even this substantive shift remained tentative. In *Horse v. The Queen,*[61] a case decided before *Sioui* but after *Simon,* the appellants were charged and convicted of violating provincial game laws when they hunted on private farm property. The appellants argued that they were entitled to do so by virtue of Treaty 6. The text of the treaty supported the Crown's case, in that it provided that the 'said Indians shall have the right to pursue their avocations of hunting and fishing throughout the tract surrendered ... saving and excepting such tracts as may from time to time be required or taken up for settlement.'[62] However, the appellants pointed to oral evidence recorded by the Crown's negotiator, Alexander Morris, that suggested that they were entitled to hunt on private land subject to the interests of the property holder and in consideration of the safety of others.[63] They argued that this oral evidence suggested that Treaty 6 contemplated that Aboriginal people were entitled to hunt over land taken up for settlement under a concept of joint use, that is, when land covered by the treaty became settled, the right to hunt was not extinguished and Aboriginal and non-Aboriginal people could use the land jointly.

In dismissing the appeal, Estey J. for the court had 'reservations'

---

60 Ibid., at 1063.
61 [1988] 1 S.C.R. 187.
62 Morris, *The Treaties of Canada*, at 353.
63 More specifically, the appellants relied on the following extract from Morris, *Treaties of Canada*, at 215: '[Chief Tee-Tee-Quay-Say:] We want to be at liberty to hunt on any place as usual ... [Lieutenant Governor Morris:] You want to be at liberty to hunt as before. I told you we did not want to take that means of living from you, you have it the same as before, only this, if a man, whether Indian or Half-breed, had a good field of grain, you would not destroy it with your hunt ...'.

about referring to oral evidence given the 'parole evidence' rule that 'extrinsic evidence is not to be used in the absence of ambiguity.'[64] Paying lip service to Chief Justice Dickson's exhortation in *Simon* that treaties 'should be liberally construed and doubtful expressions resolved in favour of the Indian'[65] while not conceding that the text of Treaty 6 is ambiguous on this point, Estey J. considered the Morris text. He claimed it 'reinforces the conclusion that the argument of the appellant for joint use of lands taken up by settlement must be rejected.'[66] Yet Estey J. studiously ignored the evidence supportive of the appellant's case and concentrated instead on parole evidence that related to three other treaties. He then argued that during the negotiations of Treaty 6, federal negotiators said that it was analogous to Treaties 1, 3, and 4. In his view, since the records of these other negotiations contained no statement by Aboriginal negotiators expressly requesting the right to hunt on occupied lands, and since federal negotiators indicated that the terms of Treaty 6 'were analogous to those of the previous treaties,' the conclusion that Treaty 6 did not contemplate hunting on occupied lands was 'inescapable.'[67] He added that the evidence relied on by the appellant 'can be read in a manner consistent with the written provision'[68] although he offered no reasons as to why one ought to read the extrinsic evidence in such a manner.

Justice Estey's reluctance to consider oral evidence in *Horse* may have been overcome by Chief Justice Dickson's statement in *Simon* that treaties are to be broadly construed, but his understanding of the text of Treaty 6 and his treatment of oral evidence surrounding the treaty's negotiation evoke the interpretive blindness of another era. His refusal to concede that the substance of the treaty might permit hunting on settled lands denies the possibility that a surrender of Aboriginal lands can be viewed in nonexclusive terms. That is, the surrender could involve an invitation by Aboriginal people to non-Aboriginal people to use the land in question and to assert priority when their use conflicts with Aboriginal interests. Justice Estey's judgment assumes it is legitimate to apply non-Aboriginal assumptions about the meaning of surrender in a context in

---

64 See Sir Rupert Cross and Colin Tapper, *Cross on Evidence*, 6th ed. London: Butterworths, 1985, at 615–16.
65 *Horse v. The Queen*, at 202.
66 Ibid., at 203.
67 Ibid., at 205, 208.
68 Ibid.

which joint use by Aboriginal and non-Aboriginal people is possible. His stubborn focus on oral evidence surrounding the negotiation of three other treaties and his claim that such evidence supports the view that Treaty 6 does not contain the right to hunt on occupied territories are at best disingenuous and at worst constitute a profoundly disturbing exercise of judicial power. Simply stating that the oral evidence surrounding the negotiation of Treaty 6 can be read consistently with the written guarantee – that is, consistently with the conclusion that the treaty does not include the right to hunt on occupied lands – begs the question of whether the written guarantee ought to exclude such activity. It also begs the question of whether the oral evidence ought to be read in a manner consistent with such a conclusion. The alternative conclusion, that the oral evidence supports a right to hunt on occupied Crown lands, is not ruled out by the language of the treaty and can be supported by the oral evidence presented by the appellant. If the evidence and the text of the treaty are ambiguous on this point, why reach the conclusion that the treaty does not authorize the activity in question? The failure by Estey J. to offer any reasons in this regard indicates an unwillingness to entertain treaty claims seriously in the face of legislative regulation.

With the enactment of subsection 35(1) of the Constitution Act, 1982, treaty rights assumed the form of constitutional rights. Treaties thus represent constitutional accords between Aboriginal people and the Canadian state and, no longer enforceable merely in the face of Crown inaction, they now constrain the exercise of legislative authority. In *R. v. Badger*,[69] the Supreme Court of Canada was given the opportunity to integrate the interpretive framework it articulated in *Simon* and *Sioui* with the new constitutional status of treaties. At issue was whether the right to hunt contained in Treaty 8 provided a defence to a charge under Alberta's Wildlife Act which prohibited hunting out of season and hunting without a licence. The court held that Treaty 8 protected hunting for food on private property that was not put to a 'visible, incompatible use,'[70] and that the right to hunt was a treaty right within

---

69 *R. v. Badger*, [1996] 1 S.C.R. 771.
70 The court defined the scope of the treaty right in light of its modification by the 1930 Natural Resources Transfer Agreement, one of three constitutionally recognized agreements entered into between Canada and the prairie provinces, which guarantee Indians the right to take game and fish 'for food.' For critical commentary, see Catherine Bell, '*R. v. Badger:* One Step Forward and Two Steps Back?' 8 Constitutional Forum 2 (1997).

the meaning of subsection 35(1) of the Constitution Act. The court stated that 'a treaty represents an exchange of solemn promises ... [and] an agreement whose nature is sacred.' It reiterated that treaties should be interpreted in 'a manner which maintains the integrity of the Crown' and that ambiguities or doubtful expressions in the wording of the treaty should be resolved in favour of Aboriginal people. The court also held that Parliament can unilaterally abridge treaty rights as long as the law in question meets justificatory standards similar to those that must be met for laws that interfere with the exercise of Aboriginal rights.[71]

Badger marks a significant transformation in the judicial understanding of a treaty's form and substance. No longer mere political agreements or contractual agreements, treaties now possess the formal status of constitutional accords. Their substance ought to be determined in a manner consistent with Aboriginal understandings, flexible to evolving practices, inclusive of reasonably incidental practices, and in a way that best reconciles the competing interests of the parties. Apart from stating that a treaty 'is an agreement whose nature is sacred,' however, the court did not explain why treaty rights warrant constitutional protection. Given the explicit textual reference to treaty rights in subsection 35(1) of the Constitution Act, 1982, it likely thought such an inquiry to be unnecessary. But text alone does not resolve questions concerning the justice of existing constitutional arrangements; it merely clarifies what requires justification.

Treaties as Constitutional Accords

A review of how the judiciary has regarded the form and substance of treaty rights does not fully capture the constitutional significance of the treaty process because beneath the surface of judicial pronouncements exist fundamental normative questions concerning the contemporary relevance of treaties between Aboriginal people and the Crown. For example, what role did the treaty process play in the establishment of the Canadian state? Is it just to distribute constitutional rights in accordance with the terms and conditions of agreements reached between Aboriginal people and the Crown? Such questions relate in part to what was accomplished by the treaty process, which in turn invites consider-

---

71 For discussion, see text accompanying notes 60–80, Chapter 6.

ation of why participants entered into treaties and what expectations they held concerning the process itself.

European powers initially saw fit to enter into treaties with Aboriginal people in part to legitimate their claims of territorial sovereignty in North America.[72] They also entered into treaties for the simple reason that colonists initially were vastly outnumbered by Aboriginal people. In the words of Jeremy Webber, '[i]t would have been impossible for such a tiny number of colonists to govern the Aboriginal nations by force, or indeed by any other means.'[73] Moreover, the Crown sought formal agreements to regularize the trading of fur, fish, and food.[74] The treaty process also enabled the Crown to develop military alliances with Aboriginal nations. By the time international law came to comprehend the distribution of sovereignty in North America and elsewhere in terms of the doctrine of discovery, the Crown no longer relied on treaties to legitimate its assertion of territorial sovereignty. During the nineteenth century, perhaps as a result of the dramatic shift in demography and in the balance of military and economic power between Aboriginal nations and the Crown, the treaty process from the Crown's perspective became a means of facilitating the relocation and assimilation of Aboriginal people. The Crown increasingly saw the treaty process as a means of formally dispossessing Aboriginal people of ancestral territory in return for reserve land and certain benefits to be provided by state authorities.

Though each treaty is unique in its terms and scope of application, Aboriginal understandings of treaties are relatively uniform. Aboriginal people entered into treaties with the Crown to formalize a relationship of continental co-existence. They initially sought military alliances before and during the war between Britain and France and also sought to maximize benefits associated with economic interdependence. As the nineteenth century progressed, Aboriginal peoples attempted to maintain their traditional ways of life in the face of railway construction, surveying activity, non-Aboriginal settlement of Aboriginal territory, and an

---

72 See Brian Slattery, 'The Hidden Constitution: Aboriginal Rights in Canada,' 32 Am. J. Comp. L. 361 at 361–3 (1984). See also Royal Commission on Aboriginal Peoples, *Final Report*, vol. 2, *Restructuring the Relationship* (Ottawa: Supply and Services, 1996), at 193–9.

73 Jeremy Webber, 'Relations of Force and Relations of Justice.'

74 See Stephen Cornell, *The Return of the Native: American Indian Political Resurgence* (New York: Oxford University Press, 1988), at 17.

unprecedented rise in hunting, fishing, and trapping by non-Aboriginal people. They sought to retain traditional authority over their territories and to govern their communities in the face of colonial expansion. In James Youngblood Henderson's words, 'Aboriginal nations entered into the treaties as the keepers of a certain place.'[75] Aboriginal people regarded the treaty process as enabling the sharing of land and authority with non-Aboriginal people while at the same time protecting their territories, economies, and forms of government from non-Aboriginal incursion.[76]

The original participants viewed the treaty process as relevant to the achievement of a number of shared and divergent objectives. Treaties formalized aspects of 'the vast middle range of interactions characterized by neither absolute harmony nor total warfare, neither full understanding nor complete ignorance, neither unmarred competition nor utter contention.'[77] But why are treaties relevant today? Henderson's earlier writings with Russel Lawrence Barsh on American Indian law provide insight into this question. Barsh and Henderson claim that American jurisprudence erroneously assumes that Indian nations were conquered by the newcomers and that, as a result, they are entitled to govern themselves according to their own laws only until Congress passes a law to the contrary.[78] Barsh and Henderson argue that legal principles governing conquest have skewed understandings of treaties so that they are wrongly viewed as documents that outline the consequences of conquest and which can be overridden by Congress if cir-

---

75 James [sákéj] Youngblood Henderson, 'Interpreting Sui Generis Treaties,' 36 Alta. L. Rev. 46 at 64 (1997).

76 For a historical overview of Aboriginal and Crown policies with respect to the treaty process, see Royal Commission on Aboriginal Peoples, *Treaty Making in the Spirit of Co-existence.*

77 Matthew Dennis, *Cultivating a Landscape of Peace: Iroquois-European Encounters in Seventeenth-Century America* (Ithaca: Cornell University Press, 1993), at 3–4. See also Michael Leroy Oberg, *Dominion and Civility: English Imperialism and Native North America, 1585–1686* (Ithaca: Cornell University Press, 1999), at 3 (describing North American 'frontiers' as 'zones of intercultural contact, involving two or more groups, no single one of which can dictate unilaterally the nature of the ensuing relationships') and Richard White, *The Middle Ground: Indians, Empires, and Republics in the Great Lakes* (Cambridge: Cambridge University Press, 1991), at 52 (describing a 'middle ground' between Aboriginal peoples and settlers that emerged as a result of 'the need of people to find a means, other than force, to gain the cooperation or consent of foreigners').

78 *The Road: Indian Tribes and Political Liberty* (Berkeley: University of California Press, 1980), at 270–87.

cumstances so require. In their view, the application of the law of conquest to Indian nations 'has no historical foundation.'[79] Treaties ought to be viewed instead as a source of federal power, as spelling out the terms on which federal power can be exercised in the United States: '[t]reaties are a form of political recognition and a measure of the consensual distribution of powers between tribes and the United States.'[80] Like the compact among American states that created the federal government, treaties reserve to Indian nations those powers not expressly delegated to Congress.[81]

To the extent that the judiciary comprehends the acquisition of Crown sovereignty as arising from discovery rather than conquest, the critiques that Barsh and Henderson levy against legal principles governing conquest are of secondary importance. But to the extent that the doctrine of discovery offends basic principles of equality and distributive justice, their thesis offers an alternative way of understanding why Canada might legitimately claim a measure of sovereign authority over territory that Aboriginal people occupied and governed prior to European contact. According to Barsh and Henderson, the treaty process produced 'a consensual distribution' of constitutional power. Treaties, in other words, are constitutional accords, articulating basic terms and conditions of social co-existence and making possible the exercise of constitutional authority. Unlike legal contracts between the Crown and private citizens, which distribute power delegated by the state to private parties in the form of legally enforceable rights and obligations,[82] treaties establish the constitutional parameters of state power itself.[83]

---

79 Ibid., at 278.

80 Ibid., at 270.

81 For an elaboration of this theme in the Canadian context, see James [sákéj] Young-blood Henderson, 'Empowering Treaty Federalism,' 58 Sask. L. Rev. 241 at 268 (1994) ('[a]ll legitimate British authority in North America is derived from the compacts and treaties with First Nations').

82 See Michel Rosenfeld, 'Contract and Justice: The Relation between Classical Contract Law and Social Contract Theory,' 70 Iowa L. Rev. 751 (1985) (discussing differences between contract law and social contract theory). For discussions of the distributive dimensions of contract law, see Robert Hale, 'Coercion and Distribution in a Supposedly Non-Coercive State,' 38 Pol. Sci. Q. 470 (1923); Anthony T. Kronman, 'Contract Law and Distributive Justice,' 89 Yale L.J. 472 (1980).

83 Compare Williams Jr, *Linking Arms Together*, at 105 ('[I]n American Indian visions of law and peace, a treaty connected different peoples through constitutional bonds of multicultural unity'). For the view that treaties between Aboriginal peoples and the Crown constitute international treaties at international law, see Sharon Venne,

Accordingly, treaties do not distribute delegated state power, they distribute constitutional authority. Treaties are thus as much a part of the constitutional history of Canada as the Constitution Act, 1867, which distributes legislative power between the federal and provincial governments. Treaty rights are constitutional rights that flow to Aboriginal people in exchange for allowing European nations to exercise a measure of sovereign authority in North America.

As constitutional accords, treaties operate as instruments of mutual recognition. Negotiations occur against a backdrop of competing claims of constitutional authority. The Crown enters negotiations under the assumption that it possesses jurisdiction and rights with respect to the territory in question; an Aboriginal nation enters negotiations on the assumption that it possesses jurisdiction and rights with respect to the same territory. The treaty process is a means by which competing claims of authority and right can be reconciled with each other by each party agreeing to recognize a measure of the authority of the other.[84] Recognition can occur geographically, as with a number of contemporary land claims agreements that distribute jurisdiction between the parties based on different geographical categories of land within the territory in question. It can also occur by subject, whereby the parties distribute jurisdiction between themselves based on various subject matters suitable for legislation. As an instrument of mutual recognition, a treaty is an ongoing process, structured but not determined by the text of the original agreement, by which parties commit to resolving disputes that might arise in the future through a process of dialogue and mutual respect.

Viewing treaties as constitutional accords is consonant with recent scholarly attempts to construct alternative legal histories of Aboriginal-Crown relations. Legal histories typically trace the legal position of Aboriginal people under Canadian law over time to demonstrate the redemptive potential, or lack thereof, of Canadian law for protecting Aboriginal people from assimilation. What such histories lack, and what recent scholarship attempts to provide, is an appreciation of how Aboriginal people actively participated in the production and reproduction of

---

'Understanding Treaty 6: An Indigenous Perspective,' in Michael Asch, ed., *Aboriginal and Treaty Rights in Canada: Essays on Law, Equality, and Respect for Difference* (Vancouver: UBC Press, 1997), 173.

84 See generally Royal Commission on Aboriginal Peoples, *Treaty Making in the Spirit of Co-existence.*

legal norms that structured their relations with non-Aboriginal people on the continent. James Tully, for example, has interpreted the treaty process as a form of 'treaty constitutionalism' whereby Aboriginal people participate in the creation of constitutional norms governing Aboriginal-Crown relations.[85] Robert Williams has written of the 'long-neglected fact that ... Indians tried to create a new type of society with Europeans on the multicultural frontiers of colonial North America.'[86] Henderson has interpreted the treaty process as producing 'treaty federalism' – a constitutional order grounded in the consent of Aboriginal and non-Aboriginal people on the continent.[87] What such scholarship shares is an appreciation of the active participation by Aboriginal people in the production of basic legal norms governing the distribution of authority in North America.[88] The treaty process represents a formal manifestation of such participation through its active production of constitutional accords that distribute constitutional authority on the continent.

Social Contracts and Distributive Justice

The treaty process thus stands as a credible alternative to the doctrine of discovery as a source of legitimacy for European assertions of sovereignty in North America. European nations were entitled to exercise sovereign authority in North America not because of their grandiose claims of discovery and unilateral assertions of empire but because they entered into constitutional accords with Aboriginal nations that had the effect of distributing sovereign authority between the parties. The legitimacy of Canadian sovereignty over territory not subject to such a treaty remains dependent on establishing constitutional arrangements that protect interests associated with Aboriginal cultural difference, Aboriginal territory, and Aboriginal sovereignty, and that foster contemporary treaty processes that enable the parties themselves to reconcile their competing claims of authority.

If it is the case that treaties distribute sovereign authority, what of the

---

85 James Tully, *Strange Multiplicity: Constitutionalism in an Age of Diversity* (Cambridge: Cambridge University Press, 1995), at 117.
86 Williams Jr, *Linking Arms Together*, at 9.
87 Henderson, 'Empowering Treaty Federalism.'
88 See generally Webber, 'Relations of Force and Relations of Justice.' See also Sidney L. Harring, *White Man's Law: Native People in Nineteenth-Century Canadian Jurisprudence* (Toronto: Osgoode Society for Canadian Legal History, 1998).

justice of such distributions? Some might argue that treaties, by definition, produce just distributions because the parties consent to their
terms. Efforts to determine the conditions of a just constitutional order
by reference to a consensual social contract are common in antipositiv-
ist constitutional theory.[89] John Rawls, for example, has sought to determine the conditions of a just constitutional order by placing parties in
an 'original position' in order to ascertain the constitutional arrangements they would have agreed to had negotiations actually occurred.[90]
Jürgen Habermas has sought to elucidate the contours of a legitimate
constitutional order by reference to behavioural expectations that all
possibly affected persons could agree to as participants in rational dis-
courses.[91] At first glance, a focus on treaty making provides an even
richer justification of the legitimacy of existing constitutional arrangements than social contract theory, as treaties represent evidence of the
parties' actual, as opposed to hypothetical, consent.[92]

But relying on hypothetical consent enables the separation of questions relating to actual constitutional arrangements from questions
relating to the justice of such arrangements. Such a separation might be
unnecessary with at least some treaties entered into in the early history
of French and British settlement, because they were negotiated in the
context of relatively equal bargaining power.[93] However, many other
treaties were reached in the context of a radical inequality of bargaining

---

89 For a critical history of social contract theory, see J.W. Gough, *The Social Contract: A Critical Study of Its Development*, 2nd ed. (Oxford: Oxford University Press, 1963). For an
original defence of the claim that social contract theory affords a coherent interpretation of the common law of Aboriginal title, see Ken Avio, 'Aboriginal Property Rights in
Canada: A Contractarian Interpretation of *R. v. Sparrow*,' 20 Can. Pub. Pol. 415 (1994).

90 John Rawls, *Political Liberalism* (New York: Columbia University Press, 1993), at 23 ('the
fair terms of social cooperation are conceived as agreed to by those engaged in it').

91 Jürgen Habermas, *Between Facts and Norms: Contributions to a Discourse Theory of Law and
Democracy* (Cambridge: MIT Press, 1996), at 107.

92 Compare Seyla Benhabib, 'Liberal Dialogue versus a Critical Theory of Discursive
Legitimation,' in Nancy L. Rosenblum, ed., *Liberalism and the Moral Life* (Cambridge:
Harvard University Press, 1989), 143–56 at 149–50 ('the purpose of the [exercise] is not
to develop a blueprint for social order but to suggest a critical vantage point from
which to judge power relations in our societies').

93 For the claim that the early treaty process occurred under conditions close to those
governing Rawls's 'original position,' see Williams, Jr, *Linking Arms Together*, at 27
('Both groups approached cultural group negotiations with each other with little
knowledge of what each side's future fortunes would be in this radically different and
new type of multicultural society. Each negotiated behind a veil of ignorance.').

power between the parties. In such circumstances, parties agree to a particular arrangement that they would not have agreed to in a hypothetical situation of relative equality of bargaining power. For example, many treaties contain written terms that purport to strip Aboriginal people of any pre-existing rights to ancestral territory and to force their relocation onto unproductive parcels of reserve land. Often referred to as 'extinguishment clauses', these provisions purport to extinguish Aboriginal title to ancestral territory in exchange for reserve land and treaty rights to hunt, fish, and trap throughout the surrendered territory. Such clauses no doubt capture what the Crown sought to achieve through the treaty process but, given the parties' profound linguistic and cultural differences, as well as the fact that Aboriginal negotiators saw the treaty process as a mechanism for sharing territory and protecting Aboriginal ways of life from non-Aboriginal incursion, it is highly unlikely that Aboriginal signatories actually understood their meaning, let alone consented to their terms.[94] In such circumstances, it would be unjust to enforce such a clause in a court of law.

Even assuming that Aboriginal signatories understood and consented to the extinguishment of title and self-governing authority, it is far from clear that such clauses deserve enforcement. Distributive justice consists of more than keeping one's agreements;[95] it requires an examination of the conditions under which an agreement was entered into and whether, given the nature of the good being distributed, each party has received its fair share.[96] In other words, in the event of proof that

---

94 See, for example, Treaty 7 Elders and Tribal Council, *The True Spirit and Intent of Treaty 7* (Montreal and Kingston: McGill-Queen's University Press, 1996), at 323–4 ('[t]he elders have said that Treaty 7 was a peace treaty; none of them recalled any mention of a land surrender'); Venne, 'Understanding Treaty 6,' 173 at 192 ('[t]he Elders maintain that these words [extinguishment clause] were not included in the original treaty').

95 But see Robert Nozick, *Anarchy, State, and Utopia* (New York: Basic Books, 1974), at 152 ('[j]ustice in holdings is historical; it depends upon what actually has happened').

96 See Michael Sandel, *Liberalism and the Limits of Justice* (Cambridge: Cambridge University Press, 1982), at 102 ('we may typically assess [contracts] from two points of view. We may ask about the conditions under which the agreement was made, whether the parties were free or coerced, or we may ask about the terms of the agreements, whether each party received a fair share.'). Compare Joseph Raz, *The Morality of Freedom* (Oxford: Clarendon Press, 1986), at 84 ('[c]onsent is an act purporting to change the normative situation' but '[n]ot every act of consent succeeds in doing so, and those that succeed do so because they fall under reasons, not themselves created by consent, that show why acts of consent should, within certain limits, be a way of creating rights and duties').

Aboriginal negotiators understood and agreed to the extinguishment of title or self-governing authority, distributive justice requires scrutiny of the adequacy of consideration received in return for extinguishment. At the very least, it requires interpreting vague treaty language to reflect what Aboriginal signatories would have agreed to had they possessed greater equality of bargaining power. Properly understood, the court's interpretive framework ought to be geared towards producing interpretations that reflect not only the true intent of the parties but also what the parties would have agreed to under conditions of relative equality of bargaining power.

The judiciary has not yet grasped the full implications of the fact that treaties, as constitutional accords, distribute constitutional power in Canada. It continues to regard treaty rights as rights to exercise delegated state power as opposed to consideration for the legitimate exercise of constitutional authority. Nor has the judiciary fully accepted the responsibility of assessing the justice of such distributions. It continues to assume that Aboriginal signatories consented to the extinguishment of Aboriginal title and to downplay inequalities of power that existed among the parties. In the following chapter, I argue that the distributive dimensions of the treaty process, as well as the court's new interpretive framework, entail a dramatically different constitutional understanding of extinguishment clauses.

Chapter Six

Interests, Rights, and Limitations

An interest is a demand or desire or expectation which human beings either individually or in groups seek to satisfy, of which, therefore, the ordering of human behavior in civilized society must take account.

Roscoe Pound, *Lectures on Jurisprudence*[1]

Legal rights – whether common law, statutory or constitutional, Aboriginal or otherwise – serve to protect certain interests from unjustifiable interference.[2] Property rights, for example, protect an owner's interest in the use and enjoyment of his or her property.[3] Similarly, the constitutional right of freedom of expression protects a number of interests,

---

1 Roscoe Pound, *Outlines of Lectures on Jurisprudence*, 4th ed. (Cambridge: Harvard University Press, 1928), at 60.
2 In addition to Pound, many others have made a similar claim. See, for example, P.J. Fitzgerald, ed., *Salmond on Jurisprudence*, 12th ed. (London: Sweet & Maxwell, 1966), at 218 ('[a] legal right ... is an interest recognized and protected by a rule of law – an interest the violation of which would be a legal wrong done to him whose interest it is, and respect for which is a legal duty'), and Joseph Raz, *The Morality of Freedom* (Oxford: Clarendon, 1986), at 180–3 (addressing the relation between rights and interests). For an illuminating account of the relationship between interests and rights, see Leon Trakman and Sean Gatien, *Rights and Responsibilities* (Toronto: University of Toronto Press, 1999).
3 See, for example, A.M. Honoré, 'Ownership,' in A.G. Guest, ed., *Oxford Essays in Jurisprudence* (Oxford: Clarendon Press, 1961) 107–47 (describing property as a bundle of rights that includes the right to personal use and enjoyment of the commodity or resource in question).

including an interest in the free flow of ideas.[4] But what often goes unexplored in legal scholarship is the precise relationship between interests and rights. In his *Lectures on Jurisprudence*, the great American legal sociologist Roscoe Pound attempted to define the term 'interest.' Several aspects of Pound's definition merit attention. For instance, he defines an interest both simply and broadly as a 'demand or desire or expectation.' He also contemplates individual and collective interests, opening the door to a conception of collective rights. But perhaps the most striking aspect of Pound's definition is what is left unsaid.

Specifically, Pound leaves two important questions unanswered. First, by deploying a strategic 'therefore' in the heart of his definition, Pound artfully bridges the gulf between fact and norm, masking a failure to explain why 'the ordering of human relations in civilized society must take account' of a 'demand or desire or expectation which human beings ... seek to satisfy.' Must the law take account of all such interests? Why? Simply because human beings seek their satisfaction? Or, more likely, do only certain interests warrant legal protection? Second, assuming that at least some interests warrant legal protection, how should the law protect them?

In this chapter, I explore the relationship between interests associated with indigenous difference and subsection 35(1) of the Constitution Act, 1982. Properly understood, the purpose of constitutional recognition and affirmation of existing Aboriginal and treaty rights is to protect Aboriginal interests associated with culture, territory, sovereignty, and the treaty process. The nature and scope of such rights, including the kinds of activities, practices, and authority that they ought to protect, are outlined below. Understanding Aboriginal and treaty rights in light of their underlying interests also assists in determining when governments can justifiably interfere with the exercise of those rights.

Aboriginal Interests and Purposive Interpretation

In Canadian constitutional jurisprudence, the dominant method of attempting to answer the two questions left unanswered by Roscoe

---

4 See, for example, *Abrams v. United States*, 250 U.S. 616 at 630 (1919), per Holmes J. dissenting ('when men have realized that time has upset many fighting faiths, they may come to believe even more than they believe the very foundations of their own conduct that the ultimate good desired is better reached by free trade in ideas – that the best test of truth is the power of the thought to get accepted in the competition of the market, and that truth is the only ground upon which their wishes safely can be carried out').

Pound's definition of 'interest' is to engage in a method of interpretation that has been coined a purposive analysis. Courts attempt to ascertain what interests underlie a particular constitutional guarantee by a purposive inquiry into the character and larger objects of the constitution, the language chosen to articulate the specific right or freedom in question, the historical origins of the concepts enshrined in the guarantee and, where applicable, the meaning and purpose of other specific rights and freedoms found in the constitution.[5] Such an approach is thought to be justified by the need to render the constitution 'capable of growth and development over time to meet new social, political and historical realities often unimagined by the framers.'[6] It stands in stark contrast to the dominant interpretive approach that the judiciary applied to the Canadian Bill of Rights. Courts sought to interpret the Bill of Rights by reference to its meaning at the time of its enactment, resulting in narrow and legalistic interpretations of its guarantees.[7]

The Supreme Court of Canada has called for a purposive approach to the interpretation of Aboriginal and treaty rights recognized and affirmed by subsection 35(1) of the Constitution Act, 1982. In *R. v. Sparrow*, the court held that '[t]he approach to be taken with respect to interpreting the meaning of subsection 35(1) is derived from general principles of constitutional interpretation, principles relating to aboriginal rights, and the purposes behind the constitutional provision itself.'[8] At issue in Sparrow was the validity of a fishing permit issued under the federal Fisheries Act to the Musqueam First Nation that required members to use a drift net with a maximum length of twenty-five fathoms. The appellant was apprehended fishing with a net that was forty-five fathoms in length. He admitted violating the terms and conditions of the permit but asserted an Aboriginal right to fish and argued that the permit's length restriction was inconsistent with subsection 35(1) and therefore invalid. Although the court held that the Musqueam possessed an Aboriginal right to fish in waters near its reserve, it offered few reasons as to why they possessed this right and little insight into what interests Aboriginal rights ought to protect. It noted that 'the Musqueam have lived in the area as an organized society long before the

---

5 *R. v. Big M Drug Mart Ltd.*, [1985] 1 S.C.R. 295 at 344.

6 *Hunter v. Southam Inc.*, [1984] 2 S.C.R. 145 at 155.

7 See generally Walter S. Tarnopolsky, 'The Supreme Court and the Canadian Bill of Rights,' 53 Can. Bar Rev. 649 (1975).

8 [1990] 1 S.C.R. 1075 at 1106.

coming of the European settlers, and that the taking of salmon was an integral part of their lives and remains so to this day,' intimating that the Musqueam possess a right to fish because they form an 'organized society,' because they occupied their territory prior to contact, and because the taking of salmon is integral to their collective identity. But the Court did not examine these possible justifications of an Aboriginal right to fish in any detail and it did not explore whether or why these social facts might give rise to constitutionally protected rights.

The relationship between Aboriginal interests and Aboriginal rights received more judicial attention in *R. v. Van der Peet*, where the court was faced with a claim by the Sto:lo First Nation that it possessed an Aboriginal right to engage in commercial fishing. In developing a general approach to the interpretation of Aboriginal rights, Chief Justice Lamer for a majority of the court stated that 'when the court identifies a constitutional provision's purposes, or the interests the provision is intended to protect, what it is doing in essence is explaining the rationale of the provision; it is articulating the reasons underlying the protection that the provision gives. With regards to s. 35(1), then, what the court must do is explain the rationale and foundation of the recognition and affirmation of the special rights of aboriginal peoples; it must identify the basis for the special status that aboriginal peoples have within Canadian society as a whole.'[9] In the chief justice's view, constitutional recognition of existing Aboriginal and treaty rights is based on the 'simple fact' that 'when Europeans arrived in North America, aboriginal peoples were already here, living in distinctive communities on the land, and participating in distinctive cultures, as they had done for centuries.'[10] The purpose of subsection 35(1), is his opinion, is twofold: to constitutionally recognize the fact of Aboriginal prior occupancy and to reconcile this fact with the assertion of Crown sovereignty over Canadian territory. In light of this purpose, the court defined an Aboriginal right in terms of an activity that is 'an element of a practice, custom or tradition integral to the distinctive culture of the aboriginal group claiming the right' at the time of contact.[11]

In Chapter 2, I argued that the court's definition of what constitutes an Aboriginal right does not follow from its view of the purpose of subsection 35(1). First, its definition unreasonably restricts constitutional

---

9 *R. v. Van der Peet*, [1996] 2 S.C.R. 507 at 537.

10 Ibid., at 538 (emphasis deleted).

11 Ibid., at 549.

protection of Aboriginal cultural interests to pre-contact cultural practices integral to Aboriginal cultures. Second, the court failed adequately to explain why Aboriginal prior occupancy justifies regarding Aboriginal cultural difference as an interest worthy of constitutional protection. Moreover, the court's definition treats Aboriginal cultural difference as though it were the only aspect of indigenous difference worthy of constitutional recognition. Not only does the court's definition of an Aboriginal right not follow from the purpose it ascribes to subsection 35(1), but, more fundamentally, the court mischaracterizes the purpose of that section.

Perhaps the most challenging aspect of a purposive analysis is that a right's purpose does not magically arise from the text and announce its presence to the interpreter.[12] While resort to structure and precedent helps to illuminate the purpose of a constitutional guarantee, structure and precedent tend to raise more questions than they answer. Structure may provide interpretive guidance but it does not provide clarity or certainty. Precedent may identify the purpose of a guarantee but it is only as stable as the reasons it provides in support of such a purpose. A right's purpose is ultimately a conclusion that the judge reaches after examining a range of interests that the right in question might seek to further. Determining the purpose of a right involves the selection of certain interests that the right ought to protect. One or more interests are selected from a universe of potential candidates, and the right's purpose becomes the protection of those interests worthy of constitutional attention. Interests deemed worthy of constitutional attention might be cast in broad terms, thereby generating a potentially expansive definition of the purpose of the right in question, or they might be cast in more specific terms, resulting in a narrow definition of the right's purpose. Despite the fact that the purpose of a right is a function of its underlying interests, it often is announced in the absence of an explicit inquiry into the interests it ought to protect, leaving the reader with the task of discerning the right's underlying interests by comparing the purpose ascribed to the right with the types of activities that it authorizes.

Take, for example, the Supreme Court's reasoning in *Van der Peet*. As stated, a majority of the court held that the purpose of constitutional recognition and affirmation of existing Aboriginal rights is to reconcile

---

12 See Joel Bakan, *Just Words: Constitutional Rights and Social Wrongs* (Toronto: University of Toronto Press, 1997), at 24 (a right's purpose cannot be 'identified without the intervention of judicial subjectivity').

Aboriginal prior occupancy with the assertion of Crown sovereignty over Canadian territory. But the court did not ascertain this purpose by explicitly examining which Aboriginal interests ought to receive constitutional protection. Instead, it concluded that the right's purpose is a function of Aboriginal prior occupancy, stating that 'it is this fact, and this fact above all others, which separates aboriginal peoples from all other minority groups in Canadian society and which mandates their special legal, and now constitutional, status.' The court made reference to text, precedent, and academic scholarship to support the purpose it ascribed to the provision. None of these sources, however, effectively determines the issue. The textual argument is based on the French wording of the provision, which intimates that Aboriginal rights are 'temporally rooted in the historical presence – the ancestry – of aboriginal peoples in North America,'[13] and is at best an inference. Given that the court had not yet addressed this issue, precedent was not decisive either. The court referred to academic literature that regards Aboriginal rights as forming part of intersocietal law specific to the meeting of two vastly dissimilar legal cultures.[14] This scholarship supports the position that Aboriginal prior occupancy possesses legal significance but it does not suggest that prior occupancy is the sole or even the most salient aspect of indigenous difference that merits constitutional attention. Confusing the matter further is that the test promulgated by Chief Justice Lamer in *Van der Peet* for what constitutes an Aboriginal right has little to do with protecting interests associated with the fact of Aboriginal prior occupancy, that is, Aboriginal territorial interests. Instead, he defines an Aboriginal right as 'an element of a practice, custom or tradition integral to the distinctive culture' of an Aboriginal nation, effectively saying that the purpose of Aboriginal rights is to protect interests associated with cultural difference. But it is by no means clear why protecting cultural interests – as opposed to other Aboriginal interests – reconciles Aboriginal prior occupancy with the fact of Canadian sovereignty.

---

13 The French version of s. 35(1) translates 'Aboriginal rights' as 'les droits ancestraux.'
14 Brian Slattery, 'The Legal Basis of Aboriginal Title,' in Frank Cassidy, ed., *Aboriginal Title in British Columbia: Delgamuukw v. The Queen* (Lantzville: Oolichan Books, 1992), at 121–2 (law of Aboriginal title is 'a form of intersocietal law that evolved from long-standing practices linking the various communities'); Mark Walters, 'British Imperial Constitutional Law and Aboriginal Rights: A Comment on Delgamuukw v. British Columbia,' 17 Queen's L.J. 350 at 412 (1992) (Aboriginal rights are 'rights peculiar to the meeting of two vastly different legal cultures').

These deficiencies in the court's reasons in *Van der Peet*, as well as those discussed in Chapter 2 – the failure to extend constitutional protection to post-contact practices, the lack of an explanation of why Aboriginal cultural difference merits constitutional protection, and the tendency to treat Aboriginal cultural difference as the only aspect of indigenous difference that warrants constitutional protection – manifest a more basic problem with the court's approach. The court fails to explicitly identify the purpose of Aboriginal and treaty rights in light of the interests they protect. The purpose it does ascribe to subsection 35 is instead derived by a balancing exercise that wrongly excludes certain interests associated with indigenous difference and wrongly includes countervailing state interests. Specifically, the court focuses solely on Aboriginal prior occupancy, excluding from consideration interests associated with culture, sovereignty, and the treaty process.[15] And it defines the purpose of the provision as the reconciliation of Aboriginal prior occupancy with the fact of Canadian sovereignty. But Canadian sovereignty, while relevant to determining whether and to what extent the state can limit the exercise of Aboriginal and treaty rights, is irrelevant to determining what purpose is served by constitutionally recognizing and affirming such rights.[16] In contrast, an approach that seeks to determine the interests underlying Aboriginal and treaty rights yields a definition of the purpose of subsection 35(1) that differs in a number of important respects from the court's formulation and provides greater insight into the nature and scope of existing Aboriginal and treaty rights.

It is true that interests – like purposes – do not magically emerge from the text of the constitution. The choice of which interests merit constitutional attention requires argument. But defining a right's purpose in light of the interests that underlie it helps to specify the values associated with that right and illuminates the role that distributive justice plays in constitutional interpretation.[17] I have argued that the interests

---

15 Compare Steve Sheppard, 'The State Interest in the Good Citizen: Constitutional Balance between the Citizen ad the Perfectionist State,' 45 Hastings L.J. 969 at 982–93 (1994) (criticizing the manipulation of balancing exercises by the selection of one interest to the exclusion of others).

16 Compare David Beatty, *Constitutional Law in Theory and Practice* (Toronto: University of Toronto Press, 1995), at 89–90 (criticizing 'definitional-balancing,' i.e., the inclusion of state interests in the definition of a constitutional right).

17 Compare Stephen E. Gottlieb, 'The Paradox of Balancing Significant Interests,' 45 Hastings L.J. 825 at 864 (1994) (a focus on interests 'helps to clarify and simplify other constitutional categories by allowing us to disaggregate them and deal directly with the values at stake rather than with derivative concepts that mask the issues').

underlying Aboriginal and treaty rights correspond to certain aspects of indigenous difference worthy of constitutional protection: Aboriginal people belong to distinctive cultures threatened by assimilation; they lived on and occupied territories in North America prior to European contact; they exercised sovereign authority over such territories; and they participated and continue to participate in a treaty process with the Crown. If constitutional law is an interpretive enterprise that aspires to distributive justice, each of these four aspects of indigenous difference corresponds to a set of interests that merits constitutional protection. Properly understood, the purpose of constitutional recognition and affirmation of Aboriginal and treaty rights is to protect these interests in the wake of Canada's emergence as a sovereign state.

Cultural and Territorial Rights

If Aboriginal cultural and territorial interests merit constitutional protection, how should the law protect them? As discussed above, Chief Justice Lamer in *Van der Peet* proposed defining Aboriginal rights as activities that are elements of practices, customs or traditions integral to distinctive cultures of Aboriginal nations. His approach to the protection of Aboriginal cultural difference, however, is flawed in two respects. First, it relies on a core-periphery distinction that excludes from the ambit of constitutional recognition practices that are not 'integral' to the cultural identity of an Aboriginal community. In defence of this distinction, the court states that its approach reconciles the pre-existence of Aboriginal societies with the existence of Canadian sovereignty. In Chapter 4, I discussed the extent to which the judiciary tends to assume the constitutional legitimacy of the assertion of Canadian sovereignty over Aboriginal people, and *Van der Peet* is no exception. But assuming it is a legitimate consideration at this stage of the inquiry, the fact of Canadian sovereignty is no reason to limit constitutional protection of Aboriginal cultural practices by a core-periphery distinction. The chief justice stated that '[t]o reconcile aboriginal societies with Crown sovereignty it is necessary to identify the distinctive features of those societies; it is precisely those distinctive features which need to be acknowledged and reconciled with the sovereignty of the Crown.'[18] As a result, 'incidental practices, customs and traditions cannot qualify as aboriginal rights through a process of piggybacking on integral practices, customs

18 *R. v. Van der Peet*, at 554.

and traditions.'[19] But is it truly 'necessary' to rely on a core-periphery distinction to reconcile the fact of pre-existing Aboriginal societies with Canadian sovereignty?

Drawing a distinction between a core and periphery within Aboriginal cultures seeks to identify what is truly important to Aboriginal cultural reproduction in order to shield it from the exercise of state power, but it presents judges with a dilemma: they, and not Aboriginal people themselves, must define what is essential and what is peripheral to Aboriginal cultures.[20] Aboriginal cultures become constructed as sets of practices and traditions that can be identified through legal inquiry, displacing or at least disrupting individual and communal processes of negotiation over questions of Aboriginal cultural identity. In the words of Martha Minow, '[t]he use of a specific notion of identity to resolve a legal dispute can obscure the complexity of lived experiences while imposing the force of the state behind the selected notion of identity.'[21] This dilemma cannot be resolved in the absence of constitutional recognition of an Aboriginal right of self-government that would allow Aboriginal people themselves to determine and protect what is essential to cultural identity. Even constitutional recognition of a right of self-government would not completely resolve this dilemma, given that the judiciary presumably would be charged with the responsibility of policing the boundaries of Aboriginal jurisdiction. To offset some of the costs associated with judicial definition of Aboriginal cultures, the judiciary ought to defer to what cultural participants themselves regard as integral to their cultural identities. And to acknowledge that the production and reproduction of cultural identities involve practices that are dependent and mutually reinforcing, the judiciary ought to relax the core-periphery distinction to allow for the protection of at least some practices that are incidental but related to core practices.[22]

---

19 Ibid., at 560.
20 Compare Russel Lawrence Barsh and James [sákéj] Henderson, 'The Supreme Court's Van der Peet Trilogy: Native Imperialism and Ropes of Sand,' 42 McGill L.J. 993 at 1000 (1997) ('[t]he extent to which an idea, symbol or practice is central to the cultural identity of a particular society is inescapably subjective to that society'); John Borrows, 'Frozen Rights in Canada: Constitutional Interpretation and the Trickster,' 22 American Indian L. Rev. 37 at 52 (1997) (the court's approach establishes 'non-Aboriginal characterizations of Aboriginality, evidence, and law as the standards against which Aboriginal rights are measured').
21 Martha Minow, 'Identities,' 3 Yale J. Law & Hum. 97 at 111 (1991).
22 Compare Barsh and Henderson, in 'The Supreme Court's Van der Peet Trilogy,' at 1000 ('distinguishing between what is "'central'" to a culture, and what is merely "incidental"' ... presupposes that cultural elements can exist independently of one another,

The second way in which the test in *Van der Peet* is flawed is that it requires a pre-contact referent. That is, only practices, customs and traditions 'having continuity with the practices, customs and traditions that existed prior to contact' with Europeans can serve as the basis of Aboriginal rights.[23] Such practices can evolve and take a modern form but they must possess a pre-contact referent. For example, if hunting was a practice integral to an Aboriginal culture prior to contact, the practice of hunting constitutes an Aboriginal right; if not extinguished by Canadian law prior to 1982, the right to hunt in accordance with modern methods would receive constitutional protection. The court's allowance of modernized pre-contact practices attempts to find common ground with a 'frozen rights' approach, which would restrict Aboriginal rights to practices as they were engaged in prior to contact, and a more open-ended approach, which would acknowledge that Aboriginal cultures have adapted and changed over time.

In Chapter 2, I argued that, although culture provides a common intelligibility to human experience and therefore merits a measure of respect, constitutional protection of cultural difference must first take into account its conceptual elasticity. As a constitutional category, Aboriginal cultural difference conceivably includes a vast set of Aboriginal interests, ranging from interests in engaging in ancient customs, practices, and traditions to interests associated with Aboriginal territory and sovereignty. As well, constitutional protection of Aboriginal cultural difference must be sensitive to the fact that Aboriginal people are not locked into particular cultures but instead express plural cultural allegiances; they also assimilate, break cultural bonds, and change cultural allegiances over time. Finally, Aboriginal cultures undergo dramatic transformations in response to internal and external circumstances and developments. A frozen rights approach ignores the dynamic nature of cultural identity and the fact that cultures undergo deep transforma-

---

so that the loss of one element does not compromise the perpetuation or enjoyment of the others'). Indeed, the court has since signalled that it might be willing to soften the core-periphery distinction as it relates to Aboriginal rights: see *R. v. Coté*, [1996] 3 S.C.R. 139 at 176 ('a substantive Aboriginal right will normally include the incidental right to teach such a practice, custom and tradition to a younger generation'); *R. v. Adams*, [1996] 3 S.C.R. 101 at 128 (requiring a practice only to be 'an important source of sustenance,' not necessarily integral to one's distinctive culture). The court has not insisted on a core-periphery distinction in the context of treaty rights: see *R. v. Sundown*, [1999] 1 S.C.R. 393 (treaty hunting right includes activities that are reasonably incidental to the act of hunting).

23 *Van der Peet*, at 556.

tions over time. It risks stereotyping Aboriginal people in terms of historical differences with non-Aboriginal people that may or may not have existed in the distant past and profoundly under-describes important aspects of contemporary Aboriginal cultural identities. But a more open-ended approach risks the constitutional recognition of all aspects of Aboriginal social existence.

Although the requirement of a pre-contact referent reins in the scope of Aboriginal rights in a way that avoids the severity of a purely frozen rights approach, *Van der Peet* unjustifiably excludes from constitutional protection practices that do not possess pre-contact referents but are integral to Aboriginal cultures. If Aboriginal cultural difference is worthy of constitutional recognition, why do only those aspects of Aboriginal culture that possess a pre-contact referent receive protection? Chief Justice Lamer states that the need for a pre-contact referent flows from the fact that 'distinctive aboriginal societies lived on the land prior to the arrival of Europeans.'[24] But prior occupancy possesses constitutional significance because it justifies constitutional protection of Aboriginal title; its significance is in no way related to a requirement that Aboriginal cultural practices possess a pre-contact referent. Just because distinctive Aboriginal societies lived on the land pre-contact does not mean that constitutional recognition of this fact should be restricted to the protection of pre-contact cultural activities. Chief Justice Lamer hints that the pre-contact referent furthers a reconciliation of the pre-existence of Aboriginal societies with Canadian sovereignty. In his words, '[i]t is not the fact that aboriginal societies existed prior to Crown sovereignty that is relevant; it is the fact that they existed prior to the arrival of Europeans in North America.'[25] But this debate is beside the point; neither a pre-contact nor a pre-sovereignty referent furthers the reconciliation sought by the court for the simple reason that the fact of Aboriginal prior occupancy (be it before contact or before the assertion of Crown sovereignty) does not justify restricting constitutional protection of Aboriginal cultural practices to those with a pre-contact referent.

One way out of the dilemma presented by the choice between a frozen rights approach and a more open-ended approach is to insist that a disputed practice relate to the continued vitality of the culture in question and to treat the fact that a particular cultural practice has been engaged

---

24 Ibid., at 555.
25 Ibid. (emphasis deleted).

in for a long time as evidence of its significance.[26] This approach would allow for the constitutional protection of certain post-contact cultural practices and acknowledge both the dynamic nature of cultural identity and the dramatic transformations undergone by Aboriginal cultures since contact. The potential risk of constitutionalization of all aspects of Aboriginal existence could be avoided by adopting a categorical approach that identifies certain background conditions that merit constitutional protection. The fact that the concept of culture is elastic, in other words, does not necessitate stretching it to cover every aspect of Aboriginal existence. Eliminating the pre-contact referent would thus allow for constitutional protection not only of traditional practices and their modern variants but also of other cultural interests, for example, spirituality, language, and education, depending on the strength of arguments that assert their relation to Aboriginal cultural difference.

The judiciary has recently grappled with the relationship between traditional Canadian legal understandings of Aboriginal title and the constitutional recognition of Aboriginal rights accomplished by subsection 35(1). Does that subsection constitutionalize Aboriginal title in its entirety? Or does it only constitutionalize particular rights to engage in particular practices, customs, and traditions? The former approach would result in the constitutionalization of Aboriginal territorial interests, including the freedom to decide how to use that territory. As stated by Chief Justice Marshall of the U.S. Supreme Court in *Johnson v. M'Intosh*,[27] Aboriginal people are 'the rightful occupants of the soil, with a legal as well as just claim to retain possession of it, and to use it according to their own discretion.'[28] The latter approach would result in the disentanglement of the bundle of rights traditionally referred to by Canadian law as Aboriginal title in order to elevate some rights of use to constitutional status.[29]

Before its resolution, the relevance of this ambiguity lay in the uncertainty it reflected regarding the extent to which the preservation and protection of Aboriginal territory is an interest underlying the constitu-

---

26 Compare *R. v. Van der Peet*, at 601, per L'Heureux-Dubé J. dissenting (the activity must have 'formed an integral part of a distinctive Aboriginal culture ... for a substantial continuous period of time').

27 (1823), 21 U.S. (8 Wheat.) 543.

28 Ibid.; quoted with approval in *Van der Peet*, at 507, per Lamer C.J.

29 See, for example, *Adams v. The Queen*, 55 Q.A.C. 19 (C.A.), per Proulx J.A. concurring (Aboriginal fishing right cannot exist independently of Aboriginal title).

tional recognition and affirmation of Aboriginal rights. In *Delgamuukw v. British Columbia*, the Supreme Court of Canada resolved the issue when it held that subsection 35(1) recognized and affirmed an existing Aboriginal right to title in addition to recognizing a set of rights to engage in certain practices, customs, or traditions. The court held further that Aboriginal title is a communally held right in land and, as such, contemplates more than the right to engage in specific activities which may themselves constitute Aboriginal rights. Based on the fact of prior occupancy, Aboriginal title confers the right to exclusive use and occupation of land for a variety of purposes, not all of which need be aspects of practices, customs, or traditions integral to the distinctive cultures of Aboriginal societies. By interpreting subsection 35(1) in an expansive manner, as opposed to recognizing only certain rights of use and enjoyment of land, the court in *Delgamuukw* acknowledged the constitutional significance of Aboriginal territorial interests.

Understood as the right to exclusive use and occupation of the land for a variety of purposes, Aboriginal title protects territorial interests that arise by virtue of the constitutional significance of Aboriginal prior occupancy. But it also protects many cultural interests that arise by virtue of the constitutional significance of Aboriginal cultural difference, namely, those interests that a community has in engaging in customs, practices, and traditions on territory to which it enjoys Aboriginal title. Because such activities possess territorial and cultural dimensions, Aboriginal prior occupancy and Aboriginal cultural difference interact normatively to justify their constitutional protection. The significance of Aboriginal prior occupancy reaches beyond the significance of Aboriginal cultural difference, however, by justifying constitutional protection of a set of activities on territory subject to Aboriginal title that is not limited to culturally significant activities. Aboriginal cultural difference, on its own, justifies only the constitutional protection of extra-territorial customs, practices, and traditions integral to the distinctive identity of an Aboriginal nation. Given the threshold problems associated with ascribing constitutional significance to cultural difference, it is perhaps appropriate that, at the end of the day, Aboriginal cultural difference does relatively little independent constitutional work.

Aboriginal Rights of Self-Government

In 1985, the Eagle Lake First Nation, whose members live on a reserve near Dryden, Ontario, passed a resolution enacting a lottery law that authorized and regulated gaming activities on the reserve. The First Nation then began to conduct regular bingo games that attracted a significant number of non-Aboriginal participants and generated an annual profit of over a million dollars. The operation enabled the First Nation to build a community arena, a resort, a lodge, a conference centre, and a local school and gymnasium. But federal law prohibits certain forms of gaming without provincial authorization and the Eagle Lake First Nation, acting on the assumption that it alone possessed the authority to regulate economic activity on the reserve, did not seek Ontario's authorization for its activities. Members of the First Nation were charged with and convicted of keeping a common gaming house contrary to the Criminal Code.

On appeal to the Supreme Court of Canada, in *R. v. Pamajewon,*[30] the Eagle Lake First Nation unsuccessfully argued that it possessed an Aboriginal right to manage its economic affairs on its reserve land free of federal and provincial interference. According to Chief Justice Lamer, '[a]ssuming that s. 35(1) encompasses claims to self-government, such claims must be considered in light of the purposes underlying the provision and must, therefore, be considered against the test derived from consideration of those purposes.'[31] At the time the court rendered its decision, the test for determining the content of an Aboriginal right was that found in *R. v. Van der Peet,* which, as stated, defined an Aboriginal right as an element of a custom, practice, or tradition integral to the distinctive culture of an Aboriginal nation. The court rejected the Eagle Lake First Nation's characterization of its claim as an assertion of a broad right to manage the use of its reserve lands, characterizing the claim instead as involving the assertion of a narrow right to participate in and regulate high stakes gambling on the reserve. It concluded that the claim did not relate to a custom, practice, or tradition integral to the distinctive culture of the First Nation at the time of contact.

The court's decision in *Pamajewon* should be read in light of its subsequent decision in *Delgamuukw,* in which the Gitksan and Wet'suwet'en nations asserted an Aboriginal right of self-government over lands to which they possessed Aboriginal title. The court in *Delgamuukw* held that errors of the trial judge made it 'impossible ... to determine

---

30 [1996] 2 S.C.R. 821. *R. v. Pamajewon* also involved the trial and conviction of, and subsequent appeals by, members of the Shawanaga First Nation for similar violations of the Criminal Code.

31 Ibid., at 832.

whether the claim to self-government has been made out.' [32] Nonetheless, it also held that Aboriginal title confers an exclusive right to use and occupy land for a variety of activities that need not relate to customs, practices, or traditions integral to the distinctive culture of the Aboriginal nation in question. It held further that 'the same legal principles governed the aboriginal interest in reserve lands and lands held pursuant to aboriginal title.'[33] In other words, *Delgamuukw* contemplates the very possibility that *Pamajewon* sought to foreclose: a First Nation successfully asserting a broad Aboriginal right to regulate and engage in economic activity on reserve lands unrelated to traditional patterns of territorial use and enjoyment. Viewed together, *Delgamuukw* and *Pamajewon* suggest that the Canadian Constitution recognizes and affirms an inherent Aboriginal right of self-government – specifically, a right to make laws in relation to customs, practices, and traditions integral to the distinctive culture of the Aboriginal nation and in relation to the use of reserve lands and lands subject to Aboriginal title.

Whether the constitution ought to be interpreted as recognizing an Aboriginal right of self-government, however, turns less on precedent and more on the distributive justice of recognizing an Aboriginal order of government within the Canadian constitutional order. The legitimacy of the Canadian constitutional order rests in part on the extent to which it protects interests associated with indigenous difference. Because protection of interests associated with prior Aboriginal sovereignty promotes both formal and substantive equality, such interests ought to receive protection in the form of an existing Aboriginal right of self-government. Constitutional recognition of an Aboriginal right of self-government formally acknowledges that Aboriginal nations were and continue to be self-governing despite the establishment of the Canadian state and begins to ameliorate the substantive inequalities that Aboriginal people face in contemporary society by enabling them to exercise greater control over their individual and collective identities.

If interests associated with Aboriginal sovereignty merit constitutional protection in the form of an existing Aboriginal right of self-government, how would an Aboriginal order of government relate to the distribution of power between Parliament and provincial legislatures? The constitution assigns to provincial legislatures subject matters over which

---

32 *Delgamuukw v. British Columbia*, [1997] 3 S.C.R. 1010 at 1114.
33 Ibid., at 1085.

they enjoy exclusive jurisdiction.[34] Parliament is assigned jurisdiction over specific subject matters, as well as residual authority 'to make Laws for the Peace, Order, and good Government of Canada.'[35] The judiciary generally takes a purposive approach to the delineation of the distribution of legislative authority, and subject matters are often viewed as possessing both federal and provincial 'aspects.'[36] A central feature of the distribution of legislative authority in Canada is that both levels of government can regulate the same activity as long as each is acting within its sphere of jurisdiction. This approach permits a great deal of overlap in the exercise of legislative authority. Perhaps the most common example of such overlap is highway traffic legislation, where a federal and a provincial law, for different purposes, can regulate the same activity.[37] In the event of a conflict between a federal and a provincial law, where one law prohibits what the other requires, federal law is paramount.[38] In the absence of conflict, where an individual can obey both federal and provincial laws, the presence of a federal law does not invalidate a provincial law regulating the same or similar conduct.

Regardless of the precise means by which interests associated with Aboriginal sovereignty receive constitutional protection, recognition of Aboriginal governmental authority will throw current law governing the distribution of legislative authority into a state of confusion. For example, both Parliament and provincial legislatures are currently entitled to pass laws regulating Aboriginal people. A fundamental issue surrounding constitutional recognition of Aboriginal governmental authority will be whether and to what extent federal or provincial laws continue to apply to Aboriginal people. Suppose an Aboriginal nation is viewed by agreement, law, or constitutional right as possessing jurisdiction to pass laws or otherwise to regulate certain matters that affect community life.

---

34 See, e.g., s. 92 of the Constitution Act, 1867.

35 See s. 91 of the Constitution Act, 1867.

36 *Hodge v. The Queen* (1883), 9 A.C. 117.

37 Provincial traffic offences prohibiting careless driving, enacted pursuant to provincial jurisdiction over 'Property and Civil Rights in the Province' in accordance with s. 92(13) of the Constitution Act, 1867, often co-exist with federal criminal offences prohibiting dangerous driving, enacted pursuant to federal jurisdiction over 'Criminal Law' in accordance with s. 91(27) of the Constitution Act, 1867. See, e.g., *O'Grady v. Sparling*, [1960] S.C.R. 804; *Stephens v. The Queen*, [1960] S.C.R. 823; *Mann v. The Queen*, [1966] S.C.R. 776.

38 See, e.g., *Multiple Access v. McCutcheon*, [1982] 2 S.C.R. 161; *Bank of Montreal v. Hall*, [1990] 1 S.C.R. 121.

To what extent should Aboriginal jurisdiction be exclusive to the Aboriginal nation and to what extent should it be shared with Parliament or a provincial legislature? And which level of government – federal, provincial, or Aboriginal – should prevail in the event of a conflict between or among laws regulating subjects that fall within shared jurisdiction?

Pre-existing principles governing the current distribution of legislative authority in Canada can be extended to account for three instead of two levels of government. Traditional principles suggest that the mere fact that a federal law and a provincial law regulate the same subject matter does not render either unconstitutional as long as each level of government is acting within its sovereign sphere of authority.[39] This approach to the distribution of legislative authority could easily operate in a tri-federal system of government. Subject matters could potentially be regulated by all three levels of government, assuming that each acts within its jurisdiction; as long as an individual could conform to all three laws, there would be no conflict and no need to determine which law is paramount. A great deal of overlap among federal, provincial, and Aboriginal law would result. For example, if an Aboriginal community decides to levy a tax on the sale of alcohol already taxed by federal and provincial governments, the purchaser could conform to all three laws by paying all three taxes. The enactment of an Aboriginal tax would not result in a direct conflict among laws. Other federal, and possibly provincial, laws would continue to apply to Aboriginal people even after an Aboriginal government entered the field with legislation of its own. The judiciary would need to develop principles to address actual conflict between laws but the mere fact of duplication or overlap would not limit the operation of a federal or provincial law.

Alternatively, recognizing an Aboriginal order of government could involve carving out a sphere of exclusive Aboriginal jurisdiction into which no other level of government could enter. Such exclusivity would operate even when no conflict existed between a federal or provincial law and an Aboriginal law, that is, where an individual could conform to both laws by adhering to the stricter prohibition. Although the dominant judicial approach to the current distribution of legislative authority is to permit considerable duplication and overlap among federal and

---

39 Parliament is entitled to raise 'Money by any Mode or System of Taxation': see s. 91(3) of the Constitution Act, 1867; provinces are entitled to pass laws that constitute direct taxation within the province to raise revenue for provincial purposes: see s. 92(2) of the Constitution Act, 1867.

provincial laws, a competing approach is to view each sphere of authority as immune from the legislative reach of the other.[40] This approach suggests that some 'matters' are exclusively federal and others exclusively provincial. Extended to apply to a tri-federal system, some matters would be exclusively within the jurisdictional domain of Aboriginal governments, beyond the reach of federal or provincial regulation even if such regulation does not actually conflict with Aboriginal law. This approach would entail the identification of an exclusively Aboriginal sphere of jurisdictional authority into which neither Parliament nor provincial legislatures, for whatever reason, could enter. It would suggest, for example, that the taxation of certain economic activity perhaps ought to be viewed as within the exclusive jurisdiction of Aboriginal governments, and that federal and provincial taxes that invade Aboriginal jurisdiction would be unconstitutional, even if they did not actually conflict with Aboriginal law.

A third possibility is to seek a compromise between these two competing approaches to the distribution of legislative authority. Overlap and duplication would in some cases be an appropriate attribute of a tri-federal system. All levels of government would be permitted to regulate certain subject matters, assuming that each could point to a valid legislative purpose and that overlap or duplication did not result in actual conflict. Other matters, however, would be exclusively Aboriginal and beyond the reach of federal or provincial legislative authority. This compromise would involve distinguishing between core and peripheral jurisdiction and maintaining a core of jurisdiction into which neither the federal nor provincial governments could enter. Matters on the periphery of Aboriginal jurisdiction could allow for concurrent regulation, overlap, and duplicative laws.

---

40 The most prominent example of this doctrinal counter-tendency is what is known as the 'inter-jurisdictional immunity' doctrine, which provides that certain activities are immune from the regulatory reach of one jurisdiction: see, e.g., *McKay v. The Queen*, [1977] 2 S.C.R. 1054. A similar approach has been proposed with respect to Indian reserves. See *Cardinal v. A.G. Alberta*, [1974] S.C.R. 695, per Laskin C.J. dissenting ('Indian Reserves are enclaves which, so long as they exist as Reserves, are withdrawn from provincial regulatory power ... If provincial legislation is applicable at all, it is only by referential incorporation through adoption by the Parliament of Canada'). For an exhaustive account of this counter-tendency, and the argument that it ought to regulate the existing distribution of federal and provincial power in the context of Aboriginal peoples, see Bruce Ryder, 'The Demise and Rise of the Classical Paradigm in Canadian Federation: Promoting Autonomy for the Provinces and First Nations,' 36 McGill L.J. 308 (1991).

Although it failed to achieve sufficient support to produce a constitutional amendment, the Charlottetown Accord offers one approach to conceptualizing Aboriginal government as one of three orders of government in Canada. The Accord proposed to define a core of Aboriginal jurisdiction. Matters essential or 'integral'[41] to an Aboriginal community's ability 'to safeguard and develop' its language, culture, economy, identity, institutions, and traditions and 'to develop, maintain and strengthen' its relationship to its land, water, and environment were to fall within the exclusive jurisdiction of Aboriginal governments. The Royal Commission on Aboriginal Peoples also proposed that Aboriginal governmental authority could be clarified by distinguishing between a core and a periphery. The commission identified the core of Aboriginal jurisdiction as the authority to make laws in relation to matters of vital concern to the life and welfare of the community, which do not have a major impact on adjacent jurisdictions and which are not otherwise the object of overarching federal or provincial concern. Such a core would prevent Parliament and provincial legislatures from enforcing against Aboriginal people laws that regulated matters central to Aboriginal identity. Subject to the above principles, Aboriginal governments would have the authority to establish a national constitution, governmental and judicial institutions, and citizenship criteria, and enact laws in relation to education, health, family matters, and certain economic activity as well as aspects of criminal law and procedure. On the other hand, matters that do not fall within the core of Aboriginal jurisdiction could support overlapping and duplicative laws enacted by all three levels of government. Aboriginal authority over matters on the periphery of Aboriginal jurisdiction, such as those that would have a major impact on adjacent jurisdictions, would require intergovernmental agreement.[42]

Assuming that the judiciary would permit some degree of overlap among federal, provincial, and Aboriginal laws, which law will be paramount in the event of actual conflict? The current approach is one of federal paramountcy: in the event of an actual conflict between federal and provincial law, where compliance with one results in breach of the

---

41 Compare *Van der Peet*, where the Supreme Court of Canada viewed customs, practices, and traditions 'integral' to an Aboriginal community's 'distinctive culture' to be protected against governmental interference by virtue of s. 35(1) of the Constitution Act, 1982.

42 Royal Commission on Aboriginal Peoples, *Final Report*, vol. 2, *Restructuring the Relationship* (Ottawa: Ministry of Supply and Services, 1996), at 219.

other, federal law prevails. Regardless of which reform initiatives usher in an Aboriginal order of government, principles will be necessary to govern conflicts among exercises of legislative authority. If, for example, an Aboriginal community passes a law that requires persons to engage in activity prohibited by an otherwise-applicable federal or provincial law, which law ought to be paramount? Four possibilities present themselves: (a) Aboriginal law is paramount over federal and provincial law; (b) Aboriginal law is paramount over federal but not provincial law; (c) Aboriginal law is paramount over provincial but not federal law; and (d) both federal and provincial law are paramount over Aboriginal law.

The Charlottetown Accord attempted to provide guidance on this issue. It proposed that '[n]o Aboriginal law or any exercise of the inherent right of self-government ... may be inconsistent with federal or provincial laws that are essential to the preservation of peace, order and good government in Canada.'[43] This provision can be read in at least two different ways. One interpretation is that it said nothing concerning paramountcy; the provision was directed to the scope of Aboriginal jurisdiction and not to which law was paramount, assuming each was a valid exercise of legislative authority. On this view, an Aboriginal government would not have possessed the authority to pass laws that address matters essential to peace, order, and good government in Canada. Instead of providing guidance on the nature of the hierarchy that ought to structure the three orders of government, the Accord would have declared Aboriginal laws that regulated matters essential to peace, order, and good government in Canada unconstitutional regardless of whether they actually conflicted with federal or provincial legislation.

Another interpretation, however, is that a federal or provincial law essential to the peace, order, and good government of Canada is paramount if it conflicts with an otherwise valid exercise of Aboriginal jurisdiction. This interpretation would have opened the door for partial Aboriginal paramountcy. Aboriginal laws that did not conflict with federal or provincial laws essential to peace, order, and good government but which did conflict with other federal or provincial laws would have been paramount over those other laws. The Royal Commission on Aboriginal Peoples proposed another version of this interpretation. In the commission's view, Aboriginal laws regulating the core of Aboriginal jurisdiction would be paramount over conflicting provincial legislation

---

43 Draft Legal Text, s. 29 (proposed s. 35.4(2)).

and paramount over federal legislation if the federal law in question did not serve a compelling and substantial need or was inconsistent with the Crown's fiduciary responsibilities to Aboriginal peoples.[44] Either version is far-reaching: Aboriginal law would be paramount over some or all conflicting provincial laws and paramount over federal laws that do not serve a compelling or substantial need.

How should the constitution address these concerns? Respecting a core of Aboriginal jurisdiction into which neither the federal nor provincial government can enter is consistent with the constitutional significance of Aboriginal prior sovereignty. It is distributively unjust to constitutionally enshrine the proposition that European settlement of lands previously occupied by Aboriginal people triggers a complete transfer of sovereignty over those lands and peoples to the nation responsible for settlement. European settlement should be regarded in less absolutist terms, as justifying the establishment of states to which non-Aboriginal and Aboriginal people can claim allegiance but not displacing modified forms of Aboriginal governance that maintain and reproduce distinct Aboriginal identities. A just distribution of sovereignty requires a constitutional order that both respects the integrity of Aboriginal governmental authority and reflects the plurality of contemporary Aboriginal allegiances. The extent to which Aboriginal people claim allegiance to their own forms of government as well as governments established by settlement ought to be reflected in a federal structure that recognizes that Aboriginal people possess the authority to make laws in relation to matters that affect their daily lives. Similarly, treating Aboriginal law as paramount over some or all conflicting provincial laws and paramount over federal laws that do not serve a compelling or substantial need conforms to a vision of contemporary Aboriginal governmental authority as a remnant of inherent Aboriginal sovereignty. Despite settlement and the establishment of the Canadian state, Aboriginal law ought to continue to govern Aboriginal people and their lands and, in certain circumstances, ought to be treated as paramount in the event of a conflict with an inconsistent federal or provincial law.

From Extinguishment to Co-Existence

In Chapter 9, I address a number of interests underlying the treaty process that require positive state action in the form of institutional

---

44 Royal Commission on Aboriginal Peoples, *Final Report*, vol. 2, at 224.

arrangements designed to resolve ongoing disputes between Aboriginal people and the Canadian state. But one interest associated with the treaty process merits discussion at this point. As I noted in chapter 5, numerous treaties between Aboriginal people and the Crown contain an 'extinguishment clause' that purports to extinguish all or a portion of the Aboriginal party's title in exchange for a set of treaty-based rights. Generally speaking, there are two types of extinguishment clauses. A blanket extinguishment clause purports to extinguish all Aboriginal title in exchange for treaty-based rights whereas a partial extinguishment clause purports to extinguish some, but not all, Aboriginal title in exchange for treaty-based rights. Early treaties between the Crown and Aboriginal people typically did not involve written text purporting to accomplish the blanket extinguishment of Aboriginal title. Some confirmed the respective territorial claims of the parties; others ceded a portion of Aboriginal title to the Crown while reserving the remainder to Aboriginal signatories. Beginning in the nineteenth century, treaties increasingly contained blanket extinguishment clauses, reflecting the Crown's understanding of the treaty process as a means of formally dispossessing Aboriginal people of ancestral territory in return for reserve land and certain benefits to be provided by state authorities.[45]

The written text of Treaty 9, for example, negotiated and signed in 1905 and 1906 by representatives of the federal government, the Province of Ontario, and Cree and Ojibway peoples living in northern Ontario, provides that the Aboriginal signatories 'cede, release, surrender and yield up to the Government of the Dominion of Canada, for His Majesty the King and His successors forever, all their rights, titles and privileges' to the land covered by the treaty's terms.[46] The written text also provides that the Aboriginal signatories agree to 'conduct and behave themselves as good loyal subjects of His Majesty the King' and 'in all respects, obey and abide by the law.'[47] In return, each Aboriginal person was to receive eight dollars for 1905 and four dollars for the years following, and each chief was to receive a flag and a copy of the treaty itself. The federal government also promised to pay the salaries of school teachers and to provide adequate educational facilities and

---

45 For more detail on extinguishment policy and the treaty process, see Royal Commission on Aboriginal Peoples, *Treaty-Making in the Spirit of Co-existence* (Ottawa: Minister of Supply and Services Canada, 1995).
46 *James Bay Treaty* (Ottawa: Queen's Printer, 1964), reprinted from 1931 edition.
47 Ibid.

equipment. In addition, Treaty 9 recognizes that Aboriginal people governed by the treaty have the 'right to pursue their usual vocations of hunting, trapping, and fishing throughout the tract surrendered.' Hunting, trapping, and fishing rights are subject to two qualifications. First, they are 'subject to such regulations as may from time to time be made by the Government of the Country, acting under the authority of His Majesty.'[48] Second, they do not extend to tracts of land 'as may be required or taken up from time to time for settlement, mining, lumbering, trading and other purposes.'[49]

The judiciary has interpreted extinguishment clauses such as the one contained in Treaty 9 in accordance with the Crown's understanding of the treaty process as a means of formally dispossessing Aboriginal people of ancestral territory in return for reserve land and certain state benefits. The judiciary typically holds that the legal effect of an extinguishment clause is to preclude an Aboriginal nation from asserting Aboriginal title to its ancestral territory in a Canadian court of law.[50] This is not to say that extinguishment of title precludes Aboriginal people from asserting rights to engage in particular practices on ancestral territories. Such rights may have been left unaffected by the treaty in question,[51] or they may have been expressly protected by its terms, as with the rights to hunt, trap and fish protected by Treaty 9. But the fact that the judiciary has interpreted treaties as severing the legal bonds between an Aboriginal nation and its ancestral territory is a source of profound disempowerment. However much they may vary from nation to nation, Aboriginal relationships with ancestral territory are critical to Aboriginal identities. The severing of these relationships and the relocation of Aboriginal peoples to reserves have had a devastating effect on Aboriginal peoples' ability to maintain Aboriginal ways of life. Equating the legal effect of an extinguishment clause with Crown policy operates on the assumption that treaties are instruments of dispossession, not instruments of mutual recognition.

As I argued in the previous chapter, treaties that purport to extinguish Aboriginal title ought to be understood in light of the new interpretive framework developed by the Supreme Court of Canada. The judiciary must demand strict proof that Aboriginal signatories under-

48 Ibid.
49 Ibid.
50 See, for example, *R. v. Howard*, [1994] 2 S.C.R. 299.
51 See, for example, *R. v. Adams*, [1996] 3 S.C.R. 101.

stood they were signing away their territorial interests in exchange for rights to engage in particular practices on surrendered lands and other benefits. Given cultural and linguistic differences, the written text alone should not be sufficient proof of actual consent. Without such proof, an extinguishment clause ought to declared void and of no legal effect. Assuming it can be proven that Aboriginal signatories actually consented to the extinguishment of their title, distributive justice demands more than the mere enforcement of such an agreement. It requires determining what the parties would have agreed to under conditions of equality and acknowledging that Aboriginal signatories would probably not have agreed to the extinguishment of title in such circumstances. In other words, it requires interpreting a treaty in a manner that bridges the gap between actual and hypothetical consent.

This approach is consistent with the proposition that treaties between Aboriginal peoples and the Crown are more than contractual arrangements; they represent constitutional accords that distribute constitutional authority between the parties. To ensure the justice of such distributions, the judiciary should scrutinize the adequacy of consideration received in light of any actual agreement concerning the extinguishment of Aboriginal title. At the very least, it requires interpreting vague treaty language to reflect what Aboriginal signatories would have agreed to had they possessed greater equality of bargaining power. It requires separating the extinguishment of title from the protection of rights associated with title and interpreting the former narrowly and the latter broadly.[52] Treaty 9 rights to hunt, trap, and fish, for example, ought to include rights to engage in practices reasonably incidental to hunting, trapping, and fishing;[53] rights to hunt, trap, and fish for commercial purposes;[54] and the right to expect that hunting, trapping and fishing will continue to be successful, measured by reference to the fruits of past practice.[55]

---

52 See *R. v. Adams*, at 117 ('while claims to Aboriginal title fall within the conceptual framework of Aboriginal rights, Aboriginal rights do not exist solely where a claim to Aboriginal title has been made out').

53 See *R. v. Simon*, [1985] 2 S.C.R. 387.

54 See *R. v. Horseman*, [1990] 1 S.C.R. 901 (numbered treaties protect the right to hunt for commercial purposes).

55 See generally Michael C. Blumm, 'Native Fishing Rights and Environmental Protection in North America and New Zealand: A Comparative Analysis of Profits A Prendre and Habitat Servitudes,' 4 Canterbury L. Rev. 211 (1990).

This approach also calls for narrow interpretations of provisions that qualify the exercise of such rights. As stated, Treaty 9 rights are 'subject to such regulations as may from time to time be made by the Government of the Country, acting under the authority of His Majesty.'[56] The 'Government of the Country' ought to be understood as referring to the federal government and not to provincial governments.[57] Moreover, this internal qualification should not free the government from its obligation to demonstrate that regulations that interfere with the exercise of a treaty right meet constitutional standards of justification.[58] Treaty 9's second qualification, that treaty rights do not extend to tracts of land 'as may be required or taken up from time to time for settlement, mining, lumbering, trading and other purposes' should not be interpreted as authorizing the Crown to unilaterally restrict Aboriginal access to and use of ancestral territories for any purpose. The judiciary should interpret 'other purposes' to refer to purposes that do not conflict with the exercise of treaty rights.[59] More generally, it ought to interpret this clause in a way that guarantees Aboriginal people continued access to and use of ancestral territory, and requires the Crown to justify its actions.

Limiting Aboriginal and Treaty Rights

Interests associated with indigenous difference thus provide insight into the nature and scope of Aboriginal and treaty rights recognized and affirmed by subsection 35(1) of the Constitution Act, 1982. Protecting cultural interests requires an interpretation of subsection 35(1) that does not depend on either a core-periphery distinction or a pre-contact referent for Aboriginal cultural customs, practices, or traditions. Protecting Aboriginal territorial interests requires an expansive understanding of Aboriginal title. Protecting interests associated with Aboriginal sovereignty necessitates interpreting the constitution as recognizing an existing Aboriginal right of self-government. And protecting interests asso-

---

56 Ibid.
57 See, for example, *R. v. Batisse* (1987), 84 D.L.R. (4th) 377 (Ont. Dist. Ct.); *Cheecho v. R.*, [1981] 3 C.N.L.R. 45 (Ont. Dist. Ct.).
58 See Brian Slattery, 'Understanding Aboriginal Rights,' 66 Can. Bar Rev. 727 at 727 (1987).
59 See *R. v. Smith*, [1935] 3 D.L.R. 703 (Sask. C.A.); *R. v. Mirasty*, [1942] 1 W.W.R. 343 (Sask. Pol. Ct.), two cases suggesting that such a qualification should not be subject to the ejusdem generis rule, but decided well before the emergence of the new interpretive framework.

ciated with the treaty process requires interpreting treaties in a manner consistent with Aboriginal understandings, flexible to evolving practices, and inclusive of reasonably incidental practices, and in a way that best reconciles the competing interests of the parties.

But understanding the nature and scope of existing Aboriginal and treaty rights in light of their underlying interests does not end the inquiry. In *Sparrow*, the Supreme Court of Canada established that subsection 35(1) rights are not absolute. The court found that the constitution had been infringed by the federal fishing regulation in question but it also held that in certain circumstances subsection 35(1) infringements are constitutionally justifiable. Although it recognized that, unlike subsection 1 of the Charter, the text of subsection 35(1) does not mention justified limits to Aboriginal rights, the court reasoned that '[f]ederal legislative powers continue, including, of course, the rights to legislate with respect to Indians pursuant to s.91(24) of the *Constitution Act, 1867*. These powers must, however, now be read together with s.35(1). In other words, federal power must be reconciled with federal duty and the best way to achieve that reconciliation is to demand the justification of any government regulation that infringes upon or denies aboriginal rights. Such scrutiny is in keeping with the ... concept of holding the Crown to a high standard of honourable dealing with respect to the aboriginal peoples of Canada.'[60] In other words, if continuing federal legislative power means that laws and regulations may interfere with Aboriginal rights recognized by the constitution, federal duty demands the justification of such interference. The fiduciary relationship between Aboriginal people and the Crown triggers a constitutional obligation on the part of the Crown to justify state actions that interfere with the exercise of an Aboriginal right. Governments can lawfully interfere with the exercise of existing Aboriginal and treaty rights only if the interference in question meets certain standards of justification.[61]

Although 'the contours of a justificatory standard must be defined in the specific factual context of each case,'[62] the court in *Sparrow* required a two-stage analysis in the event of a prima facie infringement of subsection 35(1). The first stage asks whether the government is pursuing a compelling and substantial legislative objective; the second asks whether

---

60 *R. v. Sparrow*, at 1109.
61 See also *R. v. Badger*, [1996] 1 S.C.R. 771 (requiring justification of prima facie infringements of treaty rights).
62 *R. v. Sparrow*, at 1111.

the way in which this objective is attained is consistent with the Crown's fiduciary obligations to Aboriginal peoples. If the law seeks to achieve a compelling and substantial governmental objective in a manner consistent with the Crown's fiduciary obligation, the interference in question will be regarded as a constitutionally acceptable exercise of state power.

The fact that the relationship between the Crown and Aboriginal people is fiduciary in nature informed both stages of the justification analysis in *Sparrow*. The court saw conservation as a compelling and substantial governmental objective and noted that other 'objectives purporting to prevent the exercise of subsection 35(1) rights that would cause harm to the general populace or to aboriginal peoples themselves' would also meet this threshold.[63] Because such objectives either seek to preserve subsection 35(1) rights or to ensure that the exercise of such rights will be compatible with the rights of others, they are consistent with the more basic proposition that federal power ought to be interpreted in light of federal duty. As stated by Chief Justice Dickson and Mr Justice La Forest, 'Canada's aboriginal peoples are justified in worrying about government objectives that may be superficially neutral but which constitute *de facto* threats to the existence of aboriginal rights and interests.'[64] The existence of a fiduciary relationship between the Crown and Aboriginal people also means that the Crown at the second stage must demonstrate that 'any allocation of priorities after valid conservation measures have been implemented' gives 'top priority' to Aboriginal interests.[65] The court indicated that other cases may require determining whether the infringement has been as minimal as possible in order to effect the desired result; whether fair compensation has been made available in the event of expropriation; and whether there has been adequate consultation with affected Aboriginal people with respect to the implementation of conservation measures.[66]

In two recent decisions, however, the court has provided another, less convincing rationale for requiring justification of state action that interferes with the exercise of Aboriginal rights. In *R. v. Gladstone*, at issue was whether the Heiltsuk people in British Columbia possessed an

---

63 Ibid., at 1113.

64 Ibid., at 1110.

65 Ibid., at 1116.

66 The court in *Sparrow* ordered a retrial to allow for findings of fact to determine whether the net length restriction constituted an infringement of the Musqueam right to fish and, if so, whether such regulation was justifiable according to the two-stage inquiry.

Aboriginal right to fish for commercial purposes.[67] Chief Justice Lamer held that the Heiltsuk enjoyed such a right and went on to inquire whether the state action in question justifiably interfered with this right. Although he held that there was insufficient evidence to determine the question of justification and ordered a new trial, he took the opportunity to comment at length on *Sparrow*'s justification inquiry.

With respect to the first stage of the justification inquiry, the chief justice nudged aside the relevance of the fiduciary relationship between the Crown and Aboriginal people in favour of what he regarded as the purpose underlying constitutional recognition and affirmation of existing Aboriginal and treaty rights. He held that the purpose of subsection 35(1) rights is to reconcile Aboriginal prior occupancy with Crown sovereignty. Holding that this purpose must also inform the justifiable limits of such rights, he reasoned that it assists in determining whether an infringement furthers a compelling and substantial governmental objective. In his view,

> objectives which can be said to be compelling and substantial will be those directed at either the recognition of the prior occupation of North America by aboriginal peoples or – and at the level of justification it is this purpose which may well be most relevant – at the reconciliation of aboriginal prior occupation with the assertion of the sovereignty of the Crown ... Aboriginal rights are recognized and affirmed by s. 35(1) in order to reconcile the existence of distinctive aboriginal societies prior to the arrival of Europeans in North America with the assertion of Crown sovereignty over that territory; they are the means by which the critical and integral aspects of those societies are maintained. Because, however, distinctive aboriginal societies exist within, and are a part of, a broader social, political and economic community, over which the Crown is sovereign, there are circumstances in which, in order to pursue objectives of compelling and substantial importance to that community as a whole (taking into account the fact that aboriginal societies are a part of that community), some limitation of those rights will be justifiable. Aboriginal rights are a necessary part of the reconciliation of aboriginal societies with the broader political community of which they are part; limits placed on those rights are, where the objectives furthered by those limits are of sufficient importance to the broader community as a whole, *equally* a necessary part of that reconciliation. [68]

---

67 *R. v. Gladstone*, [1996] 2 S.C.R. 723.
68 Ibid., at 774–5 (emphasis in original).

By defining a 'compelling and substantial purpose' in light of the need to reconcile Aboriginal prior occupancy with Canadian sovereignty, Chief Justice Lamer generated a more expansive list of governmental objectives acceptable under the first stage of the justification inquiry, including 'the pursuit of economic and regional fairness, and the recognition of the historical reliance upon, and participation in, the fishery by non-aboriginal groups.' In his view, such objectives are constitutionally acceptable to the extent they are 'in the interests of all Canadians,' including Aboriginal peoples, and because 'the reconciliation of aboriginal societies with the rest of Canadian society' may depend on their successful achievement.[69]

In *Delgamuukw v. British Columbia*, Chief Justice Lamer further marginalized the relevance of the Crown's fiduciary relationship to the first stage of the justification inquiry. He interpreted *Sparrow*'s holding that conservation is an acceptable governmental objective as consistent with what he regarded as the purpose of subsection 35(1) – the reconciliation of Aboriginal prior occupancy with Canadian sovereignty. In his view, '[t]he conservation of fisheries ... simultaneously recognizes that fishing is integral to many aboriginal cultures, and also seeks to reconcile aboriginal societies with the broader community by ensuring that there are fish enough for all.'[70] Having established that the reconciliation of Aboriginal prior occupancy with Canadian sovereignty and not the Crown's fiduciary relationship with Aboriginal peoples ought to inform a finding of whether a governmental objective is compelling and substantial, the chief justice proceeded to add to *Gladstone*'s list of acceptable governmental objectives:

[I]n the wake of *Gladstone*, the range of legislative objectives that can justify the infringement of aboriginal title is fairly broad. Most of these objectives can be traced to the reconciliation of the prior occupation of North America by aboriginal peoples with the assertion of Crown sovereignty, which entails the recognition that 'distinctive aboriginal societies exist within, and are a part of, a broader social, political and economic community.' In my opinion, the development of agriculture, forestry, mining, and hydroelectric power, the general economic development of the interior of British Columbia, protection of the environment or endangered species, the

---

69 Ibid., at 775.
70 *Delgamuukw v. British Columbia*, at 1108.

building of infrastructure and the settlement of foreign populations to support those aims, are the kinds of objectives that are consistent with this purpose and, in principle, can justify the infringement of aboriginal title.[71]

The expansive nature of this list makes it clear that few laws that interfere with the exercise of Aboriginal rights will be considered as insufficiently compelling or substantial to meet the first stage of the justification inquiry.

Two problems present themselves. First, the court fails to explain why this list of acceptable governmental objectives follows from what it regards as the purpose of subsection 35(1). If the purpose underlying constitutional recognition and affirmation of existing Aboriginal rights is to reconcile Aboriginal prior occupancy with Crown sovereignty, why does such a reconciliation justify a law that interferes with the exercise of an Aboriginal or treaty right on the basis that it furthers the interests of the broader community? On the contrary, Aboriginal rights ought to operate to prevent governments from interfering with their exercise for purposes of simply advancing the broader community's interests. 'Reconciliation' just as easily supports the proposition that governmental objectives such as the development of agriculture, forestry, mining, and hydroelectric power and the general economic development of the interior of a province are not sufficiently compelling and substantial to warrant interfering with Aboriginal and treaty rights. Assuming that subsection 35(1) rights are not absolute, governments can no doubt pursue certain governmental objectives that limit their exercise. But authorizing such a wide range of acceptable governmental objectives defeats the very reconciliation purportedly embodied in the constitutionalization of existing Aboriginal and treaty rights.

Chief Justice Lamer attempts to render the concept of reconciliation more determinate by claiming that it entails that 'distinctive aboriginal societies exist within, and are a part of, a broader social, political and economic community.'[72] But this merely restates the issue, namely, under what circumstances can governments interfere with the exercise of Aboriginal and treaty rights in the name of the 'larger, social, political and economic community'? That Aboriginal people also belong to the broader community should not obscure the fact that this issue will

---

71 Ibid., at 1111 (quoting *Gladstone*).
72 Ibid., at 1107.

arise exactly when Aboriginal interests and those of the broader community are in conflict. The court's list suggests that governments can compromise constitutional rights to satisfy community interests. It ignores the fact that interests associated with indigenous difference receive constitutional protection whereas community interests, generally speaking, do not. In other words, it ignores the fact that the constitution recognizes and affirms existing Aboriginal and treaty rights precisely to protect interests associated with indigenous difference from governments seeking to satisfy community interests.[73]

Second, these deficiencies in the court's treatment of the first stage of the justification inquiry arise because its formulation of the purpose of subsection 35(1) fails to take into account its underlying interests. The purpose of subsection 35(1), properly understood, is to provide constitutional protection to interests associated with indigenous difference. This purpose should not only inform the nature and scope of Aboriginal and treaty rights recognized by the constitution, it should also assist in determining whether a governmental objective is sufficiently compelling and substantial to justify an infringement of an Aboriginal or treaty right. If the purpose of subsection 35(1) is to protect interests associated with indigenous difference from the interests of the broader community, then laws that simply embody interests of the broader community should not be seen as sufficiently compelling to justify limiting the exercise of an Aboriginal or treaty right. In contrast, the approach adopted in *Sparrow* – upholding a violation if it preserves subsection 35(1) rights, prevents the exercise of subsection 35(1) rights that would harm the general population or Aboriginal people themselves, or ensures that the exercise of subsection 35(1) rights will be compatible with the rights (and not simply interests) of others – properly acknowledges the purpose of subsection 35(1) in the first stage of the justification analysis.

Recall that in *Sparrow* the court held that the federal government, because of its fiduciary duty to Aboriginal people, is required to give priority to Aboriginal fishing interests after the implementation of valid conservation objectives. In *Gladstone*, Chief Justice Lamer emphasized the importance of the Crown's fiduciary duty to this second stage of the justification analysis but drew a distinction between a right to fish for

---

73 Compare Kent McNeil, *Defining Aboriginal Title in the Nineties: Has the Supreme Court Finally Got It Right?* (Toronto: Robarts Centre for Canadian Studies, 1998), at 19 (the list of acceptable governmental objectives in *Gladstone* turns 'the Constitution on its head by allowing interests that are not constitutional to trump rights that are').

food or social and ceremonial reasons and a right to engage in commercial fishing. He held that the former type of right involves an internal limit, as 'at a certain point the band will have sufficient fish to meet these needs.'[74] In contrast, the latter involves no such limit save for the 'external constraints of the demand of the market and the availability of the resource.'[75] In such a case, the government is not required to grant Aboriginal rights-holders an exclusive right to fish after conservation goals are met. Instead, the doctrine of priority requires that the government demonstrate that, in allocating the resource, it has taken account of the existence of Aboriginal rights and allocated the resource in a manner respectful of the fact that those rights have priority over the exploitation of the fishery by other users. This right is at once both procedural and substantive; at the stage of justification the government must demonstrate both that the process by which it allocated the resource and the actual allocation of the resource which results from that process reflect the prior interest of Aboriginal rights-holders in the fishery.[76]

This distinction allows governments, after conservation requirements have been met, to limit the extent to which Aboriginal right-holders can rely on a commercial Aboriginal right in order to allocate shares in the resource to non-Aboriginal harvesters. In other words, the Crown's fiduciary duty does not prevent the government from interfering with constitutionally protected Aboriginal interests in order to legislate for the protection of non-Aboriginal interests. Left unexplained in *Gladstone* is how non-Aboriginal interests, which do not correspond to any constitutional entitlement of the non-Aboriginal harvesters, can trump Aboriginal interests that are protected as a matter of constitutional right. It may be that the court is unwilling to regard the commercial Aboriginal right in question in exclusive terms, that is, as preventing others from participating in the fishery. But its definition of an Aboriginal right does not foreclose constitutional recognition of a custom, practice, or tradition that contemplates exclusivity of access to and use of a resource. Nor does it explain why exclusivity is inappropriate in the context of a commercial right. The court's distinction between a right that possesses an 'internal limit' and a right that possesses no such limit does not help much. While it may capture a salient descriptive differ-

---

74 *Gladstone*, at 764.
75 Ibid.
76 *Delgamuukw*, at 1109.

ence between a right to fish for food and a right to fish for commercial purposes, it does not justify either the conclusion that a commercial Aboriginal right must be non-exclusive or the proposition that interests of non-Aboriginal harvesters should take precedence over Aboriginal interests that are otherwise entitled to constitutional protection.

In *Delgamuukw*, Chief Justice Lamer also emphasized in the second stage of the justification inquiry the relevance of the Crown's fiduciary duty to Aboriginal people. However, he made it clear that the duty does not require a government to accord priority to Aboriginal interests over community interests even in circumstances where the Aboriginal right in question involves a right to exclusive use and enjoyment of the resource in question. According to the chief justice, a law that interferes with rights associated with Aboriginal title might nonetheless comply with the Crown's fiduciary duty if it can be shown that the government has provided for 'participation of aboriginal peoples in the development of ... resources ..., that the conferral of fee simples for agriculture, and of leases and licenses for forestry and mining reflect the prior occupation of aboriginal title lands, [or] that economic barriers to aboriginal uses of their lands (e.g., licensing fees) [will be] somewhat reduced.'[77] He also held that '[i]n keeping with the duty of honour and good faith on the Crown, fair compensation will ordinarily be required when aboriginal title is infringed.'[78]

In support of his conclusion that community interests can take precedence over Aboriginal interests in the above circumstances, Chief Justice Lamer acknowledged that 'the fiduciary relationship between the Crown and aboriginal peoples demands that Aboriginal interests be placed first.' However, he also stated that 'the fiduciary duty does not demand that aboriginal rights always be given priority.'[79] But it is not at all clear how Aboriginal interests are 'placed first' by a law that interferes with the exercise of an Aboriginal right and fails to give priority to Aboriginal interests when allocating a resource among citizens. In both *Gladstone* and *Delgamuukw*, the court failed to grasp the simple proposition that Aboriginal rights ought to protect interests associated with indigenous difference against laws that further wider community interests. By exploiting the flexibility inherent in the proposition that 'the requirements of the fiduciary duty are a function of the "legal and fac-

77 Ibid., at 1112.
78 Ibid., at 1114.
79 Ibid., at 1108–9.

tual context" of each appeal,' the court permits a wide range of initiatives that interfere with the exercise of Aboriginal rights in the name of community interests that do not independently merit constitutional protection.[80] Its near-total abandonment of the need to accord priority to Aboriginal interests enables governments to take away by legislation what the constitution, properly understood, guarantees.

Instead of the approach proposed by the court, the first stage of the justification analysis ought to perform a gatekeeping function, requiring laws that interfere with the exercise of Aboriginal rights to further a 'compelling and substantial purpose.' Because it is the case that all laws, at some level, further community interests, such a standard requires an examination of the actual community interest at stake and a demonstration that the community interest merits interfering with an Aboriginal right. Laws that preserve subsection 35(1) rights, prevent the exercise of subsection 35(1) rights that harm to general population or Aboriginal people themselves, or ensure compatibility between the exercise of subsection 35(1) rights and the rights of others are the type of laws that ought to be regarded as furthering a compelling and substantial purpose. Even where a law possesses such a purpose, the Crown's fiduciary duty to Aboriginal people requires not only that it provide compensation for the interference in question but also that it legislate in a manner that accords priority to Aboriginal interests in circumstances involving resource allocation.

---

80 Ibid., at 1108, quoting *Gladstone*.

Chapter Seven

Indigenous Difference and the Charter

The clan system is a social order. The clan system is a justice system. The clan system is a government. The clan system is an extended family unit.

Leonard Nelson, Roseau River, 1992[1]

Thus far I have proposed that to the extent Canada aspires to a just constitutional order, Aboriginal interests with respect to culture, territory, sovereignty, and the treaty process require constitutional protection in the form of a wide-ranging set of Aboriginal and treaty rights. In this chapter, I examine another set of rights, the rights and freedoms guaranteed to all Canadians by the Canadian Charter of Rights and Freedoms. What bearing do rights guaranteed by the Charter have on the constitutional relationship between Aboriginal people and the Canadian state? Some scholars have argued that the Charter, premised on liberal values of individual autonomy and freedom, threatens Aboriginal forms of social organization premised on collective values of community and responsibility. Standards regulating the exercise of Aboriginal power should not be imposed on Aboriginal communities from the outside; instead, they ought to emerge from within. Aboriginal communities should perhaps be afforded the opportunity to develop their own codes of conduct to constrain the exercise of Aboriginal power,

---

1 Leonard Nelson, Roseau River, Manitoba, 8 Dec. 1992, testifying before the Royal Commission on Aboriginal Peoples, quoted in Royal Commission on Aboriginal Peoples, *Final Report*, vol. 2, *Restructuring the Relationship* (Ottawa: Minister of Supply and Services, 1996), at 128.

which could serve as alternatives to the Charter.[2] In contrast, others have argued that the Charter provides protection to less powerful members of Aboriginal societies against potential abuses of Aboriginal governmental power. Certain collective values informing Aboriginal societies ought to be subject to constitutional norms embodied in the Charter, particularly those that relate to gender equality and non-discrimination.[3]

In my view, the Charter does pose a risk to the continued vitality of indigenous difference. The Charter enables litigants to constitutionally interrogate the rich complexity of Aboriginal societies according to a rigid analytic grid of individual right and state obligation. It authorizes judicial reorganization of Aboriginal societies according to non-Aboriginal values. It threatens to 'convert and corral what little is left of a culture that is so very different from the dominant one, including substantial diversity within itself.'[4] But the Charter is more indeterminate or flexible than it first appears. It presents numerous interpretive opportunities to minimize the corrosive effects that litigation might have on Aboriginal forms of social organization and to maximize the protection it affords to less powerful members of Aboriginal societies. Of course, demonstrating indeterminacy will not erase fears about the Charter's effect on indigenous difference, as the critical question is not whether the Charter is open to a range of possible interpretations but which interpretations will prevail. While I make no predictions in this regard, a number of prescriptions designed to mimimize the Charter's potential to erode legal protection of indigenous difference are offered below.

---

2 See Mary Ellen Turpel, 'Aboriginal Peoples and the Canadian Charter: Interpretive Monopolies, Cultural Differences,' 6 Canadian Human Rights Yearbook 3 at 30 (1989–90) ('[t]he collective or communal basis of Aboriginal life does not ... have a parallel to individual rights; the conceptions of law are simply incommensurable'); and Anthony Long and Katherine Beaty Chiste, 'Indian Governments and the Canadian Charter of Rights and Freedoms,' 18 American Indian Culture and Research J. 91 (1994). See also W.A. Bogart, *Courts and Country: The Limits of Litigation and the Social and Political Life of Canada* (Oxford: Oxford University Press, 1994), at 271–7.

3 See Teressa Nahanee, 'Dancing with a Gorilla: Aboriginal Women, Justice and the Charter,' in Royal Commission on Aboriginal Peoples, *Aboriginal Peoples and the Criminal Justice System* (Ottawa: Supply and Services, 1993), 359–82. See also John Borrows, 'Contemporary Traditional Equality: The Effect of the Charter on First Nations Politics,' in David Schneiderman and Kate Sutherland, eds., *Charting the Consequences: The Impact of Charter Rights on Canadian Law & Politics* (Toronto: University of Toronto Press, 1997), 169–99.

4 Bogart, *Courts and Country*, at 275.

One obvious source of constitutional flexibility lies in jurisprudence addressing section 1 of the Charter, which guarantees rights and freedoms set out in the Charter 'subject only to such reasonable limits prescribed by law as can be demonstrably justified in a free and democratic society.' Generally speaking, section 1 operates to save a law that violates a right or freedom guaranteed by the Charter if the objective of that law is of sufficient importance to warrant overriding a constitutionally protected right or freedom and the means used are proportionate to the end sought to be achieved.[5] Courts have been wary of concluding that legislation associated with indigenous difference possesses an objective insufficiently important to warrant overriding a constitutional right or freedom.[6] The judiciary has also signalled a willingness to accord deference to legislative attempts to reconcile competing social, economic, and political interests.[7] Both aspects of section 1 jurisprudence provide numerous interpretive opportunities to minimize the Charter's corrosive potential with respect to laws that seek to protect aspects of indigenous difference.

My focus here, however, is on a number of issues that are analytically prior to the role that section 1 might play in minimizing any negative effects of Charter litigation on indigenous difference. I first examine the extent to which the Charter governs the exercise of Aboriginal governmental power, which necessitates an inquiry into the relationship between Aboriginal power and state power. I then turn to the constitutionality of laws that distinguish between Aboriginal people and non-Aboriginal people. Depending on their purpose and effect, such laws may implicate a wide range of rights and freedoms guaranteed by the

---

5 See *R. v. Oakes*, [1986] 1 S.C.R. 103. For an extended analysis of the court's treatment of s. 1, see David M. Beatty, *Constitutional Law in Theory and Practice* (Toronto: University of Toronto Press, 1995), at 61–102. See also Lorraine E. Weinrib, 'The Supreme Court of Canada and Section One of the Charter,' 10 Supreme Court L. Rev. 489 (1988). For an analysis of the relationship between ss. 15 and 1, see Dale Gibson, *The Law of the Charter: Equality Rights* (Calgary: Carswell, 1990), at 264–72, 326–8.
6 See, for example, *Eastmain Band v. Gilpin*, [1988] 3 C.N.L.R. (Que. Prov. Ct.) (upholding a band by-law establishing a curfew for children under sixteen years of age).
7 See, for example, *McKinney v. University of Guelph*, [1990] 3 S.C.R. 229 (mandatory retirement); *Irwin Toy Ltd. v. Quebec*, [1989] 1 S.C.R. 927 (children's advertising). See generally David M. Beatty, *Talking Heads and the Supremes: The Canadian Production of Judicial Review* (Scarborough, Ont.: Carswell, 1990). See also Robin Elliott, 'The Supreme Court of Canada and Section One: The Erosion of the Common Front,' 12 Queen's L.J. 277 (1987).

Charter, including the right to life, liberty, and security of the person
(s. 7); the right against unreasonable search and seizure (s. 8); the right
against arbitrary detention and imprisonment (s. 9); rights to counsel
and to habeas corpus (s. 10); rights to a trial and to an independent and
impartial tribunal (s. 11(d)); and the right to be protected from cruel
and unusual punishment (s. 12). My inquiry in this chapter is restricted
to section 15 of the Charter, which prohibits governments from discrim-
inating on certain grounds when distributing benefits and burdens
among individuals but which authorizes the enactment of affirmative
action programs. I then examine section 25, which instructs the judiciary to interpret Charter rights so as to not abrogate or derogate from
rights that pertain to Aboriginal people.

Aboriginal Power and the Public/Private Distinction

The Charter is generally conceived of as primarily concerned with the
exercise of public, not private, power. Rights and freedoms guaranteed
by the Charter purport to carve out a private zone of autonomy into
which public power is restricted from entering. An individual's freedom
of expression, for example, protects his or her speech acts from certain
forms of state regulation. Similarly, the right to life, liberty, and security
of the person protects an individual's body from intrusive state actions.
The dominant understanding of the Charter is that it does not protect
individual autonomy from the exercise of private power.[8] Employees do
not enjoy a constitutional right to express themselves freely to their private employers. Tenants do not enjoy a constitutional right to be free of
discrimination by private landlords. While human rights legislation may
provide statutory protection against private actors in many instances,
Charter jurisprudence draws a distinction between public and private
spheres and seeks only to protect aspects of the latter sphere from certain actions occurring in the former.[9]

---

8 See *RWDSU, Local 580 v. Dolphin Delivery Ltd.*, [1986] 2 S.C.R. 573 at 599 ('the Charter
   applies to the common law but not between private parties').
9 For a sampling of critiques of the public/private distinction as it relates to the Charter,
   see Joel Bakan, *Just Words: Constitutional Rights and Social Wrongs* (Toronto: University
   of Toronto Press, 1997), 47–51; Allan Hutchinson, *Waiting for CORAF: A Critique of Law
   and Rights* (Toronto: University of Toronto Press, 1995), 123–53; David Beatty, 'Constitutional Conceits: The Coercive Authority of Courts,' 37 U.T.L.J. 183 (1987); Judy
   Fudge, 'The Public/Private Distinction: The Possibilities of and the Limits to the Use
   of Charter Litigation to Further Feminist Struggles,' 25 Osgoode Hall L.J. 485 (1987);

Aboriginal power – power that takes the form of Aboriginal and treaty rights by virtue of constitutional recognition of indigenous difference – appears to confound the public/private distinction. To the extent that it is recognized by but does not emanate from the Canadian state, Aboriginal power is not of the public realm. But to the extent that it addresses fundamental matters of social, economic, and political life, it is not of the private realm. Indeed, attempting to characterize Aboriginal power as either public or private exemplifies the threat that the Charter poses to the continued vitality of Aboriginal societies. Understanding Aboriginal power as either public or private requires suppressing unique aspects of indigenous difference in order to facilitate its comprehension in terms familiar to non-Aboriginal categories of understanding. To speak of Aboriginal power as though it were conceptually independent of the power of the Canadian state, however, is to ignore the multiple ways in which Aboriginal and state power reinforce and relate to each other. Judicial developments in the law of Aboriginal title, for example, have dramatic distributive effects on Aboriginal power, despite the fact that Aboriginal title is not contingent on state action but is instead rooted in Aboriginal prior occupancy. And, as discussed in Chapter 3, the relative bargaining power of parties to treaty negotiations is a function of judicial distribution of proprietary power. Moreover, Aboriginal power intersects with state power on more than the judicial plane; executive and legislative initiatives also profoundly affect the nature and extent of power that an Aboriginal community possesses under Canadian law.

The proposition that the Charter is primarily concerned with the exercise of public, not private, power finds support in judicial interpretations of section 32, which provides as follows:

32 (1) This Charter applies
(a) to the Parliament and government of Canada in respect of all matters within the authority of Parliament including all matters relating to the Yukon Territory and Northwest Territories; and

---

Hester Lessard, 'The Idea of the "Private": A Discussion of State Action Doctrine and Separate Sphere Ideology,' 10 Dalh. L.J. 107 (1986). For a discussion of the distinction as it relates to Aboriginal women, see Jennifer Koshan, 'Sounds of Silence: The Public/Private Dichotomy, Violence, and Aboriginal Women,' in Susan B. Boyd, ed., *Challenging the Public/Private Divide: Feminism, Law, and Public Policy* (Toronto: University of Toronto Press, 1997), 87–109.

(b) to the legislature and government of each province in respect of all matters within the authority of the legislature of each province.

Section 32 subjects the exercise of federal, provincial, and territorial governmental power to Charter scrutiny.[10] Accordingly, it authorizes constitutional scrutiny of federal and provincial statutes that distribute benefits and burdens based on indigenous difference. To the extent that Aboriginal power is partly constituted by statutory burdens and benefits, it is indirectly subject to the application of the Charter. For example, the federal Indian Act treats some Aboriginal people differently than non-Aboriginal people. It could be challenged as contrary to subsection 15(1) of the Charter, which guarantees that '[e]very individual is equal before and under the law and has the right to the equal protection and equal benefit of the law without discrimination.' Provincial laws that distinguish between Aboriginal and non-Aboriginal people face similar constitutional scrutiny. But are Aboriginal laws subject to the Charter? Does section 32 subject the exercise of Aboriginal governmental authority to Charter scrutiny?

Because Aboriginal governmental authority can manifest itself in a variety of ways, whether and how it implicates the Charter depends on whether it is delegated, treaty-based, or inherent in nature. Delegated authority refers to a particular kind of statutory benefit, namely, the power delegated by the federal or provincial governments to an Aboriginal government to make law, such as the statutory authority band councils currently exercise pursuant to the Indian Act. Treaty-based authority refers to Aboriginal power recognized by treaty. Inherent authority refers to Aboriginal power that flows from an inherent right of self-government recognized and affirmed by subsection 35(1) of the Constitution Act, 1982. Applying the Charter to these forms of Aboriginal governmental authority provides the judiciary with an opportunity to protect a zone of individual autonomy from the exercise of Aboriginal power, underscoring fears that the Charter will have the effect of undermining interests associated with indigenous difference.

Delegated authority, such as the authority of a band council under the Indian Act, cannot escape the requirements of the Charter because

---

10 See *RWDSU, Local 580 v. Dolphin Delivery Ltd.*, at 598 ('the Charter will apply ... [to] the legislative, executive and administrative branches of government').

Parliament cannot authorize action that violates its guarantees.[11] A legislative grant of statutory discretion will be interpreted as not conferring the power to infringe the Charter. [12] For example, the Charter has been held to apply to a municipal by-law, made under statutory authority, that prohibited postering on municipal public property.[13] But the actor exercising delegated authority must also be one to whom the Charter applies; private corporations, for instance, exercise delegated statutory authority but the Charter does not apply to them because they have not been invested with authority to implement specific governmental policies. They and other actors do not form part of 'government' within the meaning of section 32. Whether the Charter binds a band council will turn on whether the judiciary considers such a government to be a 'government actor' as defined by jurisprudence on the scope of section 32.

In *McKinney v. University of Guelph*, La Forest J., for a plurality of the court, held that an entity is a 'governmental actor' if it either performs a 'quintessentially governmental function' or operates under such a degree of government control that its decisions in fact can be said to be decisions of government itself.[14] Under this test, a band council will be hard-pressed to avoid the application of the Charter: characterizations that lessen the likelihood of it being viewed as governmental actor under the test's second branch increase the likelihood of it being viewed as such under the first. The more a band council is characterized as autonomous from government, the more likely it will be exercising 'quintessentially' governmental functions. That a band council may not exercise these functions in a typically 'Canadian' manner will probably not affect a determination of whether the Charter applies to the exercise of band council authority. Instead, the issue will be whether the exercise of band council authority runs contrary to the Charter. If a band council is characterized as not exercising 'quintessentially governmental functions,' this characterization will probably result from the

11 See, for example, *Eldridge v. British Columbia*, [1997] 3 S.C.R. 624; see also *James v. Cowan*, [1932] A.C. 542 at 558 ('[t]he Constitution is not to be mocked by substituting executive for legislative interference with freedom').

12 See, for example, *Slaight Communications Inc. v. Davidson*, [1989] 1 S.C.R. 1038 at 1078 ('[l]egislation conferring an imprecise discretion must ... be interpreted as not allowing the Charter rights to be infringed').

13 *Ramsden v. Peterborough*, [1993] 2 S.C.R. 1084. See also *Eldridge v. British Columbia.*

14 *McKinney v. University of Guelph*, at 270; see also *Douglas/Kwantlen Faculty Association v. Douglas College*, [1990] 3 S.C.R. 570; *Stoffman v. Vancouver General Hospital*, [1990] 3 S.C.R. 483; and *Lavigne v. O.P.S.E.U.*, [1991] 2 S.C.R. 211.

fact that the council is delivering services designed by the federal government and is thereby subject to the Charter on the basis that it possesses little autonomy from government.[15]

With treaty-based Aboriginal governmental authority, the Charter applies at least to federal and provincial participation in the treaty process and, by extension, to the treaty itself. In *Lavigne v. OPSEU*, the Supreme Court of Canada held that the Charter applied to an agreement between a governmental employer and a trade union. According to La Forest J., '[t]o permit government to pursue policies violating Charter rights by means of contracts or agreements with other persons or bodies cannot be tolerated.'[16] The more a treaty resembles an act of recognition of Aboriginal rights either extinguished or not previously acknowledged by Canadian law, however, the less likely it will be construed as an executive or legislative grant of power to an entity to undertake actions that, because of the Charter, the federal and provincial governments themselves could not undertake. In such a case, parties to the treaty could include specific language stipulating that the Charter is to apply to Aboriginal governmental authority recognized by the agreement.[17] Even if the Charter does not independently apply to the exercise of inherent Aboriginal governmental authority, it likely applies on consent of the parties.

But what if the agreement was silent on the question or stipulated that the Charter was not to apply? If the Charter does not apply to the exercise of inherent Aboriginal governmental authority in the absence of a treaty, it is unlikely to apply to its exercise when recognized by a treaty. But if the Charter does apply to the exercise of inherent Aboriginal governmental authority in the absence of a treaty, the judiciary probably will not look kindly upon efforts to oust Charter rights by consent of the parties. It is true that constitutional rights can be waived in certain cir-

---

15 Lower courts have held that band councils are subject to the Charter because they exercise authority delegated by Parliament pursuant to the Indian Act: see, for example, *R. v. Campbell* (1996), 112 C.C.C. (3d) 107 (Man. C.A.); *Six Nations of the Grand River Band* v. *Henderson*, [1997] 1 C.N.L.R. 202 (Ont. Gen. Div.); *Crow v. Blood Band* (1996), 107 F.T.R. 270 (F.C.T.D.). But see Kent McNeil, 'Aboriginal Governments and the Canadian Charter of Rights and Freedoms,' 34 Osgoode Hall L.J. 61 (1996) (band council authority is inherent, not delegated, authority).

16 [1991] 2 S.C.R. 211 at 313. See also *Douglas/Kwanten Faculty Association v. Douglas College*.

17 See, for example, the Nisga'a Final Agreement between the Nisga'a Nation, the Government of British Columbia, and the Government of Canada (1998).

cumstances, notably within the criminal justice system.[18] However, a permanent, negotiated waiver of third-party Charter rights by treaty negotiators is a far cry from the individualized waiver of certain legal rights by a person confronting the criminal justice system.

It is therefore critical to determine whether the Charter applies to the exercise of inherent Aboriginal governmental authority that stems from an inherent right of self-government recognized and affirmed by subsection 35(1) of the Constitution Act, 1982. An answer to this question first requires an examination of the text of the Charter itself. As stated, section 32 of the Charter provides that the Charter applies to the Parliament and government of Canada and to the legislature and government of each province in respect of all matters that fall within each level's legislative authority. Section 32 can be read either exclusively or inclusively. An exclusive interpretation holds that section 32 provides an exhaustive list of authorities subject to the Charter's terms. Under this interpretation, the Charter would apply exclusively to the exercise of federal and provincial authority and not to the exercise of Aboriginal governmental authority recognized by the constitution.[19] In contrast, an inclusive interpretation holds that section 32 does not apply exclusively to the exercise of federal and provincial governmental authority nor does it provide an exhaustive list of authorities subject to the Charter's terms. Under this interpretation, the Charter would apply to the exercise of Aboriginal governmental authority recognized by the constitution.[20]

---

18 See *R. v. Morin*, [1992] 1 S.C.R. 771 at 790 (waiver of right to be tried within a reasonable time); *Clarkson v. The Queen*, [1986] 1 S.C.R. 383 at 394 (waiver of right to counsel); and *R. v. Turpin*, [1989] 1 S.C.R. 1296 at 1314–16 (waiver of right to the benefit of trial by jury).

19 For a description, but not endorsement, of an exclusive approach, see Royal Commission on Aboriginal Peoples, *Final Report*, vol. 2, pt. 1, at 229 ('not only does the section fail to mention Aboriginal governments specifically, its wording is not broad enough to cover them. Aboriginal governments are neither creatures of federal or provincial governments nor "matters within the authority" of those bodies. They constitute a distinct order of government whose authority is constitutionally guaranteed under section 35(1).').

20 For a description, and endorsement, of an inclusive approach, see ibid., at 228 ('[w]hile the section identifies some of the main government bodies subject to the Charter, it does not state that the Charter applies exclusively to those bodies or provide a complete list of government bodies affected. In effect, then, the section leaves open the possibility that there are other government bodies, not mentioned in the section, that are subject to the Charter's provisions. The tacit recognition of an Aboriginal order of government in section 35(1) fulfils that possibility.')

Section 25 of the Charter, which specifically mentions Aboriginal and treaty rights, is equally ambiguous. Section 25 calls on the judiciary to interpret rights and freedoms guaranteed by the Charter in a manner that does not abrogate or derogate from Aboriginal and treaty rights or other rights that pertain to Aboriginal peoples. Thus, section 25 requires that the Charter not be interpreted in a way that abrogates or derogates from any rights of self-government that might be recognized and affirmed by section 35 of the Constitution Act 1982. To the extent that section 25 shields the exercise of Aboriginal governmental authority recognized by section 35 from the Charter, it suggests that the Charter does not apply to the exercise of this authority. As Kent McNeil has said, '[a]s an Aboriginal right, the right of self-government is ... shielded from the general application of the Charter by section 25.'[21] However, the text of section 25 can also support the opposite conclusion. Section 25 can be read as an instruction to the judiciary that the right of self-government recognized by section 35 should not be abrogated or diminished when the Charter is applied to its exercise. According to this interpretation, section 25 does not speak to whether the Charter applies to the exercise of Aboriginal governmental authority recognized by section 35; it assumes that the Charter does apply and cautions the judiciary to supervise the exercise of such authority in a manner that does not abrogate or derogate from the right of self-government itself.[22]

The structure of the constitution is also ambiguous on the question of whether the Charter applies to the exercise of Aboriginal governmental authority recognized by the constitution. Generally speaking, the constitution protects two distinct sets of constitutional rights and freedoms. The Charter protects rights and freedoms guaranteed to all Canadians and section 35 protects those that pertain to the Aboriginal peoples of Canada. The Charter is contained in Part I of the Constitution Act,

---

21 McNeil, 'Aboriginal Governments and the Canadian Charter of Rights and Freedoms,' at 75.

22 For an endorsement of this approach to s. 25, see Royal Commission on Aboriginal Peoples, *Final Report*, vol. 2, pt 1, at 231–2 ('[t]he application of the Charter to Aboriginal governments is moulded and tempered by the mandatory provisions of section 25. This section clearly rules out any interpretation of the Charter that would attack the existence of Aboriginal governments or undermine their basic powers. It also ensures that the Charter will receive a flexible interpretation that takes account of the distinctive philosophies, traditions and cultural practices that animate the inherent right of self-government. Section 25 prevents distinctive Aboriginal understandings and approaches from being washed away in a flood of undifferentiated Charter interpretation').

1982; section 35 is contained in Part II. To the extent that each part possesses equal constitutional stature, rights contained in Part I should not constrain rights contained in Part II.

Support for this proposition lies in the Supreme Court of Canada's decision in the *Reference Re Act to Amend the Education Act (Ontario)*. The court held that the power to distinguish between school supporters on the basis of religion was implicit in section 93 of the Constitution Act, 1867, which expressly authorizes the establishment of denominational schools, and did not infringe section 15 of the Charter. The court reasoned that governmental action mandated by one provision of the constitution cannot be rendered unconstitutional by another provision of the constitution. According to Wilson J., '[i]t was never intended that the Charter could be used to invalidate other provisions of the constitution.'[23] This interpretation, however, would be a sweeping one, and the *Education Act Reference* can be interpreted more narrowly by analogizing to the Charter's application to the exercise of federal and provincial legislative authority. That is, even if the *Education Act Reference* stands for the proposition that governmental action mandated by one provision of the constitution cannot be rendered unconstitutional by another provision of the constitution, it cannot be suggested that federal and provincial legislative authority is not subject to the Charter simply because such authority is authorized by section 91 and 92 of the Constitution Act, 1867. As stated by Peter Hogg, '[t]he fact that a power is conferred by the Constitution of Canada does not immunize the power from the Charter of Rights.'[24] Similarly, if Aboriginal governmental authority is recognized by section 35, that fact alone may be insufficient to insulate from Charter scrutiny the way in which such authority is exercised.

While the text and structure of the constitution is at best ambivalent as to whether the Charter applies to the exercise of constitutionally recognized Aboriginal governmental authority, precedent on the scope of section 32 provides greater insight. In *RWDSU, Local 580 v. Dolphin Delivery Ltd.*, at issue was whether the Charter applied to the common law in the context of a dispute between two private parties. In holding that the Charter does not apply in such circumstances, the court, per McIntyre J., reasoned that the Charter is intended to apply only to governmental action:

---

23 [1987] 1 S.C.R. 1148 at 1197. See also *New Brunswick Broadcasting Co. v. Nova Scotia*, [1993] 1 S.C.R. 319 at 373 ('one part of the Constitution cannot be abrogated or diminished by another').

24 *Constitutional Law of Canada* (Toronto: Carswell, 2000), at 697.

It is my view that s. 32 of the Charter specifies the actors to whom the Charter will apply. They are the legislative, executive and administrative branches of government. It will apply to those branches of government whether or not their action is invoked in public or private litigation. It would seem that legislation is the only way in which a legislature may infringe a guaranteed right or freedom. Action by the executive or administrative branches of government will generally depend upon legislation, that is, statutory authority. Such action may also depend, however, on the common law, as in the case of the prerogative. To the extent that it relies on statutory authority which constitutes or results in an infringement of a guaranteed right or freedom, the Charter will apply and it will be unconstitutional. The action will also be unconstitutional to the extent that it relies for authority or justification on a rule of the common law which constitutes or creates an infringement of a Charter right or freedom. In this way the Charter will apply to the common law whether in public or private litigation. It will apply to the common law, however, only in so far as the common law is the basis of some governmental action which, it is alleged, infringes a guaranteed right or freedom.[25]

While this passage clearly indicates that the Charter applies to governmental action, it does not rule out the possibility that the Charter applies to Aboriginal governmental action. However, in another passage, the court hints that the only governmental action to which the Charter will apply is that of federal, provincial, or territorial authorities:

Section 32(1) refers to the Parliament and Government of Canada and to the legislatures and governments of the provinces in respect of all matters within their respective authorities. In this, it may be seen that Parliament and the legislatures are treated as separate or specific branches of government, distinct from the executive branch of government, and therefore where the word 'government' is used in s. 32 it refers not to government in its generic sense – meaning the whole of the governmental apparatus of the state – but to a branch of government. The word 'government,' following as it does the words 'Parliament' and 'legislature,' must then, it would seem, refer to the executive or administrative branch of government. This is the sense in which one generally speaks of the Government of Canada or of a province. I am of the opinion that the word 'government' is used in s.

---

25 [1986] 2 S.C.R. 573 at 598–9.

32 of the Charter in the sense of the executive government of Canada and the Provinces.[26]

Similarly, in *McKinney v. University of Guelph*, the court in holding that the Charter did not apply to a university mandatory retirement policy stated that 'the Charter was by s. 32 limited in its application to Parliament and the legislatures, and to the executive and administrative branches of government.'[27]

The proposition that the Charter applies exclusively to federal, provincial, and territorial governmental action receives further support from three decisions that address the application of the Charter to extradition proceedings involving individuals charged with offences in foreign jurisdictions. In all three, the court ruled that the Charter does not apply to the activities of a foreign government. In *United States of America v. Allard and Charette*, for example, the court stated it to be 'obvious ... that the Charter can only apply to the activities of the governments mentioned in s. 32.'[28] Similarly, in *Harrer v. The Queen*, which addressed the admissibility of evidence obtained in the United States by American authorities in a manner inconsistent with Charter's right to counsel, the court stated the following: 'What ... is determinative against the argument that the Charter applies to the interrogation in the present case is the simple fact that the United States immigration officials and the Marshals were not acting on behalf of any of the governments of Canada, the provinces or the territories, the state actors to which, by virtue of s. 32(1), the application of the Charter is confined ... It follows that the Charter simply has no direct application to the interrogations in the United States because the governments mentioned in s. 32(1) were not implicated in these activities.'[29] These cases support the proposition that the Charter applies solely to the exercise of federal, provincial, and territorial authority and not to the exercise of Aboriginal governmental authority recognized by the constitution.[30]

---

26 Ibid., at 597–8.

27 [1990] 3 S.C.R. 229 at 263.

28 [1987] 1 S.C.R. 564 at 571. See also *Canada v. Schmidt*, [1987] 1 S.C.R. 500 and *Argentina v. Mellino*, [1987] 1 S.C.R. 536.

29 [1995] 3 S.C.R. 562.

30 For an extensive examination of the above cases, see Kerry Wilkins, 'But We Need the Eggs: The Royal Commission, the Charter of Rights and the Inherent Right of Aboriginal Self-Government,' 49 U.T.L.J. 53 (1999).

However, precedent on the issue is not as compelling as it might appear. First, the statement in *Dolphin Delivery* that 'the word "government" is used in section 32 of the Charter in the sense of the executive government of Canada and the Provinces' is made in the context of an argument that the Charter applies to the executive and administrative branches but not to the judicial branch of government. It does not rule out the possibility that inherent Aboriginal governmental authority is also subject to the Charter. Second, the statement in *McKinney* that 'the Charter was by s. 32 limited in its application to Parliament and the legislatures, and to the executive and administrative branches of government' addressed the argument that the Charter does not generally apply to the exercise of non-statutory legal authority of a non-governmental actor. Understood in this context, it likewise does not rule out the possibility that inherent Aboriginal governmental authority is subject to the Charter.

It is true that inherent Aboriginal governmental authority recognized by the constitution is not derived from a statutory grant of authority. But it differs in significant respects from the authority of a university and other entities exercising non-statutory legal authority. The Charter does not apply to the non-statutory legal authority of bodies such as a university because such bodies possess roughly the same proprietary and contractual powers as the common law confers on individuals.[31] In contrast, the non-statutory legal authority of an Aboriginal government recognized by the constitution is constitutional in nature. The power of compulsion vested in an Aboriginal government by section 35 is of a completely different order than any power of compulsion that the common law vests in private legal actors. Unlike cases that address the application of the Charter to the private sphere, at issue is the extent to which the Constitution of Canada, in so far as it constitutionally recognizes and affirms Aboriginal governmental authority, also subjects the exercise of such authority to constitutional norms enshrined in the Charter.

Finally, the cases that address the application of the Charter to foreign proceedings are of limited relevance. Aboriginal governmental authority is not authority foreign to the Canadian state. Assuming the constitution recognizes an inherent right of self-government, the exercise of such authority, unlike the authority of a foreign state, is specifically authorized by the constitution. Again, at issue is the extent to which the Con-

---

31 See, generally, Hogg, *Constitutional Law of Canada*, at 700.

stitution of Canada, given that it recognizes this authority, also subjects its exercise to constitutional norms enshrined in the Charter.

Whether the Charter applies to the exercise of Aboriginal governmental authority recognized by the constitution therefore cannot be determined solely by reference to text, structure, or precedent. Its resolution requires an inquiry into the purposes underlying both the Charter and section 35. The Supreme Court of Canada has held that both the rights and freedoms guaranteed by the Charter and the rights recognized and affirmed by section 35 are to be interpreted in light of their underlying purposes.[32] Judicial commentary on the overall purpose of the Charter – as opposed to statements about the purpose of specific Charter rights and freedoms – is surprisingly rare. In *R. v. Oakes*, however, Chief Justice Dickson outlined some of the basic values underlying the Charter's guarantee of fundamental rights and freedoms: 'respect for the inherent dignity of the human person, commitment to social justice and equality, accommodation of a wide variety of beliefs, respect for cultural and group identity, and faith in social and political institutions which enhance the participation of individuals and groups in society.'[33]

I have argued that the purpose of Aboriginal and treaty rights is to provide constitutional protection to interests associated with indigenous difference. The purpose of an Aboriginal right of self-government, recognized and affirmed by section 35 either as an Aboriginal right or as a treaty right, is to protect interests associated with Aboriginal sovereignty by affirming the authority of an Aboriginal nation to make laws in relation to critical and integral aspects of its collective identity.

Whether the Charter ought to apply to the exercise of inherent Aboriginal governmental authority should be determined in a way that attempts to accommodate the competing purposes of section 35 and the Charter. As was said earlier, critics have claimed that the Charter, because it is premised on liberal values of individual autonomy and freedom, threatens critical aspects of Aboriginal societies, which are premised on collective values of community and responsibility. In contrast, others have argued that the Charter protects less powerful members of Aboriginal societies against potential abuses of Aboriginal governmen-

---

32 See, for example, *R. v. Big M Drug Mart Ltd.*, [1985] 1 S.C.R. 295 and *R. v. Sparrow*, [1990] 1 S.C.R. 1075.

33 [1986] 1 S.C.R. 103, at 136. See also *In Re Bhindi et. al and British Columbia Projectionists, Local 348* (1986), 29 D.L.R. (4th) 47 at 53 (B.C.C.A.) (the fundamental purpose of the Charter is to 'protect the citizen from abuse of power from governmental authority').

tal authority. Interpreting section 32 of the Charter as applying to the exercise of Aboriginal governmental authority recognized by the constitution best accommodates these competing concerns. A blanket exemption from the Charter would enable Aboriginal governments to ride roughshod over interests associated with Charter rights without necessarily furthering interests associated with indigenous difference. In contrast to a blanket exemption, applying the Charter enables the judiciary to develop a much more calibrated approach.

Section 25 of the Charter instructs the judiciary not to interpret Charter rights and freedoms in a manner that abrogates or derogates from Aboriginal and treaty rights guaranteed by section 35. It requires the Charter to be interpreted in a manner sensitive to interests underlying section 35. As will be seen, section 25 enables the judiciary to soften the impact of the Charter's application to the exercise of Aboriginal governmental authority to protect interests associated with indigenous difference from a potentially rigid set of individual rights and freedoms. It also enables the judiciary to enforce Charter rights against the exercise of Aboriginal governmental authority that does not threaten interests associated with indigenous difference.[34]

In summary, the public/private distinction authorizes a number of Charter challenges to several aspects of the relation between Aboriginal

---

34 See Brian Slattery, in 'First Nations and the Constitution: A Question of Trust,' 71 Can. Bar Rev. 261 at 286–7 (1992) (footnotes removed) ('the Charter will impose some restrictions on the manner in which Aboriginal governments treat their own constituents, so long as these restrictions do not amount to an abrogation or derogation from the right of self-government proper or from other section 25 and 35 rights. At the same time, it seems clear that the Charter must be interpreted and applied in a manner consistent with the culture and traditions of the Aboriginal people in question'); Peter W. Hogg and Mary Ellen Turpel, in 'Implementing Aboriginal Self-Government: Constitutional and Jurisdictional Issues,' 74 Can. Bar Rev. 187 at 215 (1995) ('[s]ection 25 allows an Aboriginal government to design programs and laws which are different, for legitimate cultural reasons, and have these reasons considered as relevant should such differences invite judicial review under the Charter'); and Royal Commission on Aboriginal Peoples, *Final Report*, vol. 2, pt 1, at 230–1 ('in its application to Aboriginal governments, the Charter should be interpreted in a manner that allows for considerable scope for distinctive Aboriginal philosophical outlooks, cultures and traditions. This interpretive rule is found in section 25 of the Charter'). But see Wilkins, 'But We Need the Eggs'; McNeil, 'Aboriginal Governments and the Canadian Charter of Rights and Freedoms'; and Bryan Schwartz, *First Principles, Second Thoughts: Aboriginal Peoples, Constitutional Reform and Canadian Statecraft* (Montreal: Institute for Research on Public Policy, 1986), at 391–3.

power and state power. Federal and provincial laws that distribute burdens and benefits based on indigenous difference, thus affecting the nature and extent of Aboriginal power recognized by Canadian law, are subject to Charter scrutiny. In addition, the Charter governs federal and provincial delegation of law-making authority to Aboriginal governments and federal and provincial participation in treaty processes, and it likely governs the exercise of an inherent right of Aboriginal self-government. Each type of challenge enables the judiciary to subject the exercise of Aboriginal power to constitutional scrutiny, raising fears that the Charter will adversely affect Aboriginal forms of social organization. In the next few sections, using the Indian Act as an example, I focus on laws that distinguish between Aboriginal people and non-Aboriginal people to protect interests associated with indigenous difference and values associated with equality and non-discrimination.

Distinguishing Discrimination

Because the Charter applies to several aspects of the relation between Aboriginal power and state power, any law – whether federal, provincial, or Aboriginal – that treats Aboriginal people differently from non-Aboriginal people risks infringing subsection 15(1) of the Charter. Section 15 provides that '[e]very individual is equal before and under the law and has the right to the equal protection and equal benefit of the law without discrimination and, in particular, without discrimination based on race, national or ethnic origin, colour, religion, sex, age or mental or physical disability.' The Charter's drafters sought explicitly to respond to perceived shortcomings of jurisprudence on 'equality before the law' as guaranteed by the Canadian Bill of Rights.[35] Subsection 15(1) guarantees 'four equalities' – equality before and under the law and the equal protection and benefit of the law – by prohibiting discrimination based on a number of grounds.[36] Its purpose, as defined by the Supreme Court of Canada, is twofold: to express a commitment to the equal worth and dignity of all persons, and to rectify and prevent

---

35 See, generally, Lorraine E. Weinrib, 'Of Diligence and Dice: Reconstituting Canada's Constitution, 42 U.T.L.J. 207 (1992).

36 *R. v. Turpin.* See, generally, Anne Bayefsky, 'Defining Equality Rights, in Anne Bayefsky and Mary Eberts, eds., *Equality Rights and the Charter of Rights and Freedoms* (Scarborough, Ont.: Carswell, 1985), at 3–25.

discrimination against particular groups suffering social, political, and legal disadvantage in our society.'[37]

Section 15 embodies a constitutional aspiration that power be distributed in a just manner. Together with section 1, which demands justification of laws that infringe Charter guarantees, section 15 requires the judiciary to ensure that legislatures distribute statutory power in a manner that takes into account relevant similarities and differences among individuals and groups. But section 15 seems to call into question the constitutionality of legislation that treats Aboriginal people differently from non-Aboriginal people by imposing burdens or by conferring benefits on Aboriginal people that are not imposed or conferred on non-Aboriginal people. If Aboriginal interests associated with culture, territory, sovereignty, and the treaty process warrant constitutional protection, then section 15 seems to prohibit legislatures from providing what a just constitutional order demands – legal protection of interests associated with indigenous difference. Thus understood, section 15 threatens the continued vitality of Aboriginal societies by frustrating legislative initiatives that distribute statutory burdens and benefits in the name of indigenous difference.

One such initiative, the federal Indian Act,[38] distributes burdens and benefits to status Indians, that is, descendents of those Aboriginal people identified as belonging to particular bands when a treaty was negotiated or a reserve was established.[39] It creates 'bands' out of Aboriginal communities and establishes the 'band council' as the basic unit of Aboriginal governance. The Act also establishes complex rules governing band membership and Indian status, as well as detailed requirements for band council elections. It defines the nature and scope of a band council's political authority, and its relationship to federal authorities, by conferring on band councils the authority to pass by-laws, consistent with the Act and federal regulations, in relation to local matters, including aspects of band membership, health, commerce, traffic, law and order, public works, and zoning.[40] The federal cabinet retains considerable discretionary power over band funds, elections, the use and management of reserve land, the establishment of new bands, and the exemption of certain bands from the application of the Act, along with a host of other subjects.

37 *Eldridge v. British Columbia*, at 667.
38 R.S.C. 1985, c. I-5.
39 See Hogg, *Constitutional Law of Canada*, at 571.
40 Indian Act, ss. 81, 83, 85.1.

Whether the Charter proscribes legislation such as the Indian Act depends on what counts as a relevant similarity or difference for the purpose of distributing statutory benefits and burdens among individuals. Two perspectives on the nature of equality – first introduced in Chapter 4 – provide insight into this question. The first, often called formal equality, examines a law to determine if a relevant reason exists for similar or differential treatment. It requires a close fit between the ends and means of legislation.[41] The second, known as substantive equality, calls for an examination of the concrete material conditions of individuals and groups and searches for ways in which state action can ameliorate adverse social and economic circumstances.[42] Both regard equality in terms of a commitment of treating like cases alike and different cases differently, but they differ on what should count as a relevant similarity or difference. In determining relevance, formal equality is more concerned with legal form whereas substantive equality's chief concern is with material fact. Whether a law violates formal equality depends on whether it presents a valid reason for distinguishing between two classes of people; whether a law violates substantive equality depends on the extent to which it increases or decreases social or economic disparity.[43]

The distinction between formal and substantive equality informs two section 15 issues. The first relates to the list in that section of prohibited grounds of discrimination. From the perspective of formal equality, subsection 15(1) lists such grounds to illustrate, not to exhaust, the types of laws to which section 15 applies. Indeed, the logic of formal equality requires all laws to provide a relevant reason for similar or differential

---

41 See, for example, David M. Beatty, 'The Canadian Conception of Equality,' 46 U.T.L.J. 349, at 363 (1996) ('equality and discrimination simply describe two (opposite) ways the ends and the means of any law can be related when they are measured against a common metric of relevance'); Marc Gold, 'Comment: Andrews v. Law Society of British Columbia,' 34 McGill L.J. 1063 at 1065–6 (1989) (equality demands that 'legislative distinctions ... be relevant to the purposes of the law').

42 Compare Colleen Sheppard, 'Recognition of the Disadvantaging of Women: The Promise of Andrews v. Law Society of B.C.,' 35 McGill L.J. 206 (1990) (arguing for an 'effects-based' approach that furthers substantive equality).

43 American constitutional scholarship often refers to the difference between formal and substantive equality in terms of a distinction between discrimination and group disadvantage: see, for example, Owen Fiss, 'Groups and the Equal Protection Clause,' 5 Phil. & Pub. Aff. 107 (1976). For more discussion of formal and substantive equality, see Chapters 1 and 4.

treatment of any kind.[44] Moreover, formal equality is not concerned with who benefits from or is burdened by legislation. A law that distributes benefits and burdens based on sex, for example, regardless of whether it benefits or burdens men or women, must provide a relevant reason for distinguishing between them. From the perspective of substantive equality, however, section 15 is concerned with ameliorating disadvantage, not legislative rationality. It prohibits legislatures from employing only certain grounds, namely, those that correspond to historically disadvantaged groups in society, and from employing these grounds in certain ways, namely, in ways that exacerbate material inequality.[45] Thus a law that provides a benefit to women but not to men, for example, may not constitute a violation of section 15.[46] In an attempt to mediate the competing demands of formal and substantive equality, the Supreme Court of Canada has held that laws that discriminate on the basis of listed grounds or grounds analogous to those listed, such as sexual orientation, violate section 15 and require constitutional justification.[47] The court has not been consistent in its approach to what constitutes an analogous ground. In certain cases, it has held that immutable personal characteristics are analogous grounds;[48] in others, it has held that an attribute that denotes membership in a 'discrete and insular minority' is an analogous ground.[49] The court has recently held that a ground will be considered analogous to those listed in subsection 15(1) if its use by the state implicates 'human dignity.'[50]

Whether subsection 15(1) prohibits governments from distributing burdens and benefits on the basis of indigenous difference thus turns

---

44 See Beatty, 'The Canadian Conception of Equality.' See also Beatty, *Constitutional Law in Theory and Practice*, at 92–4; Peter W. Hogg, *Constitutional Law of Canada*, 2nd ed. (Scarborough Ont.: Carswell, 1998), at 799–801.

45 See, for example, *Andrews v. Law Society of British Columbia*, [1989] 1 S.C.R. 143 at 152–3, per Wilson J. concurring (analogous grounds should refer to historically disadvantaged groups).

46 Compare *Conway v. The Queen*, [1993] 2 S.C.R. 872 (cross-gender searching of male inmates but not female inmates does not violate s. 15).

47 *Egan v. Canada*, [1995] 2 S.C.R. 513 (s. 15 prohibits discrimination based on sexual orientation); see generally *Andrews v. Law Society of B.C.* (s. 15 prohibits discrimination on listed and analogous grounds).

48 See, e.g., *Andrews v. Law Society of British Columbia*, per La Forest J.; *Egan v. Canada*, per La Forest J.

49 See, e.g., *Andrews v. Law Society of British Columbia*, per Wilson J.; *Egan v. Canada*, per Cory J.

50 *Law v. Canada*, [1999] 1 S.C.R. 497 at 555.

on whether indigenous difference is a prohibited ground of discrimination. Laws such as the Indian Act may well be seen as distinguishing between persons on the basis of a listed ground, be it 'race,' 'colour,' or 'national or ethnic origin.' Even if race, colour, or national or ethnic origin does not adequately describe the classification employed by a law that treats Aboriginal people differently from non-Aboriginal people, indigenous difference can easily be seen as an immutable personal characteristic, as denoting membership in a discrete and insular minority, or as implicating human dignity so as to constitute a ground of discrimination prohibited by section 15 of the Charter.

But the constitutionality of a law that distributes burdens and benefits on the basis of indigenous difference also turns on a second issue: does the law constitute 'discrimination' within the meaning of subsection 15(1)? Some scholars have argued that this term does not narrow the application of subsection 15(1) because, properly understood, section 15 requires the state to constitutionally justify all laws that draw distinctions among individuals.[51] Others have argued that subsection 15 screens out certain statutory distinctions from constitutional scrutiny by prohibiting only those that constitute discrimination.[52] The Supreme Court has sided with the latter view. It has held that a law is discriminatory if it imposes a burden or withholds a benefit in a manner that 'reflects the stereotypical application of presumed group or personal characteristics or which otherwise has the effect of promoting the view that the individual is less capable or worthy of recognition or value as a human being or as a member of Canadian society, equally deserving of concern, respect, and consideration.'[53]

Several factors are relevant in determining whether a law promotes the view that an individual is less worthy of recognition as a human being. The court has stated that a finding of discrimination is more likely when the following conditions exist: (a) a group has experienced pre-existing disadvantage, stereotyping, prejudice, or vulnerability; (b) the law has failed to take into account the actual need, capacity, or circumstances of the claimant; (c) the law lacks an ameliorative purpose or

---

51 Beatty, 'The Canadian Conception of Equality.' See also Beatty, *Constitutional Law in Theory and Practice*, at 92–4; Hogg, *Constitutional Law of Canada*, 2nd ed., at 799–801.
52 See, for example, *Andrews v. Law Society of Upper Canada* (1986), 27 D.L.R. (4th) 600 at 610 (B.C.C.A.), per McLachlin J.A. ('unreasonable or unfair' distinctions constitute 'discrimination' within the meaning of s. 15(1)).
53 *Law v. Canada*, at 549.

effect on a more disadvantaged person or group; and (d) the consequences for the affected group are severe and localized.

Whether a law that distinguishes between Aboriginal and non-Aboriginal people constitutes discrimination thus involves a context-specific judgment, based on a mix of formal and substantive equality concerns. Not all differential treatment based on a listed or analogous ground constitutes discrimination. The fact that a law distinguishes between Aboriginal and non-Aboriginal people is insufficient to establish a violation of subsection 15. Given the above factors, it would be difficult to characterize a law that benefits Aboriginal people and burdens non-Aboriginal people as discriminatory on the basis that it draws a distinction between these two classes of persons. Section 15, in other words, does not appear to pose a serious threat to a law that distinguishes between Aboriginal people and non-Aboriginal people in order to protect or promote interests associated with indigenous difference. Moreover, such a law may merit special consideration under section 15. First, it might constitute affirmative action within the meaning of subsection 15(2). And second, section 25 of the Charter instructs the judiciary to interpret the Charter in a manner that does not abrogate or derogate from rights that pertain to Aboriginal people.

Indigenous Difference and Affirmative Action

Laws that distinguish between Aboriginal and non-Aboriginal people may benefit from subsection 15(2) of the Charter, which provides as follows:

> Subsection (1) does not preclude any law, program or activity that has as its object the amelioration of conditions of disadvantaged individuals or groups including those that are disadvantaged because of race, national or ethnic origin, colour, religion, sex, age or mental or physical disability.

It is generally agreed that subsection 15(2) is designed to permit legislatures, in the name of substantive equality, to enact affirmative action programs.[54] To the extent that a law that treats Aboriginal people differ-

---

54 See *Rebic v. Collver* (1986), 28 C.C.C. (3d) 154 at 166 (B.C.C.A.); and, generally, William Black and Lynne Smith, 'The Equality Rights,' in G.-A. Beaudoin and E. Ratushny, eds., *The Canadian Charter of Rights and Freedoms*, 2nd ed. (Scarborough, Ont.: Carswell, 1989), 557 at 596–8; K.H. Fogarty, *Equality Rights and Their Limitations in the Charter* (Scarborough, Ont.: Carswell, 1987), at 113–14.

ently from other individuals or groups has 'as its object the amelioration of conditions' of Aboriginal people, and to the extent that those to whom the law applies are 'disadvantaged individuals or groups' within the meaning of subsection 15(2), such an initiative will not infringe subsection 15(1).

Formal and substantive equality conceive of equality in terms of a relation that ought to exist between two classes of people who are similar or different in relevant respects. Formal equality restricts its inquiry into relevant similarities and differences to an examination of the law in question; substantive equality extends its inquiry to the material circumstances of individuals affected by the law. From a formal perspective, the relation between subsections 15(1) and 15(2) is one of right and exception; subsection 15(1), embodying a commitment to formal equality, provides the right and subsection 15(2), acknowledging the value of substantive equality, provides an exception. As an exception to a constitutionally guaranteed right, subsection 15(2) should be interpreted narrowly as authorizing state efforts to ameliorate economic and social disadvantage only under certain constitutionally monitored circumstances. A substantive equality perspective produces a dramatically different understanding of the relation between the two subsections. Under this approach, subsection 15(2) operates as an interpretive guide to the nature of the equality guarantee itself, suggesting that laws that have as their object the amelioration of disadvantage do not violate section 15.

Manitoba Rice Farmers Association v. Manitoba Human Rights Commission[55] illustrates the first approach. At issue was the constitutionality of a program developed by Manitoba that granted Aboriginal people rights of priority as against non-Aboriginal people to obtain licences to harvest wild rice on designated lands. The program's objective was to encourage Aboriginal people to take a leading role in the wild rice industry. The Manitoba Rice Farmers Association appealed a decision of the Manitoba Human Rights Commission that approved the special program, alleging that it violated subsection 15(1) of the Charter.

In finding for the association, Simonsen J. of the Manitoba Court of Queen's Bench held that the program violated subsection 15(1) and provided two reasons why it did not comply with subsection 15(2). First, he said: 'In order to justify a program under s. 15(2), ... there must be a

---

55 (1987), 50 Man. R. (2d) 92, affirming 37 Man. R. (2d) 50 (Q.B. Chambers). An appeal to the Manitoba Court of Appeal was dismissed on other grounds: (1988), 55 Man. R. (2d) 263.

real nexus between the object of the program declared by the government and its form and implementation. It is not sufficient to declare that the object of a program is to help a disadvantaged group if in fact the ameliorative remedy is not directed toward the cause of the disadvantage. There must be a unity or interrelationship amongst the elements in the program which will prompt the court to conclude that the remedy in its form and implementation is rationally related to the cause of the disadvantage.'[56] He concluded that the remedy was not rationally related to the cause of the disadvantage because, in his view, the disadvantage suffered by Aboriginal people was not caused by a prior inability to obtain licences but instead by an absence of capital and management assistance. The remedy of a preferential licensing scheme was therefore not directed or rationally related to the cause of the disadvantage and, as a result, could not be shielded by subsection 15(2). Second, Simonsen J. held that the remedy 'unnecessarily denie[d] the existing rights of the non-target group.'[57] Given that no evidence showed that the target and non-target groups wanted to cultivate wild rice in the same areas, that there was a shortage of existing or new areas suitable for cultivation, or that exclusivity of access by the target group was necessary to improve their condition, he held that the denial of licences to the non-target group was not 'reasonably required to ameliorate the conditions of hardship' of Aboriginal people and thus could not be protected by the Charter.[58]

To the extent that this approach is followed in subsequent cases, it offers a strict interpretation of the reach of subsection 15(2), making it difficult to predict with accuracy whether legislative efforts that accord special or differential treatment to Aboriginal people will be held to fall within its scope. Much will depend on the characterization of the objective of the legislative initiative, in particular, whether the law according special or differential treatment 'has as its object the amelioration of conditions' of Aboriginal people and whether the judiciary accepts that

---

56 (1987), 50 Man. R. (2d) 92 at 101–2.

57 Ibid., at 102.

58 Ibid., at 103. For the similar view that s. 15(2) does not protect remedial programs that infringe unnecessarily on equality rights, see Dale Gibson, *The Law of the Charter: Equality Rights* (Calgary: Carswell, 1990) at 300, 328–9. But see Patrick Monahan, *Politics and the Constitution: The Charter, Federalism and the Supreme Court of Canada* (Scarborough, Ont. Carswell, 1987), at 116 ('a restrictive approach to s. 15(2) would obviously not serve the cause of freedom').

the Aboriginal population in question is 'disadvantaged' within the requirements of subsection 15(2). Moreover, Justice Simonsen's first requirement that the cause of the disadvantage be rationally related to the remedy offered by the legislative initiative may make it difficult to support legislative reform efforts under subsection 15(2). It is no doubt the case, for example, that aspects of the criminal justice system are partly responsible for the current conditions facing Aboriginal people.[59] Enabling Aboriginal communities to assume greater responsibility in the creation and administration of criminal justice is rationally related to certain aspects of the cause of their disadvantage. However, tracing the cause or causes of the disadvantages Aboriginal people face in the current system cannot be reduced to such a discrete exercise. Given the complexity of causation, a judicial decision maker employing the approach articulated by Simonsen J. possesses a great deal of discretion to emphasize certain causal factors at the expense of others. Depending upon which causal factors are emphasized, the predictability of a test that looks for a rational relation between cause and cure in the area of Aboriginal people and criminal justice is uncertain.[60]

More generally, the approach in *Manitoba Rice Farmers* regards subsection 15(2) as an exception to the general prohibition against discrimination based on listed and analogous grounds found in subsection 15(1). This approach sees affirmative action as a measure that offends equality but is nonetheless constitutionally justified in certain circumstances. As an exception, the circumstances in which the state is justified in enacting an affirmative action measure ought to be narrowly construed. Lurking in the background of this approach is the unstated formal premise that equality is a relation that ought to exist between two classes of people who are similar or different in relevant respects but that what constitutes a relevant similarity or difference should be determined primarily by the legal position of those affected by the law immediately prior to its enactment. A law that treats certain individuals differently from others for reasons unrelated to their legal position prior to the law's enactment

---

59 See, generally, *Royal Commission on the Donald Marshall, Jr., Prosecution, Summary of Findings*, vol. 8, *Digest of Findings and Recommendations* (Halifax: Queen's Printer, 1989).

60 For a criticism of Simonsen J.'s first requirement, see Gibson, *The Law of the Charter*, at 317–21. For a holding that appears to contemplate a wider scope for s. 15(2) than the approach offered by Simonsen J., see *R. v. Youngman*, [1988] 3 C.N.L.R. 135 at 145 (B.C. Co. Ct.) (holding that a federal commercial licence requiring that a licensed vessel 'be operated by an Indian' did not violate s. 15(1) and, if it did, it had as its object the amelioration of conditions of 'disadvantaged native Indians').

should be viewed with suspicion; it may be justified as an affirmative action measure, but only if the cause and cure are rationally related and the rights of those adversely affected by the law are minimally impaired.

In contrast, a substantive equality approach figured prominently in two other cases involving equality challenges to laws that accorded differential treatment to Aboriginal people. In *R. v. Willocks*, at issue was the constitutionality of a diversion program established by the Government of Ontario. Under the program, Aboriginal offenders who agree to the facts alleged in charges brought against them are diverted out of the ordinary criminal justice system with the Crown's consent and brought before a council of Aboriginal elders. The program is an effort to introduce Aboriginal forms of administering justice to the Canadian criminal justice system. Willocks, a black man charged with assaulting his spouse, argued that the diversion program was underinclusive because it was unavailable to non-Aboriginal offenders and therefore constituted discrimination based on race.[61]

Watt J. held that the diversion program was authorized by subsection 15(2) because it was designed to ameliorate adverse conditions of Aboriginal people. He outlined an approach to subsection 15(2) that stands in striking contrast to that taken in *Manitoba Rice Farmers*. Watt J. stated that the purpose of subsection 15(2) 'is to ensure ... that subsection 15(1) does not, in the name of equality, prohibit measures which are designed to achieve equality for a disadvantaged group.'[62] He noted

---

61 (1995), 22 O.R. (3d) 552 (Gen. Div.). Ontario was involved in three Aboriginal diversion programs at the time of trial. The Attawapiskat program enabled an Aboriginal accused to consent to appear before a council of elders and to submit to any terms or conditions it imposes; the program also enabled Aboriginal elders to act as a sentencing advisory council to the presiding judge. The Sandy Lake program enabled the presiding judge to seek the guidance and recommendation of a council of elders on the appropriate sentence. The Metropolitan Toronto program enabled the Crown to stay proceedings against an Aboriginal accused who accepts responsibility for his or her criminal conduct and agrees to submit to any terms and conditions imposed by a native community council. For more discussion of Aboriginal diversion programs, see Royal Commission on Aboriginal Peoples, *Bridging the Cultural Divide: A Report on Aboriginal People and Criminal Justice in Canada* (Ottawa: Minister of Supply and Services Canada, 1996). At the time of the trial, Ontario also offered an alternative measures program, not restricted to Aboriginal offenders, that enabled the Crown to withdraw less serious charges provided the accused agreed to attend for counselling or assessment or to engage in other acts of demonstrative remorse. Willocks was unable to participate in this program because the offence with which he was charged, domestic assault, was not an offence to which the program applied.

62 *R. v. Willocks*, at 570.

that '[i]n any program which is designed to ameliorate the conditions of a disadvantaged group, others will be "disadvantaged" as a result of their non-eligibility for participation.'[63] This fact moved him to advance a far more deferential approach to subsection 15(2) than what Simonsen J. proposed in *Manitoba Rice Rice Farmers*. According to Watt J., legislatures must be free to establish priorities among disadvantaged groups as long as such initiatives are not 'grossly unfair' and do not 'unnecessarily deny any existing rights of persons outside the target group.' Fairness does not require the legislature to address at once all individuals or groups who suffer similar disadvantage. According to Watt J., no right was unnecessarily denied to Willocks because he had no legal right to a diversion program.

The constitutionality of another allegedly underinclusive affirmative action program was at issue in *Lovelace v. Ontario*.[64] Ontario Métis and non-status Indians sought a declaration that they were entitled to share in the profits of Casino Rama, a commercial casino located on an Indian reserve. The Ontario government had entered into an agreement with Indian bands in Ontario to develop the casino in order to improve the socio-economic conditions of band members and to distribute net revenues to a First Nations Fund to benefit all Ontario Indian bands. The applicants argued that their exclusion from the project and its revenues violated subsection 15(1) of the Charter.

The Supreme Court of Canada dismissed the appeal. It held that restricting the distribution of casino revenues to Indian bands did not constitute discrimination within the meaning of subsection 15(1) as it did not rely on a stereotype of non-band Aboriginal communities. Instead, by distinguishing between Indian bands and other Aboriginal communities, the distribution scheme reflected an understanding of the different needs, capacities, and circumstances of the two types of communities and did not undermine the ameliorative purpose of the distribution scheme. It therefore did not promote the view that the appellant Aboriginal communities or their members are less worthy of recognition than Indian bands or band members. The court went on to hold that 'the equality right is to be understood in substantive rather than formalistic terms' and suggested that 's. 15(2) can be understood as confirming the substantive equality approach of s. 15(1).'[65]

---

63 Ibid., at 571.
64 2000 S.C.C. 37.
65 Ibid., at paras. 93, 100.

Although it left open the possibility that subsection 15(2) might in the future be construed as being 'independently applicable ... in the future,'[66] the court therefore concluded that, generally speaking, an ameliorative program targeted at a particular group that does not exclude others in a stereotypical fashion will not run afoul of the equality guarantee.

Both *Willocks* and *Lovelace* suggest an alternative interpretation of subsection 15(2), one in which differential treatment does not constitute discrimination under subsection 15(1) when it seeks to ameliorate the conditions of disadvantaged individuals or groups. Instead of operating to save a discriminatory law, subsection 15(2) provides insight into the meaning of discrimination itself. This approach relies on subsection 15(2)'s commitment to substantive equality to answer the critical question of whether two classes of persons are sufficiently similar in relevant respects to warrant similar treatment or sufficiently different in relevant respects to warrant different treatment. Subsection 15(2) provides that differential treatment based on listed and analogous grounds is warranted, that is, it is not discriminatory, when its object is to ameliorate disadvantage and does not demean the dignity of others. This approach involves substantive equality considerations because substantive equality requires differential treatment based on the material circumstances of socially and economically disadvantaged groups in society.

In summary, laws that distinguish between Aboriginal and non-Aboriginal people may qualify as measures designed to ameliorate Aboriginal disadvantage within the meaning of subsection 15(2). The extent to which subsection 15(2) shields laws that serve this purpose will depend on whether the judiciary employs a formal or substantive approach to the relationship between subsections 15(1) and 15(2). While the latter better protects indigenous difference from the corrosive potential of the Charter, both assume that a law that distinguishes on the basis of indigenous difference merits the same scrutiny as a law that distinguishes on the basis of other grounds. In the next section, I argue that this assumption is misguided.

Derogating from Difference

Regardless of whether it constitutes affirmative action, a law that distinguishes between Aboriginal people and non-Aboriginal people merits

---

66 Ibid., at para. 100.

special consideration under section 15 because of section 25 of the Charter, which provides as follows:

> 25. The guarantee in this Charter of certain rights and freedoms shall not be construed so as to abrogate or derogate from any aboriginal, treaty or other rights or freedoms that pertain to the aboriginal peoples of Canada including
> (a) any rights or freedoms that have been recognized by the Royal Proclamation of October 7, 1763; and
> (b) any rights or freedoms that now exist by way of land claims agreements or may be so acquired.

What constitutional function does section 25 perform, and why? Does it require the judiciary to interpret rights and freedoms guaranteed by the Charter so as to shield from constitutional scrutiny all laws that extend rights to Aboriginal people? Or does section 25 play a more modest role, requiring an interpretation of Charter guarantees that protects only certain laws from Charter scrunity? Although text and precedent provide some insight into these questions, the scope of section 25 should ultimately be determined in light of the interests underlying constitutional recognition and affirmation of existing Aboriginal and treaty rights.

By its terms, section 25 does not appear to guarantee constitutional rights to Aboriginal persons; instead, it provides an interpretive instruction to the judiciary in its task of infusing vague Charter guarantees with determinate meaning.[67] It provides that Charter guarantees are 'not to be construed so as to abrogate or derogate from any Aboriginal, treaty or other rights or freedoms' that pertain to Aboriginal people. In other words, section 25 is a non-derogation clause; it shields certain rights that pertain to Aboriginal people from Charter scrutiny by requiring the judiciary to interpret constitutional guarantees in a manner that ensures

---

67 See Bruce Wildsmith, *Aboriginal Peoples and Section 25 of the Canadian Charter of Rights and Freedoms* (Saskatchewan: University of Saskatchewan Native Law Centre, 1988), at 10 ('viewing s. 25 as more than a saving provision is unwarranted'); William Pentney, 'The Rights of the Aboriginal Peoples of Canada and the Constitution Act, 1982 – Part I: The Interpretive Prism of Section 25,' 22 U.B.C. L. Rev. 21 (1987) (s. 25 is intended only as an interpretive guide and not as an independently enforceable guarantee of Aboriginal and treaty rights'); and Noel Lyon, 'Constitutional Issues in Native Law,' in Bradford W. Morse, ed., *Aboriginal Peoples and the Law: Indian, Métis and Inuit Rights in Canada* (Ottawa: Carleton University Press, 1985), at 423 ('s. 25 creates no new rights').

this result.[68] Section 25 also indicates which rights pertaining to indigenous difference are to be shielded from Charter scrutiny, because it applies expressly to 'rights or freedoms ... recognized by the Royal Proclamation of October 7, 1763; and ... any rights or freedoms that now exist by way of land claims agreements or may be so acquired.' The Royal Proclamation acknowledges the 'semi-autonomous status' of the 'Nations or Tribes' to whom it applies, and prohibits the Crown from granting unceded ancestral territory to third parties.[69] Land claims agreements can provide for a wide array of rights, including rights of self-government. For example, in the James Bay and Northern Quebec Agreement,[70] the Cree and Inuit of Quebec obtained recognition of a system of government and management in return for the surrender of title to land. Together with the Cree-Naskapi (of Quebec) Act, which grants municipal-style powers to incorporated bands, the agreement

---

68 For the view that s. 25 requires Charter provisions to be interpreted so as to avoid conflict with rights referred to in s. 25, see Norman Zlotkin, *Unfinished Business: Aboriginal Peoples and the 1983 Constitutional Conference* (Kingston: Institute of Intergovernmental Relations, Discussion Paper No. 15, 1983), at 46–7; Kent McNeil, 'The Constitutional Rights of the Aboriginal Peoples of Canada,' 4 Supreme Court L. Rev. 255 at 262 (1982); Kenneth Lysyk, 'The Rights and Freedoms of the Aboriginal Peoples of Canada,' in W. Tarnopolsky and G.-A. Beaudoin, eds., *The Canadian Charter of Rights and Freedoms, Commentary* (Scarborough, Ont.: Carswell, 1982), at 471–2. At least one author has argued that there may be cases where conflict is unavoidable, in which case s. 25 may no longer any force: see Bryan Schwartz, *First Principles: Constitutional Reform with Respect to the Aboriginal Peoples of Canada, 1982–1984* (Kingston: Institute of Intergovernmental Relations, 1985), at 271. Even Schwartz, however, acknowledges that 's. 25 will strongly discourage any court from applying the egalitarian and individualistic norms of the Charter of Rights and Freedoms against self-government legislation' (at 271). For the competing view that rights referred to in s. 25 are protected against Charter rights in the event that conflict cannot be avoided through interpretation, see Brian Slattery, 'The Constitutional Guarantee of Aboriginal and Treaty Rights,' 8 Queen's L.J. 232 at 239–40 (1982); and Wildsmith, *Aboriginal Rights and Section 25*, at 23. I argue below that the strength of s. 25 depends on the nature of the law in question.
69 Reprinted in R.S.C. 1985, App. II, No. 1. The proclamation has also been referred to as an 'Indian Bill of Rights': see *St. Catherines Milling and Lumber Co. v. The Queen* (1887), 13 S.C.R. 577 at 652 per Gwynne J. See also *Calder v. A.G.B.C.*, [1973] S.C.R. 313 at 395, per Hall J. ('its force as a statute is analogous to the status of Magna Carta'). For commentary, see Chapter 3. See also Brian Slattery, 'The Hidden Constitution: Aboriginal Rights in Canada,' 32 Am. J. Comp. Law 361 at 368–72 (1984).
70 Canada, *James Bay and Northern Quebec Agreement* (Quebec: Éditeur official du Québec, 1976).

represents a form of Aboriginal self-government that may be constitutionalized as a result of section 35 of the Constitution Act, 1982.[71] Section 25 shields from Charter scrutiny the exercise of rights associated
with the Royal Proclamation's protection of ancestral territories as well
as rights associated with land claims agreements, including rights of self-
government.

Section 25 protection, however, is not restricted to the rights
expressly listed in its subclauses. It also provides that the Charter should
not be 'construed so as to abrogate or derogate from any Aboriginal,
treaty or other rights or freedoms that pertain to the Aboriginal peoples
of Canada.' Lower courts have held that section 25 shields Aboriginal
and treaty rights recognized and affirmed by subsection 35(1). In *R. v.
Nicholas and Bear*,[72] for example, Dickson J. of the New Brunswick Court
of Queen's Bench stated that 'even though aboriginal and treaty rights
then existing and recognized under section 35 might offend against,
say, subsection 15(1), ... subsection 15(1) cannot serve to abrogate or
derogate from such rights.'[73] The greater the scope of subsection 35(1),
the greater the immunity an Aboriginal community enjoys from the
Charter's dictates. Moreover, even if a law is not in relation to an existing Aboriginal or treaty right, it might nonetheless fall within the scope
of section 25 protection because section 25 also refers to 'other rights or
freedoms that pertain to the Aboriginal peoples of Canada.'

What 'other rights' ought to be shielded from Charter scrutiny? At this
point, section 25's text underdetermines its effect because the provision
itself does not define this ambiguous phrase.[74] But if interests associated
with Aboriginal culture, territory, sovereignty, and the treaty process
merit constitutional protection, then there is no reason to restrict their
significance to section 35. Both sections 35 and 25 reflect and give effect
to the unique constitutional relationship between Aboriginal people and
the Canadian state. Both provisions provide constitutional protection to

---

71 See *Eastmain Band v. Gilpin*, [1988] 3 C.N.L.R. 15 (Que. Prov. Ct.), at 66 ('the Crees'
    rights conferred by the James Bay Agreement, as regards Category IA lands, have been
    made constitutional'). For an extended analysis of this issue, see Thomas Isaac, 'The
    Constitution Act, 1982 and the Constitutionalization of Aboriginal Self-Government in
    Canada: Cree-Naskapi (of Quebec) Act,' [1991] 1 C.N.L.R. 1.
72 [1989] 2 C.N.L.R. 131.
73 Ibid., at 134.
74 But see Pentney, 'The Rights of the Aboriginal Peoples of Canada,' at 56 ('[v]arious
    statutory or common law rights or freedoms that pertain to Aboriginal peoples natu-
    rally fall within the scope of the phrase "other rights or freedoms" in s. 25').

interests associated with indigenous difference. Section 35 protects Aboriginal people from federal and provincial action that threatens interests associated with indigenous difference; section 25 protects federal, provincial and Aboriginal initiatives that seek to further interests associated with indigenous difference from Charter scrutiny. Legislation that distinguishes between Aboriginal and non-Aboriginal people in order to protect interests associated with Aboriginal culture, territory, sovereignty, or the treaty process deserves to be shielded from Charter scrutiny. Specifically, if there are two plausible interpretations of a Charter right – one that abrogates or derogates from a right or freedom protected by section 25 and one that does not – the judiciary ought to adopt the latter over the former. If a Charter right or freedom admits of no interpretation other than one that abrogates or derogates from a right or freedom protected by section 25, then the Charter right ought not to apply.

In the context of the Charter's guarantee of equality and prohibition of discrimination, section 25 instructs the judiciary not to regard as discriminatory laws that distinguish between Aboriginal people and non-Aboriginal people for the purpose of protecting interests associated with indigenous difference. Section 15 should not be interpreted so as to unravel legislative initiatives that rely on this distinction to protect interests underlying constitutionally recognized Aboriginal and treaty rights. Because equality demands constitutional protection of interests associated with indigenous difference, it is furthered, not frustrated, by legislative protection of such interests. Indeed, in the next chapter , I argue that section 35 imposes positive obligations on the state not only to protect but to promote and fulfil Aboriginal and treaty rights. To regard such legislation as discriminatory clashes not only with the purpose of the Charter's equality guarantee but also with the purpose of section 35. Returning to the example of the Indian Act, in so far as it distinguishes between Aboriginal and non-Aboriginal people to protect Aboriginal interests associated with culture, territory, sovereignty, or the treaty process, it does not constitute discrimination within the meaning of subsection 15(1).

A law that distinguishes between Aboriginal people and non-Aboriginal people to protect interests associated with indigenous difference provides what Will Kymlicka has termed 'external protection.' It empowers an Aboriginal community against threats posed to its difference by the larger society in which it is located.[75] A broad interpretation

---

75 Will Kymlicka, *Multicultural Citizenship: A Liberal Theory of Minority Rights* (Oxford: Clarendon Press, 1995), at 35.

of section 25 minimizes the possibility that the Charter will frustrate legislative initiatives that provide external protection to indigenous difference. But what of a law that places 'internal restrictions' on some members of an Aboriginal community in a manner that appears to violate their Charter rights? Section 25 presumably governs both scenarios, but a broad interpretation of that section in the context of an internal restriction potentially sacrifices the interests of less powerful members of Aboriginal societies, in cases where the restriction may entail serious deleterious consequences to certain members and may bear only a loose relation to interests associated with indigenous difference. In these circumstances, if two plausible interpretations of a Charter right – one in which the internal restriction violates the Charter and one in which it does not – the judiciary ought to adopt the latter interpretation. If a Charter right admits of no interpretation other than one that results in a violation, section 25 should give way and the restriction should be regarded as a violation and require justification under section 1.

Requiring justification of internal restrictions that clash with Charter guarantees puts to the test the constitution's commitment to indigenous difference. Because of the constitutional significance of indigenous difference, the judiciary ought to extend a wide margin of appreciation[76] to Aboriginal forms of social and political organization when assessing the constitutionality of an internal restriction. Most Aboriginal nations in Canada, for example, place great emphasis on the interconnectedness of family and clan. Densely textured forms of social and political organization that reflect the significance of family and clan or, more generally, the unique identity of an Aboriginal nation, should not be dismantled through Charter litigation because they might appear foreign to Western norms of individualism. In the event of an infringement, an Aboriginal community should be required to justify the restriction in the name of indigenous difference by demonstrating its relevance to the community's past and future. An internal restriction should be declared unconstitutional only when it lacks a compelling and substantial objective, when alternative means exist of accomplishing

---

76 Out of respect for cultural and national diversity, the European Court of Human Rights allows states that adhere to the European Convention on Human Rights a 'margin of appreciation' when assessing compliance. See, generally, H.C. Yourow, *The Margin of Appreciation Doctrine in the Dynamics of European Human Rights Jurisprudence* (Boston: M. Nijhoff, 1993).

the objective, and when the restriction's deleterious effects on the adversely affected members outweigh its salutary effects.[77]

Aboriginal Membership and the Charter

I have argued that the Charter should be interpreted in a manner that respects the constitutional significance of indigenous difference. Laws that distinguish between Aboriginal and non-Aboriginal people to protect indigenous difference do not offend the Charter's equality guarantee; instead, they represent statutory acknowledgement of the fact that Aboriginal people enjoy a unique constitutional relationship with the Canadian state. By virtue of section 25 of the Charter, such laws do not constitute 'discrimination' within the meaning of subsection 15(1) and they may well constitute affirmative action programs within the meaning of subsection 15(2). Section 25 extends less protection to a law that imposes internal restrictions on Aboriginal people but still requires the judiciary to seek to interpret the Charter in a manner that avoids characterizing the law as violating the Charter. But what of legislation whose objective is to further Charter norms at the potential expense of Aboriginal interests associated with indigenous difference? Does legislation designed to further interests that underlie rights and freedoms guaranteed by the Charter trump interests that underlie Aboriginal and treaty rights guaranteed by subsection 35(1)?

A prime illustration of such a conflict lies in recent amendments to the Indian Act, which introduced new rules concerning the acquisition and loss of Indian status and band membership. Before 1985, Indian status and band membership went hand in hand; generally speaking, one could not be a status Indian without being a band member and vice versa. Status Indians enjoyed the right to live on Indian reserves as well as other statutory benefits under the Act, including an exemption from taxation of personal property on a reserve[78] and, in certain circumstances, the right to vote and to run for political office in band council elections.[79] Individuals could claim Indian status if they could prove that

---

77 See *R. v. Oakes*, [1986] 1 S.C.R. 103 (Charter infringement requires substantial objective and proportionality between means and ends); see also *CBC v. Dagenais*, [1994] 3 S.C.R. 835 (Charter infringement requires proportionality between the deleterious and the salutary effects of the measures').

78 Indian Act, R.S.C. 1985, s. 87 (tax-exempt status).

79 Ibid., ss. 2 and 77.

they were a descendant of a registered member of an Indian band that existed at the time of the establishment of a reserve or the negotiation of a treaty.[80] However, an Aboriginal person could lose Indian status in a variety of ways. For example, the Act provided that an Indian man, his wife, and their children lost their Indian status as a result of enfranchisement, an administrative process that provided incentives to Indian men to trade their status for the right to vote and to hold property. More important, the Act also provided that an Indian woman who married a non-Indian man lost her status under the Act. No similar provision affected the status of an Indian man who married a non-Indian woman.

The Act's rules governing Indian women who married non-Indian men came under increasing attack on a number of fronts. Aboriginal women fought a long and ultimately successful political and legal battle to amend the Act.[81] The rules were challenged as discriminatory under the Canadian Bill of Rights,[82] criticized by both a Standing Committee on Indian Affairs and Northern Development[83] and a Royal Commission on the Status of Women,[84] and held to violate article 27 of the International Covenant on Civil and Political Rights, which guarantees the right of persons belonging to 'ethnic, linguistic or religious minorities ... in community with others members of their group, to enjoy their own culture.'[85] In 1985, Parliament enacted An Act to amend the Indian Act,[86] known as Bill C-31, which sought to eliminate the discriminatory

---

80 For more description of federal enfranchisement policy, see Chapter 2.
81 See Janet Silman, ed., *Enough Is Enough: Aboriginal Women Speak Out* (Toronto: The Women's Press, 1987).
82 *A.G. Canada v. Lavell*, [1974] S.C.R. 1349.
83 Standing Committee on Indian Affairs and Northern Development, *Minutes of Proceedings and Evidence*, 1st sess., 32nd Parl., 1980-81-82, Issue no. 58, at 7 (also known as the Penner Committee) ('these discriminatory provisions have caused pain and suffering to Indian communities, and to Indian women and their children').
84 See *Report of the Royal Commission on the Status of Women in Canada* (Ottawa: Supply and Services, 1970), at 237–8, 410 (recommending that 'the Indian Act be amended to allow an Indian woman upon marriage to a non-Indian man to (a) retain her status and (b) to transmit her status to her children').
85 *Lovelace v. Canada*, Communication No. R.6/24, *Report of the Human Rights Committee*, U.N. GOAR, 36th Sess., Supp. No. 40, at 166, U.N. Doc. A/36/40, Annex 18 (1977) (views adopted 29 Dec. 1977). For commentary and critique, see Karen C. Knop, 'The Making of Difference in International Law: Interpretation, Identity and Participation in the Discourse of Self-Determination' (S.J.D. thesis, Faculty of Law, University of Toronto, 1998), at 432–51 (on file with author).
86 An Act to Amend the Indian Act, S.C. 1985, c. 27.

effects of rules governing the loss of status by marriage. As a result, no one can gain or lose Indian status by marriage. Bill C-31 also conferred Indian status and automatic band membership on several classes of persons who had lost status by marriage or enfranchisement. As well, it sought to permit bands to take greater control of band membership by authorizing them to design and implement membership codes that respect membership rights of reinstated persons. Authorizing bands to create membership codes theoretically enables bands, not the federal government, to maintain their own membership lists but codes must receive ministerial approval before they are legally binding under Canadian law.[87]

Bill C-31 creates a conflict between Charter values and indigenous difference because subsection 35(1) of the Constitution Act, 1982, understood in light of its underlying interests, recognizes and affirms the right of Indian bands to determine band membership. First, a right to determine band membership is consonant with cultural identity; a sense of belonging and a shared set of practices designed to determine who belongs and who does not are central to a community's self-definition. Second, a right to determine membership protects territorial interests to the extent that members are entitled to share in the benefits associated with the community's lands and resources. Third, a right to determine membership is at the core of interests associated with sovereignty in so far as self-government involves the freedom to enact and to enforce laws that formalize social norms of political participation. Finally, the treaty process was and continues to be predicated on the authority and capacity of Aboriginal communities to determine who should share in the distribution of treaty benefits and burdens.

Statistics released by the Department of Indian and Northern Affairs illustrate why Bill C-31, enacted in the name of gender equality, dramatically threatens interests associated with indigenous difference. While the specific effects of Bill C-31 on band membership vary from band to band, its general demographic consequences have been profound. As of

---

87 The constitutionality of Bill C-31 has been challenged in *Twinn v. Canada* (1997), 215 N.R. 133 (Fed. C.A.) (ordering a new trial on account of judicial bias). See generally John Borrows, 'Contemporary Traditional Equality: The Effect of the Charter on First Nations Politics,' in David Schneiderman and Kate Sutherland, eds., *Charting the Consequences: The Impact of Charter Rights on Canadian Law and Politics* (Toronto: University of Toronto Press, 1997), 168–99 (assessing the political effects of Bill C-31 on Aboriginal communities).

1995, membership increased in at least nine Indian bands by more than 300 per cent and in at least fifty-six bands by more than than 200 per cent. As well, in at least ninety-eight Indian bands membership more than doubled.[88] Despite promises, the federal government did not discernably increase funding to Indian bands to address these enormous increases in membership and the economic and social needs of new band members. Bands must distribute already scarce resources among an overwhelming number of newcomers. The federal government did introduce a modest housing allowance to enable homes to be built for new members wishing to live on reserves, but this initiative created problems of its own. New members were able to obtain housing funds quickly while long-time members continued to wait for funds to improve their housing.[89] Exacerbating Bill C-31's effects on reserve communities is that if they are entitled to vote and run for office, off-reserve members could theoretically control the outcome of band council elections.[90] More fundamentally, despite the fact that Bill C-31 makes limited provision for membership codes, it declares that certain persons are band members regardless of what is provided for by a membership code; as such, it is a profound interference with an Indian band's right to determine its own membership.

The federal government has defended Bill C-31 on the basis that it seeks to foster gender equality, but automatic band membership by legislative fiat reinstates persons who might have lost band membership for reasons unrelated to their gender. Moreover, Bill C-31 reinstated individuals and their descendants who had lost band membership and Indian status by virtue of federal enfranchisement policy. A less drastic interference with the right to determine membership would have been

---

88 Department of Indian and Northern Affairs, *Report S-2 Individual Status-Reinstatement of Status Information System* (1995); see also Department of Indian and Northern Affairs, *The Impacts of the 1985 Amendments to the Indian Act (Bill C-31)* (Ottawa: Supply and Services, 1990) ('the demographic effects on a status Indian population resulting from Bill C-31 were profound' and '[r]egistrations under Bill C-31 have had a significant impact on the total membership of individual bands, both on and off reserve').

89 See testimony of Chief Harry Coo, Lac la Ronge Band, in Department of Indian and Northern Affairs, *The Impacts of the 1985 Amendments to the Indian Act*.

90 Until recently, ss. 2 and 77 of the Indian Act restricted the right to vote and run for office to band members 'ordinarily resident on the reserve,' but this restriction was successfully challenged as contrary to s. 15 of the Charter: see *Corbiere v. Canada (Minister of Indian and Northern Affairs)*, [1999] 2 S.C.R. 203. See also *Goodswimmer v. Canada* (1995), 123 D.L.R. (4th) 93 (Fed. C.A.) (non-status Indian can stand as a candidate for the position of chief).

for Parliament to loosen, not tighten, the Act's restrictions on the right of Indian bands to define their own membership. It could then seek to ensure that Indian bands when exercising this right did not infringe either subsection 35(4) of the Constitution Act, 1982, which provides that 'Aboriginal and treaty rights are guaranteed equally to male and female persons,' or section 15 of the Charter, interpreted in light of section 25's instruction that Charter rights not be construed so as to abrogate or derogate from interests associated with indigenous difference. Such an approach would enable bands to develop membership laws consistent with the Charter's commitment to equality but also require individuals seeking to become members to demonstrate a connection and commitment to the reserve community.

What role should section 25 play in a constitutional challenge to a membership law that appears to violate a Charter right or freedom? I have argued that section 25 ought to be interpreted relatively broadly in the context of a challenge to a law that provides external protection to an Aboriginal community and relatively narrowly in the context of a law that imposes an internal restriction on members. But membership laws confound the distinction between laws that provide external protection and laws that impose internal restrictions; they define the border between the external and the internal. From the perspective of those who claim a right to belong to the community, a law that denies them membership amounts to an internal restriction. From the perspective of those who possess membership, a membership law provides external protection to the community in the face of outsiders wrongfully claiming membership rights and privileges. Moreover, a challenge to a membership law strikes at the core of interests associated with indigenous difference, whereas a membership law has serious adverse effects on those excluded from membership by its operation.

In these circumstances, section 25 should be interpreted in a way that maximizes the opportunity to air and accommodate the competing interests at stake.[91] With one caution, described below, a relatively nar-

---

91 Compare Ayelet Shachar, 'The Paradox of Multicultural Vulnerability: Identity Groups, the State, and Individual Rights,' in Steven Lukes and Christian Joppke, eds., *Multicultural Questions* (Oxford: Oxford University Press, 1999) ('we need to begin to develop a "reshaped" multicultural citizenship model, one which is sensitive to the diversity within groups, and takes into account not only the interests expressed by a group's acknowledged leaders, but also the *voices from within* expressed by group members, especially those who may be subject to systematic mistreatment by their group's accommodated traditions') (emphasis in original).

row interpretation of section 25 accomplishes this objective. If a Charter right admits of no interpretation other than one that results in a violation, section 25 should give way and the law in question should be regarded as a violation and require justification under section 1 of the Charter. A membership law that violates a Charter right should be declared unconstitutional only where it lacks a compelling and substantial objective, where alternative means exist of accomplishing such an objective, and where the restriction has serious deleterious effects on the adversely affected members that outweigh the restriction's salutary effects. [92] The caution is this: an assessment of a justification of a membership law that violates a Charter right must heed the fact that membership laws will always involve a measure of arbitrariness. In the words of Jean Cohen, '[w]ho belongs to the demos cannot initially be democratically established; it always involves an ascriptive, ethical-political element no matter how liberal the criteria of access for newcomers becomes.'[93] Accordingly, it is especially important that the judiciary extend a wide margin of appreciation to membership laws that infringe Charter rights.

In summary, applying the Charter to federal, provincial, and Aboriginal laws poses a real risk to the continued vitality of indigenous difference. The Charter authorizes judicial reorganization of Aboriginal societies according to non-Aboriginal values. And, as evidenced by Bill C-31, it provides new justifications for legislative incursions into matters that go to the core of indigenous difference. But the Charter also presents numerous interpretive opportunities to minimize the potentially corrosive effects that litigation might have on Aboriginal forms of social organization, and to maximize the protection it affords to less powerful

92 For a powerful argument that blood quantum requirements are necessary to protect interests associated with indigenous difference in the context of the Mohawk nation, see Gerald R. Alfred, *Heeding the Voices of Our Ancestors: Kahnawake Mohawk Politics and the Rise of Native Nationalism* (Toronto: Oxford University Press, 1995), at 173–7; but see John Borrows, '"Landed" Citizenship: Narratives of Aboriginal Political Participation,' in Will Kymlicka and Wayne Norman, eds., *Citizenship in Diverse Societies* (Oxford: Oxford University Press, 2000), 326–42.

93 Jean Cohen, 'Changing Paradigms of Citizenship and the Exclusiveness of the Demos' (unpublished paper presented at the Legal Theory Workshop, Faculty of Law, University of Toronto, November 1998), at 18 (on file with author). See also Frederick G. Whelan, 'Prologue: Democratic Theory and the Boundary Problem,' in J. Roland Pennock and John W. Chapman, eds., *Liberal Democracy* (New York: New York University Press, 1983), 13–47 at 16 ('[b]oundaries comprise a problem ... that is insoluble within the framework of democratic theory').

members of Aboriginal societies. Section 15 admits of a range of interpretations that have varying degrees of impact on interests associated with indigenous difference. Section 25 ought to shield laws that seek to advance Aboriginal interests associated with culture, territory, sovereignty, and the treaty process from Charter scrutiny. In the next two chapters, I argue that the constitution not only authorizes legislatures to enact laws aimed at protecting interests associated with indigenous difference but that, properly understood, it imposes a set of positive obligations on the Canadian state.

Chapter Eight

Indigenous Difference and State Obligations

The trappers have stolen all our beaver, so there is nothing left for them to hunt and they are too old to go anywhere else ... there are also about twenty old sick women, invalids and orphans who are very badly off and they all join me in asking you to help us.

Chief Louis Espagnol, Spanish River Indian Band, 1884[1]

In this chapter, I reflect on the following question: does constitutional recognition of indigenous difference impose positive constitutional obligations on federal, provincial, and territorial governments to provide fiscal, social, and institutional entitlements to Aboriginal people? Fiscal obligations include funding arrangements and transfer payments to facilitate the establishment and maintenance of programs and governing structures. Social obligations include the provision of health care and educational benefits. Institutional obligations include the duty to negotiate treaties in good faith with Aboriginal nations as well as to establish institutional arrangements designed to resolve ongoing disputes between Aboriginal nations and federal, provincial, and territorial governments. In addressing this question, I hope to shed light on some of the social, fiscal, and institutional implications of the unique constitutional relationship that exists between Aboriginal people and the Canadian state.

---

1 Petition (in French) of Chief Louis Espagnol to James Phipps, visiting superintendent of Indian Affairs for Manitoulin Island and Lake Huron, 15 Dec. 1884. Public Archives of Canada (PAC), Record Group 10 (RG 10), vol. 2289, file 57, 641. Chief Espagnol reiterated his request seventeen years later in a letter to Samuel Stewart of the Indian Department: Memorandum, 22 Aug. 1901, PAC RG 10, vol. 3303, file 235, 225–1.

Some might argue that Aboriginal and treaty rights are negative rights, whose sole purpose is to prevent government from interfering with their exercise. Concerns relating to judicial legitimacy and judicial competence militate against interpreting Aboriginal and treaty rights as requiring positive governmental action on social, fiscal, and institutional matters. The opposite approach would be to suggest that Aboriginal and treaty rights require federal, provincial, and territorial governments to provide Aboriginal people with a wide array of entitlements. Three reasons support this perspective. First, the fiduciary relationship between the Canadian state and Aboriginal people gives rise to a set of generous positive rights. Second, it is intuitively unfair to constitutionally distribute social, fiscal, and institutional entitlements only to those Aboriginal people sufficiently powerful or fortuitous to enjoy either the benefit of treaty protection or legislative good will. Third, principles of restitution suggest that the Canadian state ought to be constitutionally obliged to undo the damage wrought by colonization and to ameliorate Aboriginal socio-economic disadvantage.

I steer a middle course between these two perspectives, advancing the claim that all constitutional rights possess positive dimensions. I identify two types of arguments commonly employed to challenge claims that constitutional rights impose positive obligations on government, namely, arguments that question either the legitimacy or the competence of the judiciary to render such judgments. I argue that whether an Aboriginal or treaty right requires government to provide a particular social, fiscal, or institutional entitlement to Aboriginal people depends on the extent to which the entitlement in question protects one or more interests associated with indigenous difference.

Three Distinctions

Whether Aboriginal and treaty rights require governments to provide social, fiscal, or institutional entitlements to Aboriginal people is a question that implicates a well-known but elusive distinction between negative and positive rights.[2] This distinction speaks to the nature of the

---

2 The debate about positive and negative legal rights, conceived in terms of obligations of inaction and action, is related to but not strictly aligned with competing conceptions of freedom. The classic articulation of the difference between positive and negative freedom is found in Isaiah Berlin, 'Two Concepts of Liberty,' in *Four Essays on Liberty* (Oxford: Oxford University Press, 1969), 118, 121–72. For two critiques, see

obligation that rights create. Negative rights are typically imagined as checking the growth of state power into cherished areas of individual freedom; they create state obligations of inaction or non-interference. A negative right requires government not to interfere with its exercise. In contrast, a positive right requires action. Positive rights are typically imagined as requiring state intervention to correct for inequalities of wealth caused by market freedom; they require government to provide certain legal entitlements to rights-holders. Proponents of the view that Aboriginal and treaty rights require governments to provide social, fiscal and institutional entitlements to Aboriginal people might seek to characterize section 35 rights as positive rights, whereas opponents might seek to characterize them as negative rights.

An example of how a distinction between positive and negative constitutional rights works in practice is found in *Harris v. McCrae*,[3] in which the U.S. Supreme Court upheld a woman's negative right to undergo an abortion but rejected the claim that women have a positive right to state-funded abortions even if an abortion is necessary to save a woman's life. Similarly, in *DeShaney v. Winnebago County Department of Social Services*,[4] the U.S. Supreme Court dismissed the claim that state officials had violated the constitution by failing to protect a child from imminent harm because, according to the court, the government normally has no positive duties to protect citizens from imminent danger.[5]

Although popular south of the border, the distinction between negative and positive rights enjoys less currency in Canadian constitutional thought. Wilson J. stated in *McKinney v. University of Guelph*, 'Canadians have a somewhat different attitude towards government and its role from our U.S. neighbours. Canadians recognize that government has traditionally had and continues to have an important role to play in the creation and preservation of a just Canadian society. The state has been looked to and has responded to demands that Canadians be guaranteed adequate health care, access to education and a minimum level of finan-

---

C.B. MacPherson, 'Berlin's Division of Liberty,' in MacPherson, *Democratic Theory: Essays in Retrieval* (Oxford: Clarendon Press, 1973), at 118 and Charles Taylor, 'What's Wrong with Negative Liberty?' in Taylor, *Philosophy and the Human Sciences: Philosophical Papers* (Cambridge: Cambridge University Press, 1985), at 2:211.

3 448 U.S. 297 (1980).

4 489 U.S. 189 (1989).

5 See also *Jackson v. Joliet*, 715 F.2d 1200, 1203 (7th Cir. 1983), cert. denied, 465 U.S. 1049 (1984), per Posner J. ('the Constitution is a charter of negative rather than positive liberties').

cial security to name but a few examples.'[6] Canadian political culture has traditionally been wary of the libertarian premises that appear to underpin the distinction between negative and positive rights and more accepting of state action designed to promote individual and collective well-being.[7]

Moreover, at a conceptual level, a distinction between negative and positive rights is less sturdy than it might initially appear. Although a negative right is said to protect a zone of freedom from certain forms of state action, such freedom does not exist independently of or apart from state action. A right of privacy, for example, initially presents itself as a negative right, by suggesting that government should not act in certain ways. However, it also requires state action in the form of the establishment and enforcement of a host of background property and contractual entitlements. Property law prevents individuals from violating the privacy of others. Contract law protects an individual's freedom to refuse to contract with other people. Characterizing a right of privacy as a negative right ignores the myriad forms of state action embedded in the freedom contemplated by the right. Any determination of whether a constitutional provision confers a positive right requiring state action or a negative right requiring state inaction rests on one's initial vantage point. Without reference to a normative baseline understanding of the proper role of the state and a conception of human freedom, the distinction between positive and negative rights is completely uninformative.[8] In North America, judges have tended to treat traditional common law private entitlements as the essential components of an often unarticulated normative baseline.[9] What goes unsaid when this baseline is invoked is

---

6 [1990] 3 S.C.R. 229.

7 See, generally, Gad Horowitz, *Canadian Labour in Politics* (Toronto: University of Toronto Press, 1968), at 3–57.

8 For the classic articulation of this insight, see Robert L. Hale, 'Coercion and Distribution in a Supposedly Non-Coercive State,' 38 Pol. Sci. Q. 470 (1923). See also Cass R. Sunstein, *The Partial Constitution* (Cambridge: Harvard University Press, 1993), at 93–122; Susan Bandes, 'The Negative Constitution: A Critique,' 88 Mich. L. Rev. 2271 (1990); David P. Currie, 'Positive and Negative Constitutional Rights,' 53 U. Chi. L. Rev. 864 (1986); and Anna T. Majewicz, 'Baseline Analysis: Broadening the Judicial Perspective,' 65 St. John's L. Rev. 495 (1991).

9 See, e.g., *Lucas v. South Carolina Coastal Council*, 112 S. Ct. 2886 at 2901–2 (1992) ('as it would be required to do if it sought to restrain [the plaintiff] in a common law action for public nuisance, South Carolina must identify background principles of nuisance and property law that prohibit the uses [intended]'). But see *McKinney v. University of Guelph*, [1990] 3 S.C.R. 229, per Wilson J. ('[e]xperience shows ... that freedom has often required the intervention and protection of government against private action').

that property and the right to contract require extensive positive state action to be effective legal institutions. In fact, they can be seen as the structure upon which modern industrial society emerged.[10]

In light of these cultural and conceptual shortcomings, the distinction between negative and positive rights is of limited utility in understanding the nature of constitutional rights in Canada. However, it should not be jettisoned entirely. While not helpful as a means of distinguishing one type of right from another, the distinction is useful in identifying and labelling the dimensions of a right. Rights are rarely if ever purely negative or positive. Instead, they possess negative and positive dimensions, which vary according to the interests they protect. A right's positive dimensions require government to act in certain ways, whereas its negative dimensions require government to refrain from acting in other ways.

Some rights clearly contemplate positive obligations on government. For example, minority language education rights contained in the Charter impose 'positive obligations on government to alter or develop major institutional structures.'[11] Similarly, legal rights, such as the right to a fair trial, the right not to be subjected to cruel and unusual punishment, the right to an interpreter, and the right to counsel, require action and expense on the part of government. *R. v. Askov*[12] is a striking example of the positive dimensions of legal rights. In *Askov*, the Supreme Court of Canada held that a delay of up to two years between the date of committal for trial and the trial itself violated an accused's right to be tried within a reasonable time. Although the court did not order the government to build new court facilities, it suggested adapting government buildings or using portable structures to serve as courthouses and said further that, if such solutions proved 'unworkable,' some other solution would be required.[13] Other Charter rights contain less straight forward

---

10 See generally Duncan Kennedy, *A Critique of Adjudication* (Cambridge: Harvard University Press, 1997), at 240–6 (arguing that nonregulatory understandings of the common law conceal its distributive dimension and naturalize existing distributions); Joseph W. Singer, 'Property and Social Relations: From Title to Entitlement,' in G.E. van Maanen and A.J. van der Walt, eds., *Property Law on the Threshold of the 21st Century* (Apeldorn: Maklu, 1996), at 69–90 (arguing that property law is inescapably distributive); Duncan Kennedy and Frank Michaelman, 'Are Property and Contract Efficient?' 8 Hofstra L. Rev. 711 (1980) (arguing that the common law is no less regulatory than regulation).
11 See *Mahe v. Alberta*, [1990] 1 S.C.R. 342.
12 [1990] 2 S.C.R. 1199.
13 Ibid., at 1243.

positive dimensions but nonetheless have been held to require state action. For example, 'the right to life, liberty and security of the person is in one sense a negative right, but the requirement that the government respect the "fundamental principles of justice" may provide a basis for characterizing s. 7 [of the Charter] as a positive right in some circumstances.'[14] Equality rights are often construed in similarly ambivalent terms: 'the equality right is a hybrid of sorts since it is neither purely positive nor purely negative. In some contexts it will be proper to characterize s. 15 [of the Charter] as providing positive rights.'[15]

If all constitutional rights possess both positive and negative dimensions, then the key question is not whether a particular right is positive or negative but instead whether the right's positive dimensions impose a particular governmental obligation.[16] Translated to the context of section 35, do the positive dimensions of Aboriginal and treaty rights recognized by the constitution include the provision of certain social, fiscal, and institutional entitlements to Aboriginal rights-holders? The answer to this question depends in part on the nature of the interests that section 35 ought to protect, implicating in turn a second distinction commonly employed in constitutional scholarship, namely, a distinction between civil and political rights and social and economic rights.

Whereas the distinction between negative and positive rights involves differing obligations, the distinction between civil and political rights and social and economic rights identifies different interests underlying rights protection. Civil and political rights include freedom of expression, conscience, religion, assembly, and association, as well as voting rights and rights associated with a fair trial and equality. Social and economic rights include rights to health, education, culture, housing, social assistance, and nutrition. Those claiming that section 35 requires government to provide social, fiscal, and institutional entitlements to Aboriginal people might characterize Aboriginal and treaty rights as social and economic rights; their opponents might characterize them more in terms of civil and political rights.

The distinction between civil and political rights and social and eco-

---

14 *Schachter v. Canada*, [1992] 2 S.C.R. 679 at 721, per Lamer J.

15 Ibid.

16 This idea is not unfamiliar to the judiciary when cast in terms of remedial power: see, for example, *Schachter v. Canada*, at 709 ('[i]n determining whether reading in is appropriate ..., the question is not whether courts can make decisions that impact on budgetary policy, it is to what degree they appropriately do so').

nomic rights owes in part to the post-war decision to split the 1948 Universal Declaration of Human Rights[17] into two treaties: the International Covenant on Civil and Political Rights[18] and the International Covenant on Economic, Social and Cultural Rights.[19] Together with an optional protocol, the first treaty deals with civil and political rights and determinations of compliance by a quasi-judicial body, the Human Rights Committee, based on individual complaints or 'considerations.'[20] The second treaty lists economic, social, and cultural rights; it initially provided no equivalent right of individual petition and limited its monitoring mechanism to a state report procedure.[21] Broadly speaking, civil and political rights protect an individual's formal ability to participate in civil and political life. By protecting freedom of conscience, religion, expression, assembly, and association and by prohibiting certain forms of discrimination and subjecting the exercise of state power to the rule of law and principles of fundamental justice, civil and political rights purport to guarantee individual freedom and political democracy. In contrast, social and economic rights identify and protect the fundamentals of economic and social well-being. The International Covenant on Economic, Social and Cultural Rights, for example, seeks to protect the right to work, the right to education and medical care, the right to social security, and rights to food, clothing, and shelter. Social and economic rights thus seek to protect interests associated with employment, education, health, housing, nutrition, and economic well-being.

Many scholars have pointed out the intimate relationship between civil and political rights and social and economic rights. As Frank Scott said in 1949, '[w]e are more aware today of the foolishness of pretending that a man is "free" when he is unemployed and without income through no fault of his own, or when he cannot pay for good health or good education for his children.'[22] Michael MacMillan claims an instru-

---

17 Adopted 10 Dec. 1948, G.A. Res. 217A (III), U.N. Doc. A/810, at 71 (1948).

18 Adopted 16 Dec. 1966, 999 U.N.T.S. 171 (entered into force 23 Mar. 1976).

19 Adopted 16 Dec. 1966, 993 U.N.T.S. 3 (entered into force 3 Jan. 1976).

20 See, generally, Dominic McGoldrick, *The Human Rights Committee: Its Role in the Development of the International Covenant on Civil and Political Rights* (Oxford: Clarendon Press, 1994).

21 See, generally, Philip Alston and Gerald Quinn, 'The Nature and Scope of State Parties' Obligations under the International Covenant on Economic, Social and Cultural Rights,' 9 Hum. Rts. Q. 156 (1987).

22 F.R. Scott, 'Dominion Jurisdiction over Human Rights and Fundamental Freedoms, 27 Can. Bar Rev. 497 at 507 (1949).

mental relation between the two sets of rights: 'It is virtually a common-place observation that the traditional political rights are chimerical in the absence of a minimum level of socioeconomic subsistence: that some minimal level of education is a prerequisite to the effective enjoyment of freedom of speech, or that an adequate supply of food or shelter is necessary for political liberty to be meaningful. If the political rights are of paramount importance, then so too are the major social rights simply because they are necessary prerequisites to the exercise of political rights.'[23] Despite this relationship, civil and political rights are often thought of as negative rights and social and economic rights as positive rights because the former require state inaction and the latter state action. Some civil and political rights, however, create positive obligations on the state whereas social and economic rights often engender obligations typically associated with negative rights. For example, a right to housing may possess positive dimensions if it requires government to provide housing but it may also possess negative dimensions if it requires government to refrain from levelling existing homes.[24]

Litigation relating to social and economic rights typically employs two powerful arguments in favour of judicial intervention. The first involves a simple maxim of distributive justice that informs many aspects of constitutional discourse, namely, that if the state is to intervene in a certain area of social, economic, or political life, it must do so properly. For example, in criminal law, the rights of an accused can be understood in terms of state obligations triggered by the exercise of state power. If the state is going to marshal its power to imprison a citizen, it must do so in a way that conforms to principles of fundamental justice. The Supreme Court of Canada in its famous abortion case, *Morgentaler v. The Queen*,[25] employed this maxim in the context of a state system regulating women's decisions about their pregnancies. Equality jurisprudence also relies heavily on it. In *Eldridge v. British Columbia*,[26] for example, the court required the state to provide funding for interpreters for hearing-impaired patients in part because, if the state is going to fund health services, it must do so in a non-discriminatory manner. And the court's

---

23 C.M. MacMillan, 'Social versus Political Rights,' 19 Can. J. Pol. Sci. 283 at 285–6 (1986).

24 Compare *Olga Tellis*, [1985] 2 Supp. S.C.R. 51 (India) (refusing to respect a right to be heard before the eviction of sidewalk dwellers violated a right to a livelihood and right to work).

25 *R. v. Morgentaler*, [1988] 1 S.C.R. 30.

26 *Eldridge v. British Columbia*, [1997] 3 S.C.R. 624.

decision in *Vriend v. Alberta*[27] which required a provincial legislature to prohibit discrimination based on sexual orientation, rests on the proposition that, if the state is going to establish a human rights code, it cannot leave out protection against discrimination based on sexual orientation.

This maxim of distributive justice is a powerful tool to protect interests associated with social and economic rights. Because it is premised on the presence of some form of limited governmental intervention, it operates most effectively in the context of underinclusive legislative schemes. In the absence of a specific legislative regime, and where the nature of the claim is that the state has failed to provide any legislative protection for interests associated with social and economic rights, the maxim begins to falter. To be effective in this context – say, where the complaint is that the state has failed to enact a human rights code as opposed to producing an underinclusive code – it must be wedded with a second, more contentious maxim of distributive justice, one implicit in the earlier critique of the distinction between positive rights and negative rights and which speaks profoundly to the relation between law and society. This second maxim has a number of versions. According to one of them non-intervention is a form of intervention. A second version says that markets do not exist in the absence of law. A third version claims that law is deeply constitutive of social, economic, and political life. Yet another version argues that the real question is not whether the state should intervene in certain spheres of social life because it is already there, but on whose behalf ought the state intervene and for what reason.

This second maxim combines with the first to enable the judiciary to directly protect interests associated with social and economic rights by requiring the state to legislate for their protection. It eliminates the need to condition judicial intervention on the existence of an underinclusive legislative scheme because it holds that the premise of the first maxim, namely, state intervention, is always present. The state is always already 'there,' regulating the field in question, either in the form of a targeted legislative regime or as a result of the existence of baseline legal entitlements established and enforced at minimum by the law of contract and the law of property. This maxim authorizes the judiciary to ensure that the state regulates social life in a manner that conforms to

---

27   *Vriend v. Alberta,* [1998] 1 S.C.R. 493.

principles of distributive justice. It underscores the fact that constitutional law is, at root, a distributive enterprise.

However, courts have generally been reluctant to invest civil and political rights with much social, economic, or institutional content.[28] Judicial reluctance stems in part from uncertainty about the extent to which social and economic matters are justiciable, or suitable for judicial determination.[29] Debates over the justiciability of a particular matter occur in the long shadow of the basic democratic principle that the will of the majority should prevail in fashioning law and policy. This principle underpins a standard doctrine of separation of powers manifested in democratic forms of governance: the legislature makes the law, the executive implements the law, and the judiciary enforces the law. Such a doctrine, according to Philip Kurland, 'encompasses the notion that there are fundamental differences in governmental functions – frequently but not universally denoted as legislative, executive, and judicial – which must be maintained as separate and distinct, each sovereign in its own area, none to operate in the realm assigned to another.'[30]

Against the backdrop of a commitment to a separation of legislative, executive, and judicial functions, debates about a particular subject matter's justiciability typically implicate a third distinction commonly employed in constitutional scholarship: the distinction between the institutional legitimacy and the institutional competence of the judiciary.[31] Concerns relating to institutional legitimacy focus on the justice

---

28 Compare *Irwin Toy v. Quebec*, [1989] 1 S.C.R. 927 at 1003–4 (expressly refraining from stating whether s. 7 of the Charter, guaranteeing a right to security of the person, protects 'economic rights fundamental to human life or survival') with *Finlay v. Canada*, [1990] 2 F.C. 790 at 816 (Fed. C.A.) ('it must not be blithely supposed that it is necessarily in the public interest to bleed those who live at or below the poverty line as a purgative for social health, even if the bleeding is only at a little at a time and only once a month'). See generally Helena Orton, 'Section 15, Benefits Programs and Other Benefits at Law: The Interpretation of Section 15 of the Charter since Andrews,' 19 Man. L. Rev. 288 (1990); Ian Johnston, 'Section 7 of the Charter and Constitutionally Protected Welfare,' 46 U.T. Fac. L. Rev. 1 (1988); and Martha Jackman, 'The Protection of Welfare Rights under the Charter,' 20 Ottawa L. Rev. 257 (1988).

29 See D.J. Galligan, *Discretionary Powers: A Legal Study of Official Discretion* (Oxford: Clarendon Press, 1990), at 241 (defining 'non-justiciable' as 'unsuited for adjudication').

30 Philip K. Kurland, 'The Rise and Fall of the "Doctrine" of Separation of Powers,' 85 Mich. L. Rev. 592 at 593 (1986).

31 See Ghislain Otis, 'La Charte et la modification des programs gouvernementaux: l'exemple de l'injonction structurelle en droit américain,' 36 McGill L.J. 1349 at 1357–60 (1991) (legitimacy versus efficacy); Martha Minow, *Making All the Difference: Inclusion,*

of providing constitutional protection to the subject matter in question and of allowing an unelected judiciary to require an elected legislature to pursue particular political programs. For example, one scholar has stated that having the judiciary 'declare that a government is lagging behind in creating the conditions under which a social right could be enjoyed' would raise 'utterly political questions.'[32]

Legitimacy concerns emanate from both conservative and progressive visions of social justice. Conservative critics of social and economic rights often decry the fact that social and economic rights would require state intervention in the market and a significant redistribution of wealth.[33] According to this view, a constitution should guard against state intervention; state initiatives that seek to institutionalize interests underlying social and economic rights should be subject to constitutional scrutiny. Rights that create and protect a zone of individual freedom from state intervention merit constitutional protection; rights that impose positive obligations on the state do not.[34] Progressive critics, on the other hand, accept the legitimacy of the interests underlying social and economic rights but are often concerned about the legitimacy of empowering the judiciary to overrule the popular will as expressed through legislative activity. Some fear the further legalization of politics;[35] others, such as Joel Bakan, warn that social and economic rights do not touch the complicated causes of poverty and disadvantage and

---

Exclusion, and American Law (Ithaca: Cornell University Press, 1990), at 241–51 (legitimacy versus competence); Jackman, 'The Protection of Welfare Rights,' at 330–7 (legitimacy versus competence); Thomas A. Cromwell, *Locus Standi: A Commentary on the Law of Standing in Canada* (Scarborough, Ont.: Carswell, 1986), at 6 (legitimacy versus adequacy); and Jamie Cassels, 'Judicial Activism and Public Interest Litigation in India: Attempting the Impossible?' 37 Am. J. Comp. L. 495 at 509–17 (1989) (examining questions of legitimacy and adequacy in the judicial function).

32 E.W. Vierdag, 'The Legal Nature of the Rights Granted by the International Covenant on Economic, Social and Cultural Rights,' 9 Neth. Y.B. Int'l L. 69 at 92–93 (1978).

33 See, for example, Richard Epstein, *Takings: Private Property and the Power of Eminent Domain* (Cambridge: Harvard University Press, 1985), at 307–12.

34 For a classic articulation of this perspective, see Milton Friedman, *Capitalism and Freedom* (Chicago: University of Chicago Press, 1962).

35 See, for example, Michael Mandel, *The Charter of Rights and the Legalization of Politics in Canada* (Toronto: Wall and Thompson, 1989); Harry Glasbeek, 'The Social Charter: Poor Politics for the Poor,' in Joel Bakan and David Schneiderman, eds., *Social Justice and the Constitution: Perspectives on a Social Union for Canada* (Ottawa: Carleton University Press, 1992) ('it may turn out that a social charter becomes a way for government and others to avoid having to engage in transformative politics').

that their symbolic message is at best ambiguous.[36] Buttressing this perspective is the concern that judges, who are traditionally almost exclusively male, white, and wealthy, will inject conservative ideological content into vague constitutional guarantees.[37]

In contrast, concerns relating to institutional competence speak to whether the judiciary is capable of making meaningful determinations regarding the nature and scope of certain types of rights, given their underlying interests and ensuing obligations. It is often said that the judiciary is an institution that, by virtue of its nature, is incapable of engaging adequately in the relatively complex task of delineating and enforcing positive legislative obligations. Social and economic rights are often characterized as vague as to the obligations they mandate, progressive and therefore requiring time to realize, and complex and diffuse in terms of the interests they protect. According to this perspective, these matters are best left to the legislature, either because the judiciary is deficient in skill, education, training, or procedure or because their adjudication touches on complex issues involving institutional design, policy choice, and contested political programs.[38] In the words of Roberto Unger, 'the difficulty arises from the disproportion between the reconstructive mission and its institutional agent.'[39]

Any discussion of the extent to which Aboriginal and treaty rights impose positive obligations on government to provide social, fiscal, or institutional entitlements to Aboriginal people is bound to refer to the distinction between negative and positive rights. It is also bound to

---

36 Joel Bakan, *Just Words: Constitutional Rights and Social Wrongs* (Toronto: University of Toronto Press, 1997), at 134–41.

37 See Joel Bakan, 'Constitutional Interpretation and Social Change: You Can't Always Get What You Want (Or What You Need),' 70 Can. Bar Rev. 307 at 318–23 (1991) (listing factors that contribute to the elitism of the judiciary) and J.A.G. Griffith, *The Politics of the Judiciary*, 3rd ed. (Manchester: Manchester University Press, 1985) at 25–31 (providing numerical breakdown of the socioeconomic backgrounds of senior British judiciary).

38 See generally Howard I. Kalodner and James J. Fishman, eds., *The Limits of Justice: The Courts' Role in School Desegregation* (Cambridge: Ballinger Publishing, 1978); Kenneth C. Davis, 'Facts in Lawmaking,' 80 Col. L. Rev. 931 (1980); Lon L. Fuller, 'The Forms and Limits of Adjudication,' 92 Harv. L. Rev. 353 (1978). See specifically J. Frémont, 'Les Tribunaux et la Charte: le pouvoir d'ordonner la depense de fonds publics en matières sociales et économiques,' 36 McGill L.J. 1323 (1991); Andrew Petter, 'The Politics of the Charter,' 8 Supreme Court L. Rev. 473 (1986).

39 Roberto Mangabeira Unger, *What Should Legal Analysis Become?* (London: Verso, 1996), at 32.

implicate the distinction between civil and political rights and social and economic rights and concerns relating to the justiciability of social and economic rights. Nonetheless, these distinctions do not fully capture what differentiates Aboriginal and treaty rights from their civil, political, social, and economic counterparts. Aboriginal and treaty rights are neither civil and political rights nor social and economic rights. They reflect qualitatively different interests and concerns, which possess unique positive dimensions and impose unique positive obligations on the Canadian state.

Rereading *Sparrow*

As I argued above, there are at least three reasons to suggest that Aboriginal and treaty rights require governments to provide a wide array of entitlements to Aboriginal people. First, governments already owe a number of positive obligations to Aboriginal people as a result of the fiduciary relationship that exists between Aboriginal people and the Crown.[40] Second, it seems intuitively unfair to distribute certain entitlements only to those Aboriginal people sufficiently powerful or fortuitous to enjoy either the benefit of treaty protection or legislative good will.[41] Third, the Canadian state should be constitutionally obligated to undo the damage wrought by colonization and to ameliorate Aboriginal socio-economic disadvantage.[42]

Despite the attractiveness of this open-ended approach, it faces a number of formidable hurdles. First, the judiciary will be extremely reluctant to interpret the constitution as requiring substantive and open-ended judicial scrutiny of social, fiscal, and institutional policy. Courts tend to raise concerns relating to institutional legitimacy and institutional competence when faced with claims that government is constitutionally obligated to provide a particular benefit to a group of

---

40 See, generally, Leonard I. Rotman, *Parallel Paths: Fiduciary Doctrine and the Crown-Native Relationship in Canada* (Toronto: University of Toronto Press, 1996).

41 Compare Ronald Dworkin, *Law's Empire* (Cambridge: Harvard University Press, 1986) (criticizing distributions that result in 'checkerboard' justice).

42 Compare Bryan Schwartz, *First Principles, Second Thoughts: Aboriginal Peoples, Constitutional Reform and Canadian Statecraft* (Montreal: Institute for Research on Public Policy, 1986), at 48 ('Most Canadians would respond better to a claim for fiscal transfers to Aboriginal governments if they were characterized as a step towards the improvement of the lives and opportunities of Aboriginal peoples, rather than as the correction of a wrong done by Canadians in the past').

people. These concerns will be heightened in the context of Aboriginal and treaty rights. Concerns about institutional legitimacy will be exacerbated by the problematic justice of differential constitutional protection. Why should governments be constitutionally obligated to provide, for example, certain education or health care benefits to Aboriginal people but not necessarily to non-Aboriginal people? Concerns about institutional competence will be magnified to the extent that claims relate not to a set of basic entitlements but to specific entitlements over and above those provided as of statutory right to non-Aboriginal people. Both sets of concerns will provide a powerful web of judicial resistance to viewing Aboriginal rights in social and economic terms. In the absence of a more minimalist approach, the judiciary will likely shy away from constitutionally requiring government to provide social, fiscal, or institutional entitlements to Aboriginal people.

Second, and related to the first point, an open-ended approach does not fit comfortably with the jurisprudence to date that addresses the nature and scope of Aboriginal rights recognized and affirmed by section 35. In *R. v. Sparrow*, the Supreme Court of Canada held that subsection 35(1) recognizes and affirms existing Aboriginal practices integral to Aboriginal identity.[43] The court accepted anthropological evidence that, 'for the Musqueam, the salmon fishery has always constituted an integral part of their distinctive culture.'[44] In contrast to such practices, social and economic rights are designed to ensure that the state provide individuals and communities with basic social and economic benefits. Aboriginal and treaty rights protect interests associated with indigenous difference, which differ from interests protected by social and economic rights. Any claim that subsection 35(1) requires government to provide a social, fiscal, or institutional entitlement to Aboriginal people needs to link the entitlement in question to interests underlying that subsection.[45]

For all of its historic significance, the court's decision in *Sparrow* was remarkably terse on what constitutes an Aboriginal right. The court

---

43 *R. v. Sparrow*, [1990] 1 S.C.R. 1075.

44 Ibid.

45 Compare *R. v. Sparrow*, at 1106 ('[t]he approach to be taken with respect to interpreting the meaning of s. 35(1) is derived from general principles of constitutional interpretation, principles relating to Aboriginal rights, and the purposes behind the constitutional provision itself'), and *R. v. Big M Drug Mart Ltd.*, [1985] 1 S.C.R. 295 at 344 ('[t]he meaning of a right or freedom guaranteed by the Charter' is 'to be understood by an analysis of the purpose of such a guarantee' and 'in light of the interests it was meant to protect').

held that subsection 35(1) recognizes and affirms an activity, fishing, that, 'for the Musqueam ... has always constituted an integral part of their distinctive culture.'[46] A narrow interpretation of this holding is that subsection 35(1) only recognizes and affirms existing Aboriginal practices integral to Aboriginal culture.[47] This reading of *Sparrow* would make it difficult to assert that subsection 35(1) requires governments to provide entitlements to Aboriginal people independent of any treaty obligations. It would be necessary to demonstrate that receipt of a particular social, fiscal, or institutional entitlement is an existing Aboriginal practice integral to Aboriginal culture. However, *Sparrow* can be interpreted more broadly by focusing on why the court was willing to view the practice of fishing as a constitutional right. In its opinion, the practice deserved the status of a constitutional right because it was and is integral to Aboriginal culture. The purpose underlying the right to fish, in other words, is the protection of Aboriginal culture. As argued in Chapter 2, Aboriginal cultural difference is an aspect of indigenous difference that possesses constitutional significance. *Sparrow* suggests that Aboriginal culture is an interest worthy of constitutional protection. Viewed this way, *Sparrow* suggests that constitutional recognition and affirmation of existing Aboriginal and treaty rights serves to protect interests associated with Aboriginal cultural difference. This purpose is furthered, but presumably not exhausted, by constitutionally protecting practices integral to Aboriginal culture.

Considering section 35 in light of its underlying interests provides a clearer picture of its positive dimensions. Governmental provision of certain social, fiscal, and institutional entitlements to Aboriginal people, such as funding and maintaining educational facilities, is essential to the protection of interests associated with Aboriginal cultural difference.[48]

---

46 *R. v. Sparrow.*

47 An even narrower reading would focus on the fact that the court noted that fishing '*always* constituted an integral part of Musqueam culture': ibid. (emphasis added). See, for example, *Delgamuukw v. British Columbia* (1991), 79 D.L.R. (4th) 185 (B.C.S.C.), per McEachern C.J. (Aboriginal practice must have existed for a 'long, long time' before contact); (1993), 104 D.L.R. (4th) 470 (B.C.C.A.). See also *R. v. Van der Peet* (1993), 80 B.C.L.R. (2d) 75 (C.A.), at 95, per Wallace J.A. concurring (the purpose of s. 35(1) is 'to protect, from unjustified interference by government legislation or regulation, the right of the Aboriginal people to participate in those customs and activities which were traditional and integral to the native society pre-sovereignty').

48 See Joseph E. Magnet, 'Interpreting Multiculturalism,' in Canadian Human Rights Foundation, ed., *Multiculturalism and the Charter* (Scarborough, Ont.: Carswell, 1987),

If withdrawal of an entitlement threatened the ability of an Aboriginal community to maintain culturally distinct ways of life, it might in some circumstances[49] constitute an infringement of section 35. The withdrawal would then require justification in accordance with the tests set out in *Sparrow* to withstand constitutional scrutiny.[50] Similarly, if fishing is a practice integral to an Aboriginal community's cultural identity, subsection 35(1) should require governments to make good faith efforts to ensure that fishing will continue to be successful, as measured by the fruits of past practice. In other words, the constitution may obligate government to legislate to conserve fisheries.

A still broader interpretation of the court's holding in *Sparrow* is that Aboriginal cultural interests are not the only interests that Aboriginal and treaty rights are designed to protect. I have argued that interests associated with Aboriginal territory, Aboriginal sovereignty, and the treaty process also merit constitutional protection. Aboriginal peoples were dispossessed of their ancestral territories by governmental and judicial action that failed to take into account the legal and constitutional significance of Aboriginal territorial interests. Constitutional protection of these interests should not proceed on the misguided assumption that the existing distribution of title to land in Canada is just and that constitutional recognition of Aboriginal title to lands not yet actively taken up by the Crown is sufficient to fulfil constitutional requirements. Constitutional protection of Aboriginal territorial interests would ring hollow without institutional processes designed to recognize and implement Aboriginal rights of access to and use and enjoyment of their ancestral territories. Properly understood, section 35

---

145 at 150 (constitutional recognition of cultural difference requires an 'institutional infrastructure' through which groups can flourish). Compare *MacDonald v. Montreal*, [1986] 1 S.C.R. 460 at 521, per Wilson J. dissenting ('there is substantial support in legal theory for the appellant's submission that right and duty are correlative terms and ... if s. 133 confers a right on a litigant to use his or her language in court ..., then there is a correlative duty on the state to respect and accommodate that right').

49 The court in *Sparrow* suggested that interferences with Aboriginal rights must be 'unreasonable' or 'undue' in order to constitute a prima facie infringement of s. 35(1).

50 According to *Sparrow*, government action interfering with the exercise of an Aboriginal right must possess a 'valid objective' and must accord Aboriginal people top priority after the implementation of such an objective. In addition, the court signalled that it might inquire into 'whether there has been as little infringement as possible in order to effect the desired result; whether, in a situation of expropriation, fair compensation is available; and whether the Aboriginal group in question has been consulted with respect to the ... measures being implemented.' *R. v. Sparrow*, at 1119.

requires governments to make good faith efforts to provide Aboriginal people with more lands and resources than they currently possess as reserve lands.

Interests associated with Aboriginal sovereignty merit constitutional protection in the form of an Aboriginal right of self-government, which might well impose positive social, fiscal, and institutional obligations on non-Aboriginal governments. The constitutional protection of interests associated with Aboriginal sovereignty requires governments to establish institutional processes to implement Aboriginal rights of self-government and to negotiate in good faith within the framework of such processes. Moreover, non-Aboriginal governmental action in the area of base funding could have a critical effect on the exercise of an Aboriginal right of self-government. In the words of C.E.S. Franks,

> The value of Aboriginal self-government is its potential for performing essential and unusual functions for unique and disadvantaged parts of the Canadian mosaic. It is not a means for saving money. To regard [it] as such could perpetuate and entrench the harms of the present system. Aboriginal self-government might well cost more, rather than less. Small governments are in their nature costly. The special functions of Aboriginal self-governments in relation to cultural preservation and adaptation, and to economic development, will make them especially costly. So also will the factors of remoteness, the health and social breakdown problems of Aboriginal communities, and the many other factors that have caused, and are part of, the present problems ...
>
> Clearly, funding arrangements, including the strings attached, the structure and form of negotiations, the clarity, objectivity and fairness of the funding formula, and the arbitrariness of the federal government in giving or withholding funds, will have a crucial effect on the success or failure of Aboriginal self-government.[51]

The positive dimensions of an Aboriginal right of self-government likely include obligations on the Crown to reach fiscal arrangements with Aboriginal governments to ensure that the right of self-government is not illusory. Such obligations might include providing social and fiscal benefits, especially base funding of Aboriginal governmental power.

---

51 C.E.S. Franks, *Public Administration Questions Relating to Aboriginal Self-Government* (Kingston: Institute of Intergovernmental Relations, 1987).

The courts, however, may seek to refrain from imposing positive obligations on governments, except where such obligations have been explicitly assumed in negotiations or by treaty. The Draft Legal Text of the Charlottetown Accord, for example, proposed to impose on governments a constitutional obligation to bargain in good faith to reach agreements addressing, among other things, 'economic and fiscal arrangements' and that rights in such agreements could constitute 'treaty rights' within the meaning of subsection 35(1).[52] But the fact that a treaty stipulates that members of an Aboriginal nation are constitutionally entitled to a particular social, fiscal, or institutional benefit should not disentitle an Aboriginal person not party to the treaty from claiming a constitutional right to a similar benefit. Whether a treaty guarantees a specific benefit raises qualitatively different questions than those raised by an assertion of an Aboriginal right to a benefit. The possibility that some nations are entitled to a benefit by treaty should not negatively affect the ability of other nations to obtain constitutional protection in the absence of a treaty. To hold otherwise would render constitutional rights unfairly contingent on the extent of bargaining power that an Aboriginal community possessed at some point in the past.

Constitutional obligations to provide certain social, fiscal, and institutional benefits to Aboriginal people thus should only be triggered if they are essential to the fundamental interests underlying constitutional recognition and affirmation of existing Aboriginal and treaty rights. A sceptic might still argue that respect for these interests should not result in the imposition of any positive constitutional obligations on the Canadian state. Concerns relating to institutional legitimacy and institutional competence militate against interpreting subsection 35(1) to require government to provide fiscal, social, or institutional benefits. Any benefits in this regard ought to be the explicit product of negotiation or legislation.

However, the approach suggested by the sceptic seems unduly narrow. It overlooks the fact that all rights possess positive dimensions and that the relevant inquiry is not whether a right imposes a positive obligation on government but whether it contemplates a particular positive

---

52 Draft Legal Text, Charlottetown Accord, 28 Aug., 1992, ss. 35.2(1)(c), 35.2(6). Compare *Reference re Canada Assistance Plan (B.C.)*, [1991] 2 S.C.R. 525 (Parliament can unilaterally change the terms of an intergovernmental agreement setting out the amount of money owed to certain provinces under a cost-sharing arrangement in relation to social assistance).

obligation. It also overlooks the significant positive obligations imposed by domestic and international law to provide certain forms of social, fiscal, and institutional entitlements to Aboriginal people. Domestic obligations flow from the fiduciary duties that govern the Crown's relationship to Aboriginal people. International obligations flow from international human rights documents that directly or indirectly call on the Canadian state to take positive action to improve the social and economic status and condition of Aboriginal people within its borders. The existence of both sets of obligations dampens concerns about the legitimacy of constitutionally requiring government to provide certain entitlements to Aboriginal people.

Fiduciary Duties of the Crown

It is well-settled in Canada that a fiduciary relationship exists between Aboriginal nations and the Crown.[53] In *R. v. Sparrow*, for example, the Supreme Court of Canada stated that:

> [t]he sui generis nature of Indian title, and the historic powers and responsibility assumed by the Crown constituted the source of such a fiduciary obligation. In our opinion, *Guerin*, together with *R. v. Taylor and Williams* (1981), 34 O.R. (2d) 360, [1981] 3 C.N.L.R. 114, ground a general guiding principle for s. 35(1). That is, the Government has the responsibility to act in a fiduciary capacity with respect to aboriginal peoples. The relationship between the Government and aboriginals is trust-like, rather than adversarial, and contemporary recognition and affirmation of aboriginal rights must be defined in light of this historic relationship.[54]

The relationship between the Crown and Aboriginal nations thus joins a number of relationships identified by the judiciary as subject to fiduciary duties, including those between trustees and beneficiaries, solicitors and clients, directors and corporations, and agents and principals.

Fiduciary law, however, draws a distinction between the existence of a fiduciary relationship and the existence of a fiduciary duty. Fiduciary duties are duties that the judiciary has created and enforced in certain circumstances as against persons who are, in law or fact, empowered to

---

53 *Guerin v. The Queen*, [1984] 2 S.C.R. 335. See, generally, Rotman, *Parallel Paths*.
54 [1990] 1 S.C.R. 1075.

act in relation to a particular matter in the interests of another person.[55] The vulnerability of the person whose interests are legally entrusted to another party's discretion is the reason for the creation or recognition of certain duties of fairness and good faith.[56] A fiduciary typically is under a duty to act in the best interests of a beneficiary[57] but the content of a fiduciary duty will vary with the specific relationship it regulates.[58] In certain circumstances, a fiduciary's freedom of action might be constrained by a standard of care less stringent than the duty to act in the best interests of a beneficiary. Depending on the context, the judiciary might simply require the fiduciary to consult, act in good faith, or provide relevant information to a beneficiary. Since fiduciary duties vary so significantly from context to context and from relationship to relationship, their content cannot be pinned down with any degree of precision. This conceptual uncertainty has led P.D. Finn to remark that 'fiduciary' is 'one of the most ill-defined, if not altogether misleading, terms in our law.'[59]

The distinction between a fiduciary relationship and a fiduciary duty, as well as the variation in the standard of care required of a fiduciary, renders uncertain what fiduciary law requires of the Crown in terms of its dealings with First Nations. The standard of care owed by the Crown to Aboriginal peoples will depend on the 'legal and factual context' of the parties' overall relationship.[60] However, fiduciary law offers the judiciary a highly flexible means of regulating the exercise of Crown discretion. The key task is to determine whether Crown discretion in particular contexts is of a type that warrants the imposition of fiduciary duties.

The Supreme Court of Canada has recognized two specific fiduciary

---

55 See *Hospital Products Ltd. v. United States Surgical Corp.* (1984), 55 A.L.R. 417 at 454 (Aust. H.C.), per Mason J. ('the fiduciary undertakes or agrees to act for or on behalf of or in the interests of another person in the exercise of a power or discretion which will affect the interests of that other person in a legal or practical sense').

56 See *H.L. Misener and Son Ltd. v. Misener* (1977), 77 D.L.R. (3d) 428 at 440 (N.S.C.A.), per Macdonald J.A. ('[t]he reason such persons are subject to the fiduciary relationship apparently is because they have a leeway for the exercise of discretion in dealing with third parties which can affect the legal position of their principals').

57 *Frame v. Frame*, [1987] 2 S.C.R. 99.

58 See, for example, *Canadian Aero Service Limited v. O'Malley*, [1974] S.C.R. 592.

59 P.D. Finn, *Fiduciary Obligations* (Sydney: The Law Book Company, 1977), at para. 1.

60 *Delgamuukw v. British Columbia*, [1997] 3 S.C.R. 1010 at 1108–9 ; *R. v. Gladstone*, [1996] 2 S.C.R. 723.

duties owed by the federal Crown to an Indian band in the context of a voluntary surrender of reserve land. First, it owes a pre-surrender fiduciary duty to provide the band with all relevant facts and information about the band's options concerning the surrender and their foreseeable consequences, in order to prevent 'exploitative bargains.'[61] Second, the federal Crown is under a post-surrender fiduciary duty to act in the best interests of an Indian band when the band surrenders land to the Crown for third-party use.[62] In *Guerin*, for example, the Musqueam First Nation surrendered a portion of reserve land to the federal Crown to be leased to a third party for use as a golf club. The Crown in turn leased the land on less attractive terms than it had led the First Nation to believe it would receive upon surrender. Dickson J., for a majority of the court, held that the Crown was under a fiduciary duty to act in the best interests of the Musqueam when dealing with third parties on their behalf with respect to surrendered Musqueam reserve land. The existence of pre- and post-surrender fiduciary duties does not necessarily mean that the federal Crown can legally prevent an Indian band from surrendering its reserve land on terms proposed by third parties, but it does mean that the federal Crown must act in the band's best interests in negotiating and seeking to reach an arrangement that results in the 'least possible impairment' of the band's rights.[63] As McLachlin J. said in *Blueberry River Indian Band*, '[l]oyalty and care [are] at the heart of the fiduciary obligation.'[64]

The court in *Guerin* held that the federal Crown owes a fiduciary duty to act in a band's best interests because the Indian Act precludes a band from alienating reserve land directly to third parties. A band must first surrender reserve land to the federal Crown, which then deals with third parties on the band's behalf. The Crown's fiduciary duty regulates the legal discretion that vests in the federal Crown upon the surrender of reserve land. According to Dickson J., because 'the relative legal positions are such that one party is at the mercy of the other's discretion,'[65]

---

61 *Blueberry River Indian Band v. Canada*, [1995] 4 S.C.R. 344 at 370, per McLachlin J. See also *Kruger v. The Queen* (1985), 17 D.L.R. (4th) 591 (Fed. C.A.).

62 *Guerin v. The Queen*.

63 *Semiahmoo Indian Band v. Canada* (1997), 148 D.L.R. (4th) 523 at 537 (F.C.A.). For commentary, see Bob Freedman, '*Semiahmoo Indian Band v. Canada* (Case Comment),' 36 Alberta L. Rev. 218 (1997).

64 *Blueberry River Indian Band v. Canada*, supra at 372.

65 Ibid. at 340, per Dickson J., quoting E.J. Weinrib, 'The Fiduciary Obligation,' 25 U.T.L.J. 1 at 7 (1975).

the federal Crown's freedom to deal with the land as it sees fit must be constrained by principles of justice and fairness. Upon surrender, the fiduciary duty arises 'to regulate the manner in which the Crown exercises its discretion in dealing with the land on the Indians' behalf.'[66] In this context, the federal Crown is obliged to act in the interests of, and to demonstrate 'utmost loyalty' to, the surrendering party.[67]

According to *Guerin*, the Crown's fiduciary duty is triggered by a voluntary surrender of reserve land. Does a similar duty attach to unilateral governmental action that regulates or extinguishes Aboriginal rights? If so, what is its content? An answer to these questions will depend on whether the governmental action occurred before or after the enactment of subsection 35(1) of the Constitution Act, 1982. The constitutionality of post-1982 governmental action that unduly interferes with an existing Aboriginal or treaty right will depend in part on whether the government responsible for the interference was acting within its sphere of legislative authority and whether it met fiduciary duties owed to Aboriginal people adversely affected by the action. Before 1982, the federal government was relatively free to regulate and even extinguish Aboriginal rights. Does this mean that it enjoyed unilateral legislative and executive authority unfettered by fiduciary obligations to Aboriginal people?

The possibility that the federal government possessed unfettered authority in this context draws support from the reason for the fiduciary duty recognized in *Guerin*. This duty attaches to the Crown because of the vulnerability of Indian bands, which cannot sell or lease reserve land directly to third parties. They must entrust the federal Crown with their land through the act of surrender and rely on the Crown to act in their interests. According to this view, the usufructuary nature of reserve land is the source of the fiduciary duty, and the discretion that the duty regulates is the discretion enjoyed by the federal Crown when it is entrusted with reserve land for the purpose of a third-party transaction. The Crown therefore should not owe pre-1982 fiduciary duties to Aboriginal peoples when it exercises general legislative or executive authority that might adversely affect Aboriginal interests. This view suggests that the Crown should not owe specific fiduciary duties to Aboriginal people

---

66 *Guerin*, at 342.
67 Ibid. at 344.

simply because they are vulnerable to the exercise of legislative or executive power.[68]

The view that fiduciary duties were not owed in relation to pre-1982, unilateral governmental actions that interfere with Aboriginal interests rests on an extremely narrow reading of *Guerin*, one that sees fiduciary duties as arising only when reserve land is voluntarily surrendered. But case law under section 35 of the Constitution Act, 1982 suggests that the Crown is subject to fiduciary duties in other contexts. In *Sparrow*, the court held that fiduciary duties are triggered on the showing of a violation of subsection 35(1). To justify a subsection 35(1) infringement, '[t]he way in which a legislative objective is to be attained must uphold the honour of the Crown and must be in keeping with the unique contemporary relationship, grounded in history and policy, between the Crown and Canada's aboriginal peoples.'[69] The court in *Sparrow* required that '[t]he constitutional nature of the Musqueam food fishing rights means that any allocation of priorities after valid conservation measures have been implemented must give top priority to Indian food fishing.'[70] In *Delgamuukw*, the court added that consultation and compensation for interference with subsection 35(1) rights will ordinarily be required.[71]

Several important implications flow from the court's approach to the relationship between fiduciary law and subsection 35(1). First, the court's approach indicates that the conservative view that fiduciary duties are triggered only upon the voluntary surrender of reserve land is to be supplemented with a more expansive view that they are also triggered upon unilateral interferences with Aboriginal rights. These duties include ensuring that a compelling and substantial governmental objec-

---

68 A description, if not an endorsement, of this restrictive view can be found in Dubé J.'s summary of the Crown's submissions in *Lower Kootenay Indian Band v.* Canada, [1991] 2 C.N.L.R. 54 (F.C.T.D.), at 104: 'The Crown also advanced the argument that the fiduciary obligations owed to the Indians "do not float above in the air." They must be grounded in a dependency. They only exist where the Indians cannot, by statute, act for themselves. The obligations only crystallize when the Crown is interposed. It is only upon surrender that it is clear that the Indians cannot act for themselves, for the fiduciary obligation owed to the Indians by the Crown is sui generis. In any instance in which the Indian people can and do act for themselves in relation to this lease, there is no fiduciary obligation on the Crown to act.' See also *Apsassin v. Canada*, [1988] 3 F.C. 20 (T.D.).
69 Ibid. at 181.
70 Ibid. at 184.
71 See, generally, *Delgamuukw v. British Columbia*, at 1080–91.

tive exists for the interference, consulting with Aboriginal people adversely affected by the governmental action, and providing compensation for interferences with Aboriginal rights.

Second, it suggests the possibility of a general fiduciary duty on the part of the Crown to protect Aboriginal lands, including reserve lands and lands subject to Aboriginal title, from interference. Brian Slattery has long maintained that '[t]he Crown has a general fiduciary duty toward native people to protect them in the enjoyment of their Aboriginal rights and in particular in the possession and use of their lands.'[72] In his view, a general fiduciary duty is a special instance of a general doctrine of collective trust that animates the Canadian constitution:

> The Crown's general duty to protect Aboriginal lands, when coupled with the statutory discretion to burden Aboriginal title, gave rise to particular fiduciary obligations controlling the exercise of the discretion. Broadly speaking, these obligations bound the Crown to strike a fair balance between the public good and Aboriginal interests in dealing with Aboriginal lands. Ideally, this balance would best be struck through voluntary agreements with the First Nations affected. Failing that, the Provincial Crown would have the power to make its own determinations, subject to the supervision of the courts, which could enforce the fiduciary duties and grant appropriate remedies.[73]

As Slattery has formulated, the source of the Crown's generalized duty lies in its duty to protect Aboriginal lands and its constitutional authority to regulate Aboriginal use and enjoyment of land. The discretion enjoyed by the Crown in this regard should be subject to positive duties that, generally speaking, would require the Crown to strike a fair balance between interests associated with the public good and interests associated with indigenous difference.

International Legal Obligations

Emerging international legal principles also require non-Aboriginal governments to provide certain social, fiscal, and institutional benefits to Aboriginal people. The Draft Declaration on the Rights of Indige-

---

72 Brian Slattery, 'Understanding Aboriginal Rights,' 66 Can. Bar Rev. 727 at 753 (1987).
73 Brian Slattery, 'First Nations and the Constitution: A Question of Trust,' 71 Can. Bar Rev. 261 at 291–2 (1992).

nous Peoples, prepared by a sub-commission of the United Nations Commission on Human Rights, proposes to recognize indigenous rights of autonomy and self-government; the right to manifest, practice, and teach spiritual and religious traditions; rights to territory, education, language, and cultural property; and the right to maintain and develop indigenous economic and social systems.[74] It is difficult to imagine that these rights do not require government to provide social, fiscal, and institutional benefits to Aboriginal people. Indeed, article 37 of the Draft Declaration provides that 'States shall take effective and appropriate measures, in consultation with the indigenous peoples concerned, to give full effect to the provision of this Declaration. The rights recognized herein shall be adopted and included in national legislation in such a manner that indigenous peoples can avail themselves of such rights in practice.'[75]

Numerous international legal instruments issuing from the United Nations also call on member states to take active steps to protect cultural minorities. Several articles of the United Nations Charter affirm cultural cooperation and cultural development.[76] Article 27 of the International Covenant on Civil and Political Rights recognizes rights of members of 'ethnic, religious or linguistic minorities ... to enjoy their own culture, to profess and practise their own religion [and] to use their own language.'[77] The United Nations Human Rights Committee has held that Article 27 may require states to enact 'positive measures' to protect minority cultural rights.[78] The U.N. Convention Against Genocide adds support to the concept of cultural autonomy,[79] as does the UNESCO Declaration of Cultural Co-operation, which affirms a right and duty of

---

74 Draft Declaration on the Rights of Indigenous Peoples, E/CN.4/Sub.2/1993/26 (released 8 June 1993) (prepared by the Chair-Rapporteur of the Working Group on Indigenous Populations).

75 Ibid.

76 Charter of the United Nations, adopted 26 June 1945 (entered into force 24 Oct. 1945), arts. 13, 55, 57, and 73.

77 Adopted 16 Dec. 1966, 999 U.N.T.S. (entered into force 23 Mar. 1976).

78 General Comment 23 (1994), paras. 6.2, 7 UN Doc HR1/GEN/1/Rev1 (1994), at 40.

79 Convention on the Prevention and Punishment of the Crime of Genocide, 9 Dec. 1948, 78 U.N.T.S. 277 (entered into force 12 Jan. 1961). Article II defines 'genocide' as 'acts committed with intent to destroy, in whole or in part, a national, ethnical, racial, or religious group, as such ...'. For links between the concept of genocide and the treatment of American Indians, see Lyman H. Legters, 'The American Genocide,' in Fremont J. Hyden and Hyman H. Legters, ed., *Native Americans and Public Policy* (Pittsburgh: University of Pittsburgh, 1992), at 101–12.

all peoples to protect and develop minority cultures throughout the world.[80] The U.N. Convention on Racial Discrimination calls for positive governmental action to 'ensure the adequate development and protection of certain racial groups or individuals belonging to them.'[81] Most recently, the United Nations' Declaration on the Rights of Persons Belonging to National or Ethnic, Religious and Linguistic Minorities requires states to protect 'the national or ethnic, cultural, religious and linguistic identity' of minorities, to 'adopt appropriate legislative and other measures to achieve those ends,' and to 'take measures to create favourable conditions to enable persons belonging to minorities to express their characteristics and to develop their culture, language, religion, traditions and customs.'[82]

In addition, Convention 107 of the International Labour Organization,[83] adopted in 1957, while advocating the 'integration' of indigenous populations into national communities, also requires governments to develop coordinated and systematic plans to protect indigenous populations and to promote their social, economic, and cultural development.[84] While the ILO Convention now seems somewhat dated in its emphasis on integration,[85] its existence suggests some degree of support at the level of international customary law for recognizing positive governmental obligations to provide social, fiscal, and institutional benefits

---

80 Declaration of the Principles of International Cultural Cooperation, proclaimed by the General Conference of the United Nations Educational, Scientific and Cultural Organization at its fourteenth session on 4 Nov. 1966, reprinted in United Nations, *Human Rights: A Compilation of International Instruments*, U.N. Doc. ST/HR/1/Rev.3 (1988), at 409.

81 International Convention on the Elimination of All Forms of Racial Discrimination, art. 2, para. 2, opened for signature 7 Mar. 1966, 660 U.N.T.S. 195 (entered into force 4 4 Jan. 1969).

82 Resolution 47/135, adopted by the General Assembly 18 Dec. 1992.

83 The Protection and Integration of Indigenous and Other Tribal and Semi-Tribal Populations in Independent Countries, *Conventions and Recommendations Adopted by the International Labour Conference, 1919–66* (Geneva: ILO, 1966), at 901 and 909. Canada is not party to the convention.

84 Ibid., arts. 2(1), 2(2).

85 For an assessment of the ILO Convention, see Patrick Thornberry, *International Law and the Rights of Minorities* (Oxford: Oxford University Press, 1991), at 334–68. See also José Martinez-Cobo, *Analytical Compilation of Existing Legal Instruments and Proposed Draft Standards Relating to Indigenous Rights*, U.N. Doc. M/HR/86/36, Annex V, for a summary of submissions by indigenous organizations sharply criticizing the convention on a number of grounds.

to Aboriginal people. In 1989, the International Labour Organization revised Convention 107 in Convention No. 169.[86] It recognizes 'the aspirations of [indigenous] peoples to exercise control over their own institutions, ways of life and economic development and to maintain and develop their identities, languages and religions, within the frameworks of the States in which they live.'[87] It then lists an impressive range of rights that attach to Aboriginal people and responsibilities that attach to governments which would facilitate the protection of Aboriginal ways of life.[88]

The American Declaration of the Rights and Duties of Man is another international legal instrument that guarantees not only civil and political rights but also social and economic rights, such as the right to health care, food, clothing, housing, and education, as well as a more general right to life.[89] The Inter-American Commission on Human Rights, an institution established by the Charter of the Organization of American States, possesses a general mandate to protect and promote human rights.[90] In the *Yanomami* case, the commission heard a petition against the Government of Brazil presented by several human rights groups, alleging violations of the rights of the Yanomami people.[91] Thousands of Yanomami had been forced to abandon their ancestral territory after a plan, approved by the Brazilian government, was implemented to exploit the natural resources of the Amazon region of the country. A

---

86 International Labour Organization Convention (No. 169) Concerning Indigenous and Tribal Peoples in Independent Countries, 27 June 1989 (entered into force 5 Sept. 5, 1990). Canada is not a party to the convention, but, in the words of one scholar, it arguably 'represents a core of expectations that are widely shared internationally and, accordingly, it reflects emergent customary international law generally binding upon the constituent units of international community': see S. James Anaya, *Fiduciary Obligation under International Law in General* (a study prepared for the Royal Commission on Aboriginal Peoples, 13 Dec. 1994), at 20.

87 Ibid., fifth preambular paragraph.

88 See Anaya, *Fiduciary Obligation under International Law*, and Lee Swepson, 'A New Step in the International Law on Indigenous and Tribal Peoples: ILO Convention No. 169 of 1989,' 15 Okla. City L. Rev. 677 (1990).

89 *Handbook of Existing Rules Pertaining to Human Rights in the InterAmerican System*, OAS Doc. OEA/Ser.L./V/II.60 Doc. 28 (1983) 21.

90 See *Charter of the Organization of American States*, 30 Apr. 1948, 2 U.S.T. 2394, 119 U.N.T.S. 48, amended by Protocol of Buenos Aires, 27 Feb. 1967, 21 U.S.T. 607.

91 Resolution No. 12/85, Case No. 7615, (1985) (Brazil), reprinted in 1985 Inter-American Commission on Human Rights & Inter-American Court of Human Rights, *Inter-American Yearbook of Human Rights* (1985), at 264.

highway was built that cut through Yanomami territory and rich mineral deposits were discovered in the area. It was alleged that the massive penetration by outsiders had devastating consequences for the Yanomami, including the disintegration of traditional social structures, the introduction of prostitution, and the epidemic spread of disease.

Although the commission has the power only to issue recommendations, the *Yanomami* case illustrates the possibility that quasi-judicial bodies can effectively adjudicate rights that impose positive obligations on government. The commission held that the Brazilian government's failure to take 'timely and effective measures' on behalf of the Yanomami resulted in violations of their rights to life, liberty, and personal security; rights of residence and movement; and rights to the preservation of health and well-being as guaranteed by the declaration.[92] It further recommended that the government continue to take 'preventive and curative health measures to protect the lives and health of Indians exposed to infectious or contagious diseases.'[93] By viewing the declaration as imposing duties to protect and fulfil certain social and economic rights, the commission in effect recommended that the government take steps to ensure the well-being of the Yanomami people.

Justiciability Revisited

As stated, constitutional entrenchment of social and economic rights raise justiciability concerns, namely, the extent to which such rights are suitable for judicial determination. Concerns grounded in institutional legitimacy question the justice of requiring the judiciary to ensure that legislatures pursue particular political programs. Concerns grounded in institutional competence speak to whether the judiciary is capable of making meaningful determinations of such rights, given their underlying interests and ensuing obligations. The presence of domestic and international positive obligations should assuage at least some concerns about the legitimacy of interpreting subsection 35(1) as requiring government to provide certain social, fiscal, and institutional benefits to Aboriginal people. The legitimacy of constitutionally requiring government to provide a particular benefit to Aboriginal people is directly proportionate to the extent to which the benefit in question is tied to an

---

92 Ibid., at 276.
93 Ibid., at 278.

interest underlying section 35. But cogent arguments remain based on a perceived judicial incapacity to adjudicate such matters effectively. Although in the words of Frank Michaelman, 'constitutional canonization of a norm can sometimes effectively motivate compliance without judicial enforcement,'[94] concerns of institutional competence are still likely to have a major effect on the extent to which the judiciary will interpret subsection 35(1) as requiring governmental action.

Social and economic rights are often characterized as vague in the obligations they mandate; progressive and therefore requiring time to realize; and complex and diffuse in the interests they protect. But a right's clarity and precision is a function of repeated application and enforcement. The lack of clarity and precision surrounding the positive dimensions of Aboriginal and treaty rights should not be held up as a reason for their nonenforcement. On the contrary, nonenforcement is to a large extent the reason for their lack of clarity and precision. Moreover, concerns about the judiciary's competence to order positive governmental action ought to be set against recent efforts to demystify perceived complications associated with the judicial role in promoting social and economic rights. A number of studies at the international level provide greater clarity and precision to the nature of obligations that social and economic rights tend to generate.[95] Such studies assist in delineating the nature and scope of governmental obligations in the context of subsection 35(1), and they suggest that the positive dimensions of Aboriginal and treaty rights possess sufficient precision and clarity to render them justiciable in a court of law.

Henry Shue, for example, has argued that social and economic rights trigger three types of obligations on government.[96] The first type is a duty to respect social and economic rights. This duty conforms to the dominant understanding of what a constitutional right requires of gov-

---

94 Frank I. Michaelman, 'Socio-Political Functions of Constitutional Protection for Private Property Holdings (In Liberal Political Thought),' in G.E. van Maanen and A.J. van der Walt, eds., *Property Law on the Threshold of the 21st Century* (Apeldorn: Maklu, 1996), 433–50 at 441.

95 See, for example, Danilo Türk, *U.N. Commission on Human Rights, Preliminary Report on the Realization of Economic, Social and Cultural Rights*, U.N. Doc. E/CN.4/Sub.2/1989/19 (1989); Danilo Türk, *Progress Report on the Realization of Social, Economic, and Cultural Rights*, U.N. ESCOR, Comm'n Hum. Rts. 42d Sess., Agenda Item 7, at 4, U.N. Doc. E/CN.4/Sub.2/1990/19 (1990).

96 Henry Shue, *Basic Rights: Subsistence, Affluence, and U.S. Foreign Policy* (Princeton: Princeton University Press, 1980).

ernment, namely, that governmental action must not unjustifiably infringe the right or unjustifiably interfere with activities contemplated by the right. The second type of obligation is a duty of protection. It requires government to prevent social and economic rights from being infringed by private actors, for example, by having in place laws and regulations that confer on individuals and groups the legal status, rights, and privileges necessary to ensure the proper protection of their rights. The third obligation, a duty of promotion and fulfilment, is truly positive. It translates into governmental obligations to provide certain benefits.[97] This obligation can take many forms and is less precise in its scope and definition than the obligations of respect and protection. But, as demonstrated in the *Yanomami* case, it can be rendered more precise by imposing on governments a duty to 'take steps' toward the fulfilment of the right.[98] This duty confers a measure of discretion on government to choose the means and schedule for the promotion and fulfilment of the right.[99] It enables the judiciary initially to take a minimalist approach to the constitutional enforcement of social and economic rights, and gradually to hold government to greater obligations over time.[100] By relying on this structure of obligations and by proceeding incrementally, courts should be able to identify the nature and scope of positive obligations that Aboriginal and treaty rights impose on government.

The judiciary has already accepted that Aboriginal and treaty rights impose on government a duty of respect. Governments are obligated not to interfere unduly with the exercise of Aboriginal and treaty rights. Constitutional recognition and affirmation of existing Aboriginal and

---

97 Compare C.M. MacMillan, 'Social versus Political Rights,' at 300 (placing the onus on the state to protect the exercise of social rights).

98 See, for example, U.N. ESCOR, Comm'n on Hum. Rts., *The Limburg Principles on the Implementation of the International Covenant on Economic, Social and Cultural Rights*, 43d Sess., Annex, Agenda Items 8 & 18, at 1, U.N. Doc. E/CN.4/1987/17 (1987) (obligation to fulfil is immediate only with respect to the most vulnerable).

99 See Phillip Alston and Gerald Quinn, 'The Nature and Scope of State Parties' Obligations under the International Covenant on Economic, Social and Cultural Rights,' 9 Human Rights Quarterly 158, at 184 (1987); and Scott Leckie, Another Step towards Indivisibility: Identifying the Key Features of Violations of Economic, Social and Cultural Rights,' 20 Human Rights Quarterly 81 (1998).

100 See Lawrence G. Sager, 'Justice in Plain Clothes: Reflections on the Thinness of Constitutional Law,' 88 Northwestern U. L. Rev. 410 (1993) (arguing that social and economic rights call for a minimalist approach to constitutional enforcement).

treaty rights impose more than a duty of respect on the state. Governments must take steps to protect, promote and fulfil such rights. In the next chapter, I argue that these steps ought to include the introduction of specific institutional arrangements that facilitate treaty negotiations and treaty renewal.

Chapter Nine

State Obligations and Treaty Negotiations

The wondrous game that power plays with Things
is to move in such submission through the world:
groping in roots and growing thick in trunks
and in treetops like a rising from the dead.

Rainer Maria Rilke, *The Book of Hours*[1]

In the Nass River valley of northwestern British Columbia, the Nisga'a people mark their relationship to their ancestral territory by holding a settlement feast – also known as a potlatch – upon the death of one of their chiefs. A successor is chosen to receive the name and title of the deceased.[2] Sharing his wealth with those in attendance, the new chief assumes his responsibilities as head of the clan, and assumes ownership of the land and its resources in the name of the community. Other chiefs attend the ceremony to witness and approve of the transfer of responsibilities. In recognition of the permanence of the office and of its relationship to Nisga'a territory, participants at the settlement feast recite the name of every mountain, every valley, and every waterway owned and occupied by the clan since time immemorial.

Nisga'a ancestral territory – 24,862 square kilometres of land and water – is rich in salmon and steelhead, wolf and moose, and includes

---

1 Rainer Maria Rilke, 'The Book of Hours,' in Stephen Mitchell, ed. and trans., *Ahead of All Parting: The Selected Poetry and Prose of Rainer Maria Rilke* (New York: Modern Library, 1995), at 9.

2 For an account of the potlatch, see Douglas Cole and Ira Chaikin, *An Iron Hand upon the People: The Law against the Potlatch on the Northwest Coast* (Vancouver: Douglas and McIntyre, 1990).

vast forests, glacier-fed lakes, spectacular Pacific fiords, and snow-capped mountains. Under Canadian law, however, the Nisga'a, until recently, possessed only rights to four small reserves, located in the villages of Kincolith, Greenville, Canyon City, and New Aiyansh. With the exception of several treaties on Vancouver Island negotiated before Confederation and Treaty 8, which primarily covers northern Alberta but extends into the northeastern corner of British Columbia, no treaties were negotiated with Aboriginal people in British Columbia. The four Nisga'a reserves, like most reserves in the province, were created by unilateral governmental action in compliance with the terms under which British Columbia joined Confederation in 1871.

Every since the establishment of the colony of British Columbia, the Nisga'a have continually sought formal recognition of their rights from imperial and Canadian authorities. In 1887, Nisga'a chiefs travelled to Victoria to demand recognition of title, self-government, and treaty talks. In 1913, the Nisga'a forwarded a petition to the Privy Council of the United Kingdom asserting Aboriginal title and rights to ancestral territory. But not until 1975 did Canada begin treaty negotiations with the Nisga'a, and not until 1990 did British Columbia formally join Canada and the Nisga'a at the negotiating table.[3] Negotiations finally bore fruit in August 1998, when federal, provincial and Nisga'a representatives participated in a signing ceremony held to inaugurate a landmark treaty known as the Nisga'a Final Agreement. It formally recognizes that the Nisga'a possess rights to a portion of their ancestral territory and establishes a Nisga'a government empowered to make laws on culture, language, employment, local and public works, land use, and marriage.

In this chapter, I trace the rise of contemporary federal and provincial treaty processes designed to resolve Aboriginal claims to ancestral territory. In light of the previous chapter's general conclusion that constitutional recognition and affirmation of existing Aboriginal and treaty rights require governments to provide certain social, fiscal, and institutional entitlements to Aboriginal people, I argue that the constitution specifically requires the reform of existing treaty processes. Parliament is constitutionally obligated to establish an independent tribunal vested with the authority to oversee and resolve Aboriginal claims to ancestral territory. Federal and provincial authorities are under a constitutional

---

3 For a history of Aboriginal politics in British Columbia, see Paul Tennant, *Aboriginal Peoples and Politics: The Indian Land Question in British Columbia, 1849–1989* (Vancouver: UBC Press, 1990).

duty to enter into treaties, to negotiate in good faith, and to make every reasonable effort to reach agreement. I go on to explore the extent to which the constitution is sufficiently flexible to allow for the negotiation of self-government agreements, such as the Nisga'a treaty, that provide for Aboriginal legislative authority and limited Aboriginal paramountcy over inconsistent federal and provincial law.

Contemporary Treaty Processes

Emphasizing the cost, time, and uncertainty of litigation, federal, provincial, and territorial governments repeatedly state that they prefer negotiating to litigating Aboriginal claims.[4] This stance echoes the nation-to-nation relationship between Aboriginal peoples and the Crown evident in colonial times, when imperial powers entered into treaties with Aboriginal nations in a spirit of co-existence. As argued above, these treaties were part of a larger set of intersocietal encounters, some friendly, others hostile, through which Aboriginal and non-Aboriginal participants generated norms of conduct and recognition that structured their ongoing relationships.[5] This stance also conforms to Crown policy in the nineteenth and early twentieth centuries, when the Crown entered into the eleven numbered treaties spanning Canada from Quebec's border to the northwestern edge of the country – although Crown policy regarded the later treaty process as a means of formally dispossessing Aboriginal people of ancestral territory in return for reserve land and certain benefits to be provided by state authorities until Aboriginal people were assimilated into mainstream Canadian society. After 1923, however, when the Crown and the Mississauga and Chippewa nations entered into what are known as the Williams treaties in southwestern Ontario, there were no further treaties between Aborig-

---

4 See, for example, Minister of Public Works and Government Services Canada, *Federal Policy Guide: Aboriginal Self-Government, The Government of Canada's Approach to Implementation of the Inherent Right and the Negotiation of Aboriginal Self-Government* (1995), at 3 ('[n]egotiations among governments and Aboriginal peoples are clearly preferable as the most practical and effective way to implement the inherent right of self-government'); Ministry of Aboriginal Affairs, *British Columbia's Approach to Treaty Settlements* (12 May 1995), at 2 ('the most logical and effective way of expressing these rights in modern terms will be to negotiate with respect to the ownership and management of certain lands and resources').

5 See text accompanying notes 72–88, Chapter 5.

inal peoples and the Crown until the James Bay Agreement, which covers much of northern Quebec, was successfully negotiated in 1975.[6]

Federal refusal to acknowledge claims of Aboriginal title to ancestral territory reached a high water mark in 1969, when the federal government published a proposal known as the 'White Paper.'[7] Steeped in constitutional values geared to protecting individual rights, the White Paper proposed 'a global termination of all special treatment of Indians.'[8] Arguing that differential treatment based on race was antithetical to Canadian political traditions and that claims of Aboriginal title are 'so general and undefined that it is not realistic to think of them as specific claims capable of [legal] remedy,' the White Paper advocated the repeal of the Indian Act, the phasing out of federal responsibility for Indians and reserve lands, and an end to treaty making with Aboriginal people.[9] Aboriginal people were quick to denounce the White Paper 'with a resounding nationalism unparalleled in Canadian history.'[10] The federal government's subsequent withdrawal of the White Paper marked the beginning of a series of legal, political, and constitutional victories for Aboriginal nations in Canada.

The Nisga'a, frustrated with federal and provincial unwillingness to recognize its Aboriginal title, brought an action requesting a declaration of title to certain ancestral lands on the coast and interior of British Columbia. Despite the ultimate dismissal by the Supreme Court of Canada in *Calder v. A.G.B.C.* of the Nisga'a claim,[11] the case was a significant development in the common law of Aboriginal title in Canada because a majority of the court explicitly recognized the legitimacy of a claim of Aboriginal title to land. The court viewed Aboriginal title as a bundle of common law rights of use and enjoyment of ancestral land that

---

6 *James Bay and Northern Québec Agreement* (Quebec City: Éditeur officiel du Québec, 1976).

7 Department of Indian Affairs and Northern Development, *Statement of the Government of Canada on Indian Policy* (Ottawa: Queen's Printer, 1969).

8 Sally M. Weaver, *Making Canadian Indian Policy: The Hidden Agenda, 1968–1970* (Toronto: University of Toronto Press, 1981), at 4.

9 *Statement of the Government of Canada on Indian Policy*, at 11.

10 Weaver, *Making Canadian Indian Policy*, at 5.

11 [1973] S.C.R. 313. Three members of the court (Judson J., Martland and Ritchie JJ. concurring) were of the view that title had been extinguished by Crown and legislative action; one member (Pigeon J.) held that judicial determination of the case required a fiat from the lieutenant-governor of the province. Hall J., Laskin and Spence JJ. concurring, was of the view that Nisga'a title had not been extinguished.

stemmed not from any positive legal enactment but from Aboriginal 'possession from time immemorial.'[12]

The court's decision in *Calder* led the federal government to announce that it was prepared to enter into negotiations with Aboriginal people to resolve disputes concerning claims of Aboriginal title or breaches of treaty obligations. To this end, the federal government has established a number of processes designed to facilitate negotiations on matters relating to Aboriginal claims to territory and self-governing authority. For territorial claims, the federal government established two processes, known as the comprehensive and specific claims processes. The comprehensive claims process is designed to produce treaties in areas where Aboriginal title is unextinguished. To participate in this process, an Aboriginal community must demonstrate that it has not entered into or adhered to a treaty and that it has traditionally used and occupied the territory it claims. The federal government initially required that the community also agree to the blanket extinguishment of all Aboriginal rights and title throughout its ancestral territory in return for rights guaranteed by the treaty itself. Federal extinguishment policy has evolved in recent years to require either blanket or partial extinguishment of Aboriginal title in exchange for the rights contained in the treaty.[13] These rights typically include full ownership of certain lands in the area in question; participation in land, water, wildlife, and environmental management; financial compensation; resource revenue sharing; economic development rights and responsibilities; and an ongoing role in the management of heritage resources and parks throughout the area.[14] The specific claims process is designed to resolve claims based on an alleged failure by the Crown to discharge treaty obligations, improper alienation of reserve lands or assets, and other claims based on breach of lawful obligations by the federal government.[15] With claims of self-government, the federal government has called for tripar-

---

12 Ibid., at 375, per Hall J., dissenting on other grounds.
13 Indian Affairs and Northern Development, *Comprehensive Land Claims Policy* (Ottawa: Supply and Services, 1986), at 12. See also Indian and Northern Affairs Canada, *Federal Policy for the Settlement of Native Claims* (March 1993).
14 Indian and Northern Development, *Statement Made by the Honourable Jean Chrétien, Minister of Indian Affairs and Northern Development, on Claims of Indian and Inuit People* (Ottawa: 8 Aug. 1973).
15 Indian and Northern Development, *Outstanding Business: A Native Claims Policy* (Ottawa: Supply and Services, 1982).

tite talks to establish a negotiation process acceptable to all parties.[16] Often these three processes dovetail with each other and with provincial processes established concurrently to address Aboriginal claims. The federal government, for example, participates with British Columbia and the First Nations Summit in the British Columbia treaty process, facilitated by the British Columbia Treaty Commission, a commission established by provincial statute.[17]

As stated, in 1975, the federal and Quebec governments and the Cree and Inuit of northern Quebec reached an agreement with respect to lands in the James Bay region of Québec.[18] In 1978, the agreement was extended to include the Naskapi nation of northeastern Québec.[19] In 1984, the Inuvialuit people reached an agreement with the federal government with respect to lands located in the western Arctic.[20] More recently, Inuit people reached an agreement to divide the Northwest Territories in two and to create a new political jurisdiction, known as Nunavut, out of the central and eastern part of the territory. Other settlements include the 1992 Gwich'in Comprehensive Land Claim Agreement, the 1993 Sahtu Dene and Métis Comprehensive Land Claim Agreement, and the 1994 Yukon Umbrella Final Agreement, which consists of four final agreements signed with the Vuntut Gwich'in First Nation, the First Nation of Na-cho Ny'a'k Dun, the Teslin Tlingit Council, and the Champagne and Aishihik First Nations. And, in 1998, federal, provincial, and Nisga'a negotiators signed the first treaty negotiated in British Columbia since the province joined Confederation.

Constitutional Dictates and Institutional Design

Constitutional recognition and affirmation of existing Aboriginal and treaty rights impose certain positive obligations on governments to respect, promote, and fulfil such rights. Constitutional protection of Aboriginal territorial interests, for example, would be meaningless in the absence of institutional processes designed to recognize and imple-

---

16 See, for example, Minister of Public Works and Government Services Canada, *Federal Policy Guide: Aboriginal Self-Government.*
17 S.B.C. 1993, c. 4.
18 Canada, *James Bay and Northern Quebec Agreement* (1976).
19 Canada, *Northeastern Quebec Agreement* (1978).
20 Indian Affairs and Northern Development, *The Western Arctic Claim: The Inuvialuit Final Agreement* (1984).

ment Aboriginal rights of access and use and enjoyment of their ancestral territories. The dramatic increase in band membership and the attendant housing demands on reserve communities occasioned by Bill C-31, discussed in Chapter 7, underscore the need for reform. Similarly, constitutional recognition and affirmation of an existing Aboriginal right of self-government would be rendered illusory if federal, provincial, and territorial governments fail to take steps to recognize and implement the right within the Canadian constitutional order. Although I have argued that subsection 35(1) of the Constitution Act, 1982 authorizes Aboriginal communities to assert jurisdiction over certain subject matters notwithstanding the absence of a treaty that formally acknowledges Aboriginal law-making authority, such initiatives are bound to trigger extensive litigation and impose enormous costs on scarce community resources.

The merits of existing federal treaty processes need to be assessed in light of the constitutional requirement that the state respect, promote, and fulfil Aboriginal and treaty rights. Many criticisms have been levied against existing federal processes,[21] of which four are relevant to the present inquiry. First, the existing claim processes are not grounded in

21 See, for example, Royal Commission on Aboriginal Peoples, *Final Report*, vol. 2, *Restructuring the Relationship* (Ottawa: Supply and Services, 1996), at 527–56; Royal Commission on Aboriginal Peoples, *Treaty-Making in the Spirit of Co-existence: An Alternative to Extinguishment* (Ottawa: Supply and Services, 1995); Indian Commission of Ontario, *Discussion Paper Regarding First Nation Land Claims* (Toronto, 1990), reprinted in Indian Claims Commission Proceedings [ICCP] 177 (1995); Chiefs Committee on Claims/ First Nations Submission on Claims (Ottawa: 14 Dec. 1990), reprinted in 1 ICCP 187 (1994); Canadian Human Rights Commission, *Annual Report* (1990); *Report of the Canadian Bar Association on Aboriginal Rights in Canada: An Agenda for Action* (1988); Darlene M. Johnston, 'A Theory of Crown Trust towards Aboriginal Peoples,' 18 Ottawa L. Rev. 307 (1986); Task Force to Review Comprehensive Claims Policy, *Living Treaties, Lasting Agreements – Report of the Task Force* (Ottawa: Indian and Northern Development, 1985); Special Committee on Indian Self-Government, *Indian Self-Government in Canada: Report of the Special Committee* (Ottawa: House of Commons, 1983); Eric Colvin, *Legal Process and the Resolution of Indian Claims* (Saskatoon: University of Saskatoon Native Law Centre, 1981); Public Inquiry into the Administration of Justice and Aboriginal People, *Report of the Aboriginal Justice Inquiry of Manitoba* (Winnipeg: Queen's Printer, 1991); John A. Olthuis and Roger Townshend, *Is Canada's Thumb on the Scales? An Analysis of Canada's Comprehensive and Specific Claims Policies and Alternatives* (research study prepared for the Royal Commission on Aboriginal Peoples, 1995) (on file with author); William B. Henderson and Derek Ground, 'Survey of Aboriginal Land Claims,' 26 Ottawa L. Rev. 187 (1994); A.C. Hamilton, *Canada and Aboriginal Peoples: A New Partnership* (Ottawa: Indian Affairs and Northern Development, 1995).

legislation but are the product of policy statements that possess a dubious legal status. Aboriginal participants possess no statutory right to participate in either the comprehensive or the specific claims process; any 'rights' created by policy statements can be changed at the whim of departmental officials. Second, existing processes require the federal government to judge the validity of claims against itself, placing it in a conflict of interest. Both the comprehensive and specific claims processes authorize the federal government to determine the criteria used to assess the merits of a claim and to determine whether a claim meets the criteria employed. Third, neither process contemplates any legal avenue of redress available to a participant who wishes to challenge federal determinations of either the criteria or their application in particular cases. Fourth, neither process provides a formal, let alone effective, means of effectively supervising federal or provincial negotiating strategies. For example, the federal government has long required that Aboriginal nations agree to the extinguishment of Aboriginal title as a precondition to negotiations. It has also stated that it will refuse to negotiate with an Aboriginal participant if the participant commences a legal action in relation to matters under discussion. Until recently, it has also required that territorial issues be settled before the negotiation of self-government arrangements. And it continues to require the consent of the relevant provincial or territorial government before agreeing to the constitutional protection of treaty-based rights of self-government. These negotiating tactics have a dramatic effect on both the process and outcome of negotiations, but the processes currently in place offer no means of assessing their procedural or substantive fairness.

Constitutional recognition and affirmation of existing Aboriginal and treaty rights obligate government to rectify these deficiencies. Subsection 35(1) of the Constitution Act, 1982 should be interpreted as requiring the federal government to legislate treaty processes that establish statutory rights of Aboriginal participants. This legislation should set out basic criteria to be employed to assess the merits of particular claims. These criteria, of course, must not interfere with the exercise of existing Aboriginal and treaty rights. Requiring Parliament to establish robust statutory treaty processes is relatively uncontroversial; it flows from the claim that subsection 35(1) imposes positive obligations on government to respect, promote, and fulfil Aboriginal and treaty rights. Given their constitutional status, Aboriginal and treaty rights are too important to be left to the vagaries of departmental politics.

Federal legislation should also establish an independent tribunal and vest it with the authority to resolve any dispute that may arise during comprehensive or specific negotiations. An independent tribunal is necessary to eliminate the conflict of interest currently confronting the federal government when it acts as the sole adjudicator of comprehensive and specific claims. Although such a tribunal would implicate provincial interests, Parliament, by virtue of subsection 91(24) of the Constitution Act, 1867, which confers on it legislative jurisdiction over 'Indians and Lands reserved for the Indians,' possesses the requisite authority to enact such legislation. Aboriginal rights and title are at the core of subsection 91(24); therefore Parliament possesses the exclusive authority to legislate in relation to these matters.[22] Provincial legislatures possess no authority to legislate in relation to Aboriginal title and Aboriginal rights, and provincial laws of general application that possess a valid provincial purpose apply to these matters only by virtue of federal permission to the extent provided for by section 88 of the Indian Act.[23] A federal law establishing a tribunal to oversee disputes arising out of claims of Aboriginal title and Aboriginal rights therefore would fall well within federal legislative authority.[24]

It is true that claims of Aboriginal and treaty rights, in contrast to

---

22 *Delgamuukw v. British Columbia*, [1997] 3 S.C.R. 1010 at 1117.

23 Ibid., at 1121–2.

24 For a similar conclusion, but calling for provincial cooperation in the establishment of a tribunal, see Royal Commission on Aboriginal Peoples, *Final Report*, vol. 2, pt. 2, at 604–606.

   One potential constitutional obstacle to the establishment of such a tribunal lies in the 'judicature provisions' of the constitution. Sections 96–100 of the Constitution Act, 1867 prevent legislatures from authorizing certain tribunals to exercise powers of a judicial nature that are identical or analogous to jurisdiction historically exercised exclusively by superior, district, or county courts. However, the judiciary has held that legislatures need not conform to the judicature provisions if the powers of the tribunal in question are 'necessarily incidental to the achievement of a broader policy goal of the legislature.' *Reference re Residential Tenancies Act*, [1981] 1 S.C.R. 714 at 736. For a recent reiteration of this approach, see *Chrysler Canada Ltd. v. Canada (Competition Tribunal)*, [1992] 2 S.C.R. 394. This aspect of the inquiry is 'designed to allow the courts to consider new approaches to old problems, approaches which are more responsive to changing social conditions.' *Sobeys Stores v. Yeomans*, [1989] 1 S.C.R. 238 at 255. The establishment of an Aboriginal tribunal would be tied to a broader policy goal of the legislature, namely, the objective of vesting Aboriginal people with greater control over their ancestral territories. For more discussion of the relation between the judicature provisions and the establishment of a federal tribunal to oversee specific and comprehensive claims, see Royal Commission on Aboriginal Peoples, *Final Report*, vol. 2, pt 2, at 606–8.

claims of Aboriginal title, typically involve assertions of the right to engage in activities on provincial Crown lands or on lands subject to third-party interests. But simply because provincial interests are implicated in such claims does not mean that Parliament would exceed its authority by establishing a tribunal to oversee such claims. Provincial Crown lands, according to section 109 of the Constitution Act, 1867, are 'subject to any Trusts existing in respect thereof, and to any interest other than that of the province,' and the judiciary has held that Aboriginal title and rights constitute an interest within the meaning of s. 109.[25] As Chief Justice Lamer said in *Delgamuukw v. British Columbia*, 'separating federal jurisdiction over Indians from jurisdiction over their lands would have a most unfortunate result – the government vested with primary constitutional responsibility for securing the welfare of Canada's aboriginal peoples would find itself unable to safeguard one of the most central of native interests – their interest in their lands.'[26]

A Duty to Negotiate in Good Faith

Federal and provincial authorities have proceeded on the assumption that the constitution does not require negotiations with Aboriginal communities who assert Aboriginal title or rights. But if the constitution imposes positive obligations on the state to respect, promote, and fulfil interests associated with indigenous difference, one such obligation must be to negotiate in good faith in relation to matters arising out of comprehensive and specific claims. We saw in the previous chapter that the federal Crown owes a pre-surrender fiduciary duty to an Indian band to provide all relevant facts and information as to its options concerning the surrender of reserve land and their foreseeable consequences in order to prevent 'exploitative bargains.'[27] The federal Crown is also under a post-surrender fiduciary duty to act in the best interests of an Indian band when the band surrenders reserve land to the Crown for third-party use.[28] The existence of these fiduciary duties does not necessarily mean that the federal Crown can legally prevent an Indian band from surrendering its reserve land on terms proposed by third parties,

---

25 *Delgamuuku v. British Columbia*, at 1117.

26 Ibid., at 1118.

27 *Blueberry River Indian Band v. Canada*, [1995] 4 S.C.R. 344 at 370, per McLachlin J. See also *Kruger v. The Queen* (1985), 17 D.L.R. (4th) 591 (Fed. C.A.).

28 *Guerin v. The Queen*, [1984] 2 S.C.R. 335.

but it does mean that it must act in the band's best interests and try to reach an arrangement that results in the 'least possible impairment' of the band's rights.[29] It is only appropriate that the federal Crown live up to both of these duties when it participates in a treaty process aimed at formally acknowledging the Aboriginal title of an Aboriginal nation to certain lands otherwise subject to provincial Crown title and jurisdiction.

Specifically, the federal Crown, when participating in a treaty process, is legally obligated to explore all reasonable options available to the Aboriginal nation. This duty includes exploring options other than those preferred by provincial authorities and attempting to reach an agreement that impairs the Aboriginal nation's rights as minimally as possible. Thus, the federal Crown is under a fiduciary duty to determine whether a treaty arrangement that removes Indian Act protections from reserve lands, that fails to extend Indian Act protections to lands subject to Aboriginal title, or that fails to exempt lands subject to Aboriginal title from the application of certain federal and provincial laws, is in the Aboriginal nation's best interests. If, after reviewing all the options, an Aboriginal nation decides that its best course of action is to attempt to retain or secure certain Indian Act protections of its lands or to negotiate a treaty that exempts lands subject to Aboriginal title from the application of certain federal and provincial laws, the federal government is legally obligated to explore with provincial authorities all possible means of achieving this objective.

How a duty to negotiate in good faith might operate in the comprehensive land claims process is illustrated in the recent decision of *Makivik Corp. v. Canada (Minister of Canadian Heritage)*.[30] This case arose out of the federal government's refusal to undertake that it would proceed with the creation of a national park in Labrador only with the consent of Nunavik Inuit. At the time, Canada and Nunavik Inuit were engaged in treaty negotiations under the umbrella of the federal comprehensive claims process. In the negotiations, Nunavik Inuit claimed Aboriginal title to land contemplated as part of the national park. Associate Chief Justice Richard of the Federal Court – Trial Division held that the federal government has a duty to consult and negotiate in good faith with the Nunavik Inuit in relation to its claims of Aboriginal rights to the

---

29 *Semiahmoo Indian Band v. Canada* (1997), 148 D.L.R. (4th) 523 at 537 (F.C.A.). For commentary, see Bob Freedman, '*Semiahmoo Indian Band v. Canada* (Case Comment)' (1997), 36 Alberta L. Rev. 218.
30 [1999] 1 F.C. 58 (T.D.).

land in question before establishing the national park. In noting that different land uses may affect the content of the duty, he stated: 'Where a national park reserve is established, there is a minimal impact on the rights and the use of land. There is ... a duty to consult in such circumstances. Any consultation must be meaningful. Where a national park itself is established, the impact will occur on the title, the rights and the use of land. There is, therefore, a duty to consult and negotiate in good faith in such circumstances.'[31] He concluded that the federal government owed a duty to consult with Nunavik Inuit, including a duty to inform and to listen, and a duty to negotiate in good faith with Nunavik Inuit concerning its claims to Aboriginal rights to parts of Labrador before establishing a national park in the area.

The federal government should also be under a fiduciary duty to enter into bilateral negotiations with an Aboriginal nation if a province refuses to negotiate a treaty that does not conform to provincial treaty objectives. No doubt provincial participation is politically desirable. But given that Parliament possesses exclusive legislative authority over 'Indians, and Lands reserved for the Indians,' and given that such authority includes exclusive jurisdiction over lands subject to Aboriginal title, provincial participation is not legally required. Just as provincial consent is not necessary to obtain a surrender of reserve land to enable an Indian band to deal directly with third parties, it is not necessary to extend the application of Indian Act protections to lands subject to Aboriginal title or to specify which federal or provincial laws apply to such lands. If a provincial government refuses to continue negotiations, the federal government should be legally obligated to establish a bilateral process with the Aboriginal nation aimed at reaching agreement without provincial participation.

Why must the federal Crown live up to these specific fiduciary duties in treaty negotiations? An Aboriginal nation seeking to transform the legal status of lands subject to Aboriginal title into some other form of legal entitlement, such as treaty settlement lands, must by law first surrender its legal interests in the lands to the federal Crown, which in turn possesses the authority to transform the legal interests into a form acceptable to the Aboriginal nation and a third party. The Crown's legal discretion to deal with third parties in this context is directly analogous to its legal discretion in the context of a surrender of reserve land.

---

31 Ibid., at 84.

It does not matter whether the land already falls under Indian Act protection because it constitutes reserve land, or whether it is subject to the Aboriginal nation's title. As Dickson J. stated in *Guerin v. The Queen*: 'It does not matter, in my opinion, that the present case is concerned with the interest of an Indian Band in a reserve rather than with unrecognized aboriginal title in traditional tribal lands. The Indian interest in the land is the same in both cases.'[32] Legal equation of Aboriginal title and reserve land was also recently affirmed in *Delgamuukw v. British Columbia*.[33] Because '[t]he Indian interest in the land is the same in both cases,'[34] as is the nature of federal authority, federal duties ought also to be the same in both cases.

Is the provincial Crown under a similar set of duties to an Aboriginal nation seeking to negotiate a treaty with federal and provincial authorities? Case law is unclear on whether the provincial Crown must act in the best interests of an Aboriginal nation in these circumstances.[35] To be sure, the provincial Crown is responsible for representing third-party interests and the public interest. A duty to act in the best interests of Aboriginal people might unduly compromise the provincial Crown's responsibilities to all citizens in the province. But a duty to act in a beneficiary's best interests is not the only duty that structures fiduciary relationships. The provincial Crown could be required to provide a less stringent standard of care in these circumstances. Within the confines of a treaty process, the provincial Crown should at least be under a duty to negotiate fairly and in good faith and to make every reasonable effort to reach agreements with Aboriginal nations.

The source of this duty lies in the legal discretion that the treaty process affords the provincial Crown in its dealings with Aboriginal nations. For example, British Columbia, by establishing a process designed to reach binding agreements with Aboriginal nations, has assumed wide discretion to pursue policies that seek to balance the interests of Aboriginal nations with those of third parties and the public. Fiduciary law ought to ensure that Aboriginal interests are not unduly compromised

---

32 Ibid., at 379.

33 *Delgamuukw v. British Columbia*, at 1085.

34 Ibid.

35 See *Mitchell v. Peguis Indian Band*, [1990] 2 S.C.R. 95, per Dickson C.J.; *Ontario (A.G.) v. Bear Island Foundation*, [1991] 2 S.C.R. 570; *Cree Regional Authority v. Robinson*, [1991] 4 C.N.L.R. 84 (F.C.T.D.); *Delgamuukw v. British Columbia* (1991), 79 D.L.R. (4th) 185 (B.C.S.C.); *Gardner v. Ontario* (1984), 45 O.R. (2d) 760 (H.C.); and *Smith v. The Queen*, [1983] 1 S.C.R. 554.

by negotiating tactics employed by provincial negotiators to achieve such a balance. Alternatively, the source of a provincial duty to negotiate fairly and in good faith could lie in subsection 5(1) of the provincial Treaty Commission Act, which provides that '[t]he purpose of the commission is to facilitate, in British Columbia, the negotiation of treaties among one or more first nations, Her Majesty in right of Canada and Her Majesty in right of British Columbia.'[36] Given that the province has established a treaty commission to facilitate treaty negotiations, it can be taken to have expressed a statutory desire that parties act fairly and in good faith and make every reasonable effort to reach an agreement.[37]

Even if a court is unwilling to imply a duty to negotiate fairly and in good faith from the enactment of the Treaty Commission Act, the judiciary has held that governmental officials owe a general duty of fairness, independent of any statute, when the nature of the decision, the relationship between the parties, and the effect of the decision on the rights of the affected party require procedural fairness.[38] In addition, the judiciary has required government officials to act fairly because of expectations generated in the affected party.[39]

Parties to treaty negotiations should be afforded great leeway in discussing possible options and arrangements for reconciling competing interests. A duty to negotiate fairly and in good faith is not breached simply because one party has proposed an arrangement that the other finds undesirable. But refusing at the outset of negotiations to explore options not contemplated by provincial treaty policy frustrates the negotiating process. Exemption from taxation, for example, forms part of a package of legal protections that many Aboriginal nations regard as critical to their efforts to preserve the integrity of what remains of their ancestral territories for future generations. This package constitutes the heart of federal protection of Aboriginal lands – protection that formally began with the Royal Proclamation, 1763 and enshrined in law

---

36 S.B.C. 1993, c. 4.

37 A similar, implied duty was held to govern employers in early collective bargaining legislation despite the lack of an express statutory duty to this effect: see *National Lock Co.* (1934), 1 N.L.B. 26; *Hall Baking Co.* (1934), 1 N.L.B. 83; and *S. Drenner & Son* (1934), 1 N.L.B. 26.

38 See *Board of Education of the Indian Head School Division No. 19 of Saskatchewan v. Knight*, [1990] 1 S.C.R. 653.

39 See, for example, *Volker Stevin NWT (1992) Ltd. v. Northwest Territories (Commissioner)* (1994), 113 D.L.R. (4th) 639 (N.W.T.C.A.); *Ottawa-Carleton Dialysis Services v. Ontario (Minister of Health)* (1996), 41 Admin. L.R. (2d) 211 (Ont. Div. Ct.).

since before Confederation.[40] It may be that some Aboriginal nations will emerge from treaty negotiations with a set of protections that does not include an exemption from taxation. But, in light of the exemption's historical significance and its centrality to efforts to preserve Aboriginal lands from non-Aboriginal incursion, to rule out the possibility of taxation-exempt status from the outset and to declare the elimination of the exemption to be a precondition of negotiations represents a failure by a province to make every reasonable effort to reach an agreement. Accordingly, requiring as a precondition of negotiations that an Aboriginal nation agree to the elimination of the Indian Act tax exemption likely constitutes a breach of the province's duty to negotiate fairly and in good faith. For the same reasons, requiring as a precondition of negotiations that an Aboriginal nation agree to convert existing reserves into treaty settlement lands to avoid the application of the Indian Act likely also constitutes a breach of the province's duty to negotiate fairly and in good faith.

According to the Treaty Commission Act, the purpose of the Treaty Commission is 'to facilitate, in British Columbia, the negotiation of treaties among one or more first nations, Her Majesty in right of Canada and Her Majesty in right of British Columbia.'[41] The commission 'must ... encourage timely negotiations' and 'perform any other duties that are consistent with ... this Act.'[42] The commission therefore possesses the legal authority to determine whether these provincial preconditions constitute a breach of the duty to negotiate fairly and, if so, to make a declaration to this effect. While the Act does not confer on the commission explicit statutory authority to order remedies in the context of a breach of the duty to negotiate in good faith, a declaration to this effect, by prodding the province to alter its negotiating stance, might have a salutary effect on negotiations.

From Consultation to Co-Management

I have proposed that the Crown has a duty to negotiate in good faith in comprehensive land claims negotiations, whether the negotiations occur under the rubric of federal or provincial treaty processes. But what about Aboriginal claims that arise outside of existing processes, in

---

40 See, generally, *Mitchell v. Peguis Indian Band*, per La Forest J.
41 Treaty Commission Act, s. 5(1).
42 Ibid., ss. 5(3)(c), 5(3)(f).

cases in which an Aboriginal nation alleges that a proposed governmental action will interfere with existing Aboriginal or treaty rights? Courts have held that in the event of an infringement of an existing Aboriginal or treaty right, the Crown must involve the Aboriginal nation 'in decisions taken with respect to their lands.'[43] 'There is always,' stated Chief Justice Lamer in *Delgamuukw*, 'a duty of consultation.'[44] But subsequent lower court jurisprudence has failed to appreciate the capacity of the duty to act as an incentive on the parties to forgo litigation by negotiating the nature and scope of their respective rights.

In *Delgamuukw*, the court held that the content of the duty of consultation will vary with the circumstances:

> [I]n occasional cases, when the breach is less serious or relatively minor, it will be no more than a duty to discuss important decisions that will be taken with respect to lands held pursuant to aboriginal title. Of course, even in these rare cases when the minimum acceptable standard is consultation, this consultation must be in good faith, and with the intention of substantially addressing the concerns of the aboriginal peoples whose lands are at issue. In most cases it will be significantly deeper than mere consultation. Some cases may even require the full consent of an aboriginal nation, particularly when provinces enact hunting and fishing regulations in relation to aboriginal lands.[45]

Despite this holding, lower courts have not held the Crown to requirements that are 'significantly deeper than consultation.' In most, if not all, cases, the duty to consult has been defined simply as a duty to inform, listen, and share information with Aboriginal people whose land is at issue. The consultation must be meaningful,[46] and the duty includes a requirement to provide full notice[47] and other necessary information to Aboriginal people. In determining whether the duty to consult has been fulfilled, the judiciary will consider whether consultations effectively informed the Crown of the practices and views of the

---

43 *Delgamuukw*, at 1113.
44 Ibid.
45 Ibid.
46 Ibid.; see also *Nunavik Inuit v. Canada (Minister of Canadian Heritage)* (1998), 164 D.L.R. (4th) 463 (Fed. T.D.).
47 *Kitkatla Band v. British Columbia (Minister of Small Business, Tourism and Culture)*, [1999] 1 C.N.L.R. 72.

Aboriginal people in question.[48] Courts have also held that the duty is not fulfilled by meetings between Aboriginal people and any private company carrying out the actual resource extraction.[49] Other cases have suggested that delegation of the duty to a private entity might occasionally be sufficient, but they have also cited the potential for mistrust and conflict of interest inherent in such an arrangement.[50] Generally, the Crown must remain in an overseeing role, even when it has obligated the permit holder to determine the extent to which the activity in question might infringe Aboriginal title or rights.

Judicial reluctance to consider the duty to consult as an obligation on the Crown to negotiate in good faith no doubt stems in part from an unwillingness to handcuff the Crown in the exercise of its legislative and executive authority. But a duty to negotiate is not a duty to agree. Holding the Crown to a duty to negotiate when proposed Crown actions threaten Aboriginal interests is consistent with the proposition that subsection 35(1) contemplates the active participation of federal and provincial governments, as well as Aboriginal peoples themselves, in determining the scope and content of each party's rights. It would increase the likelihood that the parties would reach agreements detailing rights and obligations concerning ownership and authority over natural resources and the sharing in the profit and other benefits that flow from the activity in question. Such arrangements, often called co-management agreements, are consistent with three of the central principles underlying Canadian jurisprudence on Aboriginal title: that Aboriginal title includes the right to choose the uses to which the land should be put; that Aboriginal consent is required before proposed Crown action that significantly impairs Aboriginal rights; and that Aboriginal communities should be compensated for infringements of their title.[51]

Negotiating Self-Government

The 1998 Nisga'a treaty, formally known as the Nisga'a Final Agreement, recognizes that the 'Nisga'a Nation has the right of self-govern-

---

48 *R. v. Bones*, [1990] 4 C.N.L.R. 37 (B.C.P.C.); *Halfway River First Nation v. B.C. (Minister of Forests)*, [1997] 4 C.N.L.R. 45 (B.C.S.C.), at 73–4.

49 *Halfway River*, at 72.

50 *Tsilhqot'in National Government v. British Columbia*, [1998] B.C.E.A. No. 23, Appeal no. 97-PES-08.

51 *Delgamuukw*, at 1113–14.

ment.' It recognizes two levels of Nisga'a government, Nisga'a Lisims Government and Nisga'a Village Government. Nisga'a Lisims Government constitutes the government of the Nisga'a Nation as a whole; it can make laws in relation to a wide range of subject matters, including citizenship, culture, Nisga'a lands, employment, social services, health services, child and family services, and education. Nisga'a Village Governments are local governments of four existing Nisga'a villages and any additional village on Nisga'a lands established in accordance with the terms of the agreement; they possess the authority to make laws in relation to a number of local matters. Generally speaking, the agreement also provides that in the event of an inconsistency or conflict between a Nisga'a law and a federal or provincial law, the Nisga'a law prevails to the extent of the inconsistency.

By recognizing Nisga'a lawmaking authority and providing for Nisga'a paramountcy in certain circumstances, the Nisga'a Final Agreement establishes the Nisga'a government as a third order of government in Canada and appears to challenge two fundamental structural features of the Canadian constitutional order. First, it has long been a maxim of Canadian constitutional law that the distribution of legislative authority is exhaustive – no subject matter exists that cannot form the basis of legislation by Parliament or a provincial legislature.[52] Second, it is a basic feature of the distribution of legislative power that federal law is paramount in the event of conflict with an inconsistent provincial law.[53] Does the Nisga'a Final Agreement violate either principle, making it necessary to formally amend the constitution to implement the terms of the agreement? Stated differently, to what extent does the constitution authorize parties to negotiate treaty rights of self-government that contemplate Aboriginal legislative authority?

The text and the legislative history of section 35 suggest that parties to a treaty process are free to accord constitutional recognition and affirmation to a wide array of rights. Nothing in its wording suggests any restriction on the type of rights that can constitute 'treaty rights' within the meaning of the provision. Indeed, subsection 35(3), which provides

---

52 See *A.G. Ont. v. A.G. Can.*, [1912] A.C. 571 at 581, 583 ('whatever belongs to self-government in Canada belongs either to the Dominion or to the provinces, within the limits of the British North America Act').

53 See *Re Exported Natural Gas Tax*, [1982] 1 S.C.R. 1004; see generally W.R. Lederman, 'The Concurrent Operation of Federal and Provincial Laws in Canada,' 9 McGill L.J. 185 (1963).

that '"treaty rights" includes rights that now exist by way of land claims agreements or may be so acquired,' suggests that subsection 35(1) 'treaty rights' are not restricted to rights contained in historical treaties. Section 35 was drafted against the backdrop of a number of historical and modern treaties, most notably the James Bay Agreement, which contain a wide array of treaty rights addressing many diverse matters, including self-governing authority, co-management, fiscal arrangements, and land and resource ownership and use.

Precedent also supports a broad interpretation of the meaning of 'treaty rights' in section 35. The judiciary has held that what characterizes a 'treaty' under law is not its content or the rights it provides but instead the intention to create obligations, the presence of mutually binding obligations, and a certain measure of solemnity.[54] Section 88 of the Indian Act, which shields treaty rights from the application of provincial law and therefore performs a function similar but not identical to section 35, has been interpreted as applying to agreements about political and social rights, as well as to agreements about the sharing of territory.[55] Rights contained in the James Bay and Northern Quebec Agreement, for example, have been held to constitute 'treaty rights' within the meaning of section 35.[56]

Moreover, it is far from clear that the Nisga'a Final Agreement, by providing for Nisga'a legislative authority and limited paramountcy over inconsistent federal and provincial law, conflicts with structural features of the constitutional order. With respect to the principle of exhaustiveness, the Nisga'a Agreement explicitly states that it does not alter the distribution of legislative authority between Parliament and the provincial legislatures. The same classes of subject matters that fell within federal and provincial authority before the agreement came into force continue to fall within federal and provincial authority. Parliament and provincial legislatures remain free to enact the same laws that they were entitled to enact before the agreement came into force. The principle of exhaustiveness refers to the proposition that no subject matter exists that cannot form the basis of legislation by Parliament or a provincial legislature. It does not suggest that Parliament and provincial legislatures are the only bodies entitled to exercise legislative authority in Canada. This point is

---

54 *Simon v. The Queen*, [1985] 2 S.C.R. 387 at 401, 410.

55 *R. v. Sioui*, [1990] 1 S.C.R. 1025 at 1043.

56 *Cree Regional Authority v. Robinson*, supra, at 102 per Rouleau J.; *Eastmain Band v. Gilpin*, [1987] 3 C.N.L.R. 54 (Que. Prov. Ct.).

illustrated by the fact that the judiciary considered the distribution of legislative authority between Parliament and provincial legislatures to be exhaustive at a time when the Imperial Parliament possessed concurrent legislative authority over matters that fall within federal and provincial jurisdiction. Accordingly, the principle of exhaustiveness does not preclude an Aboriginal government from exercising concurrent legislative authority over matters that also fall within federal or provincial legislative authority. With respect to the principle of paramountcy, the Nisga'a Agreement provides that Aboriginal laws are paramount over federal and provincial laws in certain circumstances. But nothing in the agreement seeks to alter federal paramountcy over conflicting provincial law. And the fact that federal laws are paramount over conflicting provincial laws does not mean that they automatically trump other constitutional imperatives. Federal laws are subject to section 35 of the Constitution Act, 1982 and to treaty rights recognized and affirmed by section 35. As with all rights recognized by section 35, a treaty right of self-government can check the exercise of federal legislative authority in certain circumstances.

At best, text, structure, and precedent support the position that it is unnecessary to amend the constitution to implement the terms of the Nisga'a Agreement; at worst, they are ambiguous on this question. Understanding the constitutional relationship between Aboriginal people and the Canadian state in terms of the normative significance of indigenous difference sheds more light on this issue. For reasons central to the thesis of this book, the constitution ought to be seen as authorizing parties to negotiate self-government agreements that provide for Aboriginal legislative authority and limited Aboriginal paramountcy in the face of inconsistent federal and provincial law. If Aboriginal sovereignty merits constitutional protection in the form of an Aboriginal right of self-government, and if an Aboriginal nation possesses the right to make laws in relation to matters that affect the daily lives of its members, then the constitution contemplates the emergence of Aboriginal government as a third order of government in Canada. This does not mean that it contemplates that parties are free to negotiate a treaty that authorizes an Aboriginal nation to exercise limitless legislative authority. The scope of Aboriginal legislative authority recognized by treaty should bear a rational relation to the interests that section 35 serves to protect. But in certain circumstances, the application of an inconsistent federal or provincial law in the face of a valid Aboriginal law might not meet the standards of justification that the constitution imposes on federal or provincial actions that interfere with the exercise of an Aboriginal right. Limited paramountcy of Aboriginal law in the face of conflicting federal or provincial law, in other words, is but a consequence of the constitutional recognition and affirmation of an Aboriginal right of self-government.

No court has held that an Aboriginal nation independently possesses a right of self-government on the scale contemplated by the Nisga'a Final Agreement.[57] But judicial prudence does not, and should not, foreclose the possibility that the parties themselves can determine the nature and scope of Aboriginal governing authority through a treaty process. The framework that the constitution provides for reconciling Aboriginal interests and Canadian sovereignty contemplates the active participation of federal and provincial governments, as well as Aboriginal peoples themselves, in the process of determining the scope and content of the parties' rights. Indeed, the judiciary is not capable of adequately engaging in complex and detailed assessments of the ongoing legal relationship between Aboriginal nations and the Crown. The judicial role in this process of reconciliation is to define the background legal entitlements of Aboriginal nations, the federal government, and the provincial governments. Section 35 contemplates parties to a treaty process, not the judiciary, assuming the primary responsibility of identifying and reconciling their competing interests in a manner consistent with a just distribution of legislative authority.

---

57 But see *Campbell et al. v. A.G.B.C. and Nisga'a Nation et al.*, [2000] B.C.S.C. 1123 (upholding the constitutionality of the Nisga'a Final Agreement).

Conclusion

Due north of Manitowaning Bay, across the North Channel that separates Manitoulin Island from the north shore of Lake Huron and Georgian Bay, is the La Cloche mountain range. Extending from Killarney
west to the mouth of the Spanish River, the ancient white quartzite hills
of La Cloche include Dreamer's Rock, a sacred place where Ojibway
youth undergo traditional rites of passage. Shawonoswe, a great Ojibway
chief and healer, was once praying and fasting on Dreamer's Rock when
a thunderbird swooped down and commanded him to climb on its back.
Through the air they soared until the thunderbird left Shawonoswe on
the peak of a nearby mountain known as Nehahupkung. It was on this
mountain that Shawonoswe saw the Great Spirit sitting in a cloud holding a bowl of water. The Great Spirit asked Shawonoswe to look inside
the bowl, and Shawonoswe saw men and animals. He saw the coming of
white men and war. The Great Spirit told Shawonoswe that he had been
brought to Nehahupkung to learn harmony and order. And he told him
that, although the visions he had seen would come to pass, Shawonoswe
must have faith that the Ojibway would survive, and he instructed
Shawonoswe of the laws by which he was to rule his people.[1]

The visions that Shawonoswe saw on Nehahupkung have come to
pass, and his people have survived. But their arduous survival – and the
survival of all Aboriginal peoples in Canada – has been scarred by injustice. Throughout Canada's history, governments and courts systematically ignored the spirit and intent of treaties between Aboriginal

---

1 This account of Dreamer's Rock and Shawonoswe is adapted from Andrea Gutsche,
  Barbara Chisholm, and Russell Floren, *The North Channel and St. Mary's River: A Guide to
  the History* (Toronto: Lynx Images, 1997), at 11–12, 24–5.

peoples and the Crown, devalued ancient forms of Aboriginal sovereignty, dispossessed Aboriginal peoples of their ancestral territories, and regarded as inferior the diverse cultures to which Aboriginal people claim allegiance. Against this history, the central claim of this book is relatively straightforward: constitutional recognition of indigenous difference promotes a just distribution of constitutional power. Aboriginal and treaty rights – the constitutional power that Aboriginal people possess by virtue of their indigenous difference – authorize Aboriginal people to engage in customs, practices, and traditions integral to their distinctive identities; preserve ancestral territories from unwarranted state interference; enable Aboriginal governments to make laws governing their communities; and entrench promises made by the Crown in treaty negotiations. Constitutional recognition of indigenous difference also gives rise to corresponding state obligations to establish the fiscal, social, and institutional arrangements necessary to promote and fulfil Aboriginal and treaty rights, including treaty processes that will enable the negotiation of treaties that recognize Aboriginal claims to ancestral territory and Aboriginal law-making authority.

While the central claim of the book is relatively straightforward, the reasons supporting it are more complex. Distributions of constitutional power protect certain interests and the justice of a particular distribution depends on the nature of the interest at stake. Indigenous difference corresponds to Aboriginal interests associated with culture, territory, sovereignty, and the treaty process. Each merits constitutional protection for relatively distinct reasons. Aboriginal cultural interests warrant constitutional protection because Aboriginal cultural practices provide a shared intelligibility to Aboriginal existence and shape the formation of individual and collective identities, and because Aboriginal people face steep challenges in their efforts to maintain and reproduce their cultures. Aboriginal territorial interests warrant constitutional protection because Aboriginal people have unique spiritual relationships with their ancestral lands and lived on and occupied their lands before the establishment of the Canadian state. Interests associated with Aboriginal sovereignty merit constitutional protection because a just distribution of sovereignty requires both constitutionally recognizing the fact that Aboriginal peoples were sovereign prior to European contact and vesting greater law-making authority in Aboriginal communities. And Aboriginal interests associated with the treaty process warrant constitutional protection because treaties distribute constitutional authority by establishing basic terms and conditions of Aboriginal and non-Aboriginal co-existence.

Although the reasons why interests associated with indigenous difference merit constitutional protection are relatively distinct, they share one common trait: each appeals to a principle of equality. Protecting Aboriginal cultural interests is necessary to ensure that Aboriginal people possess equal resources to maintain and reproduce their cultural identities. Protecting Aboriginal territorial interests is necessary to ensure that Aboriginal interests in land receive no less protection than what the law extends to non-Aboriginal interests in land, and to respect the fact that Aboriginal territorial interests predated the establishment of the Canadian state. Protecting Aboriginal sovereign interests acknowledges that Aboriginal nations were formal equals to European powers at the time of contact and seeks to remedy the substantive inequalities facing Aboriginal people in contemporary life. And protecting interests associated with the treaty process formalizes the nation-to-nation relationship between Aboriginal peoples and the Canadian state.

Constitutional protection of interests associated with indigenous difference yields a unique constitutional relationship between Aboriginal people and the Canadian state. This relationship reflects the fact that Aboriginal people belonged and continue to belong to distinctive cultures threatened by forces of assimilation. It recognizes the legitimacy of ancient Aboriginal relationships with territory and Aboriginal forms of government. And it respects the fact that Aboriginal peoples are in an ongoing treaty process with the Canadian state. Far from compromising the value of equal citizenship, the constitutional relationship between Aboriginal people and the Canadian state promotes equal citizenship by acknowledging the constitutional relevance of indigenous difference.

When European powers first established colonies in North America, they sought to legitimate their grandiose claims of territorial sovereignty by ignoring the constitutional significance of indigenous difference. European powers viewed Aboriginal nations as different, but saw in difference Aboriginal inferiority. The Canadian constitutional order owes its origins to a European world-view that regarded Aboriginal nations as insufficiently civilized to merit membership in the community of nations. As a founding principle of a modern state, a belief in Aboriginal inferiority casts long shadows over the legitimacy of Canadian claims of territorial sovereignty. In contrast, recognizing constitutional significance of indigenous difference equates difference with equality. In so doing, it extends a measure of constitutional legitimacy not only to the fact of indigenous difference but to the Canadian constitutional order itself.

Bibliography

Books

Alfred, Gerald R. *Heeding the Voices of Our Ancestors: Kahnawake Mohawk Politics and the Rise of Native Nationalism*. Toronto: Oxford University Press, 1995.

Amoss, Pamela. *Coast Salish Spirit Dancing: The Survival of an Ancient Religion*. Seattle: University of Washington Press, 1978.

Anaya, S. James. *Indigenous Peoples in International Law*. New York: Oxford University Press, 1996.

An-Na'im, Abdullahi Ahmed. *Toward an Islamic Reformation: Civil Liberties, Human Rights, and International Law*. Syracuse: Syracuse University Press, 1990.

Aristotle. *Nichomachean Ethics*. Ed. and trans. Martin Ostwald. Indianapolis: Bobbs-Merrill, 1962.

– *Politics*. Ed. G.P. Goold, trans. H. Rackham. Cambridge: Harvard University Press, 1990.

Asch, Michael. *Home and Native Land: Aboriginal Rights and the Canadian Constitution*. Toronto: Methuen, 1984.

Atiyah, Patrick. *The Rise and Fall of Freedom of Contract*. Oxford: Clarendon Press, 1979.

Austin, John. *The Province of Jurisprudence Determined*. Ed. W.E. Rumble. Cambridge: Cambridge University Press, 1995.

Bakan, Joel. *Just Words: Constitutional Rights and Social Wrongs*. Toronto: University of Toronto Press, 1997.

Baldwin, James. *The Fire Next Time*. New York: Dell, 1963.

Barman, J., Y. Hébert, and D. McCaskill, eds. *Indian Education in Canada*. Vancouver: UBC Press, 1986.

Barsh, Russel Lawrence and James Youngblood Henderson. *The Road: Indian Tribes and Political Liberty*. Berkeley: University of California Press, 1980.

Bartleson, Jens. *A Genealogy of Sovereignty*. Cambridge: Cambridge University Press, 1995.

Beatty, David M. *Constitutional Law in Theory and Practice*. Toronto: University of Toronto Press, 1995.

— *Talking Heads and the Supremes: The Canadian Production of Judicial Review*. Scarborough, Ont.: Carswell, 1990.

Becker, Lawrence C. *Property Rights: Philosophic Foundations*. London: Routledge and Kegan Paul, 1977.

Benedict, Ruth. *Patterns of Culture*. Boston: Houghton Mifflin, 1934.

Berger, Thomas R. *Fragile Freedoms: Human Rights and Dissent in Canada*. Toronto: Clarke, Irwin, 1981.

Bernstein, Richard J. *Beyond Objectivism and Relativism: Science, Hermeneutics, and Praxis*. Philadelphia: University of Pennsylvania Press, 1983.

Bhabha, Homi. *The Location of Culture*. London: Routledge, 1994.

Bickel, Alexander. *The Least Dangerous Branch*. New Haven: Yale University Press, 1965.

Black, Charles L., Jr. *Structure and Relationship in Constitutional Law*. Woodbridge: Ox Bow Press, 1968.

Blackstone, William. *Commentaries on the Laws of England*. Ed. E. Christian. London: A. Strathan, 1809.

Bobbitt, Philip. *Constitutional Fate: Theory of the Constitution*. New York: Oxford University Press, 1982.

Bogart, W.A. *Courts and Country: The Limits of Litigation and the Social and Political Life of Canada*. Oxford: Oxford University Press, 1994.

Brierly, J.L. *The Law of Nations: An Introduction to the International Law of Peace*. 4th ed. Oxford: Clarendon Press, 1949.

Brigham, Clarence S., ed. *British Royal Proclamations Relating to America*. Transactions and Collections of the American Antiquarian Society, Vol. 12. Worcester: American Antiquarian Society, 1911.

Brigham, John. *The Constitution of Interests: Beyond the Politics of Rights*. New York: New York University Press, 1996.

Brisbane, Robert H. *Black Activism: Racial Revolution in the United States, 1954–1970*. Valley Forge: Judson Press, 1974.

Brown, Wendy. *States of Injury: Power and Freedom in Late Modernity*. Princeton: Princeton University Press, 1995.

Brownlie, Ian. *Principles of Public International Law*. 5th ed. Oxford: Clarendon Press, 1998.

Cairns, Alan C. *Charter versus Federalism: The Dilemmas of Constitutional Reform*. Montreal and Kingston: McGill-Queen's University Press, 1992.

Campbell, Tom. *Justice*. Atlantic Highlands: Humanities Press International, 1988.

Carens, Joseph. *Culture, Citizenship and Community: A Contextual Exploration of Justice as Evenhandedness.* Oxford: Oxford University Press, 2000.

Cassese, Antonio. *Self-Determination of Peoples: A Legal Reappraisal.* Cambridge: Cambridge University Press, 1995.

Cassidy, Frank, and Robert L. Bish. *Indian Government: Its Meaning in Practice.* Halifax: Institute for Research on Public Policy, 1991.

Clifford, James. *The Predicament of Culture: Twentieth-Century Ethnography, Literature, and Art.* Cambridge: Harvard University Press, 1988.

Cole, Douglas, and Ira Chaikin. *An Iron Hand upon the People: The Law against the Potlatch on the Northwest Coast.* Vancouver: Douglas and McIntyre, 1990.

Colvin, Eric. *Legal Process and the Resolution of Indian Claims.* Saskatoon: University of Saskatoon Native Law Centre, 1981.

Coombe, Rosemary J. *The Cultural Life of Intellectual Properties: Authorship, Appropriation, and the Law.* Durham: Duke University Press, 1998.

Cooper, David E. *The Illusions of Equality.* London: Routledge and Kegan Paul, 1980.

Cornell, Stephen. *The Return of the Native: American Indian Political Resurgence.* New York: Oxford University Press, 1988.

Crawford, James. *The Creation of States in International Law.* Oxford: Clarendon Press, 1979.

Cromwell, Thomas A. *Locus Standi: A Commentary on the Law of Standing in Canada.* Scarborough, Ont.: Carswell, 1986.

Cronon, E. David. *Black Moses: The Story of Marcus Garvey and the Universal Negro Improvement Association.* Madison: University of Wisconsin Press, 1955.

Cronon, William. *Changes in the Land: Indians, Colonists, and the Ecology of New England.* 1st ed. New York: Hill and Wang, 1983.

Cross, Sir Rupert, and Colin Tapper. *Cross on Evidence.* 6th ed. London: Butterworths, 1985.

Cruse, Harold. *Plural But Equal: A Critical Study of Blacks and Minorities and America's Plural Society.* New York: William Morrow, 1987.

– *Rebellion or Revolution?* New York: William Morrow, 1968.

Culhane, Dara. *The Pleasure of the Crown: Anthropology, Law and First Nations.* Burnaby: Talonbooks, 1998.

Davis, S. Rufus. *The Federal Principle: A Journey through Time in Quest of Meaning.* Berkeley: University of California Press, 1978.

Delany, Martin R. *The Condition, Elevation, Emigration and Destiny of the Colored People of the United States.* Salem: Ayer Company, 1988.

Denis, Claude. *We Are Not You: First Nations and Canadian Modernity.* Peterborough: Broadview Press, 1997.

Dennis, Matthew. *Cultivating a Landscape of Peace: Iroquois-European Encounters in Seventeenth-Century America.* Ithaca: Cornell University Press, 1993.

Donnelly, Jack. *Universal Human Rights in Theory and Practice.* Ithaca: Cornell University Press, 1989.

Dworkin, Ronald. *Freedom's Law: The Moral Reading of the American Constitution.* Cambridge: Harvard University Press, 1996.

– *Law's Empire.* Cambridge: Harvard University Press, 1986.

– *A Matter of Principle.* Cambridge: Harvard University Press, 1985.

– *Taking Rights Seriously.* Cambridge: Harvard University Press, 1977.

Elkins, David. *Beyond Sovereignty: Territory and Political Economy in the Twenty-First Century.* Toronto: University of Toronto Press, 1995.

Ely, John Hart. *Democracy and Distrust.* Cambridge: Harvard University Press, 1980.

Epstein, Richard. *Simple Rules for a Complex World.* Cambridge: Harvard University Press, 1995.

– *Takings: Private Property and the Power of Eminent Domain.* Cambridge: Harvard University Press, 1985.

Finn, P.D. *Fiduciary Obligations.* Sydney: The Law Book Company, 1977.

Fish, Stanley. *Doing What Comes Naturally: Change, Rhetoric, and the Practice of Theory in Literary and Legal Studies.* Durham: Duke University Press, 1989.

Fitzgerald, P.J., ed. *Salmond on Jurisprudence.* 12th ed. London: Sweet & Maxwell, 1966.

Fogarty, K.H. *Equality Rights and Their Limitations in the Charter.* Scarborough, Ont.: Carswell, 1987.

Frankena, William K. *Ethics.* Englewood Cliffs, N.J.: Prentice-Hall, 1973.

Franks, C.E.S. *Public Administration Questions Relating to Aboriginal Self-Government.* Kingston: Institute of Intergovernmental Relations, 1987.

Friedman, Milton. *Capitalism and Freedom.* Chicago: University of Chicago Press, 1962.

Frye, Northrop. *The Eternal Act of Creation: Essays, 1979–1990.* Indianapolis: Indiana University Press, 1993.

Fuller, Lon. *Legal Fictions.* Stanford: Stanford University Press, 1967.

Galligan, D.J. *Discretionary Powers: A Legal Study of Official Discretion.* Oxford: Clarendon Press, 1990.

Garvey, Marcus. *Philosophy and Opinions of Marcus Garvey.* New York: Atheneum, 1992.

Geertz, Clifford. *The Interpretation of Cultures.* New York: Basic Books, 1973.

Gibson, Dale. *The Law of the Charter: Equality Rights.* Calgary: Carswell, 1990.

Gong, Gerrit W. *The Standard of 'Civilization' in International Society.* Oxford: Clarendon Press, 1984.

Gough, J.W. *The Social Contract: A Critical Study of Its Development.* 2nd ed. Oxford: Oxford University Press, 1963.

Griffith, J.A.G. *The Politics of the Judiciary.* 3rd ed. Manchester: Manchester University Press, 1985.

Gutsche, Andrea, Barbara Chisholm, and Russell Floren. *The North Channel and St. Mary's River: A Guide to the History.* Toronto: Lynx Images, 1997.

Habermas, Jürgen. *Between Facts and Norms: Contributions to a Discourse Theory of Law and Democracy.* Cambridge: MIT Press, 1996.

Hall, William E. *A Treatise on International Law.* 8th ed. Oxford: Clarendon Press, 1924.

Hamnett, Ian. *Chieftainship and Legitimacy.* Boston: Routledge and Kegan Paul, 1975.

Hannum, Hurst. *Autonomy, Sovereignty, and Self-Determination: The Accommodation of Conflicting Rights.* Rev. ed. Philadelphia: University of Pennsylvania Press, 1996.

Harjo, Joy. *Secrets from the Center of the World.* Tucson: University of Arizona Press, 1989.

Harring, Sidney L. *White Man's Law: Native People in Nineteenth-Century Canadian Jurisprudence.* Toronto: Osgoode Society for Canadian Legal History, 1998.

Harris, J.W. *Property and Justice.* Oxford: Clarendon Press, 1996.

Hart, Henry Melvin, Jr, and Albert M. Sacks, *The Legal Process.* Westbury: Foundation Press, 1994.

Hart, H.L.A. *The Concept of Law.* Oxford: Clarendon Press, 1961.

Hawkes, David C. *Aboriginal Self-Government: What Does It Mean?* Kingston: Institute of Intergovernmental Relations, 1985.

Heard, Andrew David. *Canadian Constitutional Conventions: The Marriage of Law and Politics.* Toronto: Oxford University Press, 1991.

Hegel, G.W.F. *Philosophy of Right.* Tran. T.M. Knox. Oxford: Clarendon Press, 1942.

Herbert, Christopher. *Culture and Anomie: Ethnographic Imagination in the Nineteenth Century.* Chicago: University of Chicago Press, 1991.

Herskovits, Melville J. *Man and His Works: The Science of Cultural Anthropology.* New York: Knopf, 1948.

Hogg, Peter W. *Constitutional Law of Canada.* Scarborough, Ont.: Carswell, 2000.

Horowitz, Gad. *Canadian Labour in Politics.* Toronto: University of Toronto Press, 1968.

Howard, Rhoda. *Human Rights in Commonwealth Africa.* Totowa, N.J.: Rowman & Littlefield, 1986.

Hurt, R. Douglas. *Indian Agriculture in America: Prehistory to the Present.* Lawrence: University of Kansas Press, 1987.

Hutchinson, Allan. *Waiting for CORAF: A Critique of Law and Rights.* Toronto: University of Toronto Press, 1995.

Hyde, Charles C. *International Law Chiefly as Interpreted and Applied by the United States.* Boston: Little Brown, 1922.

Jencks, C., et al., *Inequality: A Reassessment of the Effect of Family and Schooling in America.* New York: Harper & Row, 1973.

Jennings, Francis. *The Ambiguous Iroquois Empire: The Covenant Chain Confederation of Indian Tribes with English Colonies from Its Beginnings to the Lancaster Treaty of 1744.* New York: W.W. Norton, 1984.

Jennings, R.Y. *The Acquisition of Territory in International Law.* Manchester: Manchester University Press, 1963.

Johnston, Basil. *The Manitous: The Supernatural World of the Ojibway.* Toronto: Key Porter, 1995.

Kallen, Howard M. *Cultural Pluralism and the American Idea: An Essay in Social Philosophy.* Philadelphia: University of Pennsylvania Press, 1956.

Kalodner, Howard I., and James J. Fishman, eds. *The Limits of Justice: The Courts' Role in School Desegregation.* Cambridge: Ballinger Publishing, 1978.

Kant, Immanuel. *The Metaphysics of Morals.* Trans. J. Ladd. Indianapolis: Bobbs-Merrill, 1965.

Karst, Kenneth L. *Belonging to America: Equal Citizenship and the Constitution.* New Haven: Yale University Press, 1989.

Keller, A.S., O.J. Lissitzyn, and F.J. Mann. *Creation of Rights of Sovereignty through Symbolic Acts, 1400-1800.* New York: Columbia University Press, 1963.

Kelley, Ninette, and Michael J. Trebilcock. *Making of the Mosaic: History of Canadian Immigration Policy.* Toronto: University of Toronto Press, 1999.

Kelsen, Hans. *General Theory of Law and State.* Trans. A. Nedberg. Cambridge: Harvard University Press, 1945.

Kennedy, Duncan. *A Critique of Adjudication.* Cambridge: Harvard University Press, 1997.

King, Martin Luther. *Where Do We Go from Here: Chaos or Community?* Boston: Beacon Press, 1968.

Korman, Sharon. *The Right of Conquest: The Acquisition of Territory by Force in International Law and Practice.* Oxford: Clarendon Press, 1996.

Kymlicka, Will. *Liberalism, Community, and Culture.* Oxford: Oxford University Press, 1989.

– *Multicultural Citizenship: A Liberal Theory of Minority Rights.* Oxford: Clarendon Press, 1995.

Langenhove, Fernand van. *The Question of Aborigines before the United Nations: The Belgian Thesis.* Brussels: Royal Colonial Institute, 1954.

Laski, Harold J. *The Foundations of Sovereignty and Other Essays.* New York: Harcourt, Brace, 1921.

Leyden, Wolfgang von. *Aristotle on Equality and Justice: His Political Argument.* Houndsmills: Macmillan, 1985.

Locke, John. *Two Treatises of Government.* Ed. P. Laslett. Cambridge: Cambridge University Press, 1988.

Lupis, Ingrid Detter de. *International Law and the Independent State.* 2nd ed. Aldershott: Gower, 1987.

MacCormick, Neil. *Legal Reasoning and Legal Theory.* Oxford: Clarendon Press, 1978.

MacKinnon, Catherine. *Toward a Feminist Theory of the State.* Cambridge: Harvard University Press, 1989.

Maine, Henry. *Ancient Law.* 1861; London: Dent, 1917.

Mandel, Michael. *The Charter of Rights and the Legalization of Politics in Canada.* Toronto: Wall & Thompson, 1989.

McGoldrick, Dominic. *The Human Rights Committee: Its Role in the Development of the International Covenant on Civil and Political Rights.* Oxford: Clarendon Press, 1994.

McNeil, Kent. *Common Law Aboriginal Title.* Oxford: Clarendon Press, 1989.

– *Defining Aboriginal Title in the Nineties: Has the Supreme Court Finally Got it Right?* Toronto: Robarts Centre for Canadian Studies, 1998.

Milne, Courtney. *Spirit of the Land: Sacred Places in Native North America.* Toronto: Penguin Books, 1994.

Minow, Martha. *Making All the Difference: Inclusion, Exclusion, and American Law.* Ithaca: Cornell University Press, 1990.

Monahan, Patrick. *Politics and the Constitution: The Charter, Federalism and the Supreme Court of Canada.* Scarborough, Ont.: Carswell, 1987.

Moore, Sally Falk. *Law as Process.* Cambridge: Harvard University Press, 1978.

Morris, Alexander. *The Treaties of Canada with the Indians of Manitoba and the North-West Territories.* 1880. Reprint. Toronto: Coles Publishing, 1971.

Nagel, Thomas. *Equality and Partiality.* New York: Oxford University Press, 1991.

Nozick, Robert. *Anarchy, State, and Utopia.* New York: Basic Books, 1974.

Oberg, Michael Leroy. *Dominion and Civility: English Imperialism and Native North America, 1585–1685.* Ithaca: Cornell University Press, 1999.

O'Callaghan, E.B., ed. *Documents Relative to the Colonial History of the State of New York.* Albany: Weed, Parsons, 1856–61.

Oppenheim, Lassa F.L. *International Law: A Treatise.* 3rd ed. London: Longmans, 1920.

Parry, Clive, ed. *The Consolidated Treaty Series.* Vol. 9. Dobbs Ferry, N.Y.: Oceana. 1969–86.

Pentland, H.C. *Labour and Capital in Canada, 1650–1860.* Toronto: Lorimer, 1981.

Perelman, C. *The Idea of Justice and the Problem of Argument.* London: Routledge & Kegan Paul, 1963.

Phillips, Anne. *The Politics of Presence: The Political Representation of Gender, Ethnicity, and Race.* Oxford: Clarendon Press, 1995.

Plato. *Laws.* Ed. G.P. Goold, trans. R.G. Bury. London: W. Heinemann, 1984.

Ponting, J. Rick, and Roger Gibbins. *Out of Irrelevance: A Socio-Political Introduction to Indian Affairs in Canada.* Toronto: Butterworths, 1980.

Pound, Roscoe. *Outlines of Lectures on Jurisprudence.* 4th ed. Cambridge: Harvard University Press, 1928.

Purich, Donald J. *Our Land: Native Rights in Canada.* Toronto: James Lorimer, 1986.

Rae, Douglas, Douglas Yates, Jennifer Hochschild, Joseph Morone, and Carole Fessler. *Equalities.* Cambridge: Harvard University Press, 1981.

Rawls, John. *Political Liberalism.* New York: Columbia University Press, 1993.

– *A Theory of Justice.* Cambridge: Harvard University Press, 1971.

Raz, Joseph. *The Morality of Freedom.* Oxford: Clarendon Press, 1986.

Redfield, Robert. *The Primitive World and Its Transformations.* Ithaca: Cornell University Press, 1962.

Renteln, Alison Dundes. *International Human Rights: Universalism versus Relativism.* Newbury Park: Sage Publications, 1990.

Roach, Kent. *Constitutional Remedies in Canada.* Aurora: Canada Law Book, 1995.

Ronen, Dov. *The Quest for Self-Determination.* New Haven: Yale University Press, 1979.

Rose, Carol M. *Property and Persuasion: Essays on the History, Theory, and Rhetoric of Ownership.* Boulder, Colo.: Westview, 1994.

Ross, Rupert. *Dancing with a Ghost: Exploring Indian Reality.* Markham: Octopus, 1992.

Rotman, Leonard I. *Parallel Paths: Fiduciary Doctrine and the Crown–Native Relationship in Canada.* Toronto: University of Toronto Press, 1996.

Rousseau, J.J. *Discourse on Inequality.* Harmondsworth: Penguin Books, 1984.

Said, Edward. *Culture and Imperialism.* New York: Vintage Books, 1993.

Sandel, Michael. *Liberalism and the Limits of Justice.* Cambridge: Cambridge University Press, 1982.

Saunders, William L., ed. *The Colonial Records of North Carolina.* 10 vols. Raleigh, N.C.: P.M. Hale, 1886–90.

Schwartz, Bryan. *First Principles: Constitutional Reform with Respect to the Aboriginal Peoples of Canada, 1982–1984.* Kingston: Institute of Intergovernmental Relations, 1985.

– *First Principles, Second Thoughts: Aboriginal Peoples, Constitutional Reform and Canadian Statecraft.* Montreal: Institute for Research on Public Policy, 1986.

Sebok, Anthony J. *Legal Positivism in American Jurisprudence*. Cambridge: Cambridge University Press, 1998.

Seidman, Louis Michael, and Mark V. Tushnet. *Remnants of Belief: Contemporary Constitutional Issues*. Oxford: Oxford University Press, 1996.

Shue, Henry. *Basic Rights: Subsistence, Affluence, and U.S. Foreign Policy*. Princeton: Princeton University Press, 1980.

Silman, Janet, ed. *Enough Is Enough: Aboriginal Women Speak Out*. Toronto: Women's Press, 1987.

Slattery, Brian. *The Legal Status and Land Rights of Indigenous Canadian Peoples, as Affected by the Crown's Acquisition of the Territories*. Saskatoon: Native Law Centre, 1989.

Smith, Theresa S. *The Island of the Anishnaabeg: Thunderers and Water Monsters in the Traditional Ojibwe Life-World*. Moscow: University of Idaho Press, 1995.

Snyder, Gary. *The Practice of the Wild*. New York: North Point Press, 1990.

Soifer, Aviam. *Law and the Company We Keep*. Cambridge: Harvard University Press, 1995.

Sunstein, Cass. R. *After the Rights Revolution: Reconceiving the Regulatory State*. Cambridge: Harvard University Press, 1990.

– *One Case at a Time: Judicial Minimalism on the Supreme Court*. Cambridge: Harvard University Press, 1999.

– *The Partial Constitution*. Cambridge: Harvard University Press, 1993.

Tamir, Yael. *Liberal Nationalism*. Princeton: Princeton University Press, 1993.

Taylor, Charles. *Philosophy and the Human Sciences: Philosophical Papers*, vol. 2. Cambridge: Cambridge University Press, 1985.

Tennant, Paul. *Aboriginal Peoples and Politics: The Indian Land Question in British Columbia, 1849–1989*. Vancouver: UBC Press, 1990.

Thornberry, Patrick. *International Law and the Rights of Minorities*. Oxford: Clarendon Press, 1991.

Trakman, Leon, and Sean Gatien. *Rights and Responsibilities*. Toronto: University of Toronto Press, 1999.

Treaty 7 Elders and Tribal Council. *The True Spirit and Intent of Treaty 7*. Montreal and Kingston: McGill-Queen's University Press, 1996

Tremblay, Luc B. *The Rule of Law, Justice, and Interpretation*. Montreal and Kingston: McGill-Queen's University Press, 1997.

Tully, James. *An Approach to Political Philosophy: Locke in Contexts*. Cambridge: Cambridge University Press, 1993.

– *A Discourse on Property: John Locke and his Adversaries*. Cambridge: Cambridge University Press, 1980.

– *Strange Multiplicity: Constitutionalism in an Age of Diversity*. Cambridge: Cambridge University Press, 1995.

Umozurike, Umozurike Oji. *Self-Determination in International Law*. Hamden: Archon, 1972.

Unger, Roberto Mangabeira. *What Should Legal Analysis Become?* London: Verso, 1996.

Vattel, Emmerich de. *The Law of Nations*. Bk I. New York: AMS Press, 1975.

Vincent, R.J. *Human Rights and International Relations*. Cambridge: Cambridge University Press, 1986.

Waldron, Jeremy. *The Right to Private Property*. Oxford: Clarendon Press, 1988.

Walker, R.B.J. *Inside/Outside: International Relations as Political Theory*. Cambridge: Cambridge University Press, 1993.

Walzer, Michael. *Spheres of Justice: A Defense of Pluralism and Equality*. New York: Basic Books, 1983.

Washington, Booker T. *The Negro in Business*. Boston: Jenkins & Company, 1907.

Weaver, Sally M. *Making Canadian Indian Policy: The Hidden Agenda 1968–1970*. Toronto: University of Toronto Press, 1981.

Westen, Peter. *Speaking of Equality: An Analysis of the Rhetorical Force of 'Equality' in Moral and Legal Discourse*. Princeton: Princeton University Press, 1990.

Westlake, John. *Chapters on Principles of International Law*. Cambridge: Cambridge University Press, 1894.

White, James Boyd. *Justice as Translation: An Essay in Cultural and Legal Criticism*. Chicago: University of Chicago Press, 1990.

White, Richard. *The Middle Ground: Indians, Empires, and Republics in the Great Lakes*. Cambridge: Cambridge University Press, 1991.

Wightman, W.R. *Forever on the Fringe: Six Studies in the Development of Manitoulin Island*. Toronto: University of Toronto Press, 1982.

Wildsmith, Bruce. *Aboriginal Peoples and Section 25 of the Canadian Charter of Rights and Freedoms*. Saskatchewan: University of Saskatchewan Native Law Centre, 1988.

Williams, Bernard. *Ethics and the Limits of Philosophy*. London: Fontana Collins, 1985.

Williams, Robert A., Jr. *Linking Arms Together: American Indian Treaty Visions of Law and Peace, 1600–1800*. New York: Oxford University Press, 1997.

Wolf, Eric R. *Europe and the People without History*. Berkeley: University of California Press, 1982.

Woodward, Jack. *Native Law*. Scarborough, Ont.: Carswell, 1990.

X, Malcolm. *Malcolm X Speaks: Selected Speeches and Statements*. New York: Merit, 1965.

Young, Iris Marion. *Justice and the Politics of Difference*. Princeton: Princeton University Press, 1990.

Yourow, H.C. *The Margin of Appreciation Doctrine in the Dynamics of European Human Rights Jurisprudence*. Boston: M. Nijhoff, 1993.

Articles

Addis, Adeno. 'Individualism, Communitarianism, and the Rights of Ethnic Minorities.' 66 Notre Dame L. Rev. 1219 (1991).

Alston, Philip, and Gerald Quinn. 'The Nature and Scope of State Parties' Obligations under the International Covenant on Economic, Social and Cultural Rights.' 9 Hum. Rts. Q. 156 (1987).

Alvaro, Alexander. 'Why Property Rights Were Excluded from the Charter of Rights and Freedoms.' 24 C.J.P.S. 309 (1991).

Anaya, S. James. 'The Capacity of International Law to Advance Ethnic or Nationality Rights Claims.' 75 Iowa L. Rev. 837 (1990).

– 'The Rights of Indigenous Peoples and International Law in Historical and Contemporary Perspective.' 1991 Harvard Indian Law Symposium 191 (1990).

Asch, Michael. 'Aboriginal Self-Government and the Construction of Canadian Constitutional Identity.' 30 Alta. L. Rev. 465 (1992).

Augustine, Philip W. 'Protection of the Right to Property under the Canadian Charter of Rights and Freedoms.' 18 Ottawa L. Rev. 55 (1986).

Avio, Ken. 'Aboriginal Property Rights in Canada: A Contractarian Interpretation of *R. v. Sparrow*.' 20 Can. Pub. Pol. 415 (1994).

Bakan, Joel. 'Constitutional Interpretation and Social Change: You Can't Always Get What You Want (Or What You Need).' 70 Can. Bar Rev. 307 (1991).

Baker, C. Edwin. 'Outcome Equality or Equality of Respect: The Substantive Content of Equal Protection.' 131 U. Penn. L. Rev. 933 (1983).

Balkin, Jack. 'Tradition, Betrayal, and the Politics of Deconstruction.' 11 Card. L. Rev. 1613 (1993).

Bandes, Susan. 'The Negative Constitution: A Critique.' 88 Mich. L. Rev. 2271 (1990).

Barsh, Russel Lawrence. 'An Advocate's Guide to the Convention on Indigenous and Tribal Peoples.' 15 Okla. City U. L. Rev. 209 (1990).

– 'Indigenous Peoples in the 1990s: From Object to Subject of International Law?' Harv. Human Rights J. 33 (1994).

Barsh, Russel Lawrence, and James [sákéj] Henderson. 'The Supreme Court's Van der Peet Trilogy: Native Imperialism and Ropes of Sand.' 42 McGill L.J. 993 (1997).

Beatty, David. 'The Canadian Conception of Equality.' 46 U.T.L.J. 349 (1996).

– 'Constitutional Conceits: The Coercive Authority of Courts.' 37 U.T.L.J. 183 (1987).

Bell, Catherine. '*R. v. Badger:* One Step Forward and Two Steps Back?' 8 Constitutional Forum 2 (1997).

Berman, Nathaniel. 'Sovereignty in Abeyance: Self-Determination and International Law.' 7 Wisc. Int'l L.J. 51 (1988).

Bhuta, Nehal. 'Mabo, Wik and the Art of Paradigm Management.' 22 Melbourne U. L. Rev. 24 (1998).

Binder, Guyora. 'The Case for Self-Determination.' 29 Stan. J. Int'l Law 223 (1993).

Blumm, Michael C. 'Native Fishing Rights and Environmental Protection in North America and New Zealand: A Comparative Analysis of Profits A Prendre and Habitat Servitudes.' 4 Canterbury L. Rev. 211 (1990).

Borrows, John. 'Frozen Rights in Canada: Constitutional Interpretation and the Trickster.' 22 American Indian L. Rev. 37 (1997).

– 'A Genealogy of Law: Inherent Sovereignty and First Nations Self-Government.' 30 Osgoode Hall L.J. 291 (1992).

– 'Sovereignty's Alchemy: An Analysis of *Delgamuukw v. The Queen*.' 37 Osgoode Hall L.J. 537 (1999).

– 'With or Without You: First Nations Law.' 41 McGill L.J. 629 (1996).

Brest, Paul. 'Constitutional Citizenship.' 34 Cleveland State L. Rev. 175 (1986).

– 'The Fundamental Rights Controversy: The Essential Contradictions of Normative Constitutional Scholarship.' 90 Yale L.J. 1063 (1981).

Bunting, Annie. 'Theorizing Women's Cultural Diversity in Feminist International Human Rights Strategies.' 20 J. Law & Society 6 (1993).

Cassels, Jamie. 'Judicial Activism and Public Interest Litigation in India: Attempting the Impossible?' 37 Am. J. Comp. L. 495 (1989).

Chapman, Matthew. 'Indigenous Peoples and International Human Rights: Towards a Guarantee for the Territorial Connection.' 26 Anglo-Am. L. Rev. 357 (1997).

Chayes, Abram. 'The Role of the Judge in Public Law Litigation.' 89 Harv. L. Rev. 1281 (1976).

Chen, Lung-Chu. 'Self-Determination and World Public Order.' 66 Notre Dame L. Rev. 1287 (1991).

Clinton, Robert N. 'The Rights of Indigenous Peoples as Collective Group Rights.' 32 Ariz. L. Rev. 739 (1990).

Cohen, Morris. 'Property and Sovereignty.' 13 Cornell L.Q. 8 (1927).

Crenshaw, Kimberlé. 'Demarginalizing the Intersection of Race and Sex: A Black Feminist Critique of Antidiscrimination Doctrine, Feminist Theory and Antiracist Politics.' U. Chi. L. Forum 139 (1989).

Currie, David P. 'Positive and Negative Constitutional Rights.' 53 U. Chi. L. Rev. 864 (1986).

DaRe, Vern. 'Beyond General Pronouncements: A Judicial Approach to Section 27 of the Charter.' 33 Alberta L. Rev. 551 (1995).

Davis, Kenneth C. 'Facts in Lawmaking.' 80 Col. L. Rev. 931 (1980).

Donoho, Douglas Lee. 'Relativism versus Universalism in Human Rights: The Search for Meaningful Standards.' 27 Stan. J. Int'l L. 345 (1991).

Dworkin, Ronald. 'In Praise of Theory.' 29 Ariz. L.J. 353 (1997).

– 'What is Equality? Part II Equality of Resources.' 10 Phil. & Pub. Aff. 283 (1981).

Eisenberg, Melvin Aron. 'Private Ordering through Negotiation: Dispute Settlement and Rulemaking.' 89 Harv. L. Rev. 637 (1976).

Elliott, Robin. 'The Supreme Court of Canada and Section One: The Erosion of the Common Front.' 12 Queen's L.J. 277 (1987).

Emerson, T. 'Toward a General Theory of Freedom of the First Amendment.' 72 Yale L.J. 877 (1963).

Epstein, Richard. 'Possession as the Root of Title.' 13 Georgia L. Rev. 1221 (1979).

Fiss, Owen. 'Groups and the Equal Protection Clause.' 5 Phil. & Pub. Aff. 107 (1976).

– 'The Varieties of Positivism.' 90 Yale L.J. 1007 (1981).

Foster, Hamar. 'Forgotten Arguments: Aboriginal Title and Sovereignty in Canada Jurisdiction Act Cases.' 21 Man. L.J. 343 (1992).

Franck, Thomas. 'The Emerging Right to Democratic Governance.' 86 Amer. J. Int'l L. 46 (1992).

Freedman, Bob. 'Semiahmoo Indian Band v. Canada (Case Comment).' 36 Alberta L. Rev. 218 (1997).

Frémont, J. 'Les Tribunaux et la Charte: le pouvoir d'ordonner la depense de fonds publics en matières sociales et économiques.' 36 McGill L.J. 1323 (1991).

Fudge, Judy. 'The Public/Private Distinction: The Possibilities of and the Limits to the Use of Charter Litigation to Further Feminist Struggles.' 25 Osgoode Hall L.J. 485 (1987).

Fuller, Lon L. 'The Forms and Limits of Adjudication.' 92 Harv. L. Rev. 353 (1978).

Galanter, Marc. 'Justice in Many Rooms: Courts, Private Ordering, and Indigenous Law.' 19 Journal of Legal Pluralism 1 (1981).

Gold, Marc. 'Comment: Andrews v. Law Society of British Columbia.' 34 McGill L.J. 1063 (1989).

Gordon, Robert. 'Unfreezing Critical Reality: Critical Approaches to Law.' 15 Florida State U. L. Rev. 196 (1987).

– 'Critical Legal Histories.' 36 Stan. L. Rev. 57 (1984).

Gottlieb, Stephen E. 'The Paradox of Balancing Significant Interests.' 45 Hastings L.J. 825 (1994).

Green, Leslie. 'Two Views of Collective Rights.' 4 Can. J. Law & Jur. 315 (1991).

Grey, Thomas. 'Holmes and Legal Pragmatism.' 41 Stan. L. Rev. 787 (1989).

Griffiths, John. 'What Is Legal Pluralism?' 24 Journal of Legal Pluralism 1 (1986).

Grosby, Steven. 'Territoriality: The Transcendental, Primordial Feature of Modern Societies.' 1 Nations and Nationalism 143 (1995).

Gupta, Akhil, and James Ferguson. 'Beyond Culture: Space, Identity and the Politics of Difference.' 7 Cultural Anthropology 6 (1992).

Hale, Robert L. 'Coercion and Distribution in a Supposedly Non-Coercive State.' 38 Pol. Sci. Q. 470 (1923).

Hartung, Frank E. 'Cultural Relativity and Moral Judgments.' 21 Phil. Sci. 118 (1954).

Hayman, Robert L., Jr. 'The Color of Tradition: Critical Race Theory and Postmodern Constitutional Traditionalism.' 30 Harv. C.R.-C.L. L. Rev. 57 (1995).

Henderson, James [sákéj] Youngblood. 'Empowering Treaty Federalism.' 58 Sask. L. Rev. 241 (1994).

– 'Interpreting Sui Generis Treaties.' 36 Alta. L. Rev. 46 64 (1997).

Henderson, William B., and Derek T. Ground. 'Survey of Aboriginal Land Claims.' 26 Ottawa L. Rev. 187 (1994).

Hogg, Peter W., and Mary Ellen Turpel. 'Implementing Aboriginal Self-Government: Constitutional and Jurisdictional Issues.' 74 Can. Bar Rev. 187 (1995).

Howse, Robert. 'Liberal Accommodation.' 46 U.T.L.J. 311 (1996).

Iorns, Catherine J. 'Indigenous Peoples and Self-Determination: Challenging State Sovereignty.' 24 Case Western. Res. J. Int'l L. 199 (1992).

Isaac, Thomas. 'The Constitution Act, 1982 and the Constitutionalization of Aboriginal Self-Government in Canada: Cree-Naskapi (of Quebec) Act.' [1991] 1 C.N.L.R. 1.

Ivison, Duncan. 'Decolonizing the Rule of Law: Mabo's Case and Postcolonial Constitutionalism.' 17 Oxford J. Leg. Stud. 252 (1997).

Jackman, Martha. 'The Protection of Welfare Rights under the Charter.' 20 Ottawa L. Rev. 257 (1988).

Jarvis, I.C. 'Rationalism and Relativism.' 34 Brit. J. Sociology 44 (1983).

Johnston, Darlene M. 'Native Rights as Collective Rights: A Question of Group Self-Preservation.' 2 Can. J. Law & Juris. 19 (1988).

– 'A Theory of Crown Trust towards Aboriginal Peoples.' 18 Ottawa L. Rev. 307 (1986).

Johnston, Ian. 'Section 7 of the Charter and Constitutionally Protected Welfare.' 46 U.T. Fac. L. Rev. 1 (1988).

Kahn-Freund, Owen. 'Blackstone's Neglected Child: The Contract of Employment.' 93 L.Q.R. 508 (1977).

Kapashesit, Randy, and Murray Klippenstein. 'Aboriginal Group Rights and Environmental Protection.' 36 McGill L.J. 925 (1991).

Kennedy, David. 'Receiving the International.' 10 Conn. J. Int'l L. 1 (1995).

Kennedy, Duncan. 'Legal Formality.' 2 J. Legal Studies 351 (1973).

Kennedy, Duncan, and Frank Michaelman. 'Are Property and Contract Efficient?' 8 Hofstra L. Rev. 711 (1980).

Kingsbury, Benedict. 'Claims by Non-State Groups in International Law.' 25 Cornell Int'l L.J. 481 (1992).

Klare, Karl. 'Law-Making as Praxis.' 40 Telos 123 (1979).

Kleinhans, Martha-Marie, and Roderick A Macdonald. 'What Is a *Critical* Legal Pluralism?' 12 Can. J. Law & Soc. 25 (1997).

Kluckhohn, Clyde. 'Ethical Relativity: Sic et Non.' 52 J. Phil. 663 (1955).

Koskenniemi, Martti. 'National Self-Determination Today: Problems of Legal Theory and Practice.' 43 Int'l & Comp. L.Q. 241 (1994).

Kronman, Anthony T. 'Contract Law and Distributive Justice.' 89 Yale L.J. 472 (1980).

– 'Precedent and Tradition.' 99 Yale L.J. 1029 (1990).

Kukathas, Chandran. 'Explaining Moral Variety.' 11 Soc. Phil & Pol'y 1 (1994).

Kurland, Philip K. 'The Rise and Fall of the "Doctrine" of Separation of Powers.' 85 Mich. L. Rev. 592 (1986).

Laguna, Grace A. de. 'Cultural Relativism and Science.' 51 Phil. Rev. 141 (1942).

Lâm, Maivân Clech. 'Making Room for Peoples at the United Nations: Thoughts Provoked by Indigenous Claims to Self-Determination.' 25 Cornell Int'l L.J. 603 (1992).

Laurence, Robert. 'Learning to Live with the Plenary Power of Congress over the Indian Nations.' 30 Ariz. L. Rev. 413 (1988).

Leckie, Scott. 'Another Step towards Indivisibility: Identifying the Key Features of Violations of Economic, Social and Cultural Rights.' 20 Human Rights Quarterly 81 (1998).

Lederman, W.R. 'The Concurrent Operation of Federal and Provincial Laws in Canada.' 9 McGill L.J. 185 (1963).

Lessard, Hester. 'The Idea of the "Private": A Discussion of State Action Doctrine and Separate Sphere Ideology.' 10 Dalh. L.J. 107 (1986).

Lipkin, Robert Justin. 'Can Liberalism Justify Multiculturalism?' 45 Buff. L. Rev. 1 (1997).

– 'Liberalism and the Possibility of Multi-Cultural Constitutionalism: The Distinction between Deliberative and Dedicated Cultures.' 29 U. Rich. L. Rev. 1263 (1995).

Long, Anthony, and Katherine Beaty Chiste. 'Indian Governments and the

Canadian Charter of Rights and Freedoms.' 18 American Indian Culture and Research J. 91 (1994).

Lytwyn, Victor P. 'Ojibwa and Ottawa Fisheries Around Manitoulin Island: Historical and Geographical Perspectives on Aboriginal and Treaty Fishing Rights.' 6 Native Studies Review 1 (1990).

MacMillan, C.M. 'Social versus Political Rights.' 19 Can. J. Pol. Sci. 283 (1986).

Majewicz, Anna T. 'Baseline Analysis: Broadening the Judicial Perspective.' 65 St. John's L. Rev. 495 (1991).

Margalit, Avishai, and Joseph Raz. 'National Self-Determination.' 87 J. Philo. 439 (1990).

McDonald, Leighton. 'Can Collective and Individual Rights Coexist?' 22 Melbourne U. L. Rev. 310 (1998).

– 'Regrouping in Defence of Minority Rights: Kymlicka's Multicultural Citizenship.' 34 Osgoode Hall L.J. 291 (1996).

McGoldrick, Dominic. 'Canadian Indians, Cultural Rights and the Human Rights Committee.' 40 Int. & Comp. L.Q. 658 (1991).

McNeil, Kent. 'Aboriginal Governments and the Canadian Charter of Rights and Freedoms.' 34 Osgoode Hall L.J. 61 (1996).

– 'The Constitutional Rights of the Aboriginal Peoples of Canada.' 4 Supreme Court L. Rev. 255 (1982).

– 'Envisaging Constitutional Space for Aboriginal Governments.' 19 Queen's L.J. 95 (1993).

Merry, Sally Engle. 'Resistance and the Cultural Power of Law.' 29 Law & Society Rev. 11 (1995).

Minow, Martha. 'Identities.' 3 Yale J. Law & Hum. 97 (1991).

Minow, Martha, and Elizabeth Spelman. 'In Context.' 63 S. Cal. L. Rev. 1597 (1990).

Monaghan, Henry P. 'Our Perfect Constitution.' 56 N.Y.U. L. Rev. 353 (1981).

Morgan, Edward M. 'The Imagery and Meaning of Self-Determination.' 20 N.Y.U. J. Int'l Law 355 (1988).

Morse, Bradford W. 'Common Roots but Modern Divergences: Aboriginal Policies in Canada and the United States.' 10 St. Thomas L. Rev. 115 (1997).

Newton, Nell Jessup. 'Federal Power over Indians: Its Sources, Scope, and Limitations.' 132 U. Pa. L. Rev. 195 (1984).

Nunn, Kenneth B. 'Law as a Eurocentric Enterprise.' 15 Law & Inequality 323 (1997).

Olivecrona, Karl. 'Locke's Theory of Appropriation.' 24 Philosophical Quarterly 220 (1974).

Orton, Helena. 'Section 15, Benefits Programs and Other Benefits at Law: The

Interpretation of Section 15 of the Charter since Andrews.' 19 Man. L. Rev. 288 (1990).

Otis, Ghislain. 'La Charte et la modification des programs gouvernementaux: l'exemple de l'injonction structurelle en droit américain.' 36 McGill L.J. 1349 (1991).

Pannikar, Raimundo. 'Is the Notion of Human Rights a Western Concept?' 120 Diogenes 76 (1982).

Peller, Gary. 'Race Consciousness (Frontiers of Legal Thought).' [1990] Duke L.J. 758.

Pentney, William. 'The Rights of the Aboriginal Peoples of Canada and the Constitution Act, 1982 – Part I: The Interpretive Prism of Section 25.' 22 U.B.C. L. Rev. 21 (1987).

Petter, Andrew. 'The Politics of the Charter.' 8 Supreme Court L. Rev. 473 (1986).

Pommersheim, Frank. 'Tribal-State Relations: Hope for the Future?' 36 S. Dak. L. Rev. 239 (1991).

Putnam, Ruth Anna. 'Justice in Context.' 63 S. Cal. L. Rev. 1797 (1990).

Réaume, Denise. 'Justice between Cultures: Autonomy and the Protection of Cultural Affiliation.' 29 U.B.C. L. Rev. 117 (1995).

Riles, Annelise. 'Aspiration and Control: International Legal Rhetoric and the Essentialization of Culture.' 106 Harv. L. Rev. 723 (1993).

Roach, Kent. 'Remedies for Violations of Aboriginal Rights.' 21 Man. L.J. 498 (1992).

Rosenfeld, Michael. 'Contract and Justice: The Relation between Classical Contract Law and Social Contract Theory.' 70 Iowa L. Rev. 751 (1985).

Rotman, Leonard I. 'Taking Aim at the Canons of Treaty Interpretation in Canadian Aboriginal Rights Jurisprudence.' 46 U.N.B.L.J. 11 (1997).

Ryder, Bruce. 'The Demise and Rise of the Classical Paradigm in Canadian Federalism: Promoting Autonomy for the Provinces and First Nations.' 36 McGill L.J. 308 (1991).

Sager, Lawrence G. 'Fair Measure: The Legal Status of Underenforced Constitutional Norms.' 91 Harv. L. Rev. 1212 (1978).

– 'Justice in Plain Clothes: Reflections on the Thinness of Constitutional Law.' 88 Northwestern U. L. Rev. 410 (1993).

Schauer, F. 'Precedent.' 39 Stan. L. Rev. 571 (1987).

Schmidt, Paul F. 'Some Criticisms of Cultural Relativism.' 70 J. Philo. 780 (1955).

Schneiderman, David. 'Theorists of Difference and the Interpretation of Aboriginal and Treaty Rights.' 14 Int'l J. Can. Stud. 35 (1996).

Schulte-Tenckhoff, Isabelle. 'Reassessing the Paradigm of Domestication: The Problematic of Indigenous Treaties.' 4 Rev. Const. Stud. 239 (1998).

Scott, F.R. 'Dominion Jurisdiction over Human Rights and Fundamental Freedoms.' 27 Can. Bar Rev. 497 (1949).

Segall, Eric J. 'The Skeptic's Constitution.' 44 U.C.L.A. L. Rev. 1467 (1997).

Sheppard, Colleen. 'Recognition of the Disadvantaging of Women: The Promise of Andrews v. Law Society of B.C.' 35 McGill L.J. 206 (1990).

Sheppard, Steve. 'The State Interest in the Good Citizen: Constitutional Balance between the Citizen ad the Perfectionist State.' 45 Hastings L.J. 969 (1994).

Sierra, María Teresa. 'Indian Rights and Customary Law in Mexico: A Study of the Nahuas in the Sierra de Puebla.' 29 Law & Society Rev. 227 (1995).

Simmons, A. John. 'Historical Rights and Fair Shares.' 14 Law and Philosophy 149 (1994).

Singer, Joseph W. 'The Player and the Cards: Nihilism and Legal Theory.' 94 Yale L.J. 1 (1984).

–   'Sovereignty and Property.' 86 Northwestern L. Rev. 1 (1991).

Slattery, Brian. 'Aboriginal Sovereignty and Imperial Claims.' 29 Osgoode Hall L.J. 681 (1991).

–   'The Constitutional Guarantee of Aboriginal and Treaty Rights.' 8 Queen's L.J. 232 (1982).

–   'First Nations and the Constitution: A Question of Trust.' 71 Can. Bar Rev. 261 (1992).

–   'The Hidden Constitution: Aboriginal Rights in Canada.' 32 Am. J. Comp. Law 361 (1984).

–   'Understanding Aboriginal Rights.' 66 Can. Bar Rev. 727 (1987).

Sousa, Boaventura de. 'Law: A Map of Misreading: Toward a Postmodern Conception of Law.' 14 J. Law and Society 279 (1987).

Spaulding, Richard. 'Peoples as National Minorities.' 47 U.T.L.J. 35 (1997).

Spiro, M. 'Cultural Relativism and the Future of Anthropology.' 1 Cultural Anthropology 259 (1986).

Strauss, David A. 'Common Law Constitutional Interpretation.' 63 U. Chi. L. Rev. 877 (1996).

Sunstein, Cass R. 'Against Tradition.' 13 Soc. Phil & Policy 207 (1996).

–   'General Propositions and Concrete Cases (With Special Reference to Affirmative Action and Free Speech).' 31 Wake Forest L. Rev. 369 (1996).

Swepson, L., and R. Plant. 'International Standards and the Protection of the Land Rights of Indigenous and Tribal Populations.' 124 International Lab. Rev. 91 (1985).

Swepson, Lee. 'A New Step in the International Law on Indigenous and Tribal Peoples: ILO Convention No. 169 of 1989.' 15 Okla. City L. Rev. 677 (1990).

Symmons-Symonolewicz, Konstantin. 'The Concept of Nationhood: Toward a

Theoretical Clarification.' 12 Canadian Review of Studies in Nationalism 215 (1985).

Tarnopolsky, Walter S. 'The Supreme Court and the Canadian Bill of Rights.' 53 Can. Bar Rev. 649 (1975).

Townshend, Roger. 'Interlocutory Injunctions in Aboriginal Rights Cases.' [1991] 3 C.N.L.R. 1.

Trakman, Leon. 'Native Cultures in a Rights Empire Ending the Dominion.' 45 Buff. L. Rev. 189 (1997).

Tribe, Laurence H., and Michael C Dorf. 'Levels of Generality in the Definition of Rights.' 57 U. Chi. L. Rev. 1057 (1990).

Turpel, Mary Ellen. 'Aboriginal Peoples and the Canadian Charter: Interpretive Monopolies, Cultural Differences.' 6 Canadian Human Rights Yearbook 3 (1989–90).

– 'Indigenous Peoples' Rights of Political Participation and Self-Determination: Recent International Legal Developments and the Continuing Struggle for Recognition.' 25 Cornell Int'l L.J. 579 (1992).

Tussman, Joseph and Jacobus TenBroek. 'The Equal Protection of Laws.' 37 Cal. L. Rev. 341 (1949).

Vierdag, E.W. 'The Legal Nature of the Rights Granted by the International Covenant on Economic, Social and Cultural Rights.' 9 Neth. Y.B. Int'l L. 69 (1978).

Waldron, Jeremy. 'Minority Cultures and the Cosmopolitan Alternative.' 25 U. Mich. L. Rev. 751 (1992).

Walker, Brian. 'Plural Cultures, Contested Territories: A Critique of Kymlicka.' 30 Can. J. Pol. Sci. 211 (1997).

Walters, Mark D. 'British Imperial Constitutional Law and Aboriginal Rights: A Comment on Delgamuukw v. British Columbia.' 17 Queen's L.J. 350 (1992).

– 'The Extension of Colonial Criminal Jurisdiction over the Aboriginal Peoples of Upper Canada: Reconsidering the Shawanakiskie Case (1822–26),' 46 U.T.L.J. 273 (1996).

Webber, Jeremy. 'Relations of Force and Relations of Justice: The Emergence of Normative Community between Colonists and Aboriginal Peoples.' 33 Osgoode Hall L.J. 623 (1996).

Weinrib, E.J. 'The Fiduciary Obligation.' 25 U.T.L.J. 1 (1975).

Weinrib, Lorraine E. 'Of Diligence and Dice: Reconstituting Canada's Constitution.' 42 U.T.L.J. 207 (1992).

– 'The Supreme Court of Canada and Section One of the Charter.' 10 Supreme Court L. Rev. 489 (1988).

Wells, C. 'Situated Decisionmaking.' 63 S. Cal. L. Rev. 1727 (1990).

Wilkins, Kerry. 'But We Need the Eggs: The Royal Commission, the Charter of

Rights and the Inherent Right of Aboriginal Self-Government.' 49 U.T.L.J. 53 (1999).

Williams, Robert A., Jr. 'The Algebra of Federal Indian Law: The Hard Trail of Decolonizing and Americanizing the White Man's Jurisprudence.' [1986] Wisc. L. Rev. 219.

– 'Encounters on the Frontiers of International Human Rights Law: Redefining the Terms of Indigenous Peoples' Survival in the World.' [1990] Duke L.J. 660.

– 'Sovereignty, Racism, Human Rights: Indian Self-Determination and the Postmodern World Legal System.' 2 Rev. Constitutional Studies 146 (1995).

Wolf, Clark. 'Contemporary Property Rights, Lockean Provisos, and the Interests of Future Generations.' 105 Ethics 791 (1995).

Worthen, Kevin J. 'One Small Step for Courts, One Giant Leap for Group Rights: Accommodating the Associational Role of "Intimate" Government Entities.' 71 N.C.L. Rev. 595 (1993).

Yukich, Kelley C. 'Aboriginal Rights in the Constitution and International Law.' 30 U.B.C. L. Rev. 235 (1996)

Essays

Anaya, S. James. 'On Justifying Special Ethnic Rights: Comments on Pogge.' In Ian Shapiro and Will Kymlicka, eds., *Ethnicity and Group Rights*. New York: New York University Press, 1997.

Anghie, Anthony. 'Francisco de Vitoria and the Colonial Origins of International Law.' In Eve Darian-Smith and Peter Fitzpatrick, eds., *Laws of the Postcolonial*. Ann Arbor: University of Michigan Press, 1999.

An-Na'im, Abdullahi Ahmed. 'Toward a Cross-Cultural Approach to Defining International Standards of Human Rights: The Meaning of Cruel, Inhuman or Degrading Treatment or Punishment.' In Abdullahi Ahmed An-Na'im, ed., *Human Rights in Cross-Cultural Perspective: A Quest for Consensus*. Philadelphia: University of Pennsylvania Press, 1992.

Asch, Michael, and Norman Zlotkin. 'Affirming Aboriginal Title: A New Basis for Comprehensive Claims Negotiations.' In Michael Asch, ed., *Aboriginal and Treaty Rights in Canada: Essays on Law, Equality, and Respect for Difference*. Vancouver: UBC Press, 1997.

Barsh, Russel Lawrence. 'Indigenous Peoples and the Right to Self-Determination in International Law.' In Barbara Hocking, ed., *International Law and Aboriginal Human Rights*. Sydney: Law Book, 1988.

Bayefsky, Anne. 'Defining Equality Rights.' In Anne Bayefsky and Mary Eberts, eds., *Equality Rights and the Charter of Rights and Freedoms.* Scarborough, Ont.: Carswell, 1985.

Bell, Catherine, and Michael Asch. 'Challenging Assumptions: The Impact of Precedent in Aboriginal Rights Litigation.' In Michael Asch, ed., *Aboriginal and Treaty Rights in Canada: Essays on Law, Equality, and Respect for Difference.* Vancouver: UBC Press, 1997.

Benhabib, Seyla. 'Liberal Dialogue versus a Critical Theory of Discursive Legitimation.' In Nancy L. Rosenblum, ed., *Liberalism and the Moral Life.* Cambridge: Harvard University Press, 1989.

Berlin, Isaiah. 'Two Concepts of Liberty.' In *Four Essays on Liberty.* Oxford: Oxford University Press, 1969.

Biersteker, Thomas J., and Cynthia Weber. 'The Social Construction of Sovereignty.' In Thomas Biersteker and Cynthia Weber, eds., *Sovereignty as a Social Construct.* Cambridge: Cambridge University Press, 1996.

Black, William, and Lynne Smith. 'The Equality Rights.' In G.-A. Beaudoin and E. Ratushny, eds., *The Canadian Charter of Rights and Freedoms.* 2nd ed. Scarborough, Ont.: Carswell, 1989.

Boldt, Menno, and J. Anthony Long. 'Tribal Traditions and European-Western Political Ideologies: The Dilemma of Canada's Native Indians.' In Menno Boldt and J. Anthony Long, eds., *The Quest for Justice: Aboriginal Peoples and Aboriginal Rights.* Toronto: University of Toronto Press, 1985.

Borrows, John. 'Contemporary Traditional Equality: The Effect of the Charter on First Nations Politics.' In David Schneiderman and Kate Sutherland, eds., *Charting the Consequences: The Impact of Charter Rights on Canadian Law and Politics.* Toronto: University of Toronto Press, 1997.

– '"Landed" Citizenship: Narratives of Aboriginal Political Participation.' In Will Kymlicka and Wayne Norman, eds., *Citizenship in Diverse Societies.* Oxford: Oxford University Press, 2000.

– 'Wampum at Niagara: The Royal Proclamation, Canadian Legal History, and Self-Government.' In Michael Asch, ed., *Aboriginal and Treaty Rights in Canada: Essays on Law, Equality, and Respect for Difference.* Vancouver: UBC Press, 1997.

Dickason, Olive Patricia. 'For Every Plant There is a Use: The Botanical World of Mexica and Iroquoians.' In Kerry Abel and Jean Friesen, eds., *Aboriginal Resource Use in Canada: Historical and Legal Aspects.* Manitoba: University of Manitoba Press, 1991.

Du Bois, W.E.B. 'A Negro Nation within the Nation.' In P.S. Foner, ed., *W.E.B. Du Bois Speaks: Speeches and Addresses, 1923–1963.* New York: Pathfinder, 1970.

Glasbeek, Harry. 'The Social Charter: Poor Politics for the Poor.' In Joel Bakan and David Schneiderman, eds., *Social Justice and the Constitution: Perspectives on a Social Union for Canada.* Ottawa: Carleton University Press, 1992.

Habermas, Jürgen. 'Struggles for Recognition in the Democratic Constitutional State.' In Amy Gutman, ed., *Multiculturalism: Examining the Politics of Recognition.* Princeton: Princeton University Press, 1994.

Handler, Joel. 'Poverty, Dependency, and Social Welfare: Procedural Justice for the Poor.' In Bryant G. Barth and Austin Sarat, eds., *Justice and Power in Sociolegal Studies.* Evanston: Northwestern University Press, 1998.

Honoré, A.M. 'Ownership.' In A.G. Guest, ed., *Oxford Essays in Jurisprudence.* Oxford: Clarendon Press, 1961.

Indian Chiefs of Canada, 'Citizens Plus.' In *The Only Good Indian.* Don Mills: New Press, 1983.

Knight, Alan. 'Racism, Revolution, and Indigenismo: Mexico, 1910–1940.' In R. Graham, ed., *The Idea of Race in Latin America, 1870–1940.* Austin: University of Texas Press, 1990.

Koshan, Jennifer. 'Sounds of Silence: The Public/Private Dichotomy, Violence, and Aboriginal Women.' In Susan B. Boyd, ed., *Challenging the Public/Private Divide: Feminism, Law, and Public Policy.* Toronto: University of Toronto Press, 1997.

Laski, Harold J. 'The Foundations of Sovereignty.' In *The Foundations of Sovereignty and Other Essays.* New York: Harcourt, Brace, 1921.

Legters, Lyman H. 'The American Genocide.' In Fremont J. Lyden and Lyman H. Legters, eds., *Native Americans and Public Policy.* Pittsburgh: University of Pittsburgh, 1992.

Lyon, Noel. 'Constitutional Issues in Native Law.' In Bradford W. Morse, ed., *Aboriginal Peoples and the Law: Indian, Métis and Inuit Rights in Canada.* Ottawa: Carleton University Press, 1985.

Lyons, David. 'The New Indian Claims and Original Rights to Land.' In J. Paul, ed., *Reading Nozick: Essays on Anarchy, State, and Utopia.* Oxford: Blackwell, 1982.

Lysyk, Kenneth. 'The Rights and Freedoms of the Aboriginal Peoples of Canada.' In W. Tarnopolsky and G.-A. Beaudoin, eds., *The Canadian Charter of Rights and Freedoms: Commentary.* Scarborough, Ont.: Carswell, 1982.

MacPherson, C.B. 'Berlin's Division of Liberty.' In C.B. MacPherson, ed., *Democratic Theory: Essays in Retrieval.* Oxford: Clarendon Press, 1973.

Magnet, Joseph E. 'Interpreting Multiculturalism.' In Canadian Human Rights Foundation, ed., *Multiculturalism and the Charter.* Scarborough, Ont.: Carswell, 1987.

McNeil, Kent. 'The Meaning of Aboriginal Title.' In Michael Asch, ed., *Aboriginal and Treaty Rights in Canada: Essays on Law, Equality and Respect for Difference.* Vancouver: UBC Press, 1997.

– 'The Temagami Indian Claim: Loosening the Judicial Straight-Jacket.' In Matt Bray and Ashley Thomson, eds., *Temagami: A Debate on Wilderness.* Toronto: Dundurn Press, 1990.

Michaelman, Frank I. 'Socio-Political Functions of Constitutional Protection for Private Property Holdings (In Liberal Political Thought).' In G.E. van Maanen and A.J. van der Walt, eds., *Property Law on the Threshold of the 21st Century.* Apeldorn: Maklu, 1996.

Nahanee, Teressa. 'Dancing with a Gorilla: Aboriginal Women, Justice and the Charter.' In Royal Commission on Aboriginal Peoples, *Aboriginal Peoples and the Criminal Justice System.* Ottawa: Supply and Services, 1993.

Nedelsky, Jennifer. 'Should Property Be Constitutionalized? A Relational and Comparative Approach.' In G.E. van Maanen and A.J. van der Walt, eds., *Property Law on the Threshold of the 21st Century.* Apeldorn: Maklu, 1996.

Oman, Natalie. 'The Role of Recognition in the Delgamuukw Case.' In *Sacred Lands: Aboriginal World Views, Claims and Conflicts.* Edmonton: Canadian Circumpolar Institute Press, 1998.

Poelzer, Greg. 'Land and Resource Tenure: First Nations Traditional Territories and Self-Governance.' In Roslyn Kunin, ed., *Prospering Together: The Economic Impact of Aboriginal Title Settlements in B.C.* Vancouver: Laurier Institution, 1998.

Rorty, Amelie Oskenberg.'Relativism, Persons, and Practices.' In Michael Kraus, ed., *Relativism: Interpretation and Confrontation.* Notre Dame: University of Notre Dame Press, 1989.

Scheinin, Martin. 'The Right to Enjoy a Distinct Culture: Indigenous and Competing Uses of Land.' In Theodore S. Orlin, Allan Rosas, and Martin Scheinen, eds., *The Jurisprudence of Human Rights: A Comparative Interpretive Approach.* Turku: Åbo Akademi University Institute for Human Rights, 2000.

Schlag, Pierre. 'Normativity and the Politics of Form.' In Paul F. Campos, Pierre Schlag, and Steven D. Smith, *Against the Law.* Durham, N.C.: Duke University Press, 1996.

Scott, Joan. 'Multiculturalism and the Politics of Identity.' In John Rajchman, ed., *The Identity in Question.* New York: Routledge, 1995.

Shachar, Ayelet. 'The Paradox of Multicultural Vulnerability: Identity Groups, the State, and Individual Rights.' In Steven Lukes and Christian Joppke, eds., *Multicultural Questions.* Oxford: Oxford University Press, 1999.

Simeon, Richard. 'Aboriginal Self-Government and Canadian Political Values.' In David Hawkes and Evelyn J. Peters, eds., *Issues in Entrenching Aboriginal Self-Government.* Kingston: Institute of Intergovernmental Relations, 1987.

Singer, Joseph W. 'Property and Social Relations: From Title to Entitlement.' In

G.E. van Maanen and A.J. van der Walt, eds., *Property Law on the Threshold of the 21st Century.* Apeldorn: Maklu, 1996.

Slattery, Brian. 'Did France Claim Canada upon "Discovery"'? In J.M. Bumsted, ed., *Interpreting Canada's Past,* vol. 1. Toronto: Oxford University Press, 1986.

– 'The Legal Basis of Aboriginal Title.' In Frank Cassidy, ed., *Aboriginal Title in British Columbia: Delgamuukw v. The Queen.* Lantzville: Oolichan Books, 1992.

Strang, David. 'Contested Sovereignty: The Social Construction of Colonial Imperialism.' In Thomas Biersteker and Cynthia Weber, eds., *State Sovereignty as a Social Construct.* Cambridge: Cambridge University Press, 1996.

Swinton, Katherine. 'Multiculturalism and the Canadian Constitution.' In H.P. Glenn and M. Ouelette, eds., *Culture, Justice and Law.* Montreal: Canadian Institute for the Administration of Justice, 1994.

Tambiah, Stanley J. 'The Nation-State in Crisis and the Rise of Ethnonationalism.' In Edwin N. Wilmsen and Patrick McAllister, eds., *The Politics of Difference: Ethnic Premises in a World of Power.* Chicago: University of Chicago. Press, 1996.

Taylor, Charles. 'The Politics of Recognition.' In Amy Gutman, ed., *Multiculturalism: Examining the Politics of Recognition.* Princeton: Princeton University Press, 1994.

– 'What's Wrong with Negative Liberty?' In *Philosophy and the Human Sciences: Philosophical Papers,* vol. 2. Cambridge: Cambridge University Press, 1985.

Taylor, John Leonard. 'Two Views on the Meaning of Treaties Six and Seven.' In Richard Price, ed., *The Spirit of the Alberta Indian Treaties.* Edmonton: Pica Press, 1987.

Thornberry, Patrick. 'The Democratic or Internal Aspect of Self-Determination with Some Remarks on Federalism.' In C. Tomuschat, ed., *Modern Law of Self-Determination.* Dordrecht: Martinus Nijhoff, 1993.

Tully, James. 'The Struggles of Indigenous Peoples for and of Freedom.' In D. Ivison et al., eds., *Political Theory and the Rights of Indigenous Peoples.* Oakleigh: Cambridge University Press, forthcoming.

Turner, Dale. 'From Valladolid to Ottawa: The Illusion of Listening to Aboriginal People.' In Jill Oakes et al., eds., *Sacred Lands: Aboriginal World Views, Claims, and Conflicts.* Edmonton: Canadian Circumpolar Institute, 1998.

Venne, Sharon. 'Understanding Treaty 6: An Indigenous Perspective.' In Michael Asch, ed., *Aboriginal and Treaty Rights in Canada: Essays on Law, Equality, and Respect for Difference.* Vancouver: UBC Press, 1997.

Vitoria, Francisco de. 'De Indis' (1539). In Anthony Pagden and Jeremy Lawrence, eds.. *Francisco de Vitoria: Political Writings.* Cambridge: Cambridge University Press, 1991.

Whelan, Frederick G. 'Prologue: Democratic Theory and the Boundary Problem.' In J. Roland Pennock and John W. Chapman, eds., *Liberal Democracy*. New York: New York University Press, 1983.

Williams, Bernard. 'The Idea of Equality.' In Bernard Williams, ed., *Problems of the Self*. Cambridge: Cambridge University Press, 1973.

Unpublished

Cohen, Jean. 'Changing Paradigms of Citizenship and the Exclusiveness of the Demos.' Paper presented at the Legal Theory Workshop, Faculty of Law, University of Toronto, November 1998.

Knop, Karen C. 'The Making of Difference in International Law: Interpretation, Identity and Participation in the Discourse of Self-Determination.' S.J.D. thesis, Faculty of Law, University of Toronto, 1998.

Oman, Natalie Benva. 'Sharing Horizons: A Paradigm for Political Accommodation in Intercultural Settings.' Ph.D. thesis, McGill University, 1997.

Strelein, Lisa Marie. 'Indigenous Self-Determination Claims and the Common Law in Australia.' Ph.D. thesis, Australian National University, April 1998.

Wa, Gisday, and Delgam Uukw. 'The Spirit in the Land.' Opening statement of the Gitksan and Wet'suwet'en Hereditary Chiefs in the Supreme Court of British Columbia, 11 May 1987.

Documents and Reports

Anaya, S. James. *Fiduciary Obligation under International Law in General*. Research study prepared for the Royal Commission on Aboriginal Peoples, 13 Dec. 1994.

Bear, Leroy Little. *The Relationship of Aboriginal People to the Land and the Aboriginal Perspective on Aboriginal Title*. Research study prepared for the Royal Commission on Aboriginal Peoples, 1993.

Canada. *James Bay and Northern Québec Agreement*. Quebec: Éditeur official du Québec, 1976.

– *Northeastern Quebec Agreement* (1978).

– *Indian Treaties and Surrenders*, 3 vols. Saskatoon: Fifth House Publishers, 1992.

Canadian Human Rights Commission. *Annual Report* (1990).

Charter of the Organization of American States, 30 Apr. 1948, 2 U.S.T. 2394, 119 U.N.T.S. 48, amended by Protocol of Buenos Aires, 27 Feb. 1967, 21 U.S.T. 607.

Chiefs Committee on Claims/First Nations Submission on Claims. Ottawa: 14 Dec. 1990, reprinted in 1 ICCP 187 (1994).

Convention on the Prevention and Punishment of the Crime of Genocide, 9 Dec. 1948, 78 U.N.T.S. 277 (entered into force 12 Jan.).

Daes, Erica-Irene. *Explanatory Note concerning the Draft Declaration on the Rights of Indigenous Peoples.* E/CN.4/Sub.2/1993/26/Add.1 (released 19 July 1993).

Declaration on the Granting of Independence to Colonial Territories. G.A. Res. 1514, 15 U.N. GAOR Supp. (No. 16), U.N. Doc. A/7218 (1969).

Declaration of the Principles of International Cultural Cooperation, proclaimed by the General Conference of the United Nations Educational, Scientific and Cultural Organization at its fourteenth session on 4 Nov. 1966, reprinted in *United Nations, Human Rights: A Compilation of International Instruments,* U.N. Doc. ST/HR/1/Rev.3 (1988).

Declaration on the Rights of Persons Belonging to National or Ethnic, Religious and Linguistic Minorities, Resolution 47/135, adopted by the General Assembly 18 Dec. 1992.

Department of Indian Affairs. *Annual Report* (1889).

– *Annual Report* (1890).

Department of Indian Affairs and Northern Development. *Comprehensive Land Claims Policy.* Ottawa: Supply and Services, 1986.

– *Statement of the Government of Canada on Indian Policy.* Ottawa: Queen's Printer, 1969.

– *The Western Arctic Claim: The Inuvialuit Final Agreement* (1984).

Department of Indian and Northern Affairs. *Federal Policy for the Settlement of Native Claims* (March 1993).

– *The Impacts of the 1985 Amendments to the Indian Act (Bill C-31).* Ottawa: Supply and Services, 1990.

– *Report S-2 Individual Status-Reinstatement of Status Information System* (1995).

– *Outstanding Business: A Native Claims Policy.* Ottawa: Supply and Services, 1982.

– *Statement Made by the Honourable Jean Chrétien, Minister of Indian Affairs and Northern Development, on Claims of Indian and Inuit People.* Ottawa: 8 Aug. 1973.

Deschenes, Jules. *Proposal concerning a Definition of the Term 'Minority.'* U.N. Doc. E/CN.4/Sub.2/1985/31.

Draft Declaration on the Rights of Indigenous Peoples (as agreed to by the members of the working group at its 11th session) E/CN.4/Sub.2/1994/2/Add.1 (20 Apr. 1994).

Egremont (Secretary of State for the Southern Department) to Amherst (Commander in Chief of the British forces in America), 27 Jan. 1763, 'Fitch Papers,' *Collections of the Connecticut Historical Society.* Vol. 18. Hartford: Connecticut Historical Society, 1860-1967.

Espagnol, Chief Louis. Memorandum to Samuel Stewart, the Indian Department, 22 Aug. 1901, PAC RG 10, vol. 3303, file 235, 225-1.

– Petition (in French) to James Phipps, Visiting Superintendent of Indian Affairs for Manitoulin Island and Lake Huron, 15 Dec. 1884. Public Archives of Canada (PAC), Record Group 10 (RG 10), vol. 2289, file 57, 641.

European Convention for the Protection of Human Rights and Fundamental Freedoms 213 U.N.T.S. 222 (1950).

Grand Council of the Crees (of Quebec). *Submission: Status and Rights of the James Bay Crees in the Context of Quebec's Secession from Canada* (Commission on Human Rights, 48th Sess., 1992).

Hamilton, A.C. *Canada and Aboriginal Peoples: A New Partnership*. Ottawa: Indian Affairs and Northern Development, 1995.

Handbook of Existing Rules Pertaining to Human Rights in the InterAmerican System, OAS Doc. OEA/Ser.L./V/II.60 Doc. 28 (1983) 21.

Indian Claims Commission. *Indian Claims Commission Proceedings*, vol. 2. Special Issue on Land Claims Reform. Ottawa: Supply and Services, 1995.

Indian Commission of Ontario. *Discussion Paper Regarding First Nation Land Claims* (Toronto, 1990), reprinted in 2 Indian Claims Commission Proceedings [ICCP] 177 (1995).

International Covenant on Civil and Political Rights, adopted 16 Dec. 1966, 999 U.N.T.S. 171 (entered into force 23 Mar. 1976).

International Covenant on Economic, Social and Cultural Rights, adopted 16 Dec. 1966, 993 U.N.T.S. 3 (entered into force 3 Jan. 1976).

International Convention on the Elimination of All Forms of Racial Discrimination, opened for signature 7 Mar. 1966, 660 U.N.T.S. 195 (entered into force 4 Jan. 1969).

International Labour Organization Convention (No. 169) concerning Indigenous and Tribal Peoples in Independent Countries, 27 June 1989 (entered into force 5 Sept. 1990).

James Bay Treaty. 1931. Reprint. Ottawa: Queen's Printer, 1964.

Labaree, Leonard Woods, ed. *Royal Instructions to British Colonial Governors, 1670–1776*. 1935. Reprint. New York: Octagon, 1967.

Martinez-Cobo, José. *Analytical Compilation of Existing Legal Instruments and Proposed Draft Standards Relating to Indigenous Rights*, U.N. Doc. M/HR/86/36.

Minister of Public Works and Government Services Canada. *Federal Policy Guide: Aboriginal Self-Government, The Government of Canada's Approach to Implementation of the Inherent Right and the Negotiation of Aboriginal Self-Government* (1995).

Ministry of Aboriginal Affairs. *British Columbia's Approach to Treaty Settlements* (12 May 1995).

Nisga'a Final Agreement between the Nisga'a Nation, the Government of British Columbia, and the Government of Canada (1998).

Olthuis, John A. and Roger Townshend. *Is Canada's Thumb on the Scales? An Analysis of Canada's Comprehensive and Specific Claims Policies and Alternatives.* Research study prepared for the Royal Commission on Aboriginal Peoples, 1995.

Protection and Integration of Indigenous and Other Tribal and Semi-Tribal Populations in Independent Countries, *Conventions and Recommendations Adopted by the International Labour Conference, 1919–66.* Geneva: ILO, 1966.

Public Inquiry into the Administration of Justice and Aboriginal People. *Report of the Aboriginal Justice Inquiry of Manitoba.* Winnipeg: Queen's Printer, 1991.

Report of the Canadian Bar Association on Aboriginal Rights in Canada: An Agenda for Action (1988).

Royal Commission on Aboriginal Peoples. *Bridging the Cultural Divide: A Report on Aboriginal People and Criminal Justice in Canada.* Ottawa: Minister of Supply and Services Canada, 1996.

– *Final Report,* 5 vols. Ottawa: Minister of Supply and Services Canada, 1996.

– *Treaty Making in the Spirit of Co-existence: An Alternative to Extinguishment.* Ottawa: Supply and Services Canada, 1995.

Royal Commission on the Donald Marshall, Jr., Prosecution, Summary of Findings. Vol. 8, Digest of Findings and Recommendations. Halifax: Queen's Printer, 1989.

Royal Commission on the Status of Women in Canada. Report. Ottawa: Supply and Services, 1970.

Special Committee on Indian Self-Government. *Indian Self-Government in Canada: Report of the Special Committee.* Ottawa: House of Commons, 1983.

Standing Committee on Indian Affairs and Northern Development. *Minutes of Proceedings and Evidence,* 1st sess., 32d Parl., 1980-81-82, Issue no. 58.

Task Force to Review Comprehensive Claims Policy. *Living Treaties, Lasting Agreements – Report of the Task Force.* Ottawa: Indian and Northern Development, 1985.

Türk, Danilo. *Progress Report on the Realization of Social, Economic, and Cultural Rights.* U.N. ESCOR, Comm'n Hum. Rts. 42d Sess., Agenda Item 7, at 4, U.N. Doc. E/CN.4/Sub.2/1990/19 (1990).

– *U.N. Commission on Human Rights, Preliminary Report on the Realization of Economic, Social and Cultural Rights.* U.N. Doc. E/CN.4/Sub.2/1989/19 (1989).

United Nations. *Charter of the United Nations,* adopted 26 June 1945 (entered into force 24 Oct. 1945).

– Human Rights Committee. General Comment 23 (1994) paras. 6.2, 7 UN Doc HR1/GEN/1/Rev1 (1994).

U.N. ESCOR. Commission on Human Rights. *Limburg Principles on the Implementation of the International Covenant on Economic, Social and Cultural Rights.*

43d Sess., Annex, Agenda Items 8 & 18, at 1, U.N. Doc. E/CN.4/1987/17 (1987).

U.N. Subcommission on Prevention of Discrimination and Protection of Minorities. *Study of the Problem of Discrimination against Indigenous Populations.* U.N. Doc. E/CN.4/Sub.2/1986/7/Add. 4 (1986).

Universal Declaration of Human Rights, adopted 10 Dec. 1948, G.A. Res. 217A, U.N. GAOR, 3d Sess., p.1, U.N. Doc. A/810 (1948).

Zlotkin, Norman. *Unfinished Business: Aboriginal Peoples and the 1983 Constitutional Conference.* Discussion Paper No. 15. Kingston: Institute of Intergovernmental Relations, 1983.

Cases

A.G. Can. v. A.G. Ont. (Labour Conventions), [1937] A.C. 326 (P.C.).

A.G. Canada. v. Lavell, [1974] S.C.R. 1349.

A.G. Ont. v. A.G. Can., [1912] A.C. 571.

A.G. Ont. v. Bear Island Foundation, [1985] 1 C.N.L.R. 1 (Ont. S.C.).

Abrams v. United States, 250 U.S. 616 (1919).

Adams v. The Queen, 55 Q.A.C. 19 (Que. C.A.).

Amodu Tijani v. Secretary, Southern Nigeria, [1921] 2 A.C. 399 (P.C.).

Andrews v. Law Society of British Columbia, [1989] 1 S.C.R. 143.

Andrews v. Law Society of Upper Canada (1986), 27 D.L.R. (4th) 600 (B.C.C.A.).

Apsassin v. Canada, [1988] 3 F.C. 20 (T.D.).

Argentina v. Mellino, [1987] 1 S.C.R. 536.

Attorney-General v. De Keyser's Royal Hotel Ltd., [1920] A.C. 508.

Baker v. Canada, [1999] S.C.J. No. 39,

Bank of Montreal v. Hall, [1990] 1 S.C.R. 121.

Blades v. Higgs (1865), 11 H.L.C. 621.

Blueberry River Indian Band v. Canada, [1995] 4 S.C.R. 344.

Board of Education of the Indian Head School Division No. 19 of Saskatchewan v. Knight, [1990] 1 S.C.R. 653.

British Columbia v. Tener, [1985] 1 S.C.R. 533.

Calder v. A.G.B.C. (1973), 34 D.L.R. (3d) 145, [1973] S.C.R. 313.

Campbell et al. v. A.G.B.C. and Nisga'a Nation et al., [2000] B.C.S.C. 1123.

Canada v. Schmidt, [1987] 1 S.C.R. 500.

Canadian Aero Service Limited v. O'Malley, [1974] S.C.R. 592.

Canadian Pacific Ltd. v. Paul, [1988] 2 S.C.R. 654.

Cardinal v. A.G. Alberta, [1974] S.C.R. 695.

Cayuga Indians (Great Britain) v. United States (1926), 6 R.I.A.A. 173.

CBC v. Dagenais, [1994] 3 S.C.R. 835.

Cheecho v. R., [1981] 3 C.N.L.R. 45 (Ont. Dist. Ct.).

Cherokee Nation v. Georgia, 30 U.S. (5 Pet.) 1 (1831).

Chrysler Canada Ltd. v. Canada (Competition Tribunal), [1992] 2 S.C.R. 394.

Clarkson v. The Queen, [1986] 1 S.C.R. 383.

Clipperton Island Arbitration, 26 Am. J. Int'l L. 390 (1932).

Coe v. Commonwealth of Australia (1979), 53 A.L.J.R. 403.

Conway v. The Queen, [1993] 2 S.C.R. 872.

Cook v. Sprigg, [1899] A.C. 572.

Corbiere v. Canada (Minister of Indian and Northern Affairs), [1999] 2 S.C.R. 203.

Coté v. The Queen, [1996] 3 S.C.R. 139.

Cree Regional Authority v. Robinson, [1991] 4 C.N.L.R. 84 (F.C.T.D.).

Crow v. Blood Band (1996), 107 F.T.R. 270 (F.C.T.D.).

Delgamuukw v. British Columbia (1991), 79 D.L.R. (4th) 185, [1991] 3 W.W.R. 97
    (B.C.S.C.), rev'd, (1993), 104 D.L.R. (4th) 470 (B.C.C.A.).

Delgamuukw v. British Columbia, [1997] 3 S.C.R. 1010.

DeShaney v. Winnebago County Department of Social Services, 489 U.S. 189 (1989).

Dick v. The Queen, [1985] 2 S.C.R. 309.

Doherty v. Giroux (1915), 24 Que. K.B. 433.

Douglas/Kwantlen Faculty Association v. Douglas College, [1990] 3 S.C.R. 570.

Dreaver v. The King (Ex. Ct.) [unreported].

Eastmain Band v. Gilpin, [1987] 3 C.N.L.R. 54 (Que. Prov. Ct.).

Eastmain Band v. Gilpin, [1988] 3 C.N.L.R. 15 (Que. Prov. Ct.).

Egan v. Canada, [1995] 2 S.C.R. 513.

Eldridge v. British Columbia (A.G.), [1997] 3 S.C.R. 624.

Finlay v. Canada, [1990] 2 F.C. 790 (C.A.).

Four B Manufacturing v. United Garment Workers of America, [1980] 1 S.C.R. 1031.

Frame v. Frame, [1987] 2 S.C.R. 99.

Gardner v. Ontario (1984), 45 O.R. (2d) 760 (H.C.).

Goodswimmer v. Canada (1995), 123 D.L.R. (4th) 93 (Fed. C.A.).

Guerin v. The Queen, [1984] 2 S.C.R. 335.

H.L. Misener and Son Ltd. v. Misener (1977), 77 D.L.R. (3d) 428 (N.S.C.A.).

Halfway River First Nation v. B.C. (Minister of Forests), [1997] 4 C.N.L.R. 45
    (B.C.S.C.).

Hall Baking Co. (1934), 1 N.L.B. 83.

Hamlet of Baker Lake v. Minister of Indian Affairs and Northern Development, [1980] 1
    F.C. 518 (T.D.).

Harrer v. The Queen, [1995] 3 S.C.R. 562.

Harris v. McCrae, 448 U.S. 297 (1980).

Hodge v. The Queen (1883), 9 A.C. 117.

Horse v. The Queen, [1988] 1 S.C.R. 187.

Hospital Products Ltd. v. United States Surgical Corp (1984), 55 A.L.R. 417 (Aust. H.C.).

Hunter v. Southam Inc., [1984] 2 S.C.R. 145.

In Re Bhindi et. al and British Columbia Projectionists, Local 348 (1986), 29 D.L.R. (4th) 47 (B.C.C.A.).

In re Southern Rhodesia, [1919] A.C. 211 (P.C.).

Irwin Toy Ltd. v. Quebec, [1989] 1 S.C.R. 927.

Island of Palmas, 11 R.I.A.A. 829 (1928).

Jackson v. Joliet, 715 F.2d 1200 (7th Cir. 1983), cert. denied, 465 U.S. 1049 (1984).

James v. Cowan, [1932] A.C. 542.

James Smith Indian Band v. Saskatchewan (Master of Titles), [1994] 2 C.N.L.R. 72 (Sask. Q.B.).

Johnson v. M'Intosh, 21 U.S. (8 Wheat.) 543 (1823).

Johnston v. The Queen (1966), 56 D.L.R. (2d) 749 (Sask. C.A.).

Jones v. Meehan, 175 U.S. 1 (1899).

Kitkatla Band v British Columbia (Minister of Small Business, Tourism and Culture), [1999] 1 C.N.L.R. 72.

Kitok Ivan v. Sweden (Communication 197/1985), *Official Records of the Human Rights Committee* 1987/88, vol. II, p. 442 (U.N. Doc. A/43/40 (1988)).

Kruger v. The Queen (1985), 17 D.L.R. (4th) 591 (Fed. C.A.).

Kruger and Manuel v. The Queen, [1978] 1 S.C.R. 104.

Lac La Ronge Indian Band v. Beckman, [1990] 4 W.W.R. 211 (Sask. C.A.).

Lavigne v. O.P.S.E.U., [1991] 2 S.C.R. 211.

Law v. Canada, [1999] 1 S.C.R. 497.

Logan v. Styres (1959), 20 D.L.R. (2d) 416 (Ont. C.A.).

Lone Wolf v. Hitchcock, 187 U.S. 553 (1903).

Lovelace v. Canada, U.N. Doc. CCPR/C/DR/[XII]/R6/24 (31 July 1983).

Lovelace v. Ontario [2000] S.C.C. 37.

Lower Kootenay Indian Band v. Canada, [1991] 2 C.N.L.R. 54 (F.C.T.D.).

Lucas v. South Carolina Coastal Council, 112 S. Ct. 2886 (1992).

Mabo v. Queensland [No. 2] (1992), 175 C.L.R. 1.

MacDonald v. Montreal, [1986] 1 S.C.R. 460.

Mahe v. Alberta, [1990] 1 S.C.R. 342.

Makivik Corp. v. Canada (Minister of Canadian Heritage), [1999] 1 F.C. 58 (T.D.).

Manitoba Rice Farmers Association v. Manitoba Human Rights Commission (1987), 50 Man. R. (2d) 92 (Q.B.), aff'g 37 Man. R. (2d) 50 (Q.B), appeal dismissed on other grounds (1988), 55 Man. R. (2d) 263 (C.A.).

Mann v. The Queen, [1966] S.C.R. 776.

McKay v. The Queen, [1977] 2 S.C.R. 1054.

McKinney v. University of Guelph, [1990] 3 S.C.R. 229.

Michael H. v. Gerald D., 109 S. Ct. 2333 (1989).

Mitchel v. U.S., 9 Pet. 717 (U.S. Fla., 1835).

Mitchell v. Peguis Indian Band, [1990] 2 S.C.R. 95.

Multiple Access v. McCutcheon, [1982] 2 S.C.R. 161.

Namibia, [1971] I.C.J. 16.

National Lock Co. (1934), 1 N.L.B. 26.

New Brunswick Broadcasting Co. v. Nova Scotia, [1993] 1 S.C.R. 319.

Norris v. Thomas, [1992] 2 C.N.L.R. 139 (B.C.S.C.).

Nunavik Inuit v. Canada (Minister of Canadian Heritage) (1998), 164 D.L.R. (4th) 463 (Fed. T.D.).

O'Grady v. Sparling, [1960] S.C.R. 804.

Olga Tellis, [1985] 2 Supp. S.C.R. 51 (India).

Ominayak and the Lubicon Lake Band v. Canada, U.N. Doc. A/45/40, Vol. II, App. A (1990).

Ontario (A.G.) v. Bear Island Foundation, [1991] 2 S.C.R. 570.

Ottawa-Carleton Dialysis Services v. Ontario (Minister of Health) (1996), 41 Admin. L.R. (2d) 211 (Ont. Div. Ct.).

Pacific Fishermen's Defence Alliance v. Canada, [1987] 3 F.C. 272 (T.D.).

Pawis v. The Queen (1979), 102 D.L.R. (3d) 602 (F.C.T.D.).

Pierson v. Post, 3 Cai. R. 175 (N.Y. Sup. Ct. 1805).

R. v. Adams, [1996] 3 S.C.R. 101.

R. v. Askov, [1990] 2 S.C.R. 1199.

R. v. Baby (1855), 12 U.C.Q.B. 346.

R. v. Badger, [1996] 1 S.C.R. 771.

R. v. Batisse (1987), 84 D.L.R. (4th) 377 (Ont. Dist. Ct.).

R. v. Big M Drug Mart Ltd., [1985] 1 S.C.R. 295.

R. v. Bones, [1990] 4 C.N.L.R. 37 (B.C.P.C.).

R. v. Campbell (1996), 112 C.C.C. (3d) 107 (Man. C.A.).

R. v. Coté, [1996] 3 S.C.R. 139.

R. v. Derricksan (1976), 71 D.L.R. (3d) 159 (S.C.C.).

R. v. George, [1966] S.C.R. 267.

R. v. Gladstone, [1996] 2 S.C.R. 723.

R. v. Horseman, [1990] 1 S.C.R. 901.

R. v. Howard, [1994] 2 S.C.R. 299.

R. v. Jones, [1986] 2 S.C.R. 284.

R. v. Keegstra, [1990] 3 S.C.R. 697.

R. v. Koonungnak (1963), 45 W.W.R. 282 (N.W.T. Terr. Ct.).

R. v. Mirasty, [1942] 1 W.W.R. 343 (Sask. Pol. Ct.).

R. v. Morgentaler, [1988] 1 S.C.R. 30.

R. v. Morin, [1992] 1 S.C.R. 771.

R. v. Nicholas and Bear, [1989] 2 C.N.L.R. 131 (N.B.Q.B.).

R. v. Oakes, [1986] 1 S.C.R. 103.

R. v. Pamajewon, [1996] 2 S.C.R. 821.

R. v. Simon, [1985] 2 S.C.R. 387.

R. v. Sioui, [1990] 1 S.C.R. 1025.

R. v. Smith, [1935] 3 D.L.R. 703 (Sask. C.A.).

R. v. Sparrow, [1990] 1 S.C.R. 1075.

R. v. Sundown, [1999] 1 S.C.R. 393.

R. v. Sutherland, [1980] 2 S.C.R. 451.

R. v. Syliboy, [1929] 1 D.L.R. 307 (N.S. Co. Ct.).

R. v. Turpin, [1989] 1 S.C.R. 1296.

R. v. Van der Peet (1993), 80 B.C.L.R. (2d) 75 (C.A.).

R. v. Van der Peet, [1996] 2 S.C.R. 507.

R. v. Willocks (1995), 22 O.R. (3d) 552 (Gen. Div.).

R. v. Youngman, [1988] 3 C.N.L.R. 135 (B.C. Co. Ct.).

Ramsden v. Peterborough, [1993] 2 S.C.R. 1084.

Rebic v. Collver (1986), 28 C.C.C. (3d) 154 (B.C.C.A.).

Re Exported Natural Gas Tax, [1982] 1 S.C.R. 1004.

Reference re Act to Amend the Education Act (Ontario), [1987] 1 S.C.R. 1148.

Reference re Canada Assistance Plan (B.C.), [1991] 2 S.C.R. 525.

Reference re Public Service Employees Act (Alta.), [1987] 1 S.C.R. 313.

Reference re Residential Tenancies Act, [1981] 1 S.C.R. 714.

Reference re Secession of Québec, [1998] 2 S.C.R. 217.

RWDSU, Local 580 v. Dolphin Delivery Ltd., [1986] 2 S.C.R. 573.

S. Drenner & Son (1934), 1 N.L.B. 26.

Schachter v. Canada, [1992] 2 S.C.R. 679.

Semiahmoo Indian Band v. Canada (1997), 148 D.L.R. (4th) 523 (Fed. C.A.).

Simon v. The Queen, [1985] 2 S.C.R. 387.

Six Nations of the Grand River Band v. Henderson, [1997] 1 C.N.L.R. 202 (Ont. Gen. Div.).

Slaight Communications Inc. v. Davidson, [1989] 1 S.C.R. 1038.

Smith v. The Queen, [1983] 1 S.C.R. 554.

Sobeys Stores v. Yeomans, [1989] 1 S.C.R. 238.

St. Catherine's Milling and Lumber Co. v. The Queen, 13 S.C.R. 577 (1887).

St. Catherine's Milling and Lumber Co. v. The Queen (1888), 14 A.C. 46 (P.C.).

Stephens v. The Queen, [1960] S.C.R. 823.

Stoffman v. Vancouver General Hospital, [1990] 3 S.C.R. 483.

Sutton v. Moody, 1 Ld. Raym. 250 (1697).

Tsilhqot'in National Government v. British Columbia, [1998] B.C.E.A. No. 23, Appeal no. 97-PES-08.

Twinn v. Canada (1997), 215 N.R. 133 (Fed. C.A.).

U.S. v. Kagama, 118 U.S. 375 (1886).

United States of America v. Allard and Charette, [1987] 1 S.C.R. 564.

Uukw v. A.G.B.C. (1987), 16 B.C.L.R. (2d) 145 (C.A.).

Uukw v. B.C., [1987] 6 W.W.R. 155 (B.C.S.C.).

Vajesingji Joravarsingji v. Sec. of State for India (1924), L.R. 51.

Volker Stevin NWT (1992) Ltd. v. Northwest Territories (Commissioner) (1994), 113 D.L.R. (4th) 639 (N.W.T.C.A.).

Vriend v. Alberta, [1998] 1 S.C.R. 493.

Western Sahara, [1975] I.C.J. 12.

Williams v. Lee, 358 U.S. 217 (1959).

Worcester v. Georgia, 31 U.S. (6 Pet.) 515 (1832).

Yanomami. Resolution No. 12/85. Case No. 7615, Inter-American Commission on Human Rights (1985) (Brazil).

Index

Ross, Rupert, 42
Rousseau, Jean-Jacques, 78
Royal Commission on Aboriginal
Peoples, core of Aboriginal juris-
diction, 178
Royal Commission on the Status of
Women, 228
Royal Proclamation of 1763, 104–5,
223–4, 278–9
*RWDSU, Local 580 v. Dolphin Delivery
Ltd.* (1986), 204–5, 207

Sahtu Dene and Métis Comprehensive Land Claim Agreement
(1993), 270
Said, Edward, 52
Sami culture, reindeer husbandry, 69
Saskatchewan Hospitalization Act,
142–3
Scott, Frank, 240
Secession Reference, 63
self-determination, 33–40, 112, 125
and Belgium, 35–6; and colonial
territories, 34–6; external, 37–8,
125; internal, 37–9; international
law, 33–8, 39; rights of, 33–40, 125
Shue, Henry, 262
Simonsen, Justice, 216–18, 220
Simon v. The Queen (1985), hunting
and trapping rights, 144–5, 147–9,
147n. 59
Singer, Joseph, 96
Sioui case (1990), provincial park regulations, 146–8
Slattery, Brian, 118–19, 257
social contracts, and distributive justice, 156–9
social and economic rights, 239–40,
260, 261–2; obligations on government, 262–3

sovereignty, 62, 111–12, 167–8;
Aboriginal people and Canadian
sovereign authority, 7, 125; and
constitutional protection, 118–23,
129–30, 249–50, 287; discovery and
distribution of, 113–19, 126; doctrine of discovery, 113–14; and formal equality, 119–25, 129; internal,
109–11; under international law, 7,
39; meaning of, 108–12; rights, 6;
and substantive equality, 126–8. *See
also* prior sovereignty
Sparrow case (1990), fishing rights,
57–8, 162, 185–90, 246–52, 256
special rights, 5
spirit dance (Coast Salish), 49, 52, 65
state, and individual and collective
well-being, 237
status Indians: enfranchisement and
men, 57; legal status under federal
law, 116; women under Indian Act,
69
Sto:lo First Nation, 58–9, 163
substantive equality, 120 and formal
equality, 128; and sovereignty, 126–
8, 127n. 65
Supreme Court of Canada: *Calder v.
A.G.B.C.* (1973), 268–9; *Delgamuukw v. British Columbia* (1997),
89–91, 94–5, 100, 172–4, 188, 192,
256, 274, 277, 280; on discrimination, 214–15; on equality, 210–11,
213; fiduciary duty of the Crown,
253–7; *Harrer v. The Queen* (1995),
206; *Horse v. The Queen* (1988), 148–
50; interpretation of Aboriginal
rights, 162–3; *Lavigne v. OPSEU*
(1991), 201; on legal relationship
between Canada and Aboriginal
people, 14–15; *McKinney v. Univer-*